PRIVATE DEMONS

"*Private Demons* is written with care and intelligence. . . The biographer never loses sympathy with her strange, brilliant, sometimes impossible subject, nor with Jackson's selfish, very unsympathetic husband. . . . Presented with such clarity and good sense, the contradictions of Shirley Jackson's life seem entirely understandable."

Chicago Tribune

"Contradictions abound in this woman of dualities . . . sometimes competent, cheerful and hospitable, sometimes morose and agoraphobic. A hard-drinking, chain-smoking, cholesterol-consuming pair, Jackson and her husband Stanely Edgar Hyman (literary critic and professor at Bennington College in Vermont) reigned as the center of a wide circle of literary luminaries that included Howard Nemerov and novelist Ralph Ellison."

San Francisco Examiner Chronicle

"As Judy Oppenheimer points out often in this detailed and fascinating biography, Jackson was a study in contradictions—the rebellious daughter of conservative parents who attempted all her life to achieve a balance between the wildness of her imaginative power and the necessary compromises expected of a woman coming to maturity in the 1930s and 40s."

Cleveland Plain Dealer

"Jackson was an extraordinary woman, a 250-pound genius who was possessed of an inhuman energy. She tended to her babies, ran a 14-room house, catered to [her husband's] male chauvinist whims, gave frequent dinner parties, where she drank far into the night with her guests. . . . She was full of wit, of irony, of humor. . . . *Private Demons* is a well-written biography of this extraordinarily talented, driven woman."

Dallas Morning News

PRIVATE DEMONS

THE LIFE OF SHIRLEY JACKSON

Judy
Oppenheimer

FAWCETT COLUMBINE • NEW YORK

For my parents, Ralph and Jeanne Altman;
in love, in gratitude, and in awe

A Fawcett Columbine Book
Published by Ballantine Books
Copyright © 1988 by Judy Oppenheimer

"In Memoriam" by Stanley Edgar Hyman reprinted by permission
of Brandt & Brandt Literary Agents, Inc.

"Janice" and excerpt from *Come Along With Me* reprinted by permission
of Viking Penguin, Inc., from *Come Along With Me* by Shirley Jackson,
copyright © 1960 by Shirley Jackson.

Library of Congress Catalog Card Number: 88-92241
ISBN: 0-449-90405-9

This edition published by arrangement with G.P. Putnam's Sons

Cover design by James R. Harris

Manufactured in the United States of America

First Ballantine Books Edition: July 1989

10 9 8 7 6 5 4 3 2 1

ACKNOWLEDGMENTS

I suppose I had taken it for granted that Shirley Jackson's friends and family would be intelligent, insightful, and expressive people—these were qualities she looked for in those she knew. I was not prepared for their amazing generosity. From her childhood friends in San Francisco and Rochester to those she made late in life, everyone I contacted seemed overwhelmingly eager to help—interrupting their lives for interviews, responding to scores of follow-up phone calls, tracking down old addresses, digging into dusty files to retrieve letters. She was important to each of them, and they have not forgotten. I am grateful to all, but must add a special thanks to Frank Orenstein and June Mirken Mintz, for their endless patience.

My deepest gratitude goes to Shirley Jackson's children—Laurence Hyman, Jai Holly, Sarah Stewart, and Barry Hyman. Each faced the difficult task of looking back with honesty, integrity and courage. Their parents, who prized these traits highly, would be proud.

And my thanks to all: Linda Gould Abtalion, Jean Aldrich, Frances Woodward Bardacke, Ben Belitt, Walter Bernstein, Carol Brandt, Tom and Jean Brockway, Kenneth Burke, Fred Burkhardt, Nanci Payne Coonz, Catherine Corcoran, Malcolm Cowley, Hal Crowther, Nicholas and Elena Delbanco, Peter De Vries, Dr. Oliver Durand, Ralph Ellison, Jennifer Feeley, Dr. Anna Fels, Willie Finckel, Tom and Kit Foster, Dorothy Ayling Gielow, Robert Giroux, Dr. Dorothy Hager, Philip Hamburger, Elizabeth Young Henry, Arthur Hyman, Bunny Hyman, Scott Hyman, Barry Jackson, Jean Rathgen Jackson, Taissa Kellman Julian, Barbara Karmiller, Jeanne Krochalis, Jesse Lurie, Betty Lyddon, Ann Malamud, Uli Beigel Monaco, Howard Nemerov, Laura Nowak, Michael Palmer, Al Parsell, Junior Percey, Phoebe Pettingell, Larry Powers, Harriet Fels Price, Elsa Dorfman Rosenthal, Joan Schenkar, Anna Schlabach, Red Sdolsky, Dr. Robert Seidenberg, Florence Shapiro Siegel, Roger Straus, Marion Morton Strobel, Dr. James Toolan, Kay Turk Truman, Fred Welling, Helen Feeley Wheelwright, Barbara Williams, Kayla Zalk, and Ben Zimmerman. Thanks, too, to Mary O'Brien of Syracuse University's Arents Library; Paul Caluori of Boston University's Mugar Memorial Library; and Martha Cordova of the Bennington Free Library.

My editor, Faith Sale, defines the art; she is one of those rare people who actually transcend their reputation, no mean feat in her case. Jennifer Barth, her assistant, was a consistent help. Anna Jardine, who did the copyediting, is a true perfectionist. No one could ask for more sensitive, intelligent handling; I have, I'm afraid, been spoiled for life.

Writing a book is a little like jumping off the side of the earth; you need all the support cables you can get. I am grateful for every one of mine, but especially the members of my writers' group, Stan Field, Johnnie Thomas, Lou Anne Tuck, and Honora Jaffe, who encouraged me for years; my friend Susan Skramstad, who gave me exactly the right push at the right time; and my sisters, Debbie and Ida Altman, who kept me going, as they have all my life. My husband Jerry will never be an eighties man; he put up maybe one wash during the course of this project and made a botch of that. But his unflagging support and belief were a lot more important to me than washloads; where it counted, he came through like a prince.

PRIVATE DEMONS

CHAPTER

·1·

She was not the daughter her mother wanted; that much was clear from the start. Shirley Jackson was born on December 14, 1916, in San Francisco, into comfort, pleasant surroundings, and social position, but to parents who never truly knew what to make of her, not in childhood and not throughout her entire forty-eight years.

Particularly her mother. A few years later Zelda Fitzgerald would look down at her own newborn daughter and make a fervent wish—that she be "a fool, a beautiful little fool, the best thing a girl could be in this life." Geraldine Bugbee Jackson may have lacked the wit to make such a statement, but it was a sentiment she shared, wholeheartedly and without irony. She too would have liked a daughter who was beautiful and a fool; instead, she got Shirley, who would never for one instant be either.

Only twenty-one, tall, slim, with dark hair and liquid brown eyes, Geraldine Jackson was already terribly conscious of both where she had come from and where she was going. On her paternal grandmother's side, the family tree could be traced directly back to Revolutionary War hero General Nathanael Greene (the family showed its appreciation by sprouting a new Nathaniel nearly every generation). There was a connection by marriage to New England sculptor William Wetmore Story, and Julia Ward Howe, of "Glory, hallelujah" fame. The Bugbee side was almost as impressive—originally from Rhode Island, they had detoured to Boston and then rerooted themselves in San Francisco as early as 1854, making Geraldine part of the third generation of Bugbees to be born in the Bay City, a fact of immense pride.

The Bugbees did not just arrive in San Francisco early, they helped design it; a recurrent architect gene seemed to crop up every other generation in the family. Samuel Bugbee, Shirley Jackson's great-great-grandfather, had planned some of the town's oldest buildings, including the Stanford, Crocker, and Colton mansions on Nob Hill and the Grand Opera House. Most of these did not survive the 1906 earthquake—as Shirley put it later, wryly, "One [of her ancestors] built houses only for millionaires out west and that was where the family wealth came from, and one of them was certain that houses could be made to stand on the sand dunes of San Francisco, and that was where the family wealth went to." It wasn't completely true, of course; Shirley was never able to dip into her family's history without making a few creative changes. The houses may have toppled, but the Bugbees remained comfortably fixed even after the earthquake.

Samuel's son, John Stephenson Bugbee, born in 1841, studied law back east, at Harvard, and eventually (after a three-year stint in the Civil War) returned to practice in San Francisco; later, President Benjamin Harrison appointed him U.S. district judge for Alaska. The architect gene reappeared in his son, Shirley's grandfather, Maxwell Greene Bugbee, born in 1865, who had a long, successful career. It then went into hiding for another generation, only to appear again with Shirley Jackson—but in a very different manner. Her fascination with old houses went deep: they served, in fact, as leading characters in more than one of her books—but the structures she most liked to design and rearrange were those of reality, not mortar and brick.

Geraldine's mother, Evangeline Field, descended from the Connecticut Fields, who in turn could be traced back to the de la Fields of eleventh-century England, who came complete with a coat of arms. But Evangeline, known as Mimi, grew up in a family of eight children and seems to have been a bit lost in its midst; she was a somewhat plain, even retiring sort of woman. Certainly she had none of her daughter's pretensions or zest for the social milieu.

Mimi produced two children, a son, Clifford, in 1894, and a year later, Geraldine. Mimi's marriage to Maxwell foundered for many years and finally collapsed, although it is unlikely they were ever divorced. Maxwell Bugbee, who was no fool, relied on his architectural skills to extricate himself from his marriage: he designed a large house for his daughter and son-in-law, installed Mimi in one of the four bedrooms, and removed himself from the scene. Little was heard of him after that, although he did make the odd Christmas appearance. But throughout most of Shirley's childhood, her grandmother Mimi was a continuing presence in the home.

For a twenty-one-year-old, Geraldine Maxwell Bugbee Jackson (she later dropped the Maxwell) was a remarkably self-possessed woman. Certainly she knew what she wanted: social position and wealth. And she was sure she had found the man most likely to bring it to her, a man whose upwardly mobile instincts if anything outstripped her own.

Shirley's father, Leslie Jackson, tall, fair, dynamic, was born in England in 1891; his father, Edward, had been a school friend of Prime Minister Herbert Asquith, and apparently well situated. But some trouble had occurred, one of those dark spots that turn up in family histories from time to time. It could not have been minor, since it wiped out the family's wealth and led Edward to change his name (from Henchall to Jackson) and to emigrate to the United States in the 1890s, leaving his wife, two daughters, and son on their own in England for a number of years. But even Leslie was never able to discover what that dark spot was.

Shirley's brother, Barry, remembered seeing a letter from his father's mother to his father, when he was a teenager. "To answer some of your questions, the next time I see you I will tell you why he changed his name," she had written. But his grandmother died soon after, and as far as he knows, the questions remained unanswered.

Leslie Jackson, then only thirteen, made the long trip by sea with his mother and sisters to join his father in San Francisco, arriving in 1905— just in time for the earthquake. For Leslie, it probably seemed a propitious omen: now both he and San Francisco were even, starting at rock bottom. He promptly got a job, working for three dollars a week. By the time Geraldine met him, ten years later, he was a rising star at Traung Label Company, definitely a young man on his way up in the business world.

Leslie and Geraldine were well suited. Both had the easy California manner, which could be turned on or off at will; both enjoyed entertaining, good food, good clothes, and both had their eyes fixed firmly on their primary goal, ascending the social and economic ladder rung by rung. Their romance was a brisk one—Leslie was not one to waste time— and they were married on March 15, 1916. The groom was twenty-five, the bride only twenty. Prospects looked rosy all around.

Unfortunately, Geraldine became pregnant instantly, long before either of them was ready. Geraldine especially was upset—she had looked forward to having time alone with her dashing husband, unencumbered, and to the parties and social engagements she loved. Little more than a child herself, she had no interest in raising one.

It was too soon. Later, perhaps, it might have been different, although it is unlikely Geraldine would ever have been completely thrilled at the prospect—conventional as she was, she was far from domestic, and child-rearing held small interest for her. Isn't contraception a wonderful thing, she said in a 1962 letter to Shirley, and weren't the Catholics silly to oppose it? "I only wish I'd had it back then." It was no more than the plain truth, of course, though hardly the most tactful thing to say to one's daughter.

But Geraldine Jackson was not a tactful woman. Years later, when Shirley was struggling to make sense of her own problems, she told her daughter Joanne a chilling story: when Shirley was an adolescent, Geraldine had informed her she was an unsuccessful abortion. It could have been the simple truth—Geraldine had a tendency to blurt things out around her daughter—or one of Shirley's intuitive guesses, but one thing was certain. This was the way Geraldine had made her feel, throughout her life.

As a beautifully turned-out woman, Geraldine, having resigned herself to maternity, expected at the very least a beautifully turned-out daughter. Fashionable, superficial, and utterly conventional—a miniature version, in fact, of Geraldine Jackson herself, who was a strong adherent of the child-as-jewelry school of parenthood.

The fact that the child she gave birth to—exactly nine months and one day after her wedding—turned out to be Shirley seems almost too ironic, one of those quirks of fate second-rate novelists delight in. For Shirley was odd from the start, a restless, high-strung, difficult child; brilliant, messy, torrentially creative, and far from ornamental. "You were always a wilful child," Geraldine snapped at her daughter forty-six years after her birth, by mail, and both the sentiment and the misspelling underlined the vast gulf that had always stretched between them. "My most basic beliefs in writing are that the identity is all-important and the word is all-powerful," Shirley said once. Her mother had managed to malign both in one six-word sentence.

A goldfish giving birth to a porpoise, as one of Shirley's sons described it. But a tenacious goldfish, one who never stopped trying to rearrange her porpoise daughter along more acceptable goldfish lines. Perhaps with a little guile she might have had more luck, but Geraldine was never a subtle woman. Strong-willed, yes; subtle, no. Years after Shirley had left home, married, and given birth to her own children, her mother still sent her corsets in the mail, trying foolishly but persistently to rein in the overgrown creature she had somehow, unbelievably produced.

This was no malleable clay, however; Shirley had, as her mother soon recognized, a will surpassing her own. Even as a small child, carefully groomed, her strawberry-blond hair neatly arranged under a large bow, there was a set to the chin, a cool appraisal in the light eyes. Shirley Jackson, born to be a writer, dug her feet in and fought. Eventually she would say no to all of it, to Geraldine's whole world of proper breeding and grooming and social minutiae, would reject forever the torch of country-club conventionality. She would laugh at it, flout it, rebel against it. But she would carry her mother within her, unexorcised for the rest of her life.

Shirley's children, especially her daughters, grew up acutely aware of the terrible resentment Shirley bore her parents, particularly her mother. "She felt Geraldine had squashed her," her older daughter said flatly. "Crushed her spirit." And yet Geraldine was not a cruel woman, or even an unloving mother—simply vain, foolish, unalterably conventional. No matter how strained the relationship, it was also true that a confused, hopeless love existed between them throughout their lives, right along with the anger, pain, hatred, and lack of forgiveness.

Not that it helped. In fact, a complete break between these two utterly unlike women might well have been the best thing that could have happened. Instead they remained entangled for life, even though they were separated by the entire country for the last seventeen years. "Who is looking over my shoulder all the time?" Shirley mused to herself months before her death, wondering at her inability to confront certain parts of herself. It could only have been the worried, disapproving, unrelenting specter of Geraldine Jackson.

Shirley's early years were spent in the fashionable Ashbury Park section of San Francisco, and it seems likely she was her daddy's girl from the start. For one thing, she looked more like him, with her reddish-blond hair, light eyes, and fair complexion—the complexion of a redhead, delicate, quick to burn or chafe. Leslie Jackson himself was a person of high energy, often impatient; he had the forceful personality and sharp mind of the good business executive and thought he saw a great deal of that in his daughter. In some ways he always felt he understood her better than her mother did. Both parents were proud of Shirley's sharp mind, even if her mother's pride was tinged with uneasiness almost from the beginning. Shirley could be so unpredictable and headstrong, even as a small child. Her little brother, Barry, born twenty months later, was such a calm, easy-going child, much easier to handle. Shirley's fits of rage— so unbecoming in a little girl—were hard for her mother to cope with. Early on, Geraldine got in the habit of giving in to her a great deal of the time, just to keep the peace, in the same way she bent to her husband's will. Especially if it meant buying something for her—acquisitiveness at least was something Geraldine understood.

Ashbury Park was fine as a starting point, but the Jacksons had no intention of staying there. In 1923, when Shirley was six and Barry four, they moved to Burlingame, a gracious, well-appointed suburb sixteen miles south of the city, where the sun shone even more warmly. For a year they rented a house, while Leslie arranged to build the home Shirley's grandfather had designed for them (and the wife he was depositing with them) on Forest View Avenue.

It was a strictly modern affair, two stories high, quite spare, almost boxlike, somewhat too big for its lot, and stood out rather sharply on the street; most of the other houses were smaller and strove for more of a country-cabin effect. But Leslie and Geraldine were pleased. Their house alone, out of all the others in the neighborhood, seemed designed for a larger estate, for even lusher surroundings, and that was precisely the way its owners felt about themselves.

With its customized houses, blooming eucalyptus trees, and well-cared-for lawns, Burlingame was a small jewel of a suburb, a clean, secure enclave of Wasp homogeneity set down far enough away from the city to be safe from any stray urban influences. It would be twenty years before the massive white middle-class surge to suburbia would empty the cities, before cheap tract housing and post–World War II spending money would suddenly make the suburbs an attainable American dream. In 1923, such a move was still only for the relatively affluent; it was in all ways a satisfactory step up the ladder for the Jacksons. Unfortunately, Geraldine only had to look out her living room window to see the vast expanse of green at the end of the block that marked the edge of the Newcastle estate: a monstrously wealthy, twenty-acre domain. Moving had only been a small step, after all. The chasm between suburban affluence and true wealth still stretched wide, dark, and insurmountable.

Nonetheless, the Jacksons were pleased with the move, and especially the house. The large, airy living room housed a grand piano—Leslie and Geraldine were both fond of holding small musicales for their guests. Mimi, Shirley's grandmother, was installed in a small upstairs bedroom at the front of the house, Barry in a similar one beside her. The Jacksons themselves had a large bedroom suite facing the back of the house, next to Shirley's room, which was almost as large.

The neighborhood where the Jacksons lived consisted of a score of houses, most of them filled with young families. The children played outside year-round, taking advantage of the near perfect weather, usually congregating on Walnut Street, which ran perpendicular to Forest View. Little Barry blended into the group almost immediately and was rarely home. Shirley was another matter.

She tended to be a loner, even then, spending hours in her room, reading and writing poetry. On the one hand, Geraldine was pleased that she kept aloof from the neighborhood children; many of them were loud and vulgar, not truly the right sort at all. She herself did not socialize with any of the adults. The Jacksons were of a better class than the other families in the neighborhood, and Geraldine made sure Shirley knew it.

At the same time, she would not have minded if Shirley had spent more time out of the house, even mingling with the other children, as long as she was able to keep the proper perspective and did not really come down to their level. But Shirley did not seem to have Barry's easy mastery of social skills. She hung around the house, often making her mother uncomfortable. Geraldine did not always know what to do with her strange, lumpish, unlikely daughter and was often irritable with her. After all, why else had they moved to this squeaky-clean, homogenized community if not for the children? There was something—she was beginning to suspect with growing horror—truly different about her daughter.

And so there was. Shirley Jackson had been born with a terrifying gift: the ability to see. Straight down through the layers of appearance, of convention, of style, of hypocrisy—right into the nutty core of reality itself. And even beyond that, into the place where reality dissolved and became something very different. Such children are not born every day, but when they are, wherever they are, it is axiomatic: they always make their mothers uncomfortable.

Shirley could look at the neighborhood, with its flowers and lawns and freckle-faced children—the sort of neighborhood that would be celebrated on television again and again thirty years later, as a fit setting for the Nelsons, the Cleavers—and see beyond it, straight to its false heart. Her eyes unerringly picked up the dark edges lurking behind the suburban gauze.

She saw the man who lived with his wife and his sister-in-law, down on Walnut Street, noted the fierce jealousy between the women, the man's bland acceptance of his importance. She saw the way the families treated the local piano teacher, who looked a bit different and was possibly even (it was whispered) Jewish. She watched the couple down the street walk their handicapped child up and down the block every evening, while the other neighbors averted their eyes in distaste. She noted the odd girl who lived only a few houses away, in a dark house, with a mother who never came out of doors, the girl who talked like a much younger child and who would run out of her house suddenly, clutching handfuls of bills, insisting on buying ice cream for everyone. She saw how the other children laughed uneasily, knowing they were taking advantage, yet allowed her to do it.

She saw the neighborhood's one old crone, crouched bitterly on her porch steps, eyeing the young families with hatred; the women of the neighborhood, gossiping, backbiting, preening; the men, ineffectual, pompous, unaware. And along with this, of course, she saw her own family—her mother's ridiculous pretensions, her snobbery; her father's bland distant cheerfulness and iron hand; and herself—anxious, selfish, and, even before puberty, overweight.

It would be years before she would write it down, in her first novel, *The Road Through the Wall,* a book remarkable for its smooth style, its unpleasant view of suburbia, and the amazing fact that it features not even one truly likable character, in a cast of many. She would write about what she had seen in Burlingame, showing her neighbors exactly as they were, and call it fiction. Nothing would be lost. For now, though, it was enough to see it all, to take it in.

People were flawed and carried evil within them: this was the lesson Shirley learned in sunny Burlingame, even while Geraldine struggled to teach her lessons of a very different sort—the proper behavior and attire for a young lady, for instance. People were where the trouble lay, Shirley learned, and she already suspected, even as a child, that they would not be very different no matter where she found them.

Yet at the same time she felt a deep love for the physical surroundings of her childhood—the sunny days, the cool nights, the bright skies and fields of northern California. Years later she would weave glowing tales for her four children of mellow, temperate winds; exotic birds; fruits— oranges, pomegranates, plums—that fell ripe from the trees; of the beautiful city of hills to the north, perched on a gleaming bay, like a vision from a fairy tale.

"Most of us have a lost paradise somewhere, a place that we want to go back to," said her friend Elizabeth Young, who knew her in college. "California was Shirley's." It was her Eden, a place she was deeply attached to and would never forget, although she would leave it at age sixteen forever.

Her love for this world did not prevent her from seeing the grim, scruffy reality under the surface. But Shirley's vision went further than that . . . and this was what gave Geraldine the most trouble. Shirley had what the Irish call "the sight," the ability to see beyond reality, to pierce the veil into other realms. Shirley was, in fact, psychic: she heard conversations, even music, that no one else heard; she saw faces no one else could see. She was acutely aware, even from childhood, that there were other very different realities as true as the one her family and neighbors lived in, existing simultaneously, perhaps only a half-turn away.

In this century, in this country, we are used to discounting such things completely—the irresistible urge is to turn toward psychiatry for the answer. A child who hallucinates and sees alternate realities is obviously suffering from schizophrenia. Or at the very least is desperately unhappy and using her creativity to spin other worlds.

But Shirley herself believed in this awareness of hers, believed it was a true perception, and kept that belief all her life. It was not something she would have wished on herself necessarily; not an ability that made her life easier, certainly. It just *was*. A part of her vision, a part of her life.

She spoke of it rarely, as she got older; Geraldine had trained her too well. For at first she did tell her mother of the things she noticed: the old man with the beard hovering near her, the odd music she heard when she lay with her head on the grass. Her mother's reaction was immediate—an outright recoil in horror. These things were insane, and Geraldine wanted nothing to do with them.

Yet to a degree it was Geraldine herself, and her mother, who had helped provide the fertile ground where Shirley's odd sensitivities could flower. Geraldine had a penchant for fortune-telling, reading tea leaves. She was the one who had brought the Ouija board into the house and showed Shirley and Barry how to use it. Barry remembers sitting around it with his mother, grandmother, and Shirley, though he never took it seriously himself. "I always thought one or the other was unconsciously directing the thing," he said. "We used to laugh—there were some very strange messages."

Geraldine also had another talent. "She could always find a four-leaf clover, no matter where she was," Shirley's daughter Sally recalled. "You'd just ask her and she'd reach over and pick one up." Shirley carried one with her, encased in plastic, all her life; her daughter Joanne has it now.

Mimi, for her part, was a devout believer in Christian Science, a religion that prides itself on not taking reality at face value, viewing the trappings of reality as no more than symbols, which must be gone beyond. Both Barry and Shirley were given a thorough grounding in the religion, attending the local Burlingame Christian Science church most Sundays, even though Geraldine was far from devout.

Mimi's devotion went deep; she was truly convinced that, as her religion taught, the mind had the power to cure illness. "She believed absolutely that anything wrong with her could be cured by her mind," Barry said. "And she used to practice it on us." On the rare occasions one of the children was sick their grandmother would creep into their rooms at night, stealthily, and spend hours whispering in their ears that they could heal themselves if they wanted, all they had to do was use their powers of mind.

Barry, a good-natured fellow, accepted this as just another irritation, on a par with Mimi's chopped-egg sandwiches, which he also hated but managed to choke down. Both he and Shirley joked about it together. But Shirley was a high-strung, deeply imaginative child; no matter how silly it seemed in the daylight, Mimi's dead-of-the-night imprecations undoubtedly left their mark.

Both Mimi and Geraldine would have been shocked, though, to think their own vagaries had in any way provided the breeding ground for Shirley's strange perceptions. Mimi's beliefs, after all, were formalized into a proper religion; Geraldine's tea-leaf reading and Ouija-board playing were more on the order of lighthearted parlor tricks than anything else. Shirley's visions were a different matter altogether.

Late in her life, in the year before her death, Shirley started a new novel unlike anything she had done before. Its heroine, Angela Motorman, was age forty-four and size forty-four (like Shirley), cheery, matter-of-fact, and psychic. The novel, *Come Along with Me,* was never finished; Shirley's husband published what there was of it in 1968, three years after her death. Under the guise of fiction, it contains the truest description she ever wrote of her childhood experience:

> At first I tried to point them out to people; I was even foolish enough at first to think other people just hadn't noticed; "Look at that," I would say, "look, right over there, it's a funny man." It didn't take long for my mother to put a stop to that; "There isn't any funny man anywhere," she would say, and jerk on my arm, "what kind of sewer do you have for a mind?" Once I tried to tell a neighbor about it; it was quite accidental, because I rarely told anyone anything. He was sitting on his front porch one evening in summer and I had been lying on the grass on our lawn, watching small lights go and come among the grass blades, and listening to a kind of singing—sometimes, especially in summer, it was a kind of pleasant world I lived in—and he heard me laughing. He asked me to come and sit on his front porch and he gave me a glass of lemonade, and when he asked me what I had been doing I went ahead and told him. I told him about seeing and hearing, and he listened, which is more than anyone else ever did. "You're clairvoyant," he told me. . . .
>
> I knew a lot about people, a lot that they never knew I knew, but I never seemed to have much sense, probably because one thing I never really knew was whether what I was doing was real or not. . . .
>
> When I was about sixteen I began to get self-conscious about all of it; it wasn't that I minded them coming around asking and following me everywhere I went; most sixteen-year-old girls like to be followed, but by then I knew no one else was going to see them and sometimes I felt like a fool; you don't go around staring at empty air all the time, not when you're sixteen you don't, not without people beginning to notice. "Do you need glasses?" my mother used to ask me, or "Can't you for heaven's sake stop gawking at nothing and shut your mouth and comb your hair and get out with the other kids?" . . .
>
> That's not a good way for a girl to grow up. . . . How can anyone

handle things if her head is full of voices and her world is full of things no one else can see?

Her clairvoyance, her special perception, faded in and out throughout childhood and on through the adult years, she continued. At times it could be put aside for years. But it remained with her for good. "I could see," said Shirley, speaking as Angela Motorman, "what the cat saw."

There are areas of the mind that are wholly uncharted, questions for which there are no answers. What are the links between creativity, madness, and psychic awareness? Where does one leave off and the other begin? The lines are dim and wavering, and the science that would sort them out has yet to appear. In Shirley's case, it is enough to know that she herself—although she had her share of mental problems in her life—never considered her psychic experiences a part of them. It is highly unlikely that she even discussed them with the psychiatrist she went to late in her life. Her psychic awareness was part of her individuality, not her madness; it was part of what made her who she was, and despite the occasional pain and the terror and loneliness it caused her, she would not have been without it.

Besides, there were advantages. By high school, she said once, "I had learned that to put myself to sleep at night it was necessary only to invent music, that instead of reading a book it was more satisfactory to talk to the man who wrote it, that the solution to the great agonizing yearning of adolescence for action, for creation, for fulfillment, was to sidestep adolescence altogether by merging into one of the other worlds where adolescence was either finished with or else not possible.

"I will not tolerate having these other worlds called imaginary," she added. "In explanation of them I can only say: how do you know when you wake up in the morning that only eight or so hours have passed since the night before, that the intervening time has been spent in bed, that the affairs you take up so dully in the morning were not laid down centuries before, to wait until you got back to them from somewhere else? In the little minutes of absent-mindedness crossing the street you may without recollection have lived a life somewhere else, you may move back and forth from one of many lives to another, without perception at any time of all the others. . . . To call such a thing imaginary is the reality of one man in one place at one time, and if anyone can be really content with that then perhaps in such a life there are no other places." For her it was different, she said. She could recall fragments from many such transitions, and, she said, "I am usually content with the glimpse that reminds me that I have been there."

CHAPTER

·2·

Shirley learned early—as do many highly imaginative children—to keep most of her feelings and odder ideas locked inside her, safely away from her family. And yet she was far from shy or withdrawn at home; she liked getting her own way and was not above staging a pitched battle to do it, especially against her mother and grandmother. Her father was another matter; he represented real power, and Shirley was wary of tangling with him.

Geraldine had her own ways of handling Shirley—but Mimi was a pushover, and it was Mimi, very often, who was the only adult around. Once installed in the new house, she fell quickly into the thankless role of unpaid housekeeper, cook, and perpetually available baby-sitter. Geraldine and Leslie were avid socializers; it was not unusual for them to go out several nights a week, leaving Barry and Shirley with their grandmother. With the usual contempt of energetic children for doormat adults, they made mincemeat of her attempts to rein them in—staying up as late as they wanted, pulling their toys into the living room, making huge messes in the kitchen.

"Shirley was always the instigator, always the one," Barry said. "Let's do this or that. Lots of energy. We'd get out all kinds of stuff, blocks, make paths around the whole living room floor, little cars, houses, and leave it there for my mother and father." Most of the time the two of them got along fairly well, even though Shirley later told her own kids she had once broken his arm. ("No, I broke it myself, falling off something," said Barry Jackson. "She was always making something up.")

Public school, with its neat rules, strict order, chalk-and-eraser mentality, is traditionally a poor place for the turbulent, creative mind, and

Shirley's case was no exception. Luckily, it left few marks; her California school days were unexciting but relatively benign. She had learned to read early, deciphering the words upside down and backward as her mother sat in the chair reading to her, and reading was a continual passion— but this had little to do with school; it was something you did at home, for your own pleasure, while your mother kept nagging you to put the book down and go outside. Geraldine was not a reader and had little sympathy for her bookworm daughter. There were few books in the Jackson house, although there was one curious collection: Mimi owned the complete works of Edgar Allan Poe, which she occasionally read aloud to the children (just the thing to quiet an anxious, impressionable child). But for most books, Shirley had to look outside the home; she became an early, voracious library user.

Reading and writing posed few problems at school, but math was impossible. Shirley later said that the only correct answers she ever got were arrived at psychically. She had occasional successes at school early on— her poetry was praised in elementary school, and she was allowed to write the class play for the McKinley Grammar School graduation. But for the most part, school passed over her. It had little to give her, and she returned the favor.

Her real education—indeed, the most important part of her life—went on at home, as she sat at the desk in her room, all alone. "Every day all the way home from school she would think about going into her room and closing the door. She would think about her desk and the sunlight coming into the room and being alone with her desk and writing. . . . She would touch her pocket to make sure that the key to her desk was safe," she wrote later. The very act of going into her room, unlocking her desk, removing her poems, reading and thinking and writing down her most private thoughts, had an almost religious significance for her. This was her world, and when it was violated something inside her broke forever.

"She opened the door of her room quietly; there was no need to let them know she was home. When she opened her door she saw her grandmother at the desk; the desk was open and her grandmother was reading the papers from the desk. . . . She stood in the doorway watching and finally she said: 'You mean it doesn't lock any more? My desk doesn't lock?' "

The description occurs in a brief sketch Shirley wrote in college, but the scene recurs a number of times in Shirley's writings, published and unpublished. The sight of her grandmother bent over her desk, eagerly reading her most private papers, had the impact of a primal scene. She would never forget, never forgive, and never completely trust again.

It seems likely, too, that it happened more than once. There is little doubt that both Mimi and Geraldine, nosy, intrusive women, felt free to rifle through Shirley's papers anytime they wished, felt as do many adults that it was their right. Late in life Shirley told her own children that when she had left her parents' home for good, she burned every single page of her writings—openly, so Geraldine would know and feel bad. It probably made very little impression on her. Shirley's need for privacy was so deep, and her family's appreciation of it so limited when she was growing up, that the lack of understanding was almost complete. It probably would have shocked them considerably to know that she never forgave any of them. As a mother herself, Shirley would have faced a firing squad before going through any of her children's papers—a fact, they admitted ruefully, they took considerable advantage of as teenagers.

Because of her private bonfire, very few of Shirley's early poems remain. Those that do show little indication of any burgeoning literary talent. One, titled "Written for Mother's Day on May 1928," when Shirley was eleven, is interesting for one line. While the poem begins typically enough ("A mother is the nicest thing that ever there could be, / I have never had cause to forget, that mine means the world to me,"), there is a small instructive note toward the end: "If we ever feel that our mother is not quite fair to us, we must try to overcome this unfaithful feeling." Obviously Shirley's clear eye was not able, even in the throes of flowery verse, to avoid the truth completely.

It was not until the summer she was twelve that Shirley made her first real friend. Dorothy Ayling was one year younger, a thin, sharp-faced girl who lived a few houses down on Forest View. The two of them became inseparable. The first to wake up in the morning would stand outside her house, place two fingers in her mouth, and deliver a piercing whistle guaranteed to wake the other—and, of course, to set Geraldine's nerves permanently on edge.

Actually, Geraldine was glad to see Shirley have a friend at last, even one she would definitely not have picked for her daughter. Dorothy's father was the neighborhood's one blue-collar worker, a gardener for the Newcastle estate, whose grounds began at the edge of the Aylings' small house.

"We were poor, very poor. In those days there was a lot of prejudice. I was the gardener's daughter—so I never felt the Jacksons really wanted me tagging around with their daughter," she explained. "They had higher ideals. They were on a different level. I got that feeling." In all the years she and Shirley were best friends, Dorothy never once was invited to eat a meal at their house. "I'm sure they would have preferred Shirley to have a more fancy friend," she said. "I felt Mrs. Jackson tolerated me because I kept Shirley amused."

And Shirley, Dorothy knew, took plenty of amusing. "She was always wanting to be entertained, wanting to do this or that, or get something. She kept them hopping. There was always something stirring. She would just pester, pester, pester till she got whatever she wanted." Shirley insisted on being taken to see the fleet when it came into San Francisco Bay—and Dorothy, of course, had to come along. From the time they became friends, Shirley wanted Dorothy with her.

"She always wanted me tagging along," Dorothy remembered. "So I did." Shirley was the undisputed leader in the friendship—she decided what they were going to do, and when.

"I was a very placid person—that was my disadvantage. When we played duets, she always insisted on playing the top part, the better part. I always played the bottom part. Never did I get a chance to play the top. Any more than I'd say, no, I didn't want to go someplace. We played cards by the hour and she always cheated so she could win, and I let her cheat."

Occasionally Dorothy would stand up to Shirley and refuse to be compliant. This generally resulted in a fight, which would blow over in a day or two, with Dorothy resuming her role as sidekick once again. Annoying and overbearing as Shirley could be, she was also a lot of fun, and being around her was exciting. Under Shirley's leadership, the two girls would collaborate on baking projects, always leaving the kitchen in a mess and Geraldine furious; they would sneak up the street to watch the construction workers building the new road, giggling and making amateur attempts to flirt; sometimes they would creep up the hill to spy on one of the Newcastles' fancy parties at their estate, which was, of course, strictly off limits to all the children in the neighborhood. Left to her own devices, Dorothy would never have tried anything so risky, but it was hard to say no to Shirley.

In fact, Shirley's forcefulness was ultimately responsible for changing Dorothy's life: she had started taking violin lessons and joined the Burlingame High School orchestra, and was determined that Dorothy accompany her there too. "She insisted I had to learn a string instrument, so I took up cello, and from then on it was the center of my life." Dorothy earned enough giving cello lessons to attend San Francisco State; she has continued to play in a local symphony and teach cello all her life. Shirley dropped the violin after a couple of years.

The two girls also helped each other in school; Dorothy did Shirley's math for her and Shirley wrote Dorothy's English compositions. Dorothy, however, was a conscientious student. "I got mostly Bs, she got mostly Cs," she recalled. "She didn't apply herself."

Dorothy was a keen observer of the Jackson household, so different from her own. "Her mother was always nagging her to look nice, speak nicely, behave exactly the way she should. It was continual, all the time, in the car, wherever—reminding her to comb her hair, brush her teeth, did you do thus and so today, and so on. Every time you got into the car it was something—and before you got out, again. She wasn't kind about it—she was firm, insistent. Shirley would just listen. She wouldn't necessarily do it."

In fact, she often ignored Geraldine completely. A few times, Dorothy became so weary of hearing her nag Shirley to clean up her room that she did it herself. Shirley did tend to be messy, she knew.

At the same time, Dorothy had the definite feeling that the Jacksons treated Shirley as something special. "All the attention was on Shirley. She ruled the roost. Barry did what they wanted him to do, so they didn't pay much attention to him." Shirley's bedroom, for instance, was a large, beautiful room, while "Barry had a little cracker box." Often Dorothy would accompany Shirley and her mother and grandmother on shopping trips and be forced to watch uncomfortably as Shirley pressured Geraldine into buying her what she wanted.

The things Shirley wanted in those days were "high heels, frilly dresses—all the latest things. She was the first person I ever knew to get a permanent." At the same time, though, she was sloppy about her appearance—hemlines never hung right, the newest clothes somehow ended up looking slightly askew the minute she put them on. Part of it was due to her figure. It was not that she was terribly fat; in fact, when Dorothy first knew her she was average in weight, "but she did have this fat stomach that just popped out."

The Jacksons entertained a great deal at home, often on Sunday afternoons. The guests were "people who were their type . . . not rich, but .well-off." The entertainment often culminated in a musical performance; Geraldine and Leslie would sing light opera and Shirley and Dorothy would play a duet, often "Parade of the Wooden Soldiers." Neither Barry nor Mimi was around during these events; Barry was off with his friends and Mimi, Dorothy felt sure, was stashed in her upstairs bedroom. Shirley's grandmother was rarely brought out for formal occasions. Dorothy remembered her as being much more down-to-earth than Shirley's mother; not as snooty and full of airs. "She did most of the work in the home. Geraldine probably just sat and admired herself."

Dorothy also came to know another member of the Jackson family—Clifford Bugbee, Geraldine's brother. An odd man who lived alone, Clifford was an eccentric inventor—or at least tried to be. "I don't think he ever invented anything worth a darn," Barry Jackson said. One of his inventions, an enormous radio that came with a big horn attached and required the use of several dials to operate, sat in the Jacksons' sun room, behind the living room.

Years later Shirley would regale her children with Uncle Clifford stories. Clifford (according to Shirley) was always coming up with truly breakthrough inventions—twenty minutes too late. He would discover a brand-new principle of radio, or develop a white neon light, race madly down to the patent office, clutching his papers, only to find that someone had beaten him to the punch moments before and walked away with the patent. Clifford, as Shirley drew him, was funny, lovable, unforgettable. Dorothy found him unforgettable, too, but for more disturbing reasons.

"There was some little weirdness there," she remembered fifty-seven years later. "Sometimes he bothered me. He would call me endearing names and kind of touch me sometimes and I didn't know quite how to handle that. It bothered me. I wasn't there with him that much, but he would come and stay a little while . . . and he'd put his arm around you. I got so I realized that I better just keep a distance. I pretty quick figured out I didn't want to be near him—the way he talked to you, and the hands."

Did Clifford ever molest Shirley? Certainly he was around the house fairly often, visiting his mother; many times while Geraldine and Leslie were off on one of their party circuits. There is no way to know for sure, but the possibility is there; an older man who touches one young girl will usually have few qualms about touching another. And if true, it would help explain certain things.

Shirley rarely dealt with sex in any of her writing, and never directly. She preferred to use it, if at all, in small, disturbing touches. An early novel, *Hangsaman,* one of her most autobiographical, has one such glimpse. The teenage protagonist is either raped or molested—one never knows for sure—by an older man at a party and puts the occurrence quickly out of mind: "It never happened." But in fact, the incident has a shattering impact, contributing to her disintegration.

Was it true? Was Shirley sexually abused as an adolescent, on the green lawns behind her house in sunny Burlingame? Perhaps. It is hard not to conclude that something terribly evil happened there, something that cast a long shadow over the rest of her life. The dark current of awareness of evil that runs through her life and work seems too strong to have as its sole root the observance of suburban hypocrisy. Dorothy Ayling, a "placid person," remembered the sticky touch of Clifford Bugbee all her life. Shirley Jackson—so intense, so acutely aware—would not have been able to bear the memory. She would have had to split off from it, build walls around it, this thing that had torn through the fabric of her innocence, and never allow herself to remember it directly. But she would have emerged with a deep awareness of the evil that can exist in the human heart, and it would color everything she did.

But whatever dark knowledge had already insinuated itself, like an ice sliver, into Shirley's mind, on the surface her teenage years in California were certainly bland and pleasant enough. The small diaries she kept sporadically, writing in pencil in pocket-size datebooks given out by the G. W. Battle insurance brokerage firm, are full of the trivia of suburban life—bike riding, piano playing, brownie making and Girl Scout camp; with few exceptions, her observations are almost militantly normal, the thoughts and plans of a Typical American Girl.

"I've decided to write down just what I'd like to be at the start of 1933 and call that my New Year's resolution," she wrote on New Year's Day 1932, at age fifteen. "It will be awfully hard, cause I'm not easily satisfied. I'm just going to note down what I do every day and try to see if I'm not improving."

Among her aims: "To make myself healthier (thinner). Eating more good food and less sweets. Make myself better in my studies, kinder, friendlier, less nasty to my friends and family. To be sweeter to everybody I know, to cure myself of wanting to spend so much money and to try to make others happier. Of course I'd like to be popular—who wouldn't?—but in order to be popular I must first be good-natured and friendly. I will try to be popular because of my own cheer and happiness.

"I must lose that sense of inferiority but not go so far as vulgarity. I must cultivate charm and 'seek out the good in others rather than explore for the evil.' " Geraldine would have been proud. On a special data page provided, Shirley filled in the blanks: pal—Dorothy Ayling; boyfriend—Bud Young; favorite teacher—Professor Young; favorite color—blue; sport—tennis, baseball.

It is a rare adolescent who can maintain a diary for any length of time without a giant crush to sustain it. The object of her interest and the subject of a good eighty-five percent of the diary entries was a boy named Bud Young, who played violin and whose father conducted the school orchestra, and who was undoubtedly the prime reason behind Shirley's short-lived interest in the violin. Days were marked lucky or unlucky, depending on whether she saw him or not. At her insistence, Dorothy drew her a map of the Young house (she had been inside, Shirley hadn't) with an X marking Bud's room.

Dorothy could not remember that Shirley ever told her directly about her interest in Bud. "But he was a pretty good crush to have," she admitted. "He was a star basketball player, and a concert master of the orchestra. Nice-looking. But he couldn't have cared less about the girls back then."

Still, Shirley's crush raged on for at least two years. "O Bud—I'm crazier about you than ever and you've never seemed so far away," she wrote on August 30, 1932. "Just finished reading 'Tarzan and the Apes' and couldn't help wondering if Jane felt the same way towards her jungle lord as I do towards my girl-shy violinist. I guess not. Tarzan loved Jane."

Occasionally she wavered. "I'm cured—grand and glorious feeling," she wrote September 6. But not for long. "I spoke too soon," she admitted a month later. And then, after several more months, "I give in. I love Bud and I always will."

Her comments about school were offhand. "Had a good time in Latin. May learn how to do the trash, if I don't look out. Trig's tough—can't see it at all. History's screwy. Mrs. B. is a pill." Later—"History and trig exam. Probably flunked them both." And still later—"Flunked history test. Ethel [a schoolmate] and I are both poor guessers!"

Her writing, which she continued to do at her desk, was obviously more important. "Wrote all evening," she bragged, on February 3, 1933. "There was something in my pen tonite. I thought I'd never be able to write again, after I lost Bud, but I have noticed even an improvement. I can find nicer words, too, they were all in my pen!"

In the main, though, her diary is remarkable only for its typicality. The complaints are familiar to anyone who has ever known an adolescent. "There's never anything to do on weekends." And "sick of staying home and doing nothing." Or another time, "So despondent and miserable. Mother has been so cross all day there is no standing her. She makes me want to cry. Jumping on whatever I do. Wish I could go away."

Rarely, very rarely, she allowed her sharp intelligence to show through. After one of her parents' parties, she swiftly noted down descriptions of the guests: "A squidgy nosed old idol, condensed laughter; Cassanova plus 20 years; good natured Fu Manchu; Harlequin with a yellow streak." Returning from a neighborhood garden party, she wrote delightedly, "I feel like a package of condensed giggles. I do believe I'm potted! [L] was stewed to the gills. Mrs. K—an emotional beer keg on legs and in a yellow dress."

At a page near the end of one of her diaries, there is a curious inscription in her handwriting. "Note to Shirley: It would be very interesting to go through this book with a more open mind and find out how much is sincere and how much affectation. I'm afraid the result would be rather overwhelmingly in favor of the latter." It was almost as if the diary was in the nature of a disguise, the costume of a typical young girl that she had pulled down over her head. And that she knew it all along.

In later years Shirley would insist many times that she remembered very little of her childhood. It was, she once wrote, "pleasant and swift and easy going, and very little of it remains in conscious memory." She did at least recall that writing "used to be a delicious private thing, done in my own room with the door locked, in constant terror of the maternal knock and the summons to bed." ("Now that I am so luckily grown up and independent, there is no one to knock on the door and save me from my excruciating labors," she added sardonically.) But aside from that, very little remained: "Since ninety percent of my life went on in my head anyway, I cannot see any point in remembering odd concrete items."

But one thing she never forgot were the clothespin dolls; perhaps it was, as she said, because she had never before made so much of any one thing. It began with her mother's suggestion. "My dear friend Dorothy and I had perpetually nothing to do. It was summer and we were about fourteen, and all I can remember doing with Dorothy is sitting on a fence and eating pomegranates. . . . My mother used to be angry at us for doing nothing, and for sitting on fences, which was unladylike, and she used to think that pomegranates would stain our teeth." Finally Geraldine came up with "the bright and progressive idea" that they make clothespin dolls. She must have read it in a magazine, Shirley later figured out—her voice had that tone.

Fired with enthusiasm, she piled the girls into the car to buy clothespins, crepe paper, metallic paper, cotton, and paste. When they began to show a certain interest, at last, she happily cleared the dining room table for them and left them alone, smiling benevolently. It probably took a few days before the smile began to slip. Shirley and Dorothy had not been terribly eager to begin, but it quickly became clear that once they had, they did not intend to stop. Ever.

For the next several months, clothespin dolls of every type, nationality, and gender continued to pile up, spilling off the table, out of the dining room, down the hall, and up the stairs. Mimi's old corset boxes were commandeered to hold them, and they too began to pile up. Home entertainment was out of the question; even dinner had become a problem. The clothespin dolls had taken over the house.

It ended, finally, as suddenly as it had begun; the girls were each allowed to keep a box of their favorites, and the rest—over four hundred, all told—were donated to the Shriners' Hospital nearby. It could not have been Geraldine's favorite memory, but it was certainly one of Shirley's, and years later she sold the story as an article, then put it in one of her family collections, *Raising Demons*. It is silly to read anything into it, perhaps, but the fact is that even then Shirley took inordinate pleasure in the simple act of producing. Back then it was clothespin dolls; later it would be books and children, but the principle—and the satisfaction—would remain the same.

CHAPTER

·3·

In the spring of 1933, when Shirley was in her junior year at Burlingame High School, Leslie Jackson was given a chance to take a major leap up the ladder. His company, Traung Label, had bought the Stecher Lithograph Company in Rochester, New York, and Leslie was to be sent there as executive vice-president, to take charge of the new plant and preside over the merger. It was the sort of promotion one would turn down at one's peril, and there is no indication that either he or Geraldine ever thought of doing so for a minute. True, they would be leaving California, but the gains in money and prestige would be well worth it.

"It didn't bother me that much to be leaving Burlingame," said Barry Jackson. "But it did Shirley. She was very disturbed by it. I know it affected her the rest of her life." Barry, Geraldine, Leslie, and Mimi would all eventually return; Shirley alone would never live in California again.

The Jacksons announced the move as a fait accompli, in April. Shirley, a hothouse flower, was about to be pulled up and transplanted to a very different soil.

It may have made no difference. Maybe even if she had stayed in her beloved California, Shirley would ultimately have felt alienated, a stranger in a strange land. Certainly she had always been different, always somewhat at odds with her mother, her neighborhood, and her schoolmates. But in California she was at least rooted; she had the solid sense of place she had inherited from three generations of Bugbees to sustain her. It would never be that simple again.

Between the old life in Burlingame and the new one in Rochester, there was an intermission—a long summer sea voyage on the luxurious

SS. *California*. And the trip, oddly enough, turned out to be one of the happiest experiences the Jacksons ever shared as a family. Geraldine was in her element, socializing and dressing up every night; she was too busy to carp at her daughter. Freed from business commitments for the time being, Leslie was more relaxed than his family had ever seen him. Ship life was agreeable to all, the only problem being the heat, which was fierce. In 1933, even the most luxurious liner did not include air-conditioning. It was so hot that the impeccably uniformed waiter in the dining room had sweat beads dripping off the end of his nose; when he bent down to set the plates on the table, small droplets would fall into the food. One night Barry, who had celebrated his fifteenth birthday on board on August 15, crawled up on the awning over the deck to catch a breeze, and promptly fell asleep; he descended the next morning to general hysteria—his family was sure he had fallen overboard.

The boat stopped for twenty-four hours in Havana, and the passengers had time for a brief tour. "They were between revolutions," Barry Jackson said. "The tour guides were very proud to show us the bullet holes in the side of the capitol." The sight may have had something to do with Shirley's diary entry that night: "We leave Havana. Travel is an education in more ways than one. I have decided to be a lawyer," she wrote.

Once off the boat in New York City, the five Jacksons (Mimi had made the trip too) piled into a car driven by a staffer at the Stecher office and headed to Rochester. The shipboard honeymoon was over; the trip was long, hot, miserable, and close (freeways too were a thing of the future). They arrived, checked into a hotel, took their first deep breath of Rochester air—and Shirley burst into a series of explosive sneezes. It was the beginning of her first bout with hay fever, which would plague her throughout her life; she had never had an allergic reaction before in her life.

Shirley and Barry were immediately enrolled in a school near the hotel. It was a bad move. "I never felt so dumb in all my life," said Barry. "They were so much ahead of us." After two weeks, the Jacksons moved into a large, handsome house in Brighton, a suburb of Rochester, and switched Barry and Shirley to Brighton High School, which was at least somewhat better. The Jacksons began to settle in.

The town they had come to was considerably different from the one they had left. Physically Rochester was small and drab, with none of the bright lushness of the Bay area. Social strata were rigid, and the rules for correct behavior were plentiful and rigorously enforced. "Rochester is considered, still, to be somewhat stuffy, a closed corporation," said Betty Lyddon, a Rochester native who was a Brighton neighbor. "There were the proper clubs, the proper dancing school. There's a certain spirit to this town—very conservative, close-knit, among people of the same class and background." The town did not open its arms to strangers, and even Geraldine might have felt a bit daunted moving in. But not for long. Geraldine had been training all her life for just this situation: a small, controlled, rigorously conventional setting in which she could bloom. Rochester suited her completely; it was her kind of town.

It was not her daughter's. For over sixteen years Shirley had lived in the West, that region of open spaces and rugged individuality. It had been an atmosphere she loved and responded to; there was a vibrant sense of freedom in the air which helped counteract her mother's rigid rules of decorum. She loved to visit San Francisco, to watch the fleet come in, to enjoy the city's throbbing, exotic rhythms. Now suddenly she found herself in one of the most constricted towns in the constricted East, a place that prized conformity above all virtues, a place where no fleet would ever come in. It was as if she had been set down in a small city of Geraldines.

Playwright Thomas Babe, who grew up in the area years later, has described how it was for him there: "There was something mean about that stretch of country—nothing to encourage or reward you if you had any imagination or ambition, especially if you were not self-conscious enough to know or demand what you wanted. The life of the imagination seemed something wicked to them. At times, writing was a desperate act."

Looking back, Shirley would undoubtedly have agreed. Rochester had a stifling, even unhealthy effect on her. In the first year, though, her attention was taken up with the small, crucially important matters of adolescence—the problems of a somewhat unsure, slightly overweight sixteen-year-old facing her senior year in a brand-new school, made up almost completely of students who had known each other for years and who were divided as tightly into cliques as their parents were in the world outside. The circumstances may have been common, but the pain Shirley suffered was intense. She had never truly known loneliness before, not consciously—before, there had been Dorothy, and the familiar surroundings of Burlingame. Now suddenly, for the first time, loneliness became a constant in her life. It had the effect of driving her back into herself even more.

One of her worst moments came when she was rejected from a Brighton High School sorority she thought she had a good chance of getting into. "I think that was a severe shock to her," said Jean Rathgen, who was two years younger, lived across the street from the Jacksons, and belonged to the sorority herself. "Two girls, sisters, were responsible for black-balling her, I think. They were wheeler-dealers. Several of us felt bad. I think the reason was—Shirley was a little bit different. She was more of an intellectual, she wasn't what they used to call, in quotes, the popular type of girl. She didn't care that much about what she wore—I remember she used to wear a green sweater and a blue skirt, and in those days you didn't wear a green sweater and a blue skirt. She was on the heavy side; her hair was always sort of windblown. And her mother was a fashion plate! I think Shirley rejected that sort of thing.

"I think she never learned the techniques of being a more accepted person. My own personal feeling is that the rejection by that crazy stupid high school sorority may have had something to do with her writing 'The Lottery.' I know she was very hurt by it."

Her diary records only one sentence: "I didn't make the sorority. Damn Gene Robbins."

Instead, Shirley hung around with a group of neighborhood teens, boys and girls, many of them younger—Jean Rathgen, Betty Lyddon, Janet Walker, Marion Morton among them. It was at least a crowd to hang out with—there were games, potluck suppers, parties, treasure hunts. Jean Rathgen remembers "Monopoly games that went on all weekend. You'd go to someone's house, start a game, go home to eat, sleep, and go back." But Shirley was acutely aware that belonging to this group placed her in a lower social caste. Some years later, she poured out all her contempt and repugnance in an unfinished piece:

"Doris was fat and badly dressed and stupid, and the center of a little group of girls who did things by themselves, went to movies and had parties and went swimming in the summer, in a gay chattering body whose animation never quite concealed the fact that they were ugly and awkward and unpopular. Ginny was pale . . . and given to much giggling flirtation with her teachers. When Natalie sat with them she knew that she was marked, just as irretrievably as though they had all worn distinctive uniforms, as one of the little group around Doris, the terribly social outsiders." The pain of this knowledge was mixed with the awareness that she was, somehow, failing her parents too by her own social failure. Natalie worries that they will think she is late "because she had been having such a gay time with her new friends, the pleasant people she had met, become close to, so readily in this new high school." Yet she is careful, in her shame, "not to confess to her mother and father she was hopelessly entangled with the wrong people."

It is important to note that Natalie herself—and Shirley, speaking through her—feels strongly that she deserves better than the companionship of these girls; she at least is horribly aware of their shortcomings, as they are not. It is only by some terrible mistake that she finds herself somehow "entangled" in their midst: surely the mistake will be corrected any minute, and she will be restored to her rightful place. Yet at the same time there is the nagging suspicion that perhaps it is not a mistake at all.

The mother portrayed in the early unpublished Natalie pieces (and in Shirley's novel *Hangsaman,* in which she also takes the name Natalie) is obviously modeled on Geraldine and is a conventional, foolish, shallow woman. Her main flaw as seen through Shirley's eyes, however, is her weakness, her ineffectuality. And perhaps that was what Shirley hated in her mother more than anything. Not her occasional cruelties, not the fact that she nagged, criticized, even berated her daughter at times, not that she tried to force her into a mold obviously not made for her, but simply that she was weak and, finally, unable to protect her daughter from pain. Cruelty Shirley understood; she knew she had a streak of it herself. But all her life she would despise weakness and ineffectuality— a legacy from her business executive father, perhaps. And never more than during her first year in Rochester, when she suffered her first real rejection and saw that there was nothing Geraldine could do to help her. It would be years before Shirley would learn the awful lesson all parents know—that no one can, ultimately, protect a child from pain. But by then it would be too late for her to forgive Geraldine.

Betty Lyddon remembers the group she and Shirley were in together. "We didn't fit in. We were not the . . . I suppose you'd call it the party crowd. We were also perhaps less sophisticated than that crowd. We were not the super-popular crowd, not the athletic crowd. Just sort of went our own way."

At one point Betty, Shirley, and Janet Walker, whose house backed on Shirley's, made a list of resolutions and signed it: "Not to do: Not to go out with Edwin, worry, think, pet. Not to do in excess: smoke, drink, waste money, fall in love, talk, neck, sleep, work, day-dream, idealize, be catty, do things that involve catching colds, talk about one subject exclusively. To do: all assignments, be nice, be ambitious, be neat, be happy." It may have been a true collaboration, but the zeal for self-improvement has Shirley's name written all over it—and it is her sprawling signature that dominates the other two.

Many original, creative people have had the experience of being unpopular in high school, a setting that rewards conformity. Perhaps it is part of the price of admission to the fold, although it would be slim comfort to any unhappy sixteen-year-old to hear that. If so, though, Shirley paid her dues in her senior year at Brighton High.

"And another year skis away from under my feet," she wrote pensively in her diary that December, when she turned seventeen. "Ambition— author, actress, aviator, lawyer. (Almost all are impossible.)"

Missing California, she wrote often to Dorothy, back in Burlingame, asking for news of school, the orchestra, and Bud. ("He hasn't fallen for anyone yet," Dorothy reassured her.) Shirley's grades were no better in the new school than they'd been before, she admitted. "Don't forget to frame that 'D' in chem with the one you got in Latin," Dorothy chided her.

Lonely, unhappy, Shirley turned to the one place she felt comfortable and powerful—the fascinating country of her own mind. She was writing daily now, exercising her skill, spending hours at her desk, going over her poems again and again. "Secretly, lovingly, afraid only that someday her own reaching, poignant emotions might take her completely, carry her into an ecstasy beyond the limits of her desk, Natalie hoarded her treasures, copying and recopying, criticising and revising, building and hoping," she later described it.

But the act of writing was not quite as hidden as it had been before, back in Burlingame. Adolescence demands an identity, or at the very least a pose, and Shirley was struggling to claim one. Maybe she couldn't be popular, or hang out with the in crowd, but she could at least develop a reputation as an artist; she was not above flaunting her creativity a bit. Even her friends in the neighborhood knew about Shirley's writing; Marion Morton spent the night once at the Jackson house, and was taken aback: "Shirley got up in the middle of the night and started to write a story. If a story came into her head, she'd get up and put it on paper, no matter where she was." Once Jean Rathgen shyly asked Shirley for her opinion on a piece she had written—"she blue-penciled it but good," she recalled ruefully. With her voracious reading, Shirley was beginning to present herself as an intellectual, to toss ideas around.

"She was sort of ahead of her time," said Morton. "More like the sixties generation than we were. We were sort of squarish. She did things we didn't do, like smoking. She smoked quite a bit. Her brother was more like us."

"Shirley considered herself an intellectual," said Jean Rathgen. "There were not very many people on her plane."

She was also beginning to realize she could use her wit as a battering ram when she wanted to. It made a strong defensive armor. Besides, she was good at it.

"She was able to cut people down pretty easily," Jean Rathgen admitted. "At times, you know, she could be on the cruel side. I think that's the kind of behavior that results from rejection . . . that feeling of being on the outside." One fat, good-hearted, not terribly bright girl in the neighborhood was the particular object of her scorn, and probably the model for Doris.

She also began, now, for the first time, to explore the world of witchcraft, reading everything she could find on the subject. It was never a superficial or frivolous pursuit—Shirley was determined to find out everything she could about the world she felt she had already encountered, in psychic visions. Nothing in the outside world held the same fascination for her that her own mind did; studying witchcraft was a route to studying herself, and it became a lifelong endeavor. There are those who would always insist that her interest was purely intellectual, and her brother is among them. "She studied it like you'd study history," he said. "I always thought it was a little tongue-in-cheek."

But others, among them her children, know different. "Do you experience it and then start studying it to find out what all this weirdness is, or is it the other way around?" said Shirley's older son, Laurence Hyman. "I believe that she experienced it first and then got interested. My mother believed strongly and firmly in the supernatural. She believed it and was very tuned in to it, perhaps more than she cared to be. I always believed she believed that she was in touch with a whole ungodly assortment of demons and characters. I don't think it was very pleasant for her."

Still, Shirley felt more at home in the intensely private world of her mind than in the world Geraldine was trying diligently to cram down her throat. The senior Jacksons had taken to Rochester society with gusto. Leslie first joined one club, the Oak Hill Country Club, then dropped that for the Rochester Country Club, later adding another, the Genesee Valley Club. He and Geraldine insisted Shirley and Barry appear with them at one club or another every Sunday night for dinner. Both of them cordially detested it, but their parents were adamant.

"My mother had visions that Shirley and I would each marry somebody in Rochester society; that was a big deal to her. She was in the DAR, belonged to the clubs. You had to be a socialite," said Barry Jackson.

"Those clubs . . . if you didn't belong to the Rochester Country Club and the Genesee Valley Club you didn't belong at all. I used to hate that Genesee Valley Club with a passion. You had to be in the right family and [have] the right income to walk in the door. If you were black, forget it. Jewish too, sure, the same thing. But we had to make an appearance; that was our duty."

At the same time, Shirley continued to get a certain amount of special treatment in the home. Her room in the Rochester house was large and beautiful, with an old English four-poster bed. Her wardrobe was filled with expensive outfits.

But there was a quid pro quo for all this, and Shirley was less and less ready to pay it. The older she grew, the more restricted she felt by her parents' master plan for her life. Shirley yearned to go away to college, but Geraldine put her foot down. She would enroll in the University of Rochester, right there in town, where her parents could keep a close eye on her. Shirley argued, but Geraldine—with Leslie's iron backing—was implacable. "She was boxed in," said Jean Rathgen. "Her mother could be a bit overpowering." In the fall of 1934, Shirley began classes at the university. It would be three years, three long years, before she would finally pull away from her parents' control.

CHAPTER

·4·

Rejection at Brighton High School had made her feel like an ugly misfit, but in fact pictures taken around this time show a young woman who had lost some of her early pudginess and was far from unattractive, with her bright smile and shining eyes. The hair straggles loosely from her bun, the clothes, as always, hang a bit askew, but there is a zest that emanates from the old photos, an eagerness, a vibrancy that is terribly appealing. She looks wrenchingly young and hopeful, ready for a new world.

She didn't get it at college. Shirley hated the University of Rochester from day one. The school then had a reputation for being rather like the town itself—stuffy, constricted, dull; boys and girls were separated, attending classes at different campuses. Shirley lived in the dorm her first year but spent most of her time in the Peacock Room, smoking and playing bridge. None of her courses interested her, and she did only minimal work. But one important thing did happen to her the first year there—she made a friend.

It was not, again, someone Geraldine would have picked for her. In fact, it was probably the one girl on campus Geraldine would not have picked, which was undoubtedly part of the point. But not all. From the first, Shirley connected strongly with Jeanne Marie Bedel, known as Jeanou, an exchange student from France, who was brilliant, independent, and certainly for Rochester, wildly unconventional. "A strange girl," Barry Jackson remembered.

Elizabeth Young, who met Shirley the following year at Rochester, remembered with amusement the university's response to Jeanou. "Jeanou was a communist," she said. "Well, let's just say, radical." The university authorities were horrified at what they had brought into their midst; when the time came to choose the next exchange student, they were triply careful, finally settling on a clean-cut French youth who had a fascination with American movies. For a time he behaved impeccably, and the officials patted themselves on the back for their wise choice. Then one night he went to see a gangster film, got roaring drunk, and held up a local couple with a toy gun. It was a long time before the University of Rochester had another exchange student.

For Shirley, drowning in the atmosphere of Rochester, Jeanou was a lifeline. They wandered around the city for hours, or sat up in Shirley's room talking endlessly about their hopes and plans for the future, reassuring each other. Her loneliness was just a stage to be passed through, Jeanou told Shirley; she had beauty, wit, and talent and was destined to be wildly popular. Men would fall madly in love with her; all she had to do was wait and it would happen. Through Jeanou, Shirley met a young Russian piano player, Kostia, one of the first men to show her any real interest. Excitedly, she wrote Dorothy about it. Her friend's reply was laconic: "Your whole letter is about the Russians. They make very poor husbands," she said dismissively.

Kostia, however, didn't last long. "To sleep rather than to live," Shirley mourned extravagantly in her diary. "Why does life seem calculated to administer a deadening shock to each new jubilance?"

But the friendship with Jeanou flourished. Shirley felt she had for the first time in her life met someone on her own level, with whom she could discuss books and ideas and her own ambitions, someone who saw her as she was. The two girls eagerly exchanged their favorite reading. Shirley taught Jeanou "The Walrus and the Carpenter," and gave her the Alice books; Jeanou started Shirley reading François Villon and told her about the commedia dell'arte, which fascinated her.

In some ways, though, it was the Dorothy relationship all over again. Shirley could not help trying to dominate the friendship. Jeanou, however, was less compliant and had even fewer qualms than Dorothy about telling Shirley off. At one point she wrote her a critical note pinpointing some of her faults; Shirley, irked, mailed it off to Dorothy at once, obviously hoping her old pal would disagree with Jeanou's analysis. She didn't.

"Poor Jeanou must have a swell time arguing with you," Dorothy wrote back. "I bet she wins. I don't think that her letter is so insulting. I don't think anyone could describe you any better. I think she has you wrong when she says that you are 'terribly afraid of being ridiculous or looking sentimental,' unless you have changed a lot since you left here. I wouldn't say that is true, but you are 'sometimes of an unbearable affection.' I certainly do agree with Jeanou on that point. Tell Jeanou that I had just as many quarrels with you, but you always had to do the apologizing. If you really want my opinion, I think it is a very exact letter, and if I could write that kind of letter I would say the same things."

With Jeanou, as with Dorothy, Shirley had picked a close friend with a cool analytical eye who was not afraid to criticize her. She would continue to gravitate to people like that for the rest of her life. Shirley felt most comfortable around critics.

The intense friendship between the two girls, both of them "intellectuals," both of them so markedly different from the typical University of Rochester student, gave rise to a certain amount of talk on campus. Shirley, always sensitive, was aware there were others who thought the relationship strange, possibly even (they whispered) unnatural. Jeanou, who was French and in many ways more mature than Shirley, was amused— she had total contempt for the small-town Rochester mentality anyway. But Shirley, daughter of Geraldine, still had a foot in the other camp and could not pass it off so easily.

A few years later, she wrote about it: "when i first used to write stories and hide them away in my desk i used to think that no one had ever been so lonely as i was and i used to write about people all alone. once i started a novel . . . but i never finished because i found out about insanity about then and i used to write about lunatics after that. i thought i was insane and i would write about how the only sane people are the ones who are condemned as mad and how the whole world is cruel and foolish and afraid of people who are different. that was when i was still in high school and i was ugly and shy because of it and i didn't like to go to school because no one talked to me. then later i went to college and i had a friend and she was kind to me and together we were happy. she introduced me to a man who didn't laugh at me because i was ugly and i fell in love with him and tried to kill myself but i was happy just the same. and my friend was so strange that everyone, even the man i loved, thought we were lesbians and they used to talk about us, and i was afraid of them and i hated them, then i wanted to write stories about lesbians and how people misunderstood them. and finally this man sent me away because i was a lesbian and my friend went away and i was all alone."

The suicide attempt she mentions was not a serious one; her parents possibly never even knew about it. A number of times in her unpublished stories and again in *Hangsaman* there is a scene on a bridge, in which a young girl considers killing herself, starts to step over the railing, then changes her mind—Shirley's attempt was probably along those lines. As far as being a lesbian, despite Shirley's sharp intelligence, it is highly unlikely that at age eighteen—and an unworldly eighteen at that, despite all the reading—she even knew precisely what the word meant. But her opinion that "the whole world is cruel and foolish and afraid of people who are different" was a seasoned assessment, and one that would not change over the years.

At the close of the school year, Jeanou left to return to France. As a parting gift, she gave Shirley a volume of the works of François Villon, complete with slightly racy pen-and-ink illustrations (one showed a man urinating). Geraldine took one look, turned green, and ordered it out of the house. But Shirley refused to give the book up and kept it in her room, although she did put it in the back of the shelves, behind her other books.

The Jacksons had now moved to an even larger home, in the city, with an even larger room for Shirley. This one had a window seat and an alcove for her bed and, all in all, was a lot more inviting than the university dormitory. It was decided that Shirley would commute for her second year. The first year had gone poorly, academically, and over the summer her parents provided a tutor, whom Shirley referred to sneeringly in her diary as "that so queer Mr. Keyes." Higher education so far was having approximately the same effect on her as lower education had, which is to say, not much. And yet the Jacksons knew Shirley was bright; if only she would learn to apply herself. The fact that she was at her desk every day for hours, writing—an amazing display of discipline for an eighteen-year-old—impressed them very little.

Shirley, for her part, was willing to continue to attend classes, if that was what her parents wanted—but she was unable to force herself to care very much about what went on there. As usual, a great deal of her life was being conducted under the surface, in her mind, a much more fascinating place than the University of Rochester lecture halls. For now, she was beginning to do something different than before—she was developing her own private mythology, the mythology of one country, the country of Shirley's mind. Certain characters and symbols had a special, private meaning to her. They were almost like imaginary friends, with whom she could have a delightfully intimate relationship, friends who would not draw back in horror because she was "different." They were not real in the sense the desk in her room was real, of course, but as always Shirley was comfortable with other realities.

Two dominant characters were Pan and Harlequin: a pewter mask of the face of Pan hung in Shirley's room, as did a painting of Harlequin, possibly another legacy from Jeanou. Each of them had a special place in her mind, a presence. Especially now with Jeanou gone, Shirley needed friends—and the ones you created yourself were not likely to leave you.

She continued to spend time with the neighborhood crowd at times, occasionally dating one boy, Jimmie, whom Jean Rathgen remembered as "an odd one . . . but he was a date. It was no great love. But he paid her attention." At one point, Jean, Shirley, Jimmie, and Jean's friend

Bob visited a private island the Rathgens owned in the Adirondacks. "We were out there on the island, supposedly Jimmie and Shirley had fallen asleep, and Bob and I were kissing. Later Shirley told me she wasn't asleep at all," she recalled. Later she found it funny; at the time it seemed a sneaky thing to do.

"It has been a strange year, then, a strange year and a memorable one," Shirley wrote in her diary on January 2, 1936, midway through her second year at the university. "Things have happened and things have not happened. First there was the continuation of last year . . . which meant dreariness of remembering and eagerness of hoping. There was the thought and then the remembrance of Kostia, there was Jeanou, and then not Jeanou, in the saddest and the wisest thing that has ever happened to this compound of creatures I call Me. There was that suddenness of loss, and the tears, and the philosophy, and the realizations of education; there was the demands of the so-called education, and summer school."

In addition, she went on, there had been "Jimmie and the ruination of what we laughingly refer to as my reputation" (a possible reference to the night on the island?) and then going "back to face what Jeanou left. What did she leave? She gave me as a parting gift the ability to face people and laugh at them, because she knew that I would need it. . . . I have proven to myself this year that I can achieve what I want by not caring—and I do not care.

"As to resolutions—I have still my old one, untarnished and true though it has been true for so many years for me. I can still say, free and still uncaring—I shall be happy. . . . Life is such fun, Villon, Harlequin, Pan and Shirley!"

The reaction of others to her friendship with Jeanou only reinforced what she already knew—that people could be cruel and small-minded and carry evil in their hearts, and that it was best to face them with a mask. "Nothing has the power to hurt which doesn't have the power to frighten," she wrote in her diary. "If you keep a tight hold on the inside of that grin, Shirley, the outside can't crack."

Shirley and Jeanou carried on a correspondence, at first steady, which declined as their worlds diverged more and more. Jeanou had returned to the charged atmosphere of prewar Paris. She would eventually throw herself into Resistance work and even go to jail for a brief period near the end of the war. Afterward she would continue to work for radical causes. Though they had less and less in common over the years, they still exchanged occasional letters; Shirley named her old friend godmother to her third child, an honor Jeanou deeply appreciated until she realized Shirley had no intention of baptizing her.

In her second year at Rochester, Shirley made another close friend, Elizabeth Young. She was not the soulmate that Jeanou had been, but she was a reader, highly intelligent, and had a crisp, dry analytical manner that attracted Shirley. "i became eccentric and i found another friend and we used to wander around the city being crazy and i would wear my hair flying and always be laughing and my friend would laugh and she wore her hair in little curls all over her head. sometimes we did things like going to see santa claus and asking him for a rosebush and sometimes now when i think of the things we did i get very uncomfortable," Shirley wrote a few years later.

Shirley dubbed Elizabeth "Y," pronounced "Eee," as in French, and dubbed herself "Lee," although the latter never took. She felt close enough to her new friend to tell her about certain things—her writing ambitions, even her private characters, Pan and Harlequin. "She had these sort of fantasy figures that she would refer to. Her fantasies did turn to very imaginative things. They were her characters; she'd talk about them," Young said. Shirley also told Y about her interest in witchcraft and the commedia dell'arte.

"She had a very rich fantasy life fed by what she read, almost more than by her human contacts. I always felt that she had this rich world of imagination . . . Pan, Harlequin, the Devil, all there, that she wasn't looking at the people around her."

"It was a time of discovery in my life and in hers," Young continued. "There was an excitement about it. That's why we were friends at that time. She'd talk about these fantasies, like Pan, as though they were around. As though they had a persona, an outlook. I always felt it was a playful thing in her mind. Hers was the world of imagination, mystery, strong currents of unexplained things . . . implied things."

The girls exchanged books and talked about their new discoveries. Both were mystery buffs and would go to the library together to load up. They played an ongoing game, trying to stump each other with quotes. Shirley's reaction to books or movies could be intense. One day she walked into the Peacock Room, where Y was sitting in on the eternal bridge game, and when her friend greeted her just stared back, her face filled with emotion, then left. "I found out later she had seen *Winterset* the night before and was so emotionally overcome by it she couldn't talk."

As a close friend, Elizabeth Young was well aware that Shirley was unhappy at Rochester and doing poorly there. Shirley did, however, briefly join a writing club at the university. "I remember this very very conservative, classically inclined man, the head of the English department, read something of hers and he was impressed by it. Not because it was well written, because he made it quite clear it wasn't. But he said she was the only one in the group who had not written a story with a male and a female in it. He thought she had real promise because she was looking at things in a different sort of way."

The story was about two people who met by a river, both intending to commit suicide. "She rewrote it a number of times, with different endings. In some versions they did, in some versions they didn't," said Young.

Young found Shirley's parents quite likable, if conservative (and they for their part probably greeted her very warmly, as a major improvement upon Jeanou). "The whole family was very California-like, hearty, good-humored. I remember a lot of good-humored joking between Shirley and Barry and with her father." Shirley's father, she thought, was "breezier than her mother"; it was he who had the artistic leanings and had belonged to the Bohemian Club in San Francisco. Shirley told her that when she was little it was her father who used to make up stories for them now and then and illustrate them himself; his favorite was a running tale about a cat, Mother Tabbyskin.

Others, too, had noticed similarities between father and daughter. "She was like her father in looks and personality," Betty Lyddon said. "He was an executive but had a bit of the maverick to him."

On the other hand, he could be inflexible. "Her father was a very affable man but politically very much the Reagan type of Republican," said Young. At one point Shirley wanted to find a job and went down for an interview with a local newspaper. "The editor of the paper knew her father and told him, and her father was furious. He thought everyone would think the business was not doing well if his daughter needed a job."

As for Geraldine, "she tried very hard to dress her and groom her." At the beginning of each school year, Geraldine would make sure Shirley had a permanent and a new wardrobe—Young remembered a plaid skirt, a grape blouse, a new coat. "But inside of no time at all, her hair would be straight and tied back in a ponytail and she'd be wearing one of her old outfits—she had a tweed raincoat she would wear all the time. Her mother was very nice, but it was sort of like a hen with a duckling." She remembered Geraldine fixing Shirley's hair with a curling iron before a club dance. "She was trying to help her be what she thought girls should be," said Young. "She thought that what a girl ought to want was to get married, join the country club."

Neither of Shirley's parents had any particular interest in literature, as far as she could see. "They didn't have a lot of books, they tended to be Book-of-the-Month-ish. She was the one with the books. She was a changeling."

Yet during the time she knew her, Shirley seemed close to her parents, and genuinely fond of them. "Although who knows? We all sit on our own volcanoes, after all," Young mused. Shirley's political views, for instance, were exactly like those of her father (Jeanou having apparently made very few inroads on that front). "She certainly took her own path and followed it, later," said Young. "But there was always a strong element of her family in her. She never left it behind, I'm sure."

In spring 1936 Shirley did leave the University of Rochester behind, however—although it is fairly certain that her departure came by university request. Her neighbor Marion Morton is sure of it: "She finally flunked out," she said.

"It's very likely," Young agreed. "She was doing very badly. I was getting along okay there, but she was just out of it."

Shirley had not wanted to go to the university originally, and had hated it from the minute she got there. The courses were dull, the professors archaic; they could turn the whole thing into a pig farm and no one would ever know the difference, she said. But flunking out was humiliating—imagine, a girl of her intelligence. Her parents were horrified, and Shirley, always high-strung, was hysterical. In the following months she struggled with her first real bout of depression. Dr. James Toolan, the psychiatrist she saw toward the end of her life, confirmed that she suffered something of a breakdown at this time, although it was, he felt, relatively minor.

For the next year, Shirley stayed close to home, allowing Geraldine to put her through various social paces, appearing at country-club dinners and dances regularly. Her spirit was bruised but far from dead, and she set a goal for herself: she would write a thousand words a day, every day throughout the year. She was honing the discipline that would stand her in good stead her entire life.

"I think she felt about her writing the way joggers feel—you've got to go do it, you can't be good at it if you don't do it, and if you do it you can be really good. And she knew she was really really good, as long as she kept doing it," Shirley's older daughter explained. Her approach to writing was practical, not mystical; she went at it like a dancer warming up at the barre.

She continued, during the year, to see the old neighborhood crowd now and then, for picnics and movies and parties; her friend Y visited often. But her social life was far from exciting, and her parents decided to give her a hand. Leslie was now president of Stecher-Traung, and there were plenty of the right sort of young men working at the company. He arranged a dinner date for Shirley with one of them, Mike Palmer, a recent University of Rochester graduate whose mother was a tea-party chum of Geraldine's. Palmer was good-looking, dashing, every inch the gentleman—and Shirley quickly developed a huge crush on him.

Palmer couldn't help but be aware of it, and it put him in an uncomfortable position. After all, this was the daughter of the boss. To pursue her might look as if he were currying favor; on the other hand, to drop her would be far from politic. It was a tricky situation, made even trickier by the fact that he did not remotely return her affection. "She had a great interest in me for a short time. Poor child, I really felt bad about it," he remembered.

Palmer found Shirley simultaneously "a very brilliant girl and a gushing teenager," certainly a volatile combination. "She was nice and attractive—I wouldn't say she was beautiful. The mix of the mother and father did not turn out to be as beautiful as it could have." She was, he thought, very much her father's child. "She had all the qualities he had, the brilliance, the extraordinarily quick mind. He was magnetic, one of those people who could charm everybody in the room. The mother was very lovely but had none of his brilliance. She was very into the social end of things. Barry was the mother's child, Shirley the father's. They were as different as night and day. Barry was mild, easygoing, and Shirley was frighteningly brilliant."

Shirley went out with Mike Palmer several times, while her parents beamed approvingly—perhaps, after all, that was all it took, one right young man and their daughter would drop her foolish interests and take up the banner of country-club suburbia forever. It was probably the last time they would ever allow themselves that particular fond hope.

For Shirley had realized—after the dust settled—that flunking out of Rochester might have been the best thing that could have happened to her. If it did nothing else, it showed that she had been right all along—she needed to go away to college. Not too far, but away. Shirley announced that in fall 1937 she would be attending Syracuse University, a school with a highly respected journalism department. And this time she would not be brooked. Warily, a bit uneasily, her parents agreed.

Palmer, for one, was shocked. "At that time Syracuse was a hotbed of communism and antisocial attitudes," he said. "Leslie was aware of this. He wanted something more desirable for his daughter."

But Shirley got her way. It would mean that she would be launched into a world so different from that of her parents it might actually be called an alternative reality, and that her life would never be the same again. It was a simple decision, even an obvious one—Syracuse was the next closest university, after all. But it set into motion a chain of events that would catapult her far away from the narrow confines of Rochester, into another universe.

CHAPTER
·5·

Newly permanented, her expensive new fall wardrobe in tow, and her old typewriter under her arm, Shirley arrived at Syracuse in September 1937, having salvaged enough credits from Rochester to enroll as a sophomore. She was twenty, and more than ready for a new start. Despite Palmer's opinion, the university in the late thirties was far from being a "hotbed of radical ideas," but nonetheless, there was definitely a wider spectrum of humanity represented here than at the University of Rochester—for one thing, the entire campus was coed, no small difference. Syracuse had the usual predominance of groups typical of all big universities—the jocks; the cheerleaders; the fraternity-sorority crowd; the business, home ec, forestry, and pre-med majors—but it was also large enough to have an arty sector and even a small but thriving radical community as well.

Writing and journalism were taken seriously at Syracuse; the school newspaper, *The Daily Orange,* and the campus humor rag, *The Syracusan,* were both thriving entities. Even better for Shirley's purposes, there was a class in creative writing, which she enrolled in at once.

The teacher, Professor A. E. Johnson, was a mild-mannered gentleman who tended to be overly pleased with his own vague efforts, which consisted primarily of flowery spurts of verse. "Someone should chain me to my desk so I could do nothing but write," he would implore regularly, while his students choked back snickers. (Unfortunately, he did eventually manage to publish a book of poetry, which Shirley, by then a brash senior, tore to shreds mercilessly in a campus magazine.) Johnson did little to earn her respect, but that hardly mattered. What was important was that for the first time in her life Shirley found herself in a group of would-be writers. She herself had changed very little over the past few years; she was still the same emotional, odd, intense, intellectual girl she had been in high school. But these selfsame traits, which at one time had caused her to experience pain and rejection, now suddenly seemed actually responsible for attracting people to her. These new people didn't find her eccentricities distasteful—they found them appealing, even impressive, sure signs of an artistic temperament. It was a heady feeling.

Shirley and a handful of other students in the class quickly formed a tight group. Nearly every day they went out eagerly to encounter adventure, descending into the very bowels of the city to seek it out, then returning to write about it and compare versions. "It didn't matter what the target might be," said Al Parsell, who was one of them. "A ride on the trolley, a beer joint, a sunset, department stores, whatever." The important thing was to take it in, return to your room, filter it through one literary form or another, then meet the next day to compare your results with everyone else's.

There was a feeling of excitement, even risk. "Here we were, middle-class students, going down into the depths of Syracuse, going to bars, striking up conversations with people we didn't normally deal with," said Parsell. And no one was more eager, more ready to hit the streets for art, than Shirley.

Right away, it was clear to the others that Shirley's writing was different. "She would always be a little more mystical than the rest of us," said Parsell. "I was always the realist. This was the Depression, and I was always saying, People are starving and we've got to do something about them. Shirley was always going off into the clouds."

Many of her pieces were either about—or written to—a central figure named Y. But the Y in Shirley's work was less her friend in Rochester, it is likely, and more a presence she had developed on her own, a fantasy Y which used the real Y only as a point of departure (in the same way she had developed Pan and Harlequin, earlier, partly out of what she remembered of Jeanou). The new Y now became a part of her private mythology.

It was in one of these written dialogues with the mythical Y that Shirley first alluded to a shadowy figure that had begun to appear to her, either in a dream or in a vision, around this time—a figure that would eventually take form in her mind as the demon lover (or daemon, as she would later spell it, using the old English ballad form of the word). Whatever it was— dream, vision, alternate reality—wherever it sprang from, the idea of a daemon lover took root in Shirley's mind with extraordinary strength, appearing and reappearing for years. A desirable entity, somehow imbued with the ability to fill up an aching void, never directly seen, rarely even directly alluded to, the Daemon Lover would continue for years to flicker in and out of view—with something not quite real, not quite human, and very possibly terrible at his core.

"but all i remember is that i met him (somewhere where was it in the darkness in the light was it morning were there trees flowers had i been born) and now when i think about him i only remember that he was calling margaret. as in loneliness margaret margaret. and then (did i speak to him did he look at me did we smile had we known each other once) i went away and left him (calling to me after me) calling margaret margaret."

There would be a time when she would meet a man in real life who powerfully resembled her myth of the Daemon Lover, and in writing of him she would take the name Margaret again, but that would not be for many years.

Kay Turk, another member of the group, was older than Shirley, a cool, self-possessed young lady who was mildly amused at some of Shirley's histrionics. "She was pretty emotional at that point," she remembered. At times, Shirley could become hysterical in public, for no apparent reason, or so it seemed to Kay. "She would get very shrill, words would come tumbling out. And she would turn and say, 'Hit me in the face, hit me in the face.' " Kay, obligingly, would promptly smack her once or twice, which seemed to calm her down.

"Kay took care of me all through my first year at college," Shirley later wrote, adding that by the next year, she was tired of her: "I was in love and she was just a little dismal about it." But for the first year at Syracuse, Kay also performed another service—as a proper young lady who came from the right sort of home, she was (Shirley knew) just the sort of friend Geraldine wanted her to have. Shirley took Kay home to Rochester several times.

Kay found Shirley "intriguing"—her unusual mind, her talent. Once she sat with Shirley as Shirley tried to conjure up the devil—Shirley was beginning to do a few experiments in magic along with her witchcraft reading. "She was hoping a black dog would walk up, that would be the sign," said Kay. "She just said something like, 'Devil if there be a Devil, make yourself known.' " He didn't, at least not then.

Kay also observed, a little distastefully, Shirley's problem with her weight. "It went up and down. She would eat herself huge, then diet and get herself down to where she should be, then back up again." Shirley was, she thought, a homely girl.

But Al Parsell disagreed; in fact, he was quite taken with Shirley. "You wouldn't say she was attractive, but she was striking," he said. "A fascinating person. I reveled in the fact that I knew her. My own roommates used to think I was crazy because I went out with her. They thought she was way out. I guess my feeling then was, she was one of the most exciting people I knew."

Shirley was not seriously interested in Al, but being somebody else's fascination was a delightful new sensation, which she thoroughly enjoyed. For herself, she was still nurturing a rather perfunctory crush on Mike Palmer, much as she had with Bud Young a few years before. "Why on earth such unsuitable guys have to fall in love with me, when I can't be sure of Mike," she complained to Y (the real Y) gaily. She also wrote happily to Jeanou of her new popularity. "You see? What did I tell you years ago?" said Jeanou triumphantly. "That you would become a terribly popular girl, that boys would fall in love with you—my prophetic soul knew it." (It was amusing, Jeanou added, "to remember your fear of going out, how you refused the idea of boys being your slaves only a year ago.")

Since the cardinal rule in the group was to use one's own experience as a base for literature, it was only natural for Al to start writing about Shirley, the girl who was so different from anyone he had ever met before, and whom his friends didn't like at all. ("He could never make them see beyond her impetuous high-strung mannerisms and her seemingly fantastic ideas and actions," he wrote, casting himself in the third person. "She was just a 'screwy dame' to them.") Shirley waited a couple of years to write about him, and when she did it was with amused disdain, a new tone which had begun to creep into many of her autobiographical writings. But by then she had fallen under the influence of a champion disdainer and left Al far behind:

"We were both ardent young writers and we met through one of those little college literary groups where you sit on the floor and read poetry to each other. Al and I became friends at once because he sat there on a chair and read a long story about a whore and I sat on the floor and read a three-act play about a gangster.

"I was in that first sweet bohemian stage where all living artists are Artists, and everyone who is pursuing his happy anonymous artistic way through college is a potential satellite." She had never, she said, been to "a Man's Apartment" before, but now Al and she began regularly to visit the place he shared with three roommates, all majors in forestry. "Al and I used to take a bottle of wine and go to his place and spend all afternoon drinking wine and talking earnestly, and get a sense of delicious wickedness out of it." Once Al's landlady objected to her being there, and "that made our liaison complete."

At one point, she went on, Al had asked her to marry him, despite the fact that his roommates couldn't stand her, but she refused, claiming "a vocational call." Al, she said, was in the process of writing a long

PRIVATE DEMONS · 51

story about them and was stymied for an ending. One night when they were drunk she suggested that perhaps consummating the relationship would help him end the piece, but Al got cold feet. Later on he had a change of heart, but by then Shirley "had decided that was carrying artistic integrity too far."

While he was still on the scene, though, Al not only gave Shirley her first feeling of success in the boy-girl arena but also acted as self-appointed protector, a job he took very seriously, as a couple of practical jokers found out. The prank was a typical college foray—on a whim, two girls had scrawled a message of undying love on a postcard, addressed it to Shirley and signed it with the name "T. R. Balfour." Most girls would have been curious, even intrigued; Shirley turned it into a three-ring circus, agonizing, obsessing, and practically setting the campus on its ear in her search for the mysterious Balfour. When Al discovered the truth, he was furious:

"Perfectly harmless, anything for a laugh. Yeah! Sure!" he railed at the culprits. "Do you know that the poor kid was almost in hysterics when she got that card? I sat with her in the Savoy, Kay and Jimmie there too, while she alternated between burning rage and insatiable curiosity. You know Shirley." First she had made each of them swear they were not responsible. Next, she sent a waiter around to each table to find the mythical Balfour. Then, in "a frightful state," she made the rounds herself, in the end finding an amenable guy who said sure, that's who he was. "He played up to her," Al raged on. "Result: Shirley has been going with the biggest heel in Syracuse for the past week. She's gone nuts about this guy, or at least thinks she has. And then she found out what you had done." She was terribly shocked, deeply chagrined, and to make things worse, every time she came into the Savoy now the guy would smile at her horribly, the bastard. "He must have a sense of humor like yours."

You know how Shirley is, "impetuous and temperamental," said Al. "She's a swell kid and I think that was a low, dirty trick to play on her."

One of the perpetrators took it on herself to reply, primly. "I am certainly sorry it precipitated such an—shall I say—upheaval? It never entered my head that Shirley's sense of the dramatic would carry her to such extremes. Shirley is very high-strung, and I think the trouble lies there." The joke may have been silly and childish, but "girls get that way," she wrote him. Al accepted the apology coolly. He didn't know why it was so hard to see—Shirley was the kind of person who needed special protection. He would not be the last person to feel that way.

He continued to carry a torch for Shirley for several months. "She was a rebel against authority," he reminisced fondly. "Back then you had housemothers, but Shirley was always staying out late. Once I remember we were at my apartment, singing and drinking wine—illegal at the time, of course—and Shirley passed out. We were playing the guitar, singing, and suddenly, whoops, she went out. We panicked because we had to get her back to her place before close-up time. So we shoved her into the shower with her clothes on—this was in December. Then we called a taxi and took her back. We had to climb up the outside of the cottage to get her in, this other fellow and I. But we made a mistake and crawled in the second floor, she lived on the third. So we had to carry her up the stairs—he was at the back, I was at the front. Her feet kept clunking. I said, 'For Christ's sake, take her shoes off so it won't make so much noise.' We finally got her upstairs, then the alarm went off—someone had spotted us. We had to go out the window, down the fire escape. Later we realized we could have gotten kicked out of college for that."

Shirley, he said, never remembered any of it. "She said the next day, 'How did I get home? Why was I so wet?' "

Eventually, though, Al began to see the hopelessness of it all, with the strong encouragement of his roommates. Shirley was relieved; she was not, after all, in love with him. "That which I hoped for has occurred," she wrote in an unfinished letter to Y, back home. "Al today has gone off with his roommates. It is a sign, at last, that he is going back to them and deserting me. I feel that all my troubles are over! I am very much through with Al. Now if I could only persuade him to find some nice girl who would love him very much—everything would be OK. It's what he needs, not me."

Much more important than Al was her writing, which was flourishing. The creative-writing class was about to publish a collection of its best work, titled *The Threshold,* and Shirley was very proud of her contribution. "It's funny. I can write now more fluently and better than ever before," she told Y. "This last week I have never been anywhere without pencil and paper, and I write no matter what I am doing. I have become a mad Bohemian who curls up in corners with a pencil."

But this glow of confidence could extinguish itself almost overnight. "Michael, I can't write," she moaned in another unsent letter written only a few weeks later, to Palmer. "The typewriter leers at me when I come into the room. Why will words behave so well one day and then the next, they go all funny. I'll never be able to write again: I'm on the depressive side of my manic-depressive cycle. I feel as though I can't write, never could and don't care about anything. I can't even think!" All her life it would be like this. Whenever she allowed herself a true rush of pride for something she had done, it was followed almost immediately by a tidal wave of inadequacy; the better she got, the prouder she was, the swifter the plunge.

But now *The Threshold* was about to come out, carrying her story "Janice," only a page long, but unquestionably (as she sensed herself) the best thing she had ever done. Once again Shirley had written about a suicide attempt, but this time she had used only dialogue. The mood was chilling, her mastery unmistakable. Stuck in the middle of twenty-one pages of earnest, dull student effort, Shirley's story leapt off the page, smashing the reader with the power of a fist:

First, to me on the phone, in a half-amused melancholy: "Guess I'm not going back to school . . ."

"Why not, Jan?"

"Oh, my *mother*. She says we can't afford it." How can I reproduce the uncaring inflections of Janice's voice, saying conversationally that what she wanted she could not have? "So I guess I'm not going back."

"I'm so sorry, Jan."

But then, struck by another thought: "Y'know *what?*"

"What?"

"Darn near killed myself this afternoon."

"Jan! How?"

Almost whimsical, indifferent: "Locked myself in the garage and turned on the motor."

"But why?"

"I dunno. 'Cause I couldn't go back, I suppose."

"What happened?"

"Oh, the fellow that was cutting our lawn heard the motor and came and got me. I was pretty near out."

"But that's terrible, Jan. What ever possessed—"

"Oh, well. Say—" changing again, "—going to Sally's to-night?" . . .

And, later, that night at Sally's where Janice was not the center of the group but sat talking to me and to Bob: "Nearly killed myself this afternoon, Bob."

"What!"

Lightly: "Nearly killed myself. Locked myself in the garage with the car motor running."

"But why, Jan?"

"I guess because they wouldn't let me go back to school."

"Oh, I'm sorry about that, Jan. But what about this afternoon? What did you do?"

Sally, coming over: "What's this, Jan?"

"Oh, I'm not going back to school."

Myself, cutting in: "How did it feel to be dying, Jan?"

Laughing: "Gee, funny. All black." Then, to Sally's incredulous stare: "Nearly killed myself this afternoon, Sally . . ."

Now it seems obvious—this was no ordinary sophomore effort. Then it was less so. The other students liked her story, but were just as enamored of their own work. Professor Johnson, in a rambling introduction, did not even mention it; his own particular favorite was a verse that contained "the enchanting line 'The Havanese who having mariposa need no pearls.' " ("How does one teach anybody to write that?" he wondered; not, on the face of it, an easy question to answer.)

But Shirley's story was successful in a very real sense. It attracted the attention of the one person at the university who could grasp its real worth and, in doing that, changed the course of two lives forever.

CHAPTER

·6·

In a corner of the campus far from Shirley's cottage and far from her life, in a Jewish fraternity house, an eighteen-year-old Brooklyn boy sat at a desk reading. His hair was dark blond and curly; he wore thick glasses and an intent expression. Suddenly another student, Ben Zimmerman, burst into the room. He was waving a copy of *The Threshold*. The boy looked up over his glasses.

"Hey, Stanley, you see this yet?" said Ben. "It's from that creative-writing class, they put out a collection of their stuff."

The boy at the desk took the magazine and began to flip through it. He snorted. He flipped a few more pages and snorted again.

"Well, some of it's okay, isn't it?" said Ben, unsure. "I mean, I just looked—"

"Crap," said the boy, giving the word a ponderous, theatrical weight. "Banality. These people think they can write. Listen to this." He read a line of verse aloud. "Jesus."

"Stanley, you're flipping right through it, how can you tell?"

"I'm a critic, Ben, I told you. I know crap when I see it." He flipped some more.

"They are students, you know."

The boy laughed, one loud bark. "I'm a student. If I couldn't write better than this, I sure as hell wouldn't. . . ." His voice faded.

"What is it?"

"Hold on."

"What is it?"

"Ben, shut up."

"I gave you the magazine, at least—"

The boy looked up at him, sharply. "Who is Shirley Jackson?" he said.

"I don't know."

"This is important—who is Shirley Jackson?"

"Stanley, how the hell do I know. Some shiksa, I guess."

"I have to find her. *Now*."

"Stanley, stop banging on the table like that, it's after midnight. Why do you have to find her?"

"You see this?" he slammed his hand flat on the page with Shirley's story. "It's good. It's the only goddamn good thing in here. It's more than good. You understand? It's got something. She's got something."

"Great, put up a notice on the bulletin board, write her a letter or something," said Ben.

"You miss the point. Completely."

"So okay, what's the point?"

He leaned back in his chair, grinning. "The point is, I am going to marry her," said Stanley Edgar Hyman.

He had known his own mind practically from the beginning. It was, admittedly, some mind. His mother, Lulu, barely out of her teens when he was born, June 11, 1919, was amazed, almost a little fearful at what she had produced—even as a small child, Stanley could talk rings around everybody else and reason almost like an adult; there were times when even Moe, his father, felt a bit uneasy. A tough, stubborn man who ruled the house with an iron hand, Moe Hyman was no scholar. He had, of course, the traditional Jewish respect for any superior mind, but it was unnerving to find that mind in your own son.

Stanley was a somewhat frail and sickly child, with a heart murmur that kept Lulu fluttering around him nervously for years. He would later tell friends he had been born so prematurely the hospital in Brooklyn had told his mother he was dead, anticipating the inevitable, and sent her home, only to contact her embarrassedly two weeks later and ask if she would mind picking up her baby, who apparently had no intention of dying. A rattling good story, if almost certainly pure bunk; in all likelihood, Stanley was just taking control of his past the way he'd always taken control of everything, right from the start—with his mouth. As the Yiddish expression goes, he could throw up a dictionary.

Very early in the third-grade year at P.S. 99, Brooklyn, little June Mirken became aware of the boy in the front row who always had his hand up. It was hard not to be. For every question, he had an answer—sometimes the teacher had to ask him, a little annoyed, to give someone else in class a chance. It never bothered the boy, Stanley; two minutes later his hand would be up again. June could tell he had a really high opinion of himself, and she gave him a wide berth. Who wanted to know a little boy like that?

Moe worked hard in the family's paper company, L. Hyman and Sons, alongside his brother and his father. Hard work was a family habit: Moe's father, Louis Hyman, a Russian immigrant, had come to Brooklyn after working for several years as a peddler in North Adams, Massachusetts. As an Orthodox Jew committed to keeping kosher in that strikingly non-Jewish environment, he packed cheese and hard-boiled eggs to sustain himself on his Monday-through-Friday trips, allowing himself a full meal only when he came home on the weekend.

Now, settled in the more hospitable Brooklyn, with the company prospering, the Hymans were quite comfortable, but that was no reason to slack off. Moe was rarely home; only the Sabbath was for resting, and that he usually spent at his parents' home. Moe was devoted to his mother, a devotion that his own family rarely saw. In his own house he was harsh and demanding, often giving vent to an explosive temper, terrifying his wife and sons.

Lulu came from a large family, the Marshaks—seven girls and one boy. One of her sisters, Anna, had married Harry, Moe's brother, intensifying the ties between the two families. Stanley grew up surrounded by family, a family of stern, tough, but loyal men and warm, giving, emotional women (except for his father's mother, who seems to have been a rather cold woman). He learned early to go his own way and cultivated a cool rational approach to life, which stuck. But no child brought up with six aunts, in a large, boisterous family, is a stranger to emotional outbursts. As an adult, Stanley never felt uncomfortable around Shirley's roller-coaster emotions—after all, this had been a familiar backdrop to his life since childhood.

When he was a young boy, Stanley attended Hebrew school and studied the Torah for his bar mitzvah. He later claimed he had never darkened the door of a synagogue again after that, but in fact he continued to be involved with Jewish life, at least to the extent of observing High Holidays, until he left for college at seventeen. For his entire adult life, though, he was a proud, militant atheist, who nonetheless took pride in his Jewish background. Certainly his immense acquisition of knowledge has struck more than one person as being uncannily Talmudic in its nature. And more than one person, too, has seen his departure from Judaism, despite the innumerable rational reasons he gave for it, as more a blow against his stern father than against theology. Either way, Stanley was to leave the religion of his fathers far behind, even while he held on tenaciously to the secular faith of his native borough, a slavish, lifetime devotion to the Brooklyn Dodgers.

Stanley began early to carve out his own course, away from his family, even as Shirley had—but with a difference. For where Shirley's route led her inward, to the recesses of her own mind, which were fascinating enough to keep her enthralled, Stanley's led him outward, toward books, music, people and experiences, all of which he gobbled up with voracious hunger. There was very little of the loner about Stanley; his magnetism was as strong as his egotism, and both could overshadow everyone else in the vicinity, most days of the week. He was a born storyteller, an inveterate teacher, a champion arguer, and he thrived on having an audience.

Stanley's interests ranged far and wide. Science was an early one, and his brother, Arthur, six years younger, still remembers with a shudder the snakes, insects, and small furry animals that Stanley kept, not always in their cages, in the room they shared. "I was afraid of bugs and snakes, and he loved them," Arthur said. "We had alligators in the bathtub, a snake crawling around the bathroom, a praying mantis up on the windowsill. My parents wouldn't say a word to him, they never came into our bedroom." Later, drama superseded science; Stanley involved himself in productions at Erasmus Hall High School, building intricate set-design models. He and Walter Bernstein, one of his closest friends, were joint drama critics for *The Dutchman*, the school newspaper.

Sex was another early interest—"he was so advanced," marveled Frank Orenstein, another one of his best friends in high school. Once, discussing a girl, Stanley demolished her with adolescent scorn. "Ah, she does it for postage stamps," he said, tossing the line off casually. Frank was thrilled—"this for a fifteen-year-old kid in the thirties was so advanced." It was hands-down the most sophisticated phrase he had ever heard, and he could not keep from repeating it. He told one friend, then another, and in short order Stanley's comment had spread around the whole school, and Stanley himself was hauled into the principal's office for a severe dressing-down. "He never knew I was the one who told," said Frank, who fifty years later, in a sentimental salute to his old pal, put the phrase into his first murder mystery. Stanley also insisted to Frank that another girl had dubbed him "Buster"—Buster Hyman—which his friend, grown a bit wiser, took with a grain of salt.

While it thrilled his friends, Stanley's precociousness horrified their parents. "My mother loathed him," said Frank. "He was the sort of boy everybody's mother hated. He smoked cigarettes first, he made more noise, he didn't treat anybody's parents but his own father, who was a tyrant, with deference."

In his own home, Stanley treated his mother and his little brother cavalierly, even autocratically, obviously taking his cue from Moe. "Lulu was afraid of Stanley from the minute he was born," said his sister-in-law, Bunny Hyman, who was the recipient of Lulu's confidences for many years. "How do you deal with a genius two-year-old? He'd scare her to death, the things he said."

"Stanley and I did not get along when we were young. I was very jealous of him because he was so smart," said Arthur Hyman. "My father looked up to him and down to me." Arthur did, however, have a closer relationship with his mother than Stanley did. "Art she could understand; he was normal," said his wife.

To Stanley, Arthur was the prototypical buggy kid brother, and more than once "he fixed me," Arthur admitted. At Arthur's bar mitzvah, Stanley showed up with a couple of his friends, then walked out with a bottle of liquor under his arm. Arthur, flushed with thirteen-year-old righteousness, told his father; the next morning he woke up to find "SNITCH" written on everything he owned.

Walter Bernstein was convinced one of the keys to Stanley was his father. "He was very, very gruff, always prided himself on being tough." At the paper company, Moe would roll up his sleeves and give the guys a hand at the loading dock, just to impress everybody with his strength. It worked. "Everybody was afraid of him. Moe was a tough father to have. Stanley talked about him a lot, he felt he had to prove he was as physically tough as his father." Standing on a subway platform once, Stanley, out of the blue, proposed a contest: Walter would punch him as hard as he could in the stomach, then he would punch him back. Walter declined.

"His father was silent and very disapproving of everything," said Frank. "His mother babbled and talked and was friendly and warm—I think this drove Stanley crazy. Of course, people are never mad for their own mothers."

Stanley and his closest friends at Erasmus Hall—Walter, Frank, Robert Kahn, Sheldon Kranz—were fiercely competitive, even with board games like Monopoly. "Stanley was a killer—real tough and aggressive. He was the big winner and the big noisemaker," said Frank. All the boys would put their winnings into the pot; when they had enough, they would go to a Broadway show.

"He was always full of stories," said Frank. "He'd come into the Monopoly games and say he'd met this guy on the subway who was a magician and then the guy took him up to his apartment and tried to make a pass at him but Stanley left. He was always full of bravado-and-bravura stories." You never knew how many were true, of course—but they were always worth hearing.

"Stanley very early on was a leader—very definite in his opinions. I was in awe of his certainty. I think he was born to be a critic," said Walter Bernstein.

Stanley and his friends collaborated on writing and producing the senior class play—*Punafore, or the Class Who Loved Its Jailor* (from Gilbert and Sullivan's *Pinafore, or The Lass Who Loved a Sailor*). They were a cocky bunch, top-heavy with brains and confidence, eager to get out into the world beyond Brooklyn and test their mettle. Frank and Walter were headed for Dartmouth, but Stanley chose Syracuse. It had a good journalism department, and he'd already decided what he wanted to be—the drama critic for *The New Yorker*.

The three boys kept in close touch. Frank and Walter roomed together their first year at Dartmouth, 1936–1937, and Stanley often hitchhiked over from Syracuse to spend the night. As freshmen Stanley and Walter had both made the enthusiastic discovery of Karl Marx, and both had joined the Young Communist League. Frank, though sympathetic ("I think anybody with any sensitivity at all back then would have been if not a Communist at least a Communist sympathizer"), declined to join; he was just not that political. It was a lucky decision for him, since his first career was with the State Department.

Stanley, too, was lucky; his college fling with radical politics never came back to haunt him. Walter Bernstein alone would be burned—as a budding screenwriter some years later, his career was all but snuffed out by McCarthyism, and he was blacklisted for many years. Woody Allen later used him as a major screenwriter for *The Front,* his film treatment of Hollywood during the McCarthy years.

Even in the throes of early radical fervor, though, Stanley was not above using political theory for his own ends. On one of his visits to Dartmouth, he realized with pleasure that the college had not only one of the largest libraries in New England but an open stack system as well; what's more, anybody could go in and browse, since the library operated on the honor system. "Stanley looked at all these books and was overcome by lust," said Frank. He happily selected a large pile for himself, brought them back to the room, and began stuffing them into his suitcase.

His friends were horrified. What was he doing? Didn't he know what the honor system meant? Stanley struck one of his John Barrymore poses and delivered a ringing pronouncement: "The honor system is a device of the capitalists to enslave the workers without costing them very much money." He left it hanging in the air and went back to loading his suitcase. It had certainly sounded Marxist enough, but both Walter and Frank were sure he had made it up on the spot. Still, they knew there was no use arguing; Stanley could outtalk either one of them. Instead, they waited until he left the room, then emptied out the books and reloaded his suitcase with bricks, which Stanley, all unknowing, carted carefully back to Syracuse. He never mentioned it again.

At Syracuse, Stanley swiftly became the center of a group of like-minded students—radical, intellectual, maverick, and predominantly Jewish.

A stiff quota system still existed at the university; Jews were a small minority, but a vocal one, and no one was more vocal than Stanley. He quickly attracted satellites—Ben Zimmerman, a native Syracusan, who was awed at this brash urbanite; June Mirken, who had first noticed him wildly flailing his hand in the third grade at P.S. 99. She too had come to Syracuse for the journalism department, and met Stanley at *The Daily Orange;* this time around she was more impressed. "He had a kind of charisma. He could attract people, get people together who would otherwise be unable to do it. Most of us individually were kind of loners— these were the people he was so successful at reaching and bringing in. In some ways we were desperately grateful because we wouldn't have anybody if Stanley hadn't grabbed hold and said, 'Come here, I want you to meet somebody.' In that sense we were all dependent on him."

But Stanley too had a couple of friends he wanted to impress—two graduate students, Ted Bardacke and Dick Felmus, who lived in an apartment off campus. Both tended to treat Stanley as a kid brother; they borrowed money from him to buy a twenty-five-dollar Ford, they cheated him at craps, and they had no compunction whatsoever about putting the make on any girls he brought over. When he showed up with June Mirken, both of them pounced; they took her to a movie, each sitting on a side, each holding a hand. June begged a friend of hers, Frannie Woodward, to help her out. "I'll decide which one I like best, then you take the other off my hands," she said. Luckily, each girl had a distinct preference— Frannie for Bardacke, June for Felmus. Stanley didn't mind—he enjoyed arranging people's lives, getting them together (and on occasion, splitting them up); anyway, he and June had never really been involved.

Stanley was always at the forefront of the group, forever diving into new territory, then yelling at the others to come on in, the water was great, whether it was jazz, poetry, Marxism, or Freudianism. He reveled in his role as the discoverer. And never more than when his discovery was Shirley.

June Mirken also remembered when *The Threshold* came out in March 1938. When Stanley asked her if she'd seen it, she said she had and thought it was terrible—there was only one good thing in the whole damn magazine. Yeah, said Stanley, he'd noticed that too, nothing in it had been any good except for that piece by Shirley Jackson, and he was going to find her.

CHAPTER
·7·

Stanley indeed found Shirley. More accurately, he descended on her, with the same predatory gusto he would later display when going after rare books, coins, or two-thousand-year-old Egyptian scarabs. When Stanley was in that state, what he wanted he got; Shirley never had a chance. Stanley scooped her up, dazzled, amazed, and overwhelmed her; he tucked her in his pocket and brought her home to show off to his friends. In the years to come he would variously terrify her, amuse her, teach her, encourage her; protect, dominate, enrich, and enrage her; he drove her nuts, he kept her sane, he opened up a garden of earthly delights and responsibilities—and demanded she keep at least one foot firmly placed in its soil. Not everyone was always sure whether meeting Stanley was Shirley's greatest fortune or her worst calamity, but one thing was certain—once he strode onto the scene, all the rest was inevitable.

On the surface there could not have been a sharper contrast between the brash young Jew from the streets of Brooklyn and the odd, intense escapee from the Rochester Country Club—yet their very differences seemed calculated to unleash a powerful connection between them. He had the cool, logical, analytical mind she had always been attracted to; she had the wild imagination, the creativity, the mythic depths he was fascinated by. He was strong, sure of his opinions, sane, steady, utterly rational; she was emotional, intuitive, psychic, and turbulent. He was the critic, she the talent; he the taskmaster, she the eager self-improver; she was a loner, he the one with the perennial crowd around him. Both had the energy to keep up with each other; both had deep-seated reasons to want to spit in their family's eye. It was not so incidental that he was a scruffy radical Jew, she an upscale Republican Wasp, in a time and place when that was still a shocking combination—each was the last thing the other's parents wished to see brought home to dinner, and they both knew it.

But more important than any of this, perhaps, was a simple truth: Stanley knew just how rare Shirley was, and told her. Shirley had been waiting for someone who felt that way for a long time.

"When she met Stanley, it was nuclear fission," Shirley's friend Y described it. "And after that, everything was different. Once she met him she became completely involved—I don't think she took any boy seriously until him. He had a catalytic effect on her life."

So Stanley lassoed Shirley and brought her into his fold; he bragged about her to all his friends, and then presented her with a flourish. Some of them—particularly Frank and Walter—were initially wary. "He introduced her to me as this rich shiksa from Rochester," said Walter. "That's what he said." Neither of them could help but wonder if Stanley was once again just acting "advanced," dating a Christian girl in the same spirit he might try any new experiment, just to see what it was like. "I think he kind of liked the idea he was going with a shiksa, it was part of the revolt," said Walter. And in fact, to born-and-bred-Brooklyn-Jewish boys in the thirties, the alliance was a bit brow-raising at that. Shirley was obviously from another world, with her proper garden-club accent and her sizable wardrobe. Exactly what did Stanley think he was doing with her?

"Our first meetings were somewhat constrained," Frank admitted. The breakthrough came a few months later, in the middle of the night. "Shirley and Stanley had hitchhiked from Syracuse to Hanover, New Hampshire, in the dead of winter. This was when boys' dorms were boys' dorms. Suddenly, late at night, there was a knock at my door, on the third floor. I opened it and this great wrapped-up ball shot by me saying, 'If you touch me I'll scream,' jumped into my bed, and pulled the covers up over her head. I don't even remember her taking her shoes off." Frank philosophically got dressed and went off to sleep in another room for the night. But something about the pure chutzpah of the act had gotten to him—she was no longer just Stanley's rich shiksa. "That was the first time I knew I loved her," he remembered; from then on, he was her friend as well as Stanley's.

Either the rigors of Syracuse or the euphoria of meeting Stanley had a noticeable effect on Shirley—for the first time in her life, she was actually thin. "She was very thin when I first met her, skinny to the point of anorexia," said Walter. He found her a bit strange, eccentric, but likable enough. It was obvious that she was in awe of Stanley.

Shirley had fallen hard. Nothing before had prepared her for the intensity of her reaction to Stanley; overnight he became the single most important factor in her life. He filled up the empty spaces, made her laugh, told her what to think, and she accepted it all with a kind of stunned gratitude. There was an element of almost slavish adoration in her love for him—she trotted out her accomplishments for his approval, her wit, her writing, and lay them at his feet. Her life before Stanley now seemed entirely stale and colorless, and she was determined with all her heart never to return to it.

She had always had a penchant for self-improvement, and now she put herself eagerly in his hands. Let him remake her, if that's what it took to hold him! She would read the books he told her to read, mouth the opinions he spouted. Another, more ordinary young man, faced with such utter devotion, such dependency, might have turned tail and run— he was barely twenty, after all, while she was nearing twenty-three. But Shirley's worship did not strike Stanley as particularly outlandish at all, under the circumstances. The truth was, her opinion that Stanley was the most brilliant, exciting man in the world tallied remarkably well with his own.

"She asked me if I would use my influence with him to get her into the YCL. Shirley was not political at all, it was all Stanley," Walter recalled. Eventually she did join the Young Communist League for a brief period, though "she was as close a nonpolitical member of YCL as they ever had."

Now when she went home to the big house in Rochester she took Stanley's radical ideas with her and began to parade them in front of her friends, being careful, however, to do it well out of her parents' earshot. Some of her friends were truly horrified. Mike Palmer, for one, tried to shock her out of it. "Do you realize you are actually espousing a cause that would mark your own father for extinction and possible murder?" he demanded. Shirley stood firm. "I know it," she said.

"She was extremely headstrong," Palmer said. "She worshipped her father, but she was in the flush of violent ideas." Violent something, anyway.

Her old friend Y, on the other hand, saw it more clearly. "My feeling was, she was not a person who developed political ideas of her own. She didn't think about them. When I first knew her, her outlook was exactly like her father's. After she met Stanley, her outlook was exactly like his."

Stanley may have initiated the relationship, may have taken her by storm, may, in fact, have been as deeply smitten as she was—but Stanley Hyman was no gentleman caller. His manner, even during the first months, was brusque, rude, and dominating. "You go on home, I'll see you later," he would tell Shirley, dismissing her, when he felt like going off with his buddies. "How can you treat her like that? She's a nice girl," Walter chided him. "You should be nicer to her." Stanley only snorted, and continued to act exactly the way he felt like acting.

Their early relationship was intense and erratic, filled with fights, break-ups, and reconciliations; it was, after all, the first major involvement for both, and in many ways—despite their mutual flair for the original—an extremely typical college romance. For anyone who has had the experience, one of Shirley's unfinished letters, written around this time, strikes a highly familiar chord:

"Dear Philip," Shirley wrote to one of Stanley's minions, Philip Cohen. "I have to talk to someone and you are the one person I feel I can talk to. . . . I've left him, of course. Please don't say—'again?' along with everyone else. Every time I've left him (or every time he's left me for that matter!) I've had to come back to him because I didn't have the courage to stay away. This time I have. I've got to.

"I don't like quitting and I don't like being lonely and unhappy, but then, too, I don't like being treated like someone on a leash.

"Philip, do you think I have the guts to do this? And do you think it's a good idea? Why do I ask you these stupid questions? I've already said, 'Stanley, check out' and now I've only to abide by my decision. I don't know what he's going to do. He made it pretty plain that he was tired of having me around. He wanted to quit as much as I did. So—

"Philip, pray for me that I can keep on with this!"

The letter ends abruptly at this point for some reason—probably a call from Stanley.

Yet of course Shirley in love was still Shirley, hardly a garden-variety coed. A journal entry from around this time sounds less like a starry-eyed sophomore than a grown woman in the grips of Mephistophelian passion. In fact, there was a distinct touch of Lady Macbeth:

"I do not want to fall in love with Stanley. I want Stanley to fall in love with me and he has. Before God, he has! Now I can do whatever I want with him—hurt him, make him unhurt, watch him burn his fingers . . . and all my little weaknesses turned to strength," she gloated darkly.

As always, though, no matter what the cause, anytime she allowed herself to exult in her own power, the descent was immediate: "If I had the courage, which I haven't," she added. "I'm afraid. God WHAT AM I AFRAID OF? Why am I afraid of it? Is it Stanley—or is it part me?"

The highs and lows continued, but the relationship was steady, however stormy it got. Right from the start, Stanley and Shirley were a couple, a distinct entity. For the first time in her life, Shirley luxuriated in the glow of being wanted, being desirable, being in love, being a girl with a fellow, just like everybody else. There were other benefits, too—anyone who teamed up with Stanley got a whole new set of friends. Among them were several who would eventually be friends for life—and one who was a close friend immediately. Frank and Walter may have taken a while to warm up to their buddy's new girlfriend, but June Mirken took to Shirley at once.

"We liked each other right away, and saw each other outside of Stanley," she remembered. "I didn't know any women, mostly guys. We felt very close and strong and intellectually remote and superior and dependent on each other at the same time, and that there was nobody else we wanted to talk to. That kind of thing." Both lived in Lima Cottage. Shirley had a roommate, a rather bland girl, but after meeting June, she spent most of her time there with her, in the smoking room in the basement. Shirley took her typewriter down there to write, too, since it was the only place she could smoke.

June was bright and funny, and very early the two girls fell into what would become a lifelong habit—poking fun at Stanley. Mostly just between themselves, but not always. "It was part of our relationship, and it was good, it was what kept things in perspective," June said.

Shirley found that June, too, had an interest in witchcraft, although she was more skeptical. "Shirley had read more seriously about it, gotten into Tarot cards, and did fortunes." Both girls experimented with voodoo dolls. "I was convinced I had made this one teacher I absolutely loathed fall down the stairs and break her leg, using a wax doll," June remembered. "I didn't aim for the leg but I thought it was awfully cooperative of her to break it."

Stanley too was intrigued by Shirley's interest, and he kept his eye out for books on the subject. June felt Shirley's belief in the darker powers was "ambivalent—but I think in many ways it kept her going. I think she used it to kind of overcome hateful experiences at home, her self-doubts and everything else she had. Of course, if you have magical powers you can deal with your self-doubts because all of a sudden you become this potent person. It's like, Yeah, you think I'm not pretty? Well . . . so it gives you a sense of balance. And a sense of ritual, if you need that, and in some ways we all do. This was ritual, and deeply satisfying for her."

Rational, level-headed Stanley might not have been so sympathetic to Shirley's predilections for the demonic if he had not already met, a year or so earlier, a man he greatly respected who was deeply involved with black magic. Jay Williams had originally been Walter's friend, and all three boys, Stanley, Walter, and Frank, were greatly impressed by him. He was five years older than they, already launched on his life; he had seen tragedy—both his wife and a good friend had committed suicide; he had traveled widely, and was knowledgeable about the theater, Marxism, and black magic. "He was older, more experienced, the mentor," said Walter. "He knew a lot of things we didn't know." It was Jay Williams, in fact, who had first introduced Walter to Marxism. But what most intrigued them, Walter said, was that he was "a totally self-created personality. He wasn't a natural anything. He created Jay Williams the writer, Jay Williams the Anglophile. He even created his name."

Stanley had talked up Jay Williams to Shirley, the way he did all his friends, telling her that Jay had sent Frank a subscription to *The Christian Science Monitor* in Scandinavian, that he spoke Mandarin Chinese and was a hypnotist. Shirley was fascinated, especially when she learned about the hex he had made for Stanley to protect him against all evil—"an intricate thing with names of devil gods all over it and other names I did not even know, even after having studied witchcraft for a long time," she later wrote. But she was afraid to meet him, just as she had been uneasy meeting any of Stanley's friends, "in the way you are afraid of people you know are judging you and sizing you up." And meeting Jay Williams was worse than meeting the others; he seemed to be one of the few people Stanley looked up to. Any bad comments he made about her would be taken to heart, Shirley feared.

But in fact he turned out to be warm and likable, if unnerving—he told Shirley cheerily that his knapsack contained "a dead baby, which I shall eat tonight in the woods, roasted over a campfire." Shirley gulped but rallied. "It's always nice to have a little snack along in case you get hungry," she said bravely, earning a beneficent smile.

Several times he told Shirley he intended to perform a black mass for her and make the devil appear. "Can I ask him for anything I want?" she said.

"Anything, only you must be prepared to pay a price for it," said Williams.

Shirley laughed. "I'll pay anything except giving up Stanley," she said.

Williams's reply chilled her. "No price is too great for the devil," he said, deadly serious.

To Shirley's relief, Williams never got around to performing the black mass, but one night he did do a long drum chant for Stanley, Walter, Frank, and her. At one point during the chant he yelled for everyone to look over in the corner at what had been conjured up—Shirley, terrified, gripped Stanley's arm and refused to look, then burst into tears. Later she told Stanley she thought Jay was close to insane; Stanley scoffed at her.

"There is no logical basis for your feeling that way," he instructed her. "You are projecting a fear in yourself onto Jay; I think you resent what he stands for."

"What does he stand for?" asked Shirley.

As usual, Stanley was matter-of-fact, if hardly comforting: "All the borderline evil and darkness in the world."

Yet actually Williams was quite kind, even protective to Shirley. "You mustn't let Stanley frighten you," he warned her. Stanley, he said, had an irresistible urge to categorize people, their emotions and reactions—if she let him have his way with her, she could emerge as dried and labeled as a laboratory experiment. "Logic is an essentially bad thing," he said.

But about this, Shirley was unworried. "I never listen to Stanley," she told him. It wasn't strictly true, of course—she listened to him all the time—and yet in a sense it was. What she meant was that she would never allow Stanley's logic to change or destroy the irregular workings of her own mind. No matter how much she loved him, that was the one area that was off limits.

The crowd at Syracuse that Shirley now found herself a part of was a determinedly sophisticated bunch; they spouted Freud, they argued Marx, they spent hours sitting around drinking coffee at a place called the Cosmos (which they called "the Greek's"). A great premium was placed on experimentation of all kinds—in music, writing, politics, and of course, relationships. Bourgeois morality was abhorrent; it was as bad as capitalism (and certainly worse for your complexion). Wherever you looked there were passionately entangled couples: June Mirken and Dick Felmus; Frannie Woodward and Ted Bardacke. Fairly early in their relationship, Stanley and Shirley prepared to join the ranks.

It took some preparation, too, since Stanley still lived in a fraternity house, Shirley in a strictly off-limits-to-men housing cottage. But Stanley was a determined man. He took his problem to Felmus and Bardacke, the only people he knew with their own apartment, and begged them to let him have an evening alone there with his girl. They agreed, decided on a date for the big event, and promised they would both be safely out of the house at the set time. Stanley went off happily.

Then they got nervous. Stanley, they knew, was a chain-smoker who had little concern for where his ashes fell; in the past year he had set off innumerable small fires in their apartment. So far someone had always been on hand to put them out. But now, with both of them away, and in the heat of passion—Jesus, they could come back to find the entire place burned down. Finally they figured out the best solution: they would just have to stay in the apartment after all, and be prepared. But they didn't want to ruin Stanley's moment, either, Felmus argued. Fine, said Bardacke, they would stay there, but well hidden. If nothing happened, Stanley and Shirley would never have to know.

The magic night arrived. Stanley and Shirley showed up at the apartment—empty as promised—and repaired to the bedroom, luckily not glancing in the small bathroom off to the side, where both boys crouched behind the door, pails of water at the ready. For a while things were calm, and events seemed to be proceeding smoothly. Then suddenly an acrid gust of smoke wafted into the bathroom—the unmistakable smell of singed sheets. In an instant the rescue team was out the door with the pails; in another they had dumped the water, several gallons' worth, all over the bed and the traumatized would-be lovers, dampening their ardor for several days to come. The act, Stanley informed them grimly much later, after Shirley had stopped screaming and he had taken her home, had not been completed.

With that sort of unpleasant primal scene behind them, both Stanley and Shirley were reluctant to have another go at it in the apartment. But what to do? Finally, Stanley announced to Shirley they would just have to go down to New York City for a weekend; they could stay with married friends of his, Jesse and Irene Lurie. Stanley let Lurie know of his plan, and his friend was encouraging. He also offered some advice: "I warned him that the first time he might be unsuccessful. It's a common experience," said Lurie. "He later told me I had saved his life."

Finding privacy in the Luries' small one-bedroom apartment was not easy; Shirley and Stanley ended up sleeping on a cot in the living room, behind a strung-up curtain. Anticipation, nervousness, and lack of privacy proved too much for them the first night—but by the second night, at long last, all was well. It was Shirley's first time and, despite the thousands of ribald stories he had told his friends to the contrary, very possibly Stanley's too. They returned to Syracuse triumphant, a genuinely illicit couple at last.

Before they left, though, Shirley gave in to a thoroughly adolescent impulse—she dashed off a quick letter to Kay Turk, the proper, ladylike friend her mother had so approved of her first few months at Syracuse. In it she described the entire weekend, even down to the unsuccessful attempt their first night in New York. "She said Stanley had been too embarrassed to perform," said Kay, who was so aghast at the letter she tore it up immediately and threw it away; she had no way of knowing, of course, that she was just serving as a convenient stand-in for Geraldine.

However, it was not long before Shirley took the battle directly to the home front. She had no urge to keep her relationship with Stanley a secret; in fact, on many levels, it was deeply satisfying to let her parents know. There was nothing equivocal about their reaction, either. Leslie and Geraldine Jackson were thoroughly horror-stricken. This was what they had sent their daughter away to college for? To fall in love with a bearded, loud-mouthed, communist Jew? Leslie hit the roof; Geraldine was hysterical. For years she had striven tirelessly to imbue Shirley with a proper sense of class, groomed her to eventually take her rightful place in society. Yes, they had always known she was different—willful, odd, antisocial. But Geraldine, at least, had never stopped hoping for a blessed metamorphosis—that one day they would open the door and there would be a new Shirley, slim, coiffed, beautifully dressed, ready to take her seat at the country-club table. And now this! This Stanley Edgar Hyman! Everything about Stanley repelled them. It wasn't his Jewishness alone. There was hardly an adjective you could apply to him that didn't make things worse. A prosperous, Anglican Jew (if there was such a thing) would have been one matter—not the happiest choice, perhaps, but one they could have bravely accepted. This, this was something else. And so the arguments went, on and on, into the night.

The Jacksons were far from being rabid racists. Genteel anti-Semitism was simply endemic to the circles in which they moved, as natural to them as the air they breathed on the golf course. The daughter of the president of Stecher-Traung did not fall in love with a Jew; it was as simple as that. Couldn't Shirley see that?

Shirley saw. She and Stanley did not just understand the problem—they reveled in it. This was true freedom; they were throwing off the chains of repression, represented by Shirley's parents, and forging a brave new world. This was more, much more than just a love affair—it was Marx, it was Freud, and it was colossally exciting. Significantly, Stanley did not rush home to his own parents with the news; a confrontation with Leslie Jackson was one thing, one with Moe Hyman another, and he was in no hurry for it.

Shirley's friend Y viewed it all with a touch of cynicism. "They were working at being star-crossed," she said. "Romanticizing. I don't think the gulf was quite as much as they liked to think it was; they were dramatizing themselves. I felt it was a simple, practical matter—Shirley was well on her way to being over twenty-one [in fact, she had turned twenty-one in December 1937, even before she had met Stanley], after which it was entirely up to her what happened. So I couldn't feel it was an unresolvable problem. Of course, it took longer to be an adult in those days."

She did have the uncomfortable experience of being at the Jacksons' home for one of Stanley's brief appearances. Shirley and Stanley went for a walk almost immediately on his arrival; once they were gone, Geraldine became increasingly agitated and upset. "I sensed she was looking at me for help. She wanted me to say something, or explain something. But I couldn't." Feeling terribly ill at ease, Y left.

Stanley's visits to Rochester were brief and strained; certainly they did nothing to change Leslie's and Geraldine's minds. "It was my impression when he came to visit he came in an attack mode," said Y. Or perhaps that of a cornered animal. Barry Jackson remembered driving home one Sunday afternoon with his parents and seeing Stanley and Shirley sitting on the front porch; as the car stopped, Stanley jumped over the railing and took off down the street. Shirley's parents were understandably less than charmed. "Maybe that was part of the problem," mused Barry Jackson. "If he'd stuck around and talked . . . but my mother and father had a knack of making you feel uncomfortable, I'll say that." There were no family social occasions that included Stanley, he said.

"They were appalled by Stanley, absolutely appalled. They didn't want any part of him," said June Mirken, flatly. "They totally disapproved of the relationship. He was Jewish, he was a Communist, graceless, no class, no family. They couldn't have been more ill-matched, in that sense. I'm sure anti-Semitism played an important part—you don't want your daughter to marry a Jew."

Anti-Semitism was not exclusive to Rochester, though, Shirley was beginning to discover. There was plenty in Syracuse, too. (And of course, a great deal more of it flourishing insanely throughout Europe, but current events held little interest for Shirley, then or ever. Walter Bernstein was right, she truly was apolitical.) Stanley and his friends, Jewish all their lives, took it for granted, cynically; for Shirley, every new instance was shocking and fearful, once again enforcing what she had first become aware of in Burlingame—people carried evil inside them.

Her roommate at the cottage was the first to try to talk to her about it directly. She came into the room one day, obviously uncomfortable, and after a number of false starts blurted out a question. "Are you in love with Stanley?"

Instantly Shirley knew what was coming. She sat silent, waiting. "Some of the kids in the house asked me to talk to you," the girl went on, flustered. "We think you shouldn't be in love with him."

"Why?" Shirley said.

"You know why as well as we do."

"Because he's a Jew."

"That's right." It wasn't that they didn't like Stanley, she went on, they all did; they were worried about her. What if she married him? What about family, friends? Finally, getting no response, the girl flounced out, leaving Shirley alone, shaken.

Others too made comments, though not all were quite as direct. Several times Shirley attempted to record these first brushes with anti-Semitism, to express the way they made her feel—but the specific words people used, recorded on paper, were not enough to convey the fear and horror that clutched her. Her sensitivity, her intuition were so highly developed that even stray comments were enough to engulf her in terror. Finding Stanley had been a glorious event; he was her rock, her harbor—and yet it seemed that even here, having reached this safe shore, the tentacles of evil were still able to touch her. And it was this sense of present evil she was trying to portray. Her writing was becoming subtler, beginning to reflect mood. Anti-Semitism was, after all, only a symptom, one branch of a very old tree—what Shirley wanted to do most was to evoke a consciousness of the roots themselves.

But there is no doubt that the anti-Semitism she encountered so directly at college—and less directly later on—had a major effect on her life and work. She always refused to answer the question put to her by thousands of readers, "What is 'The Lottery' really about?"—but to a good friend she confided very matter-of-factly that it had, of course, been about the Jews.

One disturbing story she wrote in college dealt with a man who gave June and her a lift one day. He was Jewish, he told them, and had never wanted to marry a Jewish girl: "There's always a chance they would have looked Jewish. The children, I mean. And then, when they took me away, they might have gotten after the children too. I wouldn't want them to get the children." Marrying a Jew, having his children, was very much on Shirley's mind.

She was not the only one in her group to feel the sting of anti-Semitism at Syracuse. Frannie Woodward, who was also not Jewish, was called down to the office of the dean of women one day. She went nervously, positive that someone had discovered that she had been sneaking out to spend nights with her boyfriend and she was about to be expelled. To her amazement, the dean gave her a stern lecture about her friendship with June Mirken. Did her parents know she was close friends with a Jewish girl? Was she, Frannie, aware such friendships could be construed as lesbian? Relieved and astounded that the dean knew nothing about her much closer relationship with a Jewish man, Frannie laughed for at least ten minutes; the dean finally excused her. "I think my sorority had asked her to do it," she said. "They later tried to take my pin away on the grounds that I was never seen on campus with anybody but a Russian, a Jew, or a Negro. It was a very conservative time." By the end of her sophomore year, Frannie and Ted Bardacke were married. "I think marrying a Jew was easier for me; Shirley with her background was more concerned than I was. My mother was Catholic, my father Protestant, so they'd already gone through it."

Stanley took over Shirley's education, assigning her books to read, directing her to the best teachers, propping her up academically. Shirley was still no student; even Al Parsell, during their brief friendship, had helped her out more than once in her course work.

Stanley had grown very close to one of Syracuse University's bright lights, Professor Leonard Brown, who taught literature and criticism. Everyone revered Brown. "He was absolutely by far the best teacher I ever had in my life," said June Mirken. "A marvelous, brilliant guy."

Along with the more routine English courses, Brown conducted a seminar in American literature and criticism at his home, and Shirley and Stanley attended.

"She was very quiet, she let him do the talking," remembered Dr. Robert Seidenberg, now a psychiatrist but then a pre-med student with a sneaking fondness for literature. "It was a group of about ten people, mostly from the journalism and English classes; I was the only outsider. But Freud came up a lot, as part of criticism. Also Marx." Brown, like Stanley, had radical leanings.

Seidenberg found them "an odd couple. Stanley was a campus radical. He personified the Jew from New York—he even had a beard. She was the upstate shiksa. She seemed in awe of him, deferential; she thought he was a genius. Of course, she turned out to be the one."

Seidenberg was one of the rare ones who did not fall under Stanley's charm. "I didn't like him. He wasn't a warm person. I think he looked on me as an outsider, poaching on the literary intelligentsia. Very unsmiling, serious, savored his position as a radical." Seidenberg was convinced it was an act: "Maybe I'm overly cynical, but when you're on campus at Syracuse, to have an identity, that was the thing to do. He knew it made him points." In retrospect he felt there probably had been a certain tension between him and Stanley—two Jews, one following the traditional route to medical school, the other taking quite a different path. "Undoubtedly Stanley's parents wanted him to be a doctor," he said dryly.

The two of them, Shirley and Stanley, "cut quite a swath on campus, and obviously liked it. She was a dirty blonde, not unattractive. She wore glasses, had long hair, skirt and sweater, bobby socks and saddle oxfords. She was devoted to him. She took pride in that they were a pair." Even then, though, it was apparent, at least to Seidenberg, that "he talked a lot but she wrote better all the time. His essays were blustering, polemical—hers were more literate."

Looking back, Seidenberg mused about the relationship. "An upstate kid taking up suddenly with a Jew, and a radical Jew from New York at that—this is a big step. It's turning on your own heritage. She probably had not even known any Jews before Syracuse. When it's done against a prejudicial background, you know you're fighting against yourself as well, because kids incorporate the prejudices of their parents. After all these years, I find one thing—kids want to please their parents. This is what tears them apart."

On the surface, Shirley's allegiance to Stanley and Stanley's cosmos was complete—she had embraced it totally, and was moving further and further away from her parents' world every day. Yet there would always be a great deal of both Geraldine and Leslie within her; she had no problem playing lady of the manor when the occasion arose (although never, ever, to Stanley). When a male friend, who was obviously having problems and about to flunk out of school, asked her via a note during English class if her father could give him a summer job, Shirley's response was stinging, every bit the executive's daughter:

"Frankly no," she wrote back. "He would have no patience with you— I have none—and he would judge you solely from your college career and your constant demonstrations of foolishness and sheer stupidity."

"Why such enthusiasm?" he wrote.

"Because it's all your own fault and you could have done something about it. Cutting classes and not studying hardly comes under the heading of your malignant demon which pursues you. Surely you could have done something about that?" Shirley wrote back scathingly.

"I could have had I wanted to," her friend said sulkily, unleashing another abusive torrent from Shirley: "Then how can you possibly blame anyone for thinking you're a fool, and can you [wonder] when your friends are all enthusiastically disgusted with you? And can you really expect to get a job? Don't you agree you've been extremely foolish? Not failure, but low aim is the crime—I think you've been even dumber than you think, and crueller to everyone. I remember your family and I remember your sister, who couldn't come back this year because you did, dear. And I remember a lot of fine ideas you used to have. What are you going to do about your family?"

"Ditto for yourself," snapped her respondent.

"I'm not walking out of school because I was too goddamn weak to pass my courses," said the girl who had done just that at Rochester only a few short years before. Then she really let go: "You have been a stupid—I can't emphasize that enough—ungrateful, selfish child, bent on nothing but pleasing yourself and rationalizing yourself out of every difficulty. Rationalize yourself out of this. College is well rid of you. And your family would be too." And all this from a girl who not only had flunked out herself once but also was currently making her own parents tear their hair out. Shirley never let a few ambivalences stand in her way.

CHAPTER

·8·

The relationship with Stanley had a direct and immediate effect on Shirley's writing. She had always believed in her ability, her talent—she had been writing seriously ever since elementary school, after all—but now someone else believed in her too, a person of brilliance and force and certainty, whom she was both in love with and in awe of. It was a powerful validation; as long as she lived, she would always look first to Stanley's opinion, trust his judgment over anyone else's, except, perhaps, her own. Her production soared; poetry, stories, longer works flowed out of her typewriter. Writing had always been her special art, her route to competence and power; now it was something else as well—a no-fail way to keep Stanley's interest. Other girls might have better figures; she had the stories. And, as Scheherazade had learned centuries before her, sometimes stories were the most powerful aphrodisiac of all.

Falling in love with Stanley also brought her in contact with a diverse array of people—odd, dissident, quirky, fascinating—all of them grist for her mill. Her writing had always reflected her experience, what she saw. Now, pulled suddenly into the middle of a crowd, there was so much more to see—more characters, more arguments, more colors, more life. In a very real sense, Stanley threw open the door, exposing her to reams of raw copy. Of course, what she did with it was up to her; her observations would always be filtered through the beveled glass of her own private vision.

"He was very good about not interfering, respecting her writing and her ability, making suggestions that were just suggestions, never pushing," said June Mirken. "He was very admiring. He wrote painfully, it was a tedious, forced thing, whereas she—the thing flowed like you turned on a faucet."

In her second year at Syracuse, Shirley published a number of pieces in *The Syracusan*, the closest thing the university had to a literary magazine. An editorial in the October 1938 issue described her as having two ambitions: "One is to learn to play chess. The other is to write the great American novel. Consequently she majors in English and minors in chess." Both ambitions, needless to say, had a definite Hyman cast to them.

A later issue of the magazine reported on an interest closer to her own heart. "Her roommate has a pair of jade Chinese devil gods. Shirley has vainly offered her everything including the current man and a carton of cigarettes, and says that she will get them yet by hook or crook. She also swears that the Jacksons have a family ghost named 'Eric the Red' who lives in the check book." It was not the last time Shirley would flaunt her occult proclivities in public.

In March 1939 *The Syracusan* reported that Shirley was at work on a novel and had already completed the beginning and the end; only the middle remained to be done. "She says it has three characters, all of who get kicked in the face at the end of the story."

At first it seemed that her work and talent would finally result in her getting some recognition from the school—she was named the new fiction editor for *The Syracusan* for the coming year, 1939–1940. She had little time to glory in it, however; within days the editor in chief announced that the magazine would stop using fiction in the fall.

Stanley, though, had the answer. What the hell did she need *The Syracusan* for, anyway? That lightweight rag. The thing to do was start their own magazine, a true literary magazine—then they could all write for it. At once, everyone was enthusiastic. Stanley persuaded Leonard Brown to be faculty adviser and to run interference with the English department; Shirley would be editor, he managing editor, June Mirken and Frannie Bardacke on the editorial staff—it would be great.

And it was, as it turned out. *Spectre*—whose entire life spanned one school year and four issues—was amazingly ambitious for a college publication, filled with impressive writing, criticism, and art. It also managed to step on more toes, pull more noses out of joint, and set more official teeth on edge than any other publication in the history of the university. Shirley went on to become one of the university's most famous alumni, yet it was twenty-five years before college officials offered her any award, or indeed took much notice of her at all. The reason was simple: it had taken them that long to cool down.

Shirley, Stanley, June, et al. were hardly unaware that they were tweaking the lion's tail with their publication of *Spectre*. The name itself was an underground joke. It came, they announced, from a William Blake quote—"My Spectre before me night and day / Like a wild beast guards my way"—which appeared every issue above the masthead, quite properly. But of course it didn't really come from Blake at all; the actual source was the first line of *The Communist Manifesto*—"A spectre is haunting Europe—the spectre of communism." The officials were supposed to accept the respectable source, the cognoscenti to understand the real source, and everyone involved could have a good chuckle. "We called the magazine 'Spectre' for obvious reasons," Shirley hinted in her first editorial, coyly.

That one they got by. But the magazine was in hot water from the start. "Here we are, already a magazine with a lurid past," editorialized Shirley. "Just before our first issue was bound, with the pages already mimeographed, the English department tapped us on the shoulder gently and informed us that we were a menace to public morals. It seems we had two pictures of nude male bodies, and if you want to have nude bodies in a campus publication without corrupting public morals, they have to be female bodies."

Since it turned out the art department had already approved the pictures, the English department backed down and the issue did come out. "What made it particularly funny was that as soon as we went on sale (and as everyone knows, sold out in less time than it would take to burn down the Hall of Languages) the *Orange* began printing letters from indignant little coeds saying that not only were the rest of our pictures dirty too, but that our stories weren't anything to show around in mixed company. Which probably shows that even the censors weren't as dirty-minded as they could have been, and which left us with everything offensive but the table of contents."

"Some of the English department objected to my illustrations," said Frank Litto, who was art editor of *Spectre*. "They said they were too explicit. I did a naked male model, and he had a penis—in those days, the male models always wore jockstraps."

Shirley's breezy editorials set the tone of the magazine, but Stanley was definitely the mastermind. "He was the one who put it all together," said Litto. Most of the contributors, of course, were friends—Ben Zimmerman, Ted and Frannie Bardacke, Richard Posner; even Walter Bernstein sent something over from Dartmouth, about Daumier and Goya. Shirley, Stanley, and June were the most prolific—more prolific than even a reading of the table of contents would indicate, since they all wrote under pseudonyms, too. Shirley liked the name Meade Lux Lewis, which had originally belonged to a boogie-woogie pianist she and Stanley had gone to see at Café Society in New York City.

"We were so pleased with each other and ourselves," said June. "It was a wonderful time."

"All the graduates said they wouldn't write for the magazine if it sold a million copies and all the undergraduates said they wouldn't write for the magazine if it were the last magazine on earth," said Shirley in the first issue.

"Lots of people thought it was a bad time to try to start anything new because there was so much that was more important going on outside. But we think that maybe the students have a little something to say about what's going on and if the students have something to say any time is a good time to let them say it. Frequently they do approach reality.

"And if someone comes around and tells us it's art we'll use it if it's good art because we haven't got any editorial policy except printing what's good. We like experimental forms and we like traditional forms and we'll print it if it's good."

That was about all, Shirley said, except that they had bound the magazine by hand, "and if you've ever tried to lick two hundred and fifty feet of gummed tape you know how we feel."

But Shirley and her co-editors showed very little inclination to stay out of sticky territory. By the second issue, she was extrapolating freely and extravagantly from their own bout with threatened censorship to the problems of the world: "It's all part of the same thing. It is Censorship or Repression, or Dictatorship, or Reaction, or whatever you want to call it. It is the stuff Fascism fattens on.

"If we can't print nude studies and stories about prostitutes in a college magazine because 'people know these things exist and are true, but why is it necessary to base literature on such a foundation,' what can we print in a college magazine? . . . At a time when liberal thought is terrorized and in retreat, it would be too much to expect of the colleges that they be liberal strongholds. . . . Censorship of pictures for obscenity is right in tune with the dominant trends." Considering that in fact the college had decided on second thought not to censor the pictures, it was all a bit silly, but appealingly young and idealistic all the same.

Next, *Spectre* took up the banner against racism. Shirley wrote a brief prose sonnet about a lynching; Stanley, who was getting deeply interested in blues music, wrote an impressive, knowledgeable treatise on blues great Bessie Smith ("She hit the bottle a great deal, and nobody gave much of a damn because it probably made her sing better. It was nobody's business anyway"). Shirley editorialized: "Marion Anderson sells out every time she comes here, but they won't allow negro girls in the college dormitories. Maybe it's all right if you're no closer than the sixth row." Later she expanded on this: "The college is a pretty good place to fight for the rights of the negro people, and this college is a particularly good place. No one seems to know exactly why Syracuse admits so few negroes." The NAACP, she said, was attempting to get its teeth into the problem. "We wish them all the luck in the world."

Spectre devoted the first two pages of its spring issue to an enthusiastic indictment of the intellectual level represented by the bulk of Syracuse students. "They object to the lack of good lighting in the library, but don't bother about the lack of good books. . . . When the Civic Theatre runs an excellent movie or a really good play, the students pack the Regent. . . . Everybody on campus read Ulysses. No one read Finnegans Wake. In Finnegans Wake the dirty passages are harder to understand." And so on, through twenty-two separate "points."

But the best was saved for last. In the final issue of *Spectre,* Stanley and Shirley did a collaborative hatchet job on a new book of poetry written by A. E. Johnson, Shirley's old professor, a book with the unfortunate title *When Thou Hast Shut Thy Door;* they had privately renamed it *When Thou Hast Shut Thy Mouth,* although they did manage, with admirable control, to keep that out of their review. They signed it S.J. and S.E.H., but by now everyone had a pretty good idea of who they were. Fed up, enraged, university officials closed down *Spectre* for good, citing "lack of material" as one of the major reasons. It wasn't, of course. "They didn't like it—they were sure the alumni wouldn't give any money if they saw such a revolutionary, dirty magazine," said June Mirken."This was a very staid college, a very staid administration."

Spectre's founders were furious. How could they kill something that, as Stanley reminisced rosily some years later, was "a wild magazine which shocked the college, was an enormous success and made a whopping profit for its frightened backers"? Actually, the profit had been somewhere in the low two digits, but still—they had created something worthwhile, and they knew it. June, with another year to go on campus (a year of illness in childhood had placed her in the class behind Stanley's), had already been named the new editor. Shirley had signed off editorially with the wish that next year's *Spectre* be "full of advertising and great literature, with a larger circulation than the *Daily Orange* and all the contributors geniuses." The group had worked hard to make *Spectre* a thriving entity, and had succeeded; they were crushed at the university's decision. But they had also spent a good deal of time rattling cages, so perhaps it was not altogether surprising when the resident lions finally roared them down.

Shirley and Stanley's personal relationship thrived right along with *Spectre,* much as the Jacksons would have dearly loved to cut off that enterprise. As it was, they tried their best, using everything in their arsenal to discourage it—pleas and tantrums on Geraldine's part; forceful, executive-style directives from Leslie. What they never tried, to their credit, was rejection, even as the possibility of marriage grew less and less remote; Shirley was still their daughter, no matter what she did. Of course, up to the last minute they hoped they could keep her from doing it.

Undoubtedly to that end, Shirley was somehow coerced into taking a long car trip to California with her mother and brother the summer before her senior year, in 1939. Leslie was already there, on a business trip; they would join him, and who could tell? Perhaps the mellow California air would work a miracle. If nothing else, Shirley would be physically removed from Stanley for several weeks. The trip had all the earmarks of a last-ditch effort, but if so, it was a miserable failure—the minute Shirley arrived in San Francisco, her former lost Eden, she became violently sick and had to be hospitalized for the first time in her life. Doctors disagreed about the diagnosis; Barry Jackson swears he remembers the phrase "trench mouth" being bandied about at one point. Whatever the case, her illness, which had to be at least partially stress-induced, lasted for their entire three-week stay; as soon as she recovered, the family returned to Rochester. The trip had failed completely to achieve the desired effect, and Leslie and Geraldine began to suspect, uneasily, that they were going to lose the battle completely. If they had read a poem Shirley wrote at about that time, they would have known it for sure:

> o my love is long and hard and lean
> with leather gauntlets on.
> and my lover's eyes are hard and keen
>   . . . but where has my father gone? gone . . .
> o my love is lean and long and hard
> with color in his cheek
> and my lover's wrists are lean and scarred
>   . . . but my father's hands were weak . . . weak . . .
> o my love is hard and lean and long
> but silken is his tread
> and he has made my careless song,
>   . . . and he struck my father dead, dead . . .

The king was dead; long live the king. Shirley had switched allegiances forever.

Shirley kept in close touch with Stanley throughout the trip. "shirley is really sick like a dog in Frisco and may not be able to come home for weeks," Stanley wrote to Jay Williams; "that dope would get the mumps at her age period it just substantiates all walter had to say about christians period" (early on, Stanley had developed what would become a lifelong aversion to the shift key on his typewriter).

During the summer, while Shirley was being spirited away to California by her family, Stanley met the man he would come to consider his lifelong mentor. Critic Kenneth Burke, a friend of Leonard Brown, had come to Syracuse to give a series of lectures, and Stanley, as Brown's prize pupil, had managed to make a very favorable impression. At forty-two, Burke was already an almost mythic figure on the academic scene. Stories abounded of his brilliance, his generosity, and of course, the best-known story of all—of the time when, only a few weeks away from graduation at Columbia University, he had suddenly realized the utter pointlessness of a degree and refused to accept one. He would go on to teach at some of the nation's top colleges, to become one of the most respected figures in the field of American criticism, a trailblazer in the study of folklore, all without even so much as an undergraduate degree.

Stanley was truly awed by Burke. Years later he would announce grandiosely that Burke was one of the two people he had met in the world who were actually smarter than he was (poet Howard Nemerov was the other). At the time, of course, he joked to Williams in his usual wise-guy fashion about meeting Burke: "i got fairly chummy with kenneth burke when he was up here this summer. i am writing him a letter tomorrow and i have some stuff to tell him that should knock him flat on his back. he has been working on euphemistic folk distortions (jeepers creepers for jesus christ, etc.) and i want to tell him that i have discovered that 'go fly a kite' is 'go fuck' distorted, 'shiver my timbers' is 'shit,' etc. . . . any dirty phrases you want translated, you know the critic to come to. . . ." But in fact, meeting Burke had had a momentous effect, eventually changing the direction of Stanley's life and, inevitably, Shirley's as well.

Stanley had also met Malcolm Cowley, another established man of letters who was also imported to Syracuse by Brown to give summer lectures. Brown, Cowley remembered, spoke glowingly to him of Stanley—but even more so of Shirley. This was the one to keep his eye on, Brown said.

By senior year, Shirley and Stanley were virtually living together; their eventual marriage was now a certainty, and had been for some time. That previous spring Shirley had even begun wearing a ring, albeit one of dime-store origin. During a dull lecture, a classmate asked her in a note if she had been married long. "On the contrary—a year from June I'll be married if S. has $2," Shirley scrawled back. She wore the ring because "the dean started asking questions." Details of their future had already been discussed, she said. "I'm going to have 15 sons, each born in a different country. S. says if I have a daughter we'll have to eat her."

She added, sardonically: "If I can prophecy my children correctly, my sons will treat their mother just like their father does—beat me up regularly and never speak to me unless they happen to be in a very good mood."

She could make fun of it, and did, but Shirley was well aware that Stanley could be a handful. She knew he was terribly proud of her; he bragged about her to his friends constantly—"shoiley and i·go on being happy like anything," he wrote Jay Williams; "that shirley is ten times nicer than she has ever been, so smart, so beautiful. . . . this week we both wrote sonnets. hers was called lettertoasoldier and had a line in it 'bring nothing for the baby, he is dead' that knocked the class off its feet." But Stanley was also horrendously domineering, even tyrannical and worst of all an inveterate, incorrigible flirt. This last gave Shirley the most pain. She knew she was not beautiful; she had gained back the weight she had lost very quickly and would never again be called thin. Close friends are sure she accepted it: "I think she figured this was what the outside of her was supposed to look like and had nothing whatsoever to do with who she was or what she looked like inside," said June. She probably did come to terms with it, in time. But it couldn't have been easy. Especially with Stanley, in the early days.

As dedicated fighters in the war against bourgeois morality, Stanley and his friends were determined to resist the lure of fidelity, no matter how hard it might be. After all, were they not radicals? Freedom fighters? There had been, therefore, a certain amount of sexual experimentation within the group, though probably a lot more discussion than action.

"Stanley was always serious with Shirley," said Frannie Bardacke. "But I do think he felt he was educating her into this philosophical idea of fidelity being a bourgeois value. We were very philosophical about relationships. Ted and I had an open marriage all our life, though they didn't call it that then, and we settled on it then."

Shirley was not particularly bothered by the idea of sexual freedom as a philosophical ideal. It was the reality that hurt. In a long rambling piece, she discussed her reaction to one incident when Stanley had gone to bed with another girl. At first she, Frannie, and June had gone out and gotten roaring drunk and even managed to have a nice evening, with Shirley proclaiming loudly several times that she had been given horns. But later the truth had crashed down on her (possibly because the three had chosen to return to the very apartment where Stanley was conducting his liaison).

"june was so kind and she took me out on the porch where it was cold and i sobered up a little and she told me not to be a fool, that it was unimportant and i could have believed it was only it had become real suddenly so i told her she was being very logical and she was absolutely right and i agreed with her completely and i went right on crying."

The piece concluded with this sad little exchange: " 'haven't you ever been unfaithful to him?' 'why should i be?' i said. 'he wouldn't care if i were.' "

Stanley, writing to Jay Williams a few days later, on October 7, 1939, referred to the same incident as "my latest stupidity with shirley (i finally unnerved her, by screwing her next-to-best friend up here in a far-from-uncomplicated situation, most of which was that shirley was in the next room, quite drunk, shouting obscene remarks of an uncomplimentary tenor)."

Not all of Stanley's flirtations ended up in bed, of course—but all of them hurt. Even in the early flush of their relationship, in the fall of 1938, Shirley returned to campus a few weeks late after summer vacation only to find that Stanley had been spending every spare minute hanging around a cute little freshman, Florence Shapiro.

"I thought I was starting a relationship with him—and then suddenly, Shirley appeared on the scene. I hadn't even known she existed. Suddenly she appeared, and she hated me," Florence remembered. "She intimidated me completely. She was brilliant and I was a stupid kid. She could really be nasty, very witty, very sarcastic. She really knew how to put you down. I never even tried to compete—I gave up very fast."

Both Florence and Stanley belonged to the YCL club, and Florence later worked on *Spectre,* so there was no way for her to avoid running into Shirley—or her hostility. Even though nothing particular ever transpired between Stanley and Florence after the initial flurry, Shirley remained jealous. She kept her guard up and, whenever she could, fired off a volley or two in Florence's direction. Once, in the Greek's, Florence told her and Stanley of a dream she had had—both Shirley and Stanley loved playing amateur psychoanalyst—and Shirley promptly assured her, triumphantly, that it proved beyond doubt she was a latent lesbian.

"That was a terrible thing, then, one of the worst things you could suspect of yourself," Florence said. Shirley also had no compunction about using her blacker powers as well. "She was a witch, you know, and really into it. She would stick pins in wax dolls, she bragged about it. I knew I was one of the ones she was poking needles into, too. It didn't work," said Florence.

"It was strictly a physical business. Shirley had a weight problem, she was unattractive, and I wasn't, at that age. I think that was where the jealousy was. I suppose she felt threatened. I remember, people used to wonder, what did he see in her—but of course, she was brilliant, that's what he saw in her. She was a very unusual and brilliant person, and she never let you forget it. There was a lot of commitment between them, they had their own language, talked above everybody else's head.

"But I guess he must have strayed plenty. I had the feeling back then that Stanley would have liked to have two women, all the time."

There was no question that these episodes meant very little to Stanley—it almost seemed he prized them more for their anecdotal value. But that didn't keep them from hurting and infuriating Shirley. And while she might talk airily to friends about the feasibility of doing some experimentation of her own, in her case it was just talk, and she knew it. To Stanley these were minor foibles, boyish escapades hardly worthy of Shirley's notice. Unfortunately, they laid the groundwork for a pattern of jealousy and suspicion, accusation and denial, which would persist throughout their lives together.

On the other hand, there was no denying that they also added a certain spice to the relationship. There was satisfaction of a kind in knowing that no matter how far Stanley ranged, she was always going to be the one fixed point on his compass. Then too, it was not entirely unpleasant to see that her man was attractive to other women. After all, she was the one who had him, wasn't she? And finally, whatever else, it did all seem terribly sophisticated, and very far removed from Rochester. Nothing was ever simple with Shirley, certainly not where Stanley's roving eye was concerned. Always there would be an entire range of emotional reactions, hopelessly intermeshed, impossible to disentangle.

For the most part, though, especially by their senior year, Stanley and Shirley had settled into a delightfully cozy domesticity; both were taking a strikingly non-Marxist pleasure in using the little money they had to pad their nest: "shirley and i, with light housekeeping looming ahead, bought a turntable and about a dozen symphonies and things from a guy, and have become music lovers on the professional scale and even entrepreneurs after a fashion. today we went down and sunk all our october money in prokofief's 'lieutenant koje' which is really solid," Stanley wrote Jay Williams that fall.

They had also begun to try to outdo each other in gift-giving, another pattern—a bit less destructive—that would persist. Shirley had come back from her California trip, Stanley informed Williams proudly, with a present "you would give that left testicle thy centre for"—a hand-carved wooden Chinese chess set. Stanley for his part had found her a leather-bound collection of Hogarth, complete with engravings.

Under Stanley's fond gaze, Shirley's creativity seemed to bubble forth in many directions. She was writing as much poetry as prose; at the same time she was developing a talent for drawing odd, funny little sketches, and even considering a possible sideline career as a cartoonist. She had developed two cartoon alter egos, one for her and one for Stanley—Schmuyd and Schmuytle. Schmuyd was a sort of eagle-penguin mix, Schmuytle mostly turtle. Both of them show up throughout her college notebooks: despite Stanley's influence, Shirley still had little interest in most of her classes, outside the English department. Brown's classes she loved; also those of Professor H. W. Herrington, who taught "Introduction to Folklore" and "American Folksong." But Spanish and science left her cold, and her notebooks for these classes were filled with doodles. Abnormal psychology was better—at least it was concerned with the workings of the mind.

Her own mind continued to be a fearful as well as fascinating place. She knew she was prey to anxieties, to hysteria, to odd intuitions and visions, to perceptions of what seemed like reality but perhaps was not reality at all. There were times when she accepted it, even gloried in it— did others have such an interesting place to go to inside their head? But there were other times when her roiling emotions left her terrified—would she finally end up insane, was that what it all meant? To this unsettled mix had been added the effect of Stanley—Stanley with his love, his loyalty, his strength, his protection, yes, but also Stanley with his flirtations, his cool rationality, his independence, his eternal involvement with other people.

"it is a very simple problem," Shirley wrote. "i am a psychopathic case. i am abnormally jealous and he will never believe that it is because he has done so many bad things to me already that everything else he does seems bad, too—no strike that, that mustn't stay in," she stopped herself.

"it isn't jealousy, don't you see?" she insisted, continuing. "it's hurt and being left alone and being out in a safe place so he can come back to me when he is finished with the other girls, and it's being left among people who frighten me and not being able to sit and talk like he can. . . . and then it means having him look at me accusingly and say he can't have any friends, and hating myself for it."

No, it wasn't just jealousy—there was much more to it. The relationship had assumed such immense proportions that by now she considered Stanley nothing less than her anchor against insanity.

"i am a psychopathic case and i am going to go insane. right now there is no solid basis for me to think on. . . . there is an empty space inside my head. . . . if i could show you the inside of my head you would understand me better. . . . and i know perfectly well that i have no control over what i think or say right now and that whatever comes from me is not made by my mind or the thinking part of me but by the small hysterical part which has taken over the whole system. and i have nothing to hold onto to make this hysterical part go away. . . . when stanley talked like that three days ago [he had ignored her at a party, then bawled her out for her reaction] he stopped taking care of me and my one security is gone and it's not that i was basing my security so much on him as it was that i thought he was so good and i was so alone and helpless and only learning to be practical and needed something real which is now gone and all my world is unreal. . . .

"i've tried so hard to tell him what would happen when i finally broke and always it was the same words and always he consoled me and said he would take care of me and always it was all right, and now i'm going. . . . i'm really going and it's all going. . . .

"what will it feel like? . . . will he let them lock me up or will he start taking care of me again when it's too late. . . . please stanley please don't let them take me away hide me or something and don't let me go. . . ."

This was full-blown hysteria, naked and real, of the sort Shirley rarely committed to paper. Yet even here, letting it all out, she was careful to frame it, keeping the emotions—at least on paper—one step at bay: the piece was written in the third person about a girl talking to a wooden cat named Meadelux. Of course it was Shirley's cat and Shirley's hysteria, but she was still capable of controlling it. No matter how intense her feelings, one part of her mind would always stand outside, observing and taking notes. Many years later, in the grips of another torrent of fear and misery, she would pour out page after page of hysteria, then suddenly reprimand herself crisply: "Now, this is lunacy—save it for when you need a lunatic." The terror was real enough, as was the hysteria, but there was always another strong current operating too—the tough, well-tempered instinct of a natural survivor. No matter what she may have believed, it was not Stanley's power that protected her from insanity, ever—it was her own.

But it was Stanley she clung to, Stanley she adored, Stanley to whom she wrote:

> *You are like filigree of some coarse stuff*
> *That resents its being shaped into an ape of beauty.*
> *You glitter, but behind an artificial mask*
> *That, daubed, seems brighter only when adjusted.*
> *Your intellect is a half-crazed centaur*
> *That rides your body; but your body cannot part from it.*
> *How young you are:*
> *Like blood just spilled, still fragrant.*
> *How gay you are:*
> *Your laughter sounds from lips half-cracked with grief.*
> *You never smile, you always laugh.*
> *You are like a madman who dances in the dark.*

It was a fearsome thing, her attachment; a terrible devotion. He was the savior who had pulled her in out of the darkness. Any threat to the relationship was a threat to survival itself—and would be treated accordingly.

CHAPTER

·9·

Stanley, who not only rarely avoided confrontation of any kind but generally took a keen pleasure in the very process, had postponed the inevitable bout with his father as long as he could. He knew exactly how stubborn Moe Hyman could be; in that sense at least they were cut from the same cloth. The Jacksons might have a strong allegiance to country-club mores, but Moe Hyman, Stanley knew, believed he answered to an even higher authority. Orthodox Jews like Moe Hyman did not accept non-Jewish daughters-in-law. For his brilliant son, the one he was so proud of, to announce he was going to marry a shiksa would be a crushing blow. Stanley knew just how bad it was going to be, and he was right.

Somehow, God knows how, little Lulu Hyman, who had never before in her life had control over anything her husband said or did, managed to persuade him to go to Syracuse with her for one visit; perhaps he only wanted to get a look at the siren who was enticing his son away from his family. At any rate, the visit did nothing to mend matters. "It was a bad Sunday afternoon," recalled Red Stodlsky, a friend Stanley had commandeered to stick close by that day, drive them around, and run interference for him and Shirley. "I think I took them out to a restaurant. Moe didn't say much, but you could tell—he was very cold. Moe wasn't a nasty man but he lived his life the way he wanted—this was a guy brought up in a strict religious family."

Father and son faced each other down, both inflexible, iron-willed, incapable of compromise. It was a standoff. Lulu and Moe returned to Brooklyn, while back in Syracuse, Stanley comforted Shirley. It meant nothing, it changed nothing, he told her stoutly. But Shirley was shaken. She had finally met the one person capable of wringing fearful respect out of Stanley; she would be afraid of Moe Hyman the rest of her life.

They graduated in June 1940—Stanley with a magna cum laude, Shirley with "no great academic distinction," as Stanley would later put it. Still, she had made it. "What do I care if I don't learn a thing?" Shirley wrote in a poem entitled "Commencement 1940." "Who will know or give a damn. . . . What can I bring that the world will want or need? Where will I go? You made me this, so tell me kindly, what can I do?" Actually, the answer was simple. For quite some time they had known exactly what they were going to do: move to New York City, live as cheaply as possible, take menial jobs if necessary and wait for the Big Break. Not just wait—push for it. Shirley was excited. The glimpses she had had of the city on weekend trips made with Stanley had thrilled her. Her friend Elizabeth Young remembered getting an exuberant letter from her, in which she described looking out a window, taking in the whole glorious Manhattan scene. "She sounded as if she had found it," Young commented. "I was always surprised she left."

They moved into a tiny apartment at 215 West Thirteenth Street, with a small black cat they named Moe, in a spirit of defiant humor. Their first jobs were menial enough—Stanley worked at the Made-Right Novelty Company (product: shoulder straps), Shirley wrote continuity for a radio station chiefly concerned with racing results. Money was scarce, with both sets of parents having no interest whatsoever in smoothing the way for the young couple, and jobs for untrained liberal arts graduates at the tail end of the Depression not plentiful. They put off their marriage until the end of the summer—probably because they were waiting for a sign of goodwill, from either their parents or the world.

Both the Jacksons and the Hymans held fast—Moe Hyman, in fact, announced that he considered his son as good as dead. But the world was kinder. When Stanley entered a *New Republic* contest with a short piece called "The Lonely Eagle," which deftly skewered Charles Lindbergh's pro-Fascist political stance, he won handily and was offered a job as an editorial assistant, at twenty dollars a week. On August 13, 1940, the same week the piece was published, Shirley and Stanley were married in a civil ceremony at a friend's apartment in upper Manhattan. She was twenty-three, he twenty-one. It would be the last time Shirley would admit her true age on an official document—from here on, she would knock three years off, giving her birthdate as December 1919, so she would appear younger than Stanley. A small vanity, a tiny falsehood, and one Stanley understood; in the brief memoriam he wrote after her death he loyally perpetuated it.

No relatives attended the ceremony: the Jacksons, bitter and defeated, remained cloistered in Rochester; in Brooklyn, Moe Hyman huddled in a prayer shawl, sitting shivah for the son he had declared dead, while his wife tiptoed fearfully around him. But the young couple was undaunted. Shirley gave her occupation as "radio writer" on the marriage license form, but Stanley, his confidence running at full throttle, gave his as "magazine editor."

"They were free and on their own. I think everybody envied them," said Frank Orenstein. Very few young men at that time could afford to ignore the warning signs in the air—war was coming closer every day, and any career begun now would almost certainly have to be put on hold. But Stanley, with his heart murmur and bad eyesight, felt secure—he knew he would be classified 4-F. He later bragged that the doctor had told him he had the organs of a much older man.

Freedom they had; material comforts, no. Their apartment was dingy and cramped, with a window on one wall overlooking an air shaft. Stanley insisted to friends that he and Shirley often sat there expectantly while the upstairs neighbors held nightly slugfests. There would be an angry shout, a breaking of glass, and a telephone receiver would hurtle down the shaft; another shout and the rest of the phone would follow.

The fights were not confined to the apartment upstairs, though. Stanley and Shirley had plenty of their own that first year, not all of them verbal, either. "They got physical. There would be these terrible, great fights, where Shirley would smack Stanley and sometimes he'd smack her back—then she'd run off into the bathroom, crying away, and lock the door, refusing to come out," said Frank, who was the reluctant witness to several scenes. "You'd sit there and it would flare up, then stop—eventually Shirley would come out of the bathroom and it was over. They were in competition." Frank was not the only one who took a dim view of the marriage's chances of survival.

Shirley was writing diligently, mostly stories, but without great enthusiasm. After a lifetime filled with creature comforts, she took no pleasure in living close to the bone and in Stanley's "economizing by using the same coffee grounds three days running but we have to have oranges, don't we, hell, you get scurvy or something," as she wrote grumpily. "And who ever heard of giving up smoking. If we only knew someone who had a job we could go there for dinner."

She was fiercely jealous of Stanley's luck in getting a position so quickly, however small, at a respectable magazine. In a poem entitled "I Contemplate the Site of the Building in Which 'The New Republic' Is Housed" she wrote coldly: "Ere they invented moveable type, and politics and kings, there used to be fresh water here, and growing things." Just what Stanley made of this sudden burst of ecological fervor is unknown; most likely he understood the reason for it and took it in stride.

Stanley filled the tiny apartment with his friends, old and new, some dating back to Erasmus Hall, some just met at *The New Republic*. There was a sense of crisis in the air. The war in Europe was on everyone's lips, the atmosphere was charged with politics, and the arguments and ideological discussions ranged far and wide. Fueled, of course, by liquor, smoke, and any food Shirley managed to whip up—she was a complete novice as a cook, but was starting to learn and in fact enjoying the process. Baking a cake was creative, too, after a fashion. You took the ingredients, combined them, and ended up with a product. Not so different from clothespin dolls or short stories, after all. Housekeeping, on the other hand, held no charms whatsoever—where was the creativity in that? It all seemed a giant waste of her energy, and she did as little of it as possible.

The endless political discussions left her cold. Her brief fling with radical politics at college had been totally Stanley-induced, and left no marks. Now, when the boys got going, she either left the room or sat in a corner and sulked. That was their world, not hers. Irritated beyond measure, she finally wrote:

> Song for all editors, writers, theorists, political economists, idealists, communists, liberals, reactionaries, bruce bliven, marxist critics, reasoners, and postulators, any and all splinter groups, my father, religious fanatics, political fanatics, men on the street, fascists, ernest hemingway, all army members and advocates of military training, not excepting those too old to fight, the r.o.t.c. and the boy scouts, walter winchell, the terror organizations, vigilantes, all senate committees and my husband:

> > *I would not drop dead from the lack of you—*
> > *My cat has more brains than the pack of you.*

Which pretty much said it all.

She held a number of boring, low-paying jobs that first year, all of which she hated. Applying was bad enough—"I am twenty three, just out of college, authority on all books and a great writer, can type, cook, play a rather emotional game of chess, and have a republican father which is no fault of mine," she wrote, parodying her efforts. "dear sir do you have a position open in your organization for a bright young / dear sir didn't you and my father go to school together . . .

"And after a while you get to feeling like there's something you got to say and do before you float away just floating like on air and you got to tell all these people . . . and you try to tell them and all that comes out is god god life life."

Still, she did try her best to be a good little wage-earner. In late fall 1940 she got a job selling books at Macy's. "That's where everybody who had a degree in English knew they could find a job," said Taissa Kellman, another English graduate fresh out of Wayne State in Michigan, who met her there. "There were a lot of terrific people, writers, struggling artists. You had to pass a stiff exam on authors and titles so they were fairly literate types." That didn't make the job itself any more interesting, though, and both young women quit right after Christmas. Shirley went on to work at the Jack Goehring Advertising Agency for six months, "writing ads and stalling off creditors," as Stanley later described it. Her jobs, bad as they were, served a purpose. They provided her with raw material she would later use in a number of stories, and a new motivation: she was more determined than ever to succeed at her writing so that she would never have to work in an office again.

She and Stanley made a number of visits to Syracuse to see friends, staying at a cheap rooming house, with Shirley often taking a side trip to Rochester. Her parents had never closed the door completely, and now they were doing their best to make their peace with the reality. It was several months before they actually showed up at the apartment in New York. When they did, Shirley served a formal dinner, complete with turkey, to mark the occasion. Stanley, doing his best to impress his in-laws with his dignity, began solemnly to carve. Unfortunately for his image, after two passes he knocked the entire works off the platter and onto the floor. The Jacksons were not impressed, though their daughter found it hysterically funny.

Briefly, very briefly, during one of their visits to Syracuse, Stanley convinced Shirley they should both keep journals, "thus giving us every aspect and privilege of the published writer except publication," as Shirley noted caustically. "What artists we are to be sure."

Stanley's idea was that they should both write about their daily life and then compare notes; being Stanley, he then promptly went out and drummed up an incident so they would have something specific to write about: while Shirley was visiting her mother, he picked up Florence Shapiro, Shirley's old nemesis, and brought her home for an evening. He had no intention of hiding it from Shirley, far from it; he was fairly bursting with the news by the time she got back.

"Stanley met me, tremulous with moving things to tell me, all of which had to be presented in the innocent sentences he had figured out for them walking down to the station. Consequently I heard most of it before he forgot how to say it best, which meant before I had gotten my coat off," Shirley wrote. " 'I might as well tell you, dear, you'll read it in my journal and it was really very funny and I thought at the time how you would have liked it and thought it was so funny.' " Florence, according to Stanley, had "got very drunk and had to be sobered up and put in showers and have her head held and wasn't it a scream—"

Not too surprisingly, Shirley did not find it as funny as all that. "Found contemplation of Florence drooling on my husband no more pleasant than I would have expected, but obviously less pleasant than my husband found it in retrospect," she commented. "But as Junie says, if I had to marry a guy who fancies himself as a gay dog, I can hardly expect him to be housebroken so quick."

This, however, was her "mature" reaction—her real feelings, revealed over the next several pages, were distinctly less benign. A few nights later she herself served Florence wine "in hopes she would get drunk enough to say something to justify my dislike of her in Stanley's eyes." Florence, she noted, "took no more than twice her share of praise for anything that came up in conversation"; she was "coarse and vulgar" and "a piece of scum." Finally, most brutally, Shirley referred to another friend who had a wandering boyfriend: "She has the same trouble with [him], but he always picks outright whores, of course, and she doesn't care either, only she likes to know and change the sheets."

Yet there was a glimmer of wistful self-knowledge: "Whatever else I say I can't deny that she [Florence] has a beautiful body and after all I am too fat."

The amazing thing is that throughout there was hardly a touch of anger against Stanley himself, who, after all, had masterminded the entire business. Even her initial annoyance was, she quickly decided, "rather unfair to Stanley, who was really terribly thoughtful about it, and so nicely transparent."

"He got me drunk and then threw me into the shower. Nothing happened, I was too drunk," Florence Shapiro remembered. "He was playing games. He had to have been, if he told her about it. I was being used."

Shirley's journal ended abruptly after an argument with Stanley not about Florence but about art; more specifically, a lecture by Stanley on her deficiencies as art critic. "He was more interested in telling me what was good than in knowing why I didn't realize it was good—the trouble was that I wanted to talk about myself and he wanted to talk about art. [He] got me finally after several hours into a state of helplessness where I felt the whole world was standing around pointing at me and calling me names . . . went to bed furiously angry, woke up 'sulky' [Stanley's description in his journal, apparently] and stayed that way until time worked its wonders and we made friends again . . . no more. Journal finished." It would be twenty-four years before she kept another.

Stanley now came up with another plan to help them feel more like artists—"he always had these master plans, like Stalinist five-year plans," a friend said. They would take their typewriters and go off into the woods for a year. Shirley agreed immediately; she was tired of New York, tired of dead-end jobs, and extremely tired of nightly political forums. This could be a chance to get back on track with her writing.

Stanley felt the same way. Maybe the temporal world of politics and *The New Republic* (it was hard to tell where one stopped and the other began) had been distracting him from what should be his true pursuit—Art with a capital A. Over the year he had managed to develop a tenuous connection with a few people at *The New Yorker*. The magazine had always been the citadel, the giant, the one place he most wanted to be. Away from the city, undistracted by war headlines, he could concentrate on writing for it, bombarding its editors with one piece after another until they fell.

In late 1941 they rented a cheap cabin in the wilds of Keene, New Hampshire, packed their bags, and to the astonishment of nearly everyone they knew, took off. "I really didn't think they would come back married," said Frank Orenstein, who was a bit chilled at the prospect of the Hymans' urban battles transplanted to a rural landscape. Shirley wouldn't even have a bathroom to lock herself in. And the picture of Stanley spending the winter in a cabin in the woods with no heat and no *New York Times* was ludicrous. But in fact the plan worked. When they emerged from the woods months later, America had gone to war but the Hymans were at peace.

Even in the outback, they had visitors. Lulu Hyman had continued to see Stanley and Shirley while they were in New York, defying Moe, who finally admitted defeat in the face of maternal instinct and allowed her to go. That winter she visited the cabin, with Stanley's sixteen-year-old brother Arthur. Both were shocked at the primitive conditions—the cabin had no heat, no electricity, no running water, and most important, no indoor toilet. Two coal stoves provided the heat, water had to be hand-pumped from the kitchen, and the facilities were out the door and down the path. Stanley and Shirley were obviously prepared to stick it out for several more months, but after a few late-night runs to the outhouse, Lulu and Arthur beat a fast retreat.

Jay Williams also came up for a few days, bringing his new wife, Bobbie, whom he had met through his job at the Group Theater. This time there were no threatened black masses; Jay was well on his way to becoming a family man and had toned down his act considerably. The two couples played more traditional games—poker, Monopoly—and discussed their work. Williams too was trying to launch a career as a writer. (He would eventually go on to become a prolific one, turning out, among other things, the Danny Dunn science fiction series for children and a large number of detective novels under the pseudonym Michael Devlin.) Stanley, Shirley, and Williams spent hours reading manuscripts to each other, each of them keenly interested, of course, only in his or her own work. Shirley found that hilarious:

You can't refuse to talk to people just because they're writers, and what with every yearning poet in the country ducking the draft long enough to come up and read a few lines to Stanley and Stanley himself trying to get a comment or so done a week and me writing a parody of Faulkner, then Jay coming up with his unknown stories and Bobbie doing a children's book . . . and that fool poet leaving a six-inch portfolio of his "work" for us to glance at . . . what the hell, even the farmers' wives entering limerick contests . . . who the hell dares to write when there are so many other poor damn fools ready to read you what they just wrote?

Still, she managed. And in December she hit gold—*The New Republic* bought a short funny piece she wrote about working at Macy's—"My Life with R. H. Macy"—for twenty-five dollars. Her confidence soared: she was a published author at last, no more odd jobs for her. Within a month she was pregnant. She and Stanley returned to New York in the summer of 1942, triumphant: their self-imposed exile had worked. Stanley had solidified his connection at *The New Yorker* into a staff writer position, Shirley had launched her career, and there was even a baby in the works. Most of their friends felt, with Frank Orenstein, that the first hurdle had been cleared, and the Hymans "were both on their way and life was good."

CHAPTER
·10·

They first moved to Woodside, Queens, instead of Manhattan, having a vague feeling that the baby should be exposed to the country—back then, Queens was country. But shortly after their son Laurence Jackson Hyman, known as Laurie, was born, on October 3, 1942, they were back in Greenwich Village, having taken an apartment on Grove Street.

Right from the start, Shirley took to motherhood. There was something innately alien about small children, something intuitive and magical and half mad in the things they did and said that spoke directly to her. Sterilizing bottles, changing diapers, fixing schedules held no interest for her at all—that was just more housekeeping, which she despised. But children themselves were another matter. Her world had always consisted of more than one reality, unlike Stanley's—and children, when young, were by their very nature open to other realities, to the possibilities of magic. Like her, they were not bound to the limits of one time, one place. Their minds were actually more like hers—quick, intuitive, darting into strange corners. Others might see children as primitives who need to be initiated into the world of logic—Shirley delighted fiercely in their very illogic. It was their strangeness, their difference she responded to deeply, finding in it an echo of her own.

At the same time, her children grounded her, tethering her to the real world in a way even Stanley could not. She was freer to float through the odd regions of her mind, safer to contemplate terror and evil, with the sure knowledge that she would be snapped back—inevitably—to deal with a hungry baby. In a very real sense, the entire machinery of child care provided an important balance, and one she was deeply grateful for. Her children kept her safe. It was no accident that she had four—Shirley knew what she needed. For many years, her fears of insanity dimmed, even her anxieties receded. How insane could you be if you were feeding an infant, wheeling a toddler, performing the thousand and one mundane tasks necessary to keep small children alive and healthy? Where was the time to even consider insanity? It was almost as if she had developed a personal form of behavior modification, a sure-fire method of keeping the demons at bay, at least for a time. This is not how it works for every woman, certainly, but it worked for Shirley. For a long, long time.

She was a hands-on mother, while Stanley was a hands-off father. Children were her department, he made clear from the beginning. He might deign to converse with his son after he had his degree, but not before, he said, and it was not entirely a joke. Even at a time when fathers were not expected to be involved in the care of small children, Stanley was in a class by himself. He took his cues from an even earlier time, from, in fact, that master of removed Victorian fatherhood, Moe Hyman. He believed in Shirley's talent completely, respected her ability, but when it came to *Kinder*, kitchen, and cleanup, she was on her own. It amused Shirley, it occasionally annoyed her—she drew viciously funny sketches of Stanley buried under his *New York Times,* saying, "No, I don't think I'd ever want to have another, dear. It's too much of a strain for me," while she tore around after the baby. But she accepted his terms and, hard as it might be for another generation to understand, she never really minded.

Of course, there was another part of the equation operating here, too— Geraldine. Throughout her life Shirley waged an endless contest against this shallow woman who had made her feel different and unwanted when she was young. She would have twice as many children, take care of them better, enjoy them a thousand times more, never stifle their spirits; do great works, have truer friends, larger houses, better parties, a happier marriage. And she did, she did, and it was never enough. But for a long time, when the children were young and the books coming out, it must have felt as if she were vanquishing her oldest enemy at last.

Now that they were back in New York, and Shirley had an actual publication credit under her belt, Stanley turned up the pressure. She was welcome to have a baby if she wanted, just as she was welcome to practice bits of witchcraft and fool around with Tarot cards—that is to say, in her spare time. But he was going to make damn sure she continued to do what he considered her real work: writing. He did not lock her in a room, à la Colette and Willy, or dictate plots, but he took his job as curator of her talent seriously. Left to her own devices, Shirley might fritter away hours baking cakes or playing with the baby; it was up to him to keep her on the right road.

A born teacher, as well as disciplinarian, he also took up the matter of Shirley's education, which he felt had been sadly neglected, assigning her specific courses in literature. Elsa Dorfman, a friend of Stanley's from Erasmus Hall, remembers coming by once and finding Shirley lying on a sofa, popping chocolates into her mouth, and dutifully plowing her way through the entire field of English literature—she had worked her way up to the Ds, and was currently reading all of Defoe.

"He'd put her to work, he'd force her into writing," said Taissa Kellman, who after first meeting Shirley at Macy's was now being drawn into the group that clustered around the Hymans. "I was sort of an escape—when I showed up she'd stop the writing. I think I inserted a ray of hope." Stanley and Shirley tended to assign friends roles—Kellman contributed baby-sitting and cooking.

"I was the best potato pancake–maker in town, they thought, and every time I'd show up they'd railroad me into the kitchen and put the grater in my hand. Shirley loved feeding people, being the big mama. When I came, she could stop writing and start cooking. And I had fun with the kid, so we enjoyed that together."

Stanley had never had much of a problem with self-doubt; now, with his place at *The New Yorker* ensured, and not much later, with a genuine book contract for an in-depth work on criticism, his confidence shifted, if possible, into an even higher gear. The front room of the apartment was designated his office. He sat at his desk, in the exact center of the room, facing the door, with a large bowl of Indian nuts—the kind you could buy in the subway for a nickel—beside him. No one was allowed to bother him, not Shirley, not any visitors, while he sat there. He on the other hand was allowed to bother everyone.

"There he would sit in the middle of the apartment," said Taissa Kellman. "Dictating, working, telling everyone what to do, telling them how idiotic they were, how ignorant, how stupid—and everyone loved it. They took it from him. He was a terrible tyrant—but marvelous."

"Stanley was quite extraordinary," said June Mirken. "It's hard to think whether a lot of things would ever have happened if he hadn't existed. I think she would have written in any case, she'd always written—but he was so extraordinarily self-disciplined. He structured things. There was a whole routine, get up at a certain hour, do this, time the cigarette, the cigar, the going into the study, the sitting down at the typewriter, the cutoff time. You got a drink at five o'clock and not one minute before, because five was when the cocktail hour started. You ate lunch at twelve."

And inevitably, you did your best to build the same structure around your wife, no matter how unlikely the fit. Shirley had never had much use for routine schedules (possibly one more reason she enjoyed babies so much). She wrote when the mood hit, often in the middle of the night; she smoked, ate, and drank coffee throughout the day, not at specific hours. She was erratic—but then she marched to an erratic drumbeat. Still, she tried in many ways to accommodate Stanley's passion for order.

"I would often spend the night, and when I got up in the morning, Stanley would have his day planned already, and they would take five or ten minutes to discuss what the day would be for Shirley—what she would do, where she would go," said Elsa Dorfman. Even the minutiae of food shopping received his attention. "He would take out a little purse and they would count out pennies—so many grapefruits, so much for milk. He never said, Here's twenty-five dollars, give me change. Either she was incredibly careless about money or he was a pain in the ass."

"For anybody other than Shirley, Stanley would have been absolutely impossible to live with," said June. "I used to look at her in awe sometimes. I remember sort of resenting the fact that she would comply with outrageous demands he made. It went back to his own home—his father ran things, made the decisions, his mother scurried around serving the father. And this is what he demanded of Shirley in many ways. And in many ways she complied with it. I would get furious and we would both sit down and make fun of him." (Another of Shirley's sketches had Stanley again seated behind his paper: "You think you're working hard? Who do you think has been reading through the *Times* all day?" he is asking. And another has no quote at all—it simply shows Stanley, immersed in his paper, while Shirley looms above him, swinging an axe.)

Now that politics had taken a backseat, many of the people who began to come around were more to Shirley's liking. There were new friends from *The New Yorker*—Philip Hamburger, Joseph Mitchell, A. J. Liebling, Brendan Gill, even William Shawn. Stanley's oldest friends, too, were back in town, when they got a break from military commitments— Walter Bernstein, Ben Zimmerman, Frank Orenstein. And June Mirken, of course. (Frank and June had been named Laurie's godparents.) When Jay and Bobbie Williams needed a new apartment, Shirley and Stanley urged them to take the basement flat of their building on Grove Street. There was always something doing at the Hymans'. Parties were large, boisterous, and exciting.

Shirley and Stanley were among the few couples in their group with a baby—but then, they didn't act the way other people did with a baby. Philip Hamburger remembered being encouraged at one party to go into the bedroom and look at little Laurie in his crib. He dutifully trotted back, then stood staring at the crib for several minutes before he could find him. So many hats and coats had been flung into the crib by party guests that the youngest Hyman was almost completely buried from view.

Some of their more conventional friends were shocked—this was not the way it was supposed to be. "Anybody who happened to be around had the baby thrown at him," said Kellman. "I never saw such rough handling. I thought of babies as being something you adored and nurtured. There were a lot of cold and dirty-looking bottles around, diapers wherever you looked."

The Hymans were not, admittedly, neat. "They had left neatness far behind," said Hamburger; they cultivated "a genial mess."

The baby, they felt, should accommodate himself to their life, not the other way around. "Shirley usually did her writing at night, so she was a good sleeper," said Bobbie Williams, who was now living in the basement. "She could sleep through Laurie's banging his crib against the wall to get out of it—she wouldn't hear it, but I would, two floors down."

Shirley had her own ideas of what was important. Elsa Dorfman remembered her taking Laurie out to an ice cream parlor nearly every day, even when he was so small his head didn't come up to the counter. "They would sit there drinking chocolate malts, talking." Always she listened carefully. At home, she would lie on the floor next to him, making up stories with him about the cracks in the ceiling.

Dorfman reacted to this with a certain contemptuous horror—a sentiment that even today is far from uncommon: "My feeling was she would never make a real mother in the sense of a well-shaped-up kid who would go to school and get good marks and find his own career, but at least when she was alone with him, they had some good times together." Shirley followed her own lights. Her own childhood had been clean and rigid and conventional, it would certainly have received the Good Housekeeping Seal of Approval, but it had made her feel unwanted and she had no desire to pass it on. Her baby might not have the cleanest diapers— but he would know he was enjoyed, he would never be despised for the strange things he might say.

Lulu Hyman now became a regular visitor. She too was not particularly thrilled with Shirley's baby-care methods, but she was not about to be kept away from her first grandchild. "I was there one day when she came," said Dorfman. "She took one look at Laurie, who was soiled, and the gray diapers, the mess— You could tell. Shirley was very huffy. It was obvious the relationship was lousy. They both looked like they'd trade each other for anything."

Moe Hyman too, while stoutly maintaining his distance where Stanley and Shirley were concerned, insisted on having a relationship with his grandson. This led to some complicated maneuvering. Nearly every Sunday, Lulu would pick Laurie up and take him back to Brooklyn so Moe could play with him. At times Stanley and Shirley would go to pick him up and even visit for a while, which led to more complications, since Moe adamantly refused to lay eyes on his son. He would leave the house before they came and phone Lulu to make sure they had left before he returned.

On the other hand, nothing was too good for Laurie. In the most cliché scenario, the distant father had been transformed into the most foolishly devoted of grandfathers. Moe began loading Lulu down with money, gifts, and food to take to Stanley and Shirley. While still in a high chair, Laurie developed a passion for peanut-butter-and-bacon sandwiches—and Moe Hyman, that uncompromisable pillar of Orthodox Jewry, turned the city upside down (it was still wartime, after all) to find the choicest slabs of smoked pig meat for his grandson.

Geraldine and Leslie also visited, coming down from Rochester, though much more rarely. Leslie was planning an early retirement (he would in fact spend over forty years in that state), and both of them had begun taking longer and longer trips, to more and more exotic locales. Still, they were good for the occasional check, which Shirley and Stanley appreciated—money was always tight. But whenever Geraldine visited, Shirley found herself becoming tense and awkward, shot back to adolescence.

"She had an exact picture of how she wanted to look," Shirley wrote. "A gay happy young matron, terribly happy and not sentimental, well off and well liked." Not all that easy to pull off. "She always felt that it was necessary to present herself as a competent happy wife; one moment's relaxation in her mother's presence might undo all the work of justification that the years of marriage had built up so carefully." Of course, the plain fact was that Geraldine and Leslie were just as utterly horrified by Stanley as they had ever been, and nothing their daughter did was going to change that. But Shirley could not stop trying to impress on Geraldine the superiority of her life, the ultimate wisdom of her decision to marry her husband.

Luckily, she would eventually realize there was a better way to do it than in person. She could also do it by letter, using her talent to re-create her world exactly the way she wanted her mother to see it. When her parents eventually went back to California, she began to do this in earnest, pouring an amazing amount of time and energy into these letters, some of which approached the length of novellas. Around friends, of course, she was casual, flip about her family. "My father, Stonewall Jackson," she would say. "Did you know I was a descendant of the Stonewall Jacksons?"

She had given friends the impression, right from college, that she could not wait to leave her home, cut off connections, forge a new and different life. But it was not that easy; hard as she fought it, her connection to her parents remained strong. "I remember being surprised when it would recur years later, this need to prove something to her parents," said June. "She'd say she had written her mother, and I was always startled. I knew she wrote regularly, but each time it would startle me. She was never able to write her parents off, as most of us do, I guess. She wrote as she wanted and lived as she wanted, but she kept trying to pull it together—I think she did that a lot, always tried to pull things together and make a whole."

Her short-story writing proceeded apace, thanks in part to Stanley's insistence, and she was getting better and better. No longer was she simply transcribing from reality, as she often had in college; now she was becoming adept at taking the bare bones of reality and giving them a twist, infusing them with some of the fears and horrors and distortions swirling around in her own mind. It was not unlike witchcraft—you mixed a brew, threw in the people and incidents you decided on, and used your darker powers to charge the atmosphere with tension, control mood, set destiny. It was also a powerful medium for revenge, a way to control the final outcome. Her hand was growing surer all the time.

It did not, of course, hurt that Stanley was now at *The New Yorker*. In 1943 her stories began appearing there for the first time; for many years this would be her chief market. No fewer than four of her stories appeared there in 1943, another four in 1944, an almost unheard-of feat for a new writer. Her second *New Yorker* story, "Come Dance with Me in Ireland," published in May 1943, was even included in the collection *The Best American Short Stories, 1944*. Shirley was on a roll.

Most of her stories were set in a world of suburban conventionality—a familiar world, Geraldine's world, the world she had grown up in. But under Shirley's hand, that world became charged with something darker. In "After You, My Dear Alphonse," a young boy brings a black friend home for lunch; his genteel mother tries to handle it "charitably," offering the boy used clothes, carefully questioning him, revealing herself damningly with every word. In "Come Dance with Me in Ireland," three women bustle around, aglow with pride in their own virtue, fixing lunch for a tramp—who then insults them and leaves—"I never served bad liquor to my guests."

It was Shirley's genius to be able to paint homey, familiar scenes like this, and then imbue them with evil—or, more correctly, allow a reader to see the evil that had been obvious to her all along, even in sunny Burlingame. One felt the presence of a grinning skull behind the cover of surface gentility, homemade biscuits, shining floors, and this is what made the tales so disturbing. Shirley never had to search for exotic locales or strange characters. You see, her stories seemed to nudge lightly, insistently at the reader, it was right here, right in front of you all the time. Her earliest published stories did not yet play with the nature of reality itself—but that would come soon.

She liked to use odd pieces of real life in her stories, and her friends enjoyed bringing her anecdotes for possible inclusion. Once Frank Orenstein ran into a little girl in Brooklyn who had found a human leg lying on the street; he relayed this to Shirley right away and was pleased, later, to see "his leg" incorporated into a story, "Pillar of Salt." Ben Zimmerman and Taissa Kellman, who lived in apartments next to each other, became the subjects of another tale, "Like Mother Used to Make." The story is of a rather fussy young man who plans a dinner complete with cherry pie for his female neighbor, in his neat, well-appointed apartment. After dinner, another man comes to visit the woman—and she allows him to think the apartment, as well as the pie, is hers. The man settles down, impressed with her homemaking skills; the actual owner, horrified and helpless, finally leaves.

"That was Ben—it was so Ben, specifically, that she actually asked permission before she published it," said Frank. Ben Zimmerman confirmed it. The story, he said, grew out of an incident in which Stanley and Taissa were sitting in his apartment and refused to leave even though he was expecting a guest. "I had to actually leave myself and meet my guest somewhere else." He did not mind, in fact enjoyed, appearing in Shirley's story.

Taissa, however, who was not informed beforehand, was less than pleased. "I thought: unfair. It made out that Ben knew all about cooking and I had taken advantage of him to impress the guy. It was the other way around: I was the cook. It was really kind of an act of anger to me. I thought she was more approving of me than that. I was fairly sexy-looking, had a lot of guys—maybe this was what Shirley felt resentment about." Certainly it had not escaped Shirley's quick eye that Stanley, too, appreciated Taissa's good looks. "She could never get over the fact that Stanley was so attracted to good-looking women. It was a constant irritant; all day long there was this barb in her flesh. But this was Stanley— you bought the package with Stanley."

Taissa did remember "sitting around listening to a lot of Shirley's stories being created, hacked out, fought out with Stanley, seeing a lot of things from around us being integrated into the stories. It was fun, but I think if I'd known about the story about Benny and me, I would have confronted her: How dare you make me the villainess?"

The story then had many levels—it was a sly poke at Ben, a slap at Taissa, a disturbing little tale altogether. Yet somehow it was more disturbing than the mere facts seemed to warrant. The reader was left with a terrible unease—had the girl taken over the clean apartment forever? But things like that don't happen—do they? And suddenly, the comforting limits of the real world had dissolved, and the reader was left standing at a misty crossroads, gazing into an abyss—other worlds, other possibilities, unnamed terrors. This was Shirley's true territory. It was where she had always lived, and now, in her writing, she was able to convey it to others.

As time went on, she drew more and more on her own wide store of fears for her stories, from the specific—dentists, closed spaces, overhangs, traffic—to the general—chaos, loss of identity, disintegration. In "Pillar of Salt," a woman becomes agonizingly conscious of the decay, the rotting structure, of the city around her. At last she calls her husband; she has realized she is unable to cross the street. In "The Beautiful Stranger," a woman perceives her husband, suddenly, as someone completely new; the world itself seems new, fraught with fresh hope, until she is caught, standing on a suburban street, unable even to recognize her house: "Somewhere a house which was hers, with a beautiful stranger inside, and she lost out here," Shirley ended.

They were personal fears, but through her skill they expanded to envelop the reader. Suddenly they were not the obscure terrors of one unknown woman but the reader's own, pressing in on him. Her stories broke down the barrier between reader and author so the reader himself felt the icy touch of panic, the sense of unreality. She wove her fears and visions into a web she flung out at the world; it clung there, delicate, invisible, but tenacious. Not every reader appreciated the experience of being drawn into Shirley's world, but no one escaped unaffected by it.

For the three years they stayed in New York City after their stint in the woods of New Hampshire, Shirley and Stanley were the center and chief focal point for a large network of friends. Stanley was always bringing home somebody new, pulling him or her into the fold. One day he wandered by the offices of *The Negro Quarterly,* looking for a new market for his critical reviews. He and the young managing editor hit it off at once, discovering a wide band of common interests—jazz, blues, writing, the critical work of Kenneth Burke—and Ralph Ellison, too, was drawn into the group. In 1944 Stanley was responsible for Ellison's work appearing for the first time in a hardcover book.

"Stanley was helping Edwin Seaver assemble a collection of new writing. I had been working on a long story but wasn't able to finish it because it was wartime, I'd been at sea. I was back in town, visiting the Hymans, and Stanley just insisted that I finish it," said Ellison. He did not lock Ellison in a room, but he did direct him to sit down and do the writing right then, the way he often directed Shirley—and Stanley's directives could have considerable force. Ellison spent most of a day working on his story "Flying Home," which appeared in Seaver's collection, *Cross-Section.* "I certainly wouldn't have been in the book if Stanley hadn't put the pressure on," he admitted.

Shirley's work, too, made its first appearance between hard covers in

Cross-Section, with "Behold the Child Among His Newborn Blisses," which featured a mentally impaired child at a pediatrician's office—more blatantly shocking than her usual fare, but then, it was one of her very early stories. The collection was impressive, including works by Richard Wright, Norman Mailer, Jane Bowles, Langston Hughes, and Arthur Miller, along with Stanley and Jay Williams. "Stanley didn't get any credit for it, but he was more interested in helping his friends get into a book," Ellison said.

Ellison was fond of Shirley from the start, although it was Stanley he was closer to. "We'd have these long discussions, about jazz and blues [Ellison had originally majored in music in college], and criticism. Shirley often treated it as though we were a couple of nuts." Her mind was more intuitive. "Stanley used to say to me when I'd get in an argument, 'Ralph, you know Shirley's crazy.' " Shirley's interest in the occult did not appeal to Ellison: he had grown up around people who believed in the power of signs and omens; as an adult, he wanted nothing to do with that sort of thing.

Stanley could be generous and open, warmly hospitable, flinging open the door to friends—but on the other hand, he was every bit as capable of slamming the door shut. A friend who had displeased him in some way could find himself banned for good, his name erased from the blackboard. And when Stanley made up his mind, that was it.

"Shirley went along with him on his bannings—there was nothing else she could do," said June Mirken. "He said he wasn't going to have this man or woman in the house again, or ever speak to them. He could be very dogmatic and had a tendency to get furious at his friends."

One of the early bannings was Walter Bernstein. "They had some collision and Walter was banned," said June. Walter himself could not remember, but felt that if it happened, "we may have been both of us working off our wives." He had married in 1941, and on Stanley and Shirley's return to New York, his wife had loaned them a piano. "She lent it, then later on Shirley refused to give it back—she got very angry, insisted it had been given to her. So if we had an estrangement, it may have been around the piano thing."

Possibly. Neither Stanley nor Shirley was overly fond of Walter's first wife. But whatever the reason, for a time at least, Walter was out. One of the most true-to-life stories Shirley ever published was a funny sketch of Stanley refusing even to open a letter from Walter, while she tried craftily to change his mind, her irritation at his obstinacy ballooning into murderous rage. "Under the cellar steps, she thought, with his head bashed in and his goddamn letter under his folded hands, and it's worth it, she thought, oh it's worth it," she concluded. The story eventually ran in her collection *The Lottery* under the title "Got a Letter from Jimmy," but her original manuscript used Walter's name, and even mentioned Frank and Jay Williams in passing.

Even without a banning to spice things up, parties at the Hymans' were never dull. Stanley was exuberant and argumentative, and both he and Shirley could be bitingly critical—it was a rare evening in which at least one person was not mortally offended. "The insults that were hurled! The nastier the better," said Taissa Kellman. One friend from *The New Yorker* finally bawled Stanley out. "My God, you would shit on your own parlor floor!" he yelled, after several hours spent witnessing Stanley's rendition of kamikaze host. On another occasion Ellison was so appalled by Stanley and Shirley's frontal attack on a young woman he told them both that if they ever treated anybody like that again in his presence, he would never visit them again.

Yet in general, people learned to take it—or to give as good as they got—and come back eagerly for more. It was, after all, the age of the insult, the good line. Here Shirley had the advantage over Stanley. Stanley was a marathon talker, king of the harangue; but it was Shirley who had the lightning wit. Once Frank Orenstein referred to a mutual acquaintance, a lovely young woman, and Shirley's reply was instant: "I don't like her—she's the kind of woman who goes to parties and flirts with all the men and then goes home alone in a taxi." Whether accurate or not, the picture was so damning that Frank was never able to get it out of his mind.

Of course, her wit was not always nasty—it was just always instant. When the news came out that baby shoes would no longer be made in white, since white polish was needed for the war effort, Frank commiserated. "The baby's going to look like a fool in black shoes."

"Only if he wears a brown suit," Shirley shot back.

Usually at big parties Shirley receded a bit, tending to let Stanley howl. Howl he did. The Hyman parties were fueled with massive amounts of liquor, and at a certain point in the evening Stanley—who was tone-deaf—would burst into song, often one he had invented himself. A favorite was called "Schika Is a Goy" (both title and lyrics) and was, he insisted, a Russian standard. It generally brought the house down and more than once brought the cops down too.

It could be great fun, but not everyone was charmed. Taissa, for instance, recalls parties at the Hymans' that "became rough, really rough. Stanley loved to provoke, he liked to make situations. They both liked the drama. They loved to see a good old free-for-all thing right in the living room; that's what they liked best. Every party was designed to set something up and then see it explode."

And often enough, that something involved one of Stanley's myriad flirtations. "Shirley was quite jealous," said Taissa. "And Stanley would play into this. They would provoke each other and build up these terrible situations that ended in nasty explosions—but that's what they loved. All of it was incited by alcohol—gallons and gallons of it. Underneath they were very kind, generous people—but when the alcohol really took hold you would see these dramas unfold.

"It wasn't always jealousy; they were terribly critical people, they despised a lot of people. Stanley or someone would say something horrible to someone, or 'You aren't inviting that dragon woman here.' It was like a boiling cauldron. But that's what they fed on. It was like going to the theater, watching the drama play out. The rest of us were the entertainment provided.

"They liked to find a pigeon for the night and see what they could do to make him uncomfortable," said Taissa, who felt that since she came from the unsophisticated Midwest, she tended to be a sort of "ongoing pigeon."

They were not, either of them, ever the sort of people who could sit back peaceably nodding in the sun and watch the caravan go by. Both in different ways were born disturbers of the status quo—whether it meant publicizing Marxist ideas at a conservative university, or inviting two sworn enemies to the same party and watching the chips fly. It was a challenger's credo—what if I took this situation, this reality, and gave it a little twist? They both did it with life, but only Shirley could do it with fiction.

Despite the occasional bloodletting at parties, Taissa found Shirley and Stanley generous, lively, and immensely attractive. She managed to stay around, avoiding banishment, in part because she was able, finally, to persuade Stanley to stop bothering her—and thus attained the position of protected family member, like June. "Stanley was a steamroller," she said. "He'd try something with every woman, every which way—a vacuum-cleaner effect. He wasn't seducing women so much as knocking them down with heavy blows. There came a point when I got strong enough to let him know I was Shirley's friend, more than his. So it was worked out subtly, but it took some doing. And Shirley understood. She always knew, that was what was so painful, she was more aware than anybody."

Taissa may have worked it out with Shirley, but not everyone was able to. Elsa Dorfman, for example, was not. "She was very jealous. I had nothing to do with Stanley, but Shirley always acted as if I had. He was a murderer."

"Shirley was insanely jealous of other women," Walter Bernstein agreed. "I don't think she ever had much sense of herself as a woman, a sexual being." Not, perhaps, the easiest state of mind to develop when one's husband is coming on energetically with every other female in the room.

At the time, Shirley was overweight, as usual, but far from enormous.

She had not yet begun—as she would later—to let herself go. "She was rather neat. Not pretty by any means, but she made a good appearance," Ellison remembered. "She had very attractive feet and legs, then, and was admired for it." Taissa too recalled this: "It was nice, because it was something about Shirley we could all admire."

Stanley's lively interest in good-looking women was certainly real enough. Yet the image of the mad Dionysian artist, wild and lusty, unbound by the rules, also happened to be one he was particularly fond of assuming. Certainly his reputation—Stanley Steamer, Stanley the libertine—far surpassed any actual reality, and always would. There were no serious affairs, no genuine involvement outside of his marriage—the flirting, ogling, even occasional fooling around were all part of a giant lark. Unfortunately, but understandably, Shirley was not amused, any more than she had been with the story about Florence Shapiro in the shower. She could complain, she could even yell at him, but she always had trouble staying mad at Stanley. And so, inevitably, her anger went in one direction—toward the women who attracted him. Thus she despised Elsa Dorfman, who was well aware of it, and even Taissa, whom she did like, was given a passing cat-scratch, via fiction.

Stanley always felt at ease in a crowd, but Shirley still felt safest with their closest friends—Frank, June, Ben, one or two others. "They were very immersed in the life of the Hymans," Taissa said. "They were all, like me, isolated people on the periphery of the Hyman household, they leaned on them, looked to them for socializing, ideas, contacts."

Taissa felt it suited Stanley and Shirley "to have a constellation of their own, to have a lot of solitary or unaffiliated friends. It was serviceable, to have these people they could summon fast, who had no ties, no children. I always felt Shirley's greatest need was maternal, to gather people around her and have an extended family."

Both Shirley and Stanley enjoyed taking a hand in their friends' lives, finding apartments, arranging job interviews. They set Taissa up with innumerable men, urging her to "go ahead." Even more generously, Stanley managed to land her an assignment at *The New Yorker,* a real plum. Shirley for her part urged Frank to write a book about his army experiences; she would go over it chapter by chapter, and when they had enough they would try to publish it. Unfortunately, the ensuing effort was rejected so solidly it was nearly forty years before Frank wrote another book.

It was only occasionally that the Hymans' help could become a little intrusive. Talking one day with a friend who was homosexual, Shirley suddenly made a rather startling suggestion: "She decided maybe it would be a good idea if we went to bed together so I'd get over this nonsense," he remembered. Politely he turned her down. The incident stayed in her mind, however, and years later she recounted it to her older daughter—with considerable revamping. In Shirley's version, the man had begged her to try to cure him, and she had finally, out of compassion, slept with him, although it had not been successful. The new version made a better story and certainly cast her in a better light; perhaps, too, she had come to believe it.

The Hymans' tendency to meddle may have provoked resentment at times, but it rarely kept anyone away for long. The apartment on Grove Street was nearly always filled with friends. And a great many evenings were not wild or Machiavellian at all—just casual, pleasant and fun. Stanley and Shirley loved playing games, word games, board games, The Game. "She was a demon game player," said Bobbie Williams. "She always won, maybe because she was a witch." The piano too, disputed ownership or not, was a great pleasure. Shirley loved playing duets, with Frank, with Taissa, just as she had in the old days in Burlingame with Dorothy Ayling. "We were both attackers of the piano. We had the same terrible style and were good sight readers," Taissa said. Shirley also loved to sing—unlike Stanley, she had a lovely voice, a very clear soprano.

She had the rudiments of cooking down by now and was comfortable in the kitchen—so comfortable she had begun to experiment a little. A black-market steak donated by a friend was broiled to perfection—but also dyed bright blue. Mashed potatoes often arrived at the table red or green, depending on her mood. Some guests assumed it had to do with her witchcraft hobby. But June Mirken's explanation is more reasonable:

"She could be terribly conventional in many ways—her image of what a wife and mother should be was on one hand really old-fashioned. But then she would burst out of it. It was as if she could function along those lines, but periodically had to break out. To put it in its place," she said.

There was definitely a part of Shirley that leaned to the conventional—or at any rate wanted very much to master that side of life as well. Bobbie Williams often came upstairs with her young son, Chris, who was just Laurie's age, and while the youngsters played, she and Shirley would spend hours discussing "kids and shopping and how we were going to make our coupons go further. They weren't philosophical discussions at all," said Williams.

The two women got along well, having only one minor altercation during the years they were neighbors. "We used to hang our laundry outside, and she never wrung hers out, it always went out wet." Since the Hymans lived two stories above the Williamses, the dripping state of Shirley's laundry was a legitimate concern. "I went up one day and said, 'For Godsake, Shirley, can't you wring your laundry out a bit so it doesn't make mine all wet?' We had a little fight about that—it's the only one I

remember having with her. In essence, her answer was 'Drop dead.' "
Any criticism of her methods of housekeeping infuriated Shirley. She
instantly became the grande dame, enraged and imperious.

Shirley had a complex relationship with the city itself, finding it alternately appealing and terrifying. After three years, though, the terror had
started to win out. She was too conscious, walking down the street, of
all the possibilities for danger—fire, speeding cars, even the fragility of
the buildings themselves. "She had a phobia about cornices, overhangs,"
said Philip Hamburger. "She was convinced she was going to be killed
by something dropping from a building. She pretty much convinced me
it was dangerous to walk down the street." Not that she was so far wrong:
"Today there is hardly a block of New York that isn't covered by a
walkway," said Hamburger. "They passed a law a few years ago that the
overhangs had to come off. She was far ahead of her time."

She spent a great deal of time in the apartment. "A virtual hermitress,"
Elsa Dorfman called her. "She hated going out." When she had to,
though, she did—to do errands and to walk the baby. Her fears in no
way paralyzed her. She found them, in fact, rather interesting, and had
started to use them in her stories. "Mrs. Van Corn had not been out of
the house in seven months," one unpublished tale began. "She could
walk perfectly well, although she disliked it; she was not particularly afraid
of subways or taxis; she was not pregnant, sick or discouraged with the
things she saw. Mrs. Van Corn had simply not been out of the house
because she liked staying inside." Mrs. Van Corn, it seemed, had been
horrified by a small dog that had poked its nose under her skirt one day.
That was when she had made her decision to stay inside, because there
was "no need to expose oneself needlessly to these things." Shirley was
making fun of her own unease—she recognized the extravagance of her
own fears, even their innate silliness. She could not even begin to imagine
a time in the future when they would bring her life to a complete halt.

CHAPTER

·11·

In 1945, Shirley was once again pregnant, and once again on the threshold of a major change in her life.

Stanley's personal hero, Kenneth Burke, was the man responsible. He had had the greatest influence on Stanley's thought and work, including the ongoing work on his book, which was still several years away from publication (even though the original contract, in a burst of optimism, had called for delivery of the manuscript in 1944). Now Burke took a hand in Stanley's life as well. At his instigation, Stanley was offered a teaching position in the literature division at Bennington College, where Burke himself taught.

Burke painted an irresistible picture of Bennington: an idyllic setting in the Vermont hills; a progressive faculty, heavy on the arts—dancing, music, literature, criticism; barely twelve years old, independent, free-thinking, liberal, nonconformist; in short, a college that prized creativity. Why, the founders had even made the unprecedented decision not to have an alumnae board, or to engage in alumnae fund-raising, so fundamental to them was the principle of freedom from control. True, Bennington was an all-girls school—the adoring, reverent faces staring up at him in class would be one hundred percent female. Since when had Stanley minded that? It sounded like Utopia; Stanley was definitely tempted. Yet how could he leave New York?

Shirley had no reservations; she had none of Stanley's allegiance to the city. Bennington sounded terrific. It meant a way out of New York, whose streets had become so frightening; the promise of a real house, instead of a tiny apartment pressed up against millions of others; a chance to see sun, flowers, and hills; an opportunity to work in a peaceful setting, to lead a calmer, less frenetic life. And certainly it would be better to raise children in a place that had "mountains and children playing in their own gardens, and clean snow and homegrown carrots," as she later wrote.

Ben Zimmerman remembers the discussions that went on night after night for weeks at the Grove Street apartment. Stanley, with his usual passion for instilling order, listed all the reasons for and against making the move, then debated both sides loud and long with everyone else in the room. Gradually, with Shirley's crafty encouragement, Bennington began to pull ahead. It wouldn't mean dissolving his connection with *The New Yorker:* he'd still be able to do his "Talk of the Town" pieces, along with longer articles, and he could come down several times a month if he wanted. And as for the book, what better setting to work in? In the end, it was the work that won out. Stanley called Burke and accepted the post.

Bennington was, and is, extremely beautiful, the ideal backdrop for a Utopia. The college iself, with its spare, simple buildings, is set high in the hills, which roll out in all directions; in the distance, rows of pines give way to curving mountains. The clear, soft colors of grass and sky, the faint fog, the occasional deer, all help create a landscape not unlike the Scottish highlands, which is somehow apt. For in many ways, despite its determined modernity, Bennington resembles Brigadoon—the Scottish town cut off from time itself.

At the base of the hill is the small village of North Bennington, Vermont, literally and figuratively removed from the college campus. (The larger town of Bennington itself, with its shops, restaurants, and single movie theater, is a few miles to the east.) A small mill town, New England to the core, North Bennington is a place of sharp divisions between rich and poor, residents and summer vacationers, mill people and shop owners, and of course, natives and college folk; a town whose citizenry is overwhelmingly white and Christian, and innately suspicious of those who are not. Many villagers proudly trace their ancestry back to three or more generations of North Bennington forebears. A stranger here is not necessarily a person who arrived yesterday; it could well be someone who has lived in town for ten years. For the most part, town and college eye each other mistrustfully, separated by an unbridgeable gulf.

Villagers are connected by intricate webs of tradition, custom, marriage, and blood; communication among them is as swift and mysterious as that among various cells of a single body. It is a given that everyone knows everyone else's business. A body of shared knowledge has been built up over generations—the proper way to handle one's life, rules governing one's relationships with God, family, friends, the New England soil itself, rules hardened by the town's geographical isolation from the rest of the world. These people are quintessential Vermonters—rough-hewn, plainspoken, friendly enough to outsiders on the surface. But they are careful to maintain a certain distance, a certain guard. A stranger is not accepted here at face value but is tested, again and again over years, prodded for response, with the villagers always watching, patiently, coolly, not without amusement, for reaction. And of course, the presence of the college ensures that there is never a dearth of strangers on hand to observe.

In the forties most Bennington faculty members avoided the village as much as possible, choosing to live on campus, in an area of houses known as "the Orchard." Shirley and Stanley did not. Perhaps they wanted a larger house than the Orchard could provide; Shirley in particular wanted to be connected with the village, to maintain a certain distance from the college. It was in many ways a fateful decision whch would have strong effects on her life and her work. Always acutely sensitive to the dark forces in people's minds that led them to reject the outsider, the stranger, she discovered in North Bennington an almost perfect microcosm in which to study the very process of alienation itself. Their life in New York, full of odd friends, bohemian parties, loud arguments, in-house theater, had provided her with some subject matter—but North Bennington was her truest laboratory. She who had seen the face of evil in sunny California, in staid Rochester, in Syracuse, in New York City, would now find it in that most traditional American setting—a tiny, picturesque New England village, the very village, in fact, depicted in the work of Grandma Moses. Many of the natives would always treat her as a stranger; in years to come, some of the more brutish would call her names—witch and Communist and atheist and Jew; very few would ever understand or accept her. Yet all the time they studied her, she was studying them, with even greater fascination. Shirley had found her home.

The college community itself was warmly welcoming. Bennington was on the brink of a golden age—in the next few years, an amazing number of intellectuals and artists, giants in their fields, would gather there, many of them brought by Fred Burkhardt, a young mover-shaker who became president in 1947. Poets Howard Nemerov and Ben Belitt, cellist George Finckel, composer Lionel Nowak, artists Paul Feeley and Dan Shapiro, eventually novelist Bernard Malamud were but a few who came, lured by the idea of a genuinely free, creative environment, and found it close enough to ideal that they settled down to stay.

Of course, it was not perfect; earthly Utopias rarely are. Life at Bennington could become overly insular, even incestuous at times. Political in-fighting could be bloody, personal rivalry intense. Nemerov, who had written a coolly disparaging essay about Stanley's work before coming to Bennington, was warned on arrival that Stanley carried a sword-cane and he would be wise to lie low as long as he could. Being a prudent man, he did; by the time he finally met him, Stanley's rage had died down to the point that he merely informed Nemerov airily ("for the first of many times") that "we only accuse others of the sins we commit ourselves."

The atmosphere could be tense; it could be silly, it could be chaotic. But very often too, it could be wonderful. Actually, what was amazing about the college was not the occasional dissension but how well, a great deal of the time, everybody got along.

Drinking was a staple of faculty parties of the time, and it fueled many of the conflicts, of course. Kenneth Burke remembered attending an early college party with Stanley, after which the two critics struggled down the hill together back to town, alternately bumping rudely into each other and helping each other up off the path. Early the next day, Stanley was on the phone, apologizing profusely for the terrible things he had said while drunk, the insults he had hurled at his revered mentor. It was a rare moment—Stanley as humble penitent—but Burke was unable to appreciate it fully. Sadly, he had to admit that, given the state he'd been in himself, he didn't remember a single word.

The Brockways, Tom and Jean, were among the first to take Shirley and Stanley under their wing in Bennington. Brockway, an historian, had begun teaching there in 1933, when the school was barely a year old. Both he and his wife were firmly entrenched in the college and the community. Jean Brockway, along with Barbara Jones, wife of then college president Lewis Jones, spent several days looking for a house for the Hymans to rent. "Stanley said it didn't matter what kind, they just wanted a house, which wasn't very much help," said Jean Brockway.

They finally found an old house, with pillars, up Prospect Street, one of North Bennington's main residential streets, which led to the college grounds. It was quite large, with fourteen rooms and three full stories. "It wasn't in first-class condition, but it didn't seem to matter to them," said Jean Brockway. Shirley, especially, loved it at once—she was drawn to old houses, their history, their sense of other lives lived within. Such places had a presence in her mind—almost a personality, a potential for good or evil. She respected them and felt comfortable within them; she liked living, as her son Laurence said, "in the sort of house where strange things could happen." It suited her, and she would later spend pages describing it lovingly in *Life Among the Savages*. The pillars particularly pleased her; they set the house off from its neighbors. Howard Nemerov dubbed it "The Church of Christ Hyman."

The Brockways, twenty years older, did their best to initiate Stanley and Shirley into some of the ways of Vermont life. The old house came with a tricky furnace. "You had to keep stoking it, so I gave Stanley lessons on that," said Tom Brockway. They had discovered a genuine sugar maple in the backyard and were determined to make maple syrup, like real Vermonters, so the Brockways taught them that too. It wasn't entirely successful: "You have to boil the sap for ten or fifteen hours; they steamed up the house so much that the wallpaper peeled off. I think they ended up with a quarter-cup of syrup," Brockway said. But they were proud anyway. "They weren't country people—but they were willing to learn," said Jean Brockway.

Large and old, filled with hidden side rooms and attics, the house was also rather bare. Their New York furniture was ridiculously inadequate for fourteen rooms—whenever they got a chance, they padded it out with odd pieces picked up at country sales. Nanci Payne, a local junior high school girl who baby-sat for Laurie nearly every afternoon after school the first year, was surprised at the lack of amenities. "The floors were bare. Maybe one small rug in the living room. But no curtains. Just the necessities—chairs, tables. And shelves and shelves of books and records. The furniture they had was good furniture, from New York, heavy and solid. But nothing with color. I just remember the bareness."

The Hymans' first daughter, Joanne Leslie, was born in Bennington on November 9, 1945. As before, pregnancy and birth were completely trouble-free—so trouble-free, in fact, that Shirley and Stanley went out to a faculty party the very night she came out of the hospital, leaving Nanci to cope by herself. "I couldn't believe it," she marveled. "She left me with a brand-new baby!"

But as a native villager, Nanci already knew the Hymans were "different," just as most of the college families were. Intellectuals, nonconformists. She was willing to accept it: "They were very definitely individuals. Later on, some of the townspeople would tell stories . . . but I was used to being in contact with college people. For years my grandmother had rooms in her house and rented them to professors and their families. You get to know these people, you understand them." And besides, there was the practical matter to consider: college professors always paid more for baby-sitting than the locals did.

There were only two matters Nanci did not approve of at all: "The kids' favorite meal was hot dogs and canned beans—it was continuous. And they always had a bottle of orange soda to go to bed with at night, a bottle with a glass." Even as a teenager, Nanci felt wrong about feeding them that way, but "I followed her directions."

Nanci found Shirley "a very loving person, always with a smile. Even when she would scold the children, she had a smile." And of course, a lit Pall Mall as well. Her casual attitude toward cleaning and nutrition— her frank disinterest—shocked Nanci then, but less so later on. In retrospect, Shirley's absolute determination, even as a wife and mother, to be true to her own priorities impressed Nanci. "As you get older you tend to look for sincerity." Shirley, she sensed, was not trying to please anyone but herself. Once or twice, Nanci was at the house when Geraldine and Leslie visited—bringing with them a cloud of disapproval. Geraldine, she could tell, did not care for Shirley's housekeeping or child-care methods. One day, with a hoot of laughter, Shirley showed Nanci a package she had just opened—a corset sent by Geraldine. "She expects me to wear this," she said, shaking her head.

Stanley was harder to warm up to: "Even as a young man he looked like an old man, kind of walked with his shoulders hunched over. You were never quite sure what he was thinking." But Nanci did appreciate Stanley's extensive blues record collection, and his volumes of Peter Arno cartoons. Occasionally Shirley and Stanley took weekend trips to New York, and Nanci would have friends in to listen to records. "My greatest fear was that they'd come home and find all these fellows reading Peter Arno books and playing those records."

Since neither Stanley nor Shirley drove, they quickly became dependent on a local man named Junior Percey, who ran a taxicab service out of his family's store, Percey's Newsroom, located in the exact center of the village, at the corner of Prospect and Main. Over the years Percey would prove worth his weight in gold, always available at a moment's notice to drop a child off at school, to pick Stanley up at the college, to drive the family—or various visiting friends—to Albany to catch the train to New York; even, at times, to go down to New York himself to bring people up for a visit. Once Stanley told Junior he was the best driver he had ever known. Junior, who knew what a critic Stanley was, treasured the comment forever.

Percey's—which, thanks to the presence of the college, was probably the best-stocked newsroom in the state—was one of Shirley's daily stopping-off places. She and little Laurie usually walked down the steep hill once a day to Main Street, which ran pependicular to Prospect. They then began the slow climb up Main, so Shirley could pick up mail at the ancient post office near the railroad tracks, where everybody in town stopped in at least once a day. Then back to the bottom of Main to buy the New York papers at Percey's and do her grocery shopping at Powers' Market, right next door. It was a soothing ritual which allowed her mind to wander; some of her best ideas came to her on these treks.

One such trip gave a neighbor a clear glimpse of the inner workings of her marriage. Fred Welling, who lived across the street and whose family had been in Bennington for generations, was out on his front porch one morning and saw Shirley, hugely pregnant, struggling up Prospect Street, carrying mail, newspapers, and two bags of groceries. He was about to go down and offer her a hand when Stanley burst out of the house and ran down the street to meet her. But to Welling's horror, instead of relieving her, Stanley carefully removed the mail from her hand

and trotted back up the street. Shirley, still clutching her bags, continued to trudge up the hill to the house.

"I'm not sure she minded," said Jean Brockway, one of the many who heard the story. "She was so used to Stanley doing things like that." Stanley had divvied things up neatly: children, shopping, household chores were all Shirley's duties. He had apparently streamlined his down to teaching, writing, stoking the furnace, and at parties, as one friend recalled, "pouring the wine and pouring the wine and pouring the wine."

Stanley's study—it was always called Stanley's study—was off to the side of the living room. Shirley kept her typewriter in there too, although she could—and did—work in other rooms. With two small children, she still did much of her work at night. But there were times when both would sit, side by side, hard at their typewriters. Stanley's desk was always meticulously ordered, every paper clip and pencil in its place; Shirley's wasn't. "Whenever I am very very mad at Stanley, I go into his study and move one of his ashtrays one quarter inch to the side," she said once, wickedly. Bowls of sunflower seeds sat in the study—away from the subway, sunflower seeds had replaced Indian nuts as Stanley's work snack. A little later, pretzel fishies would become the snack of choice.

The Hymans were happy with the move. Vermont was clean and beautiful, the house was large enough for books and children and potential supernatural phenomena. And cats. Lots of cats. Shirley had had a deep affinity for cats since childhood—she felt they shared an almost mystical understanding, that in an odd way their minds resembled her own. There were many parts of herself Shirley kept private from everyone, and always would—perhaps there were some things that could not be conveyed even by words to another human being. But her cats, she felt, understood. "They knew her," said her youngest daughter with conviction. Everyone in the family was convinced she communicated with them telepathically.

For the rest of her life there would never be fewer than six—at first all black, later all gray—and usually a good many more than that. Later, when her reputation as a witch was better known, she would refer to them as her familiars and often give them names out of black-magic lore— Shax, for instance, the name of a devil god known to make an especially good familiar. Outsiders assumed there was a mystical reason for Shirley's insistence on monochrome cats, but actually the reason was quite practical. Stanley, no cat enthusiast, had such poor eyesight he could never tell one cat from another; as long as they all looked the same, he never knew how many she had. There would always be a dog or two as well— one, Toby, a giant sheepdog, was with them for years—but dogs were a different matter.

Life was easier and more relaxed than in New York. Stanley took to the college podium like a fish to water. Many years later a protégé of his, just starting out, begged him for a quick lesson in how to teach. "Well," said Stanley. "I've been doing it for years, and before every class, I take a piss, I check my fly, I wish I were dead—and I go into the room and begin." It worked like a charm: he was immensely popular right from the start. Later, one of his courses, "Myth and Ritual," would become the most heavily subscribed in the college.

As usual, people were drawn to Stanley; the Hymans' social life was every bit as busy in Vermont as it had been in New York, perhaps even more, since friends were constantly coming up from the city for weekends and holidays. Stanley tried to involve some of them in the college too—one of his first acts at Bennington was to invite Ralph Ellison to give a lecture. "But I've never given a public talk," Ellison objected. Stanley was firm: "If you can argue with me the way you do, you can talk to a bunch of students," he told him; Ellison caved in.

But there were plenty of new friends, too—the Brockways, Tom and Kit Foster (she had been with the literature division at Bennington since 1934), Helen and Paul Feeley. Feeley was a wild, charismatic Irish artist, a macho "Marine's Marine" who could match Stanley drink for drink and story for story; Helen had a cool, witty intelligence Shirley took to at once. She was also quite lovely, but Shirley was unthreatened—Paul, like Stanley, was enough of a handful for any woman.

Life for both Shirley and Stanley seemed to have fallen into place with the move to Bennington. There were no major problems on any front, and an old problem was about to be resolved. During Christmas week 1945, Stanley's brother, Arthur, now twenty and home on leave from the service, fell madly in love with a gorgeous blonde from Paterson, New Jersey, named Vera Shapiro. Bunny, as she had been called since childhood, happened to be pinned to his best friend, but within a night she was unpinned and a week later she and Arthur were practically engaged.

Arthur took her to meet his grandmother, Moe's mother, who had been tyrannizing the family from her bed for years, on a diet of straight champagne. The old woman took one look at the smooth blond hair, the perfect nose, and spat out a stream of Yiddish invective: Another shiksa in the family! A double disgrace! Arthur tried to get a word in, without success. His intended waited a few minutes, looking bored, then casually joined the conversation—in Yiddish. The grandmother's face dropped, then split in a huge grin, one of the first anybody had seen in years.

The wedding, planned for April 1946, was to be a glorious, no-expense-spared affair. Both bride and groom were anxious, and for more than the usual reasons. Unbeknownst to Lulu, Moe, or anyone else, they had taken the bull by the horns and asked Shirley and Stanley to attend. It was past time, Arthur felt, to mend the rift. His fiancée, who could not believe one stubborn old man could cause so much grief (her own father was a pussycat), agreed.

The crowd that gathered for the ceremony was jolly and loud, yet when Stanley and Shirley walked in, the silence fell like a stone. Every guest there knew the history of the past six years. There was a chorus of gasps, a loud rustling as people jockeyed to get a better look at the prodigal son. Shirley was shaking; Stanley kept his arm firmly around her, staring straight ahead; Arthur and Bunny held their breath.

And then, out of the crowd, his back as straight as ever, came Moe Hyman. Tears streamed from his eyes. He walked across the length of the room, put his arms around his son and kissed him, then turned and kissed Shirley. Everyone cried. The long feud was over at last.

From then on, Moe Hyman was an active force in their lives. He and Lulu visited Bennington regularly, bringing presents, clothes, and inevitably, a full carload of the finest New York delicatessen. He enticed them down to New York with World Series tickets, he kept in constant touch by phone. He had been a stern, distant father who had rejected his oldest son, and had probably suffered for it more than anyone. For hidden underneath all the tyranny was a wellspring of love and loyalty. The Moe Hyman his grandchildren knew may have been tough, cranky, occasionally mean—"an old son of a bitch," Barry Hyman calls him, affectionately—but he was nonetheless a generous man, who never scared them for a minute. Only Shirley remained tentative and slightly fearful around him, forever.

Actually, both Arthur and Bunny Hyman are convinced that Moe, for his part, was scared to death of Shirley. "I think if she had ever turned around and said one word to him, he would have crumbled—he was really authoritative, but I think he was a chicken at heart, a big sissy," said Bunny Hyman. "But she was afraid of him—she never knew what he was going to say and she felt like the outsider."

Arthur and Bunny, however, became very close to both Shirley and Stanley and often traveled to Vermont to visit. As children, the two brothers had been constantly at loggerheads, but time had wreaked magic for once, turning them into friends. And Bunny was the sort of person everyone liked—warm, bright, funny. Bunny was the only person Stanley permitted to tell Jewish jokes; only she had the accent and mannerisms down perfectly, he said. He would insist she sit next to him at dinner and push her to tell another, then another, while he roared with laughter. Ordinarily, the sight of a good-looking woman captivating her husband would have infuriated Shirley—but Bunny was different, she was family. It didn't hurt, of course, that she was also quite obviously very much in love with her own husband.

Arthur and Bunny made a great fuss about the kids, especially Joanne. Laurie, Bunny remembered, could be a stubborn mule, fiercely independent, with a flair for confrontation. But Joanne, with her blond ringlets and big blue eyes, was a gentle little doll. They were visiting on the day that Laurie, fed up to the teeth with Joanne's ringlets, cut them all off with a few swift scissor clips, and were amazed at Shirley's reaction. She was furious, and terribly upset, far more than they would have expected. Shirley had always given them the impression she cared very little for appearances of any kind. Certainly her housekeeping and her own wardrobe gave that impression. "But I guess she cared plenty," Bunny mused.

There was no question that Shirley liked having beautiful daughters— it was one more way to surpass Geraldine, whose daughter had not been beautiful at all. But that was not the only reason. It also pleased her timeless, literary sense to have daughters who could have stepped out of a Victorian novel—Kate Greenaway girls. It was one of those fond-mother labels, so easy to fasten on younger children—so impossible to keep on older ones.

But there would always be qualities beyond beauty that Shirley looked for in her children even more. Laurie's spirit struck a chord in her, even while she struggled to keep an upper hand. Shirley had no qualms about disciplining her kids, by raising her voice, imposing penalties, or delivering the occasional swift smack—another job Stanley left to her, by and large. "She did most of the discipline," said Ellison. "She did a good job of keeping the chaos away from him. She would roar, raise hell—there was nothing soft about Shirley, nothing indulgent."

There was a special closeness between her and her first son, a similarity, while Stanley and Joanne shared a closeness of their own—he appreciated her gentle ways, her early love of books. Something in Shirley, though, responded mightily to a kid who, on being given the age-old injunction to "eat up, there are starving children in Europe," would leave the table, run to a desk, bring back a large envelope, and tell her, "Go ahead— send it to them." Laurie was a challenger, a tough, restless, energetic little kid. His first memory, a clear one, is of balancing himself on a doorknob at age four, "swinging back and forth and destroying a grand piano by banging into it over and over."

Shirley's writing had always come directly out of her life, and now that her life included children and housekeeping, it was inevitable that she would start writing about that as well. Anyway, as she later said, it was a great comfort with children "to see them through a flattering veil of fiction." Tales about her children, warm, funny, instantly popular, began appearing in women's magazines—*Good Housekeeping, Woman's Home Companion*—quite a different market from *The New Yorker*. They were very different from her serious stories—and yet there were distinct similarities. Both used her keen sense of irony, of the absurd; it was amazing how suited this was, in fact, for both humor and fear. That feeling Shirley could give readers—that the earth had suddenly slipped out from under them—worked just as well for hilarity as for terror, it turned out.

But of course there were great differences, and those differences suited a genuine need. Throughout her life, Shirley loved the writing of a much earlier age—Jane Austen, Samuel Richardson, Fanny Burney. These writers "give no sense of being hurried or pressed for unique ideas; they are peaceful and gracious and write with an infinite sense of leisure that I envy greatly," she wrote once. "She was far too honest to try to write like Miss Austen or Richardson in our fragmented and fragmenting times," Stanley said after her death. Yet some of that same unhurried peace seems to flow through the stories she wrote about her children. In them she created a warm, comforting world, populated by her own family, husband and children. It resembled her own actual world in many ways, but it was not that world—it was changed, controlled, repainted.

"In those stories, everybody was so neat and clean—it fascinated me," said Helen Feeley. "Her own house was the filthiest place I've ever seen, rolls of dust. I remember once at a party getting tired and trying to fall asleep on Shirley's couch—the smell of cat pee would wake you up, it was incredible. And in the refrigerator, nasty little jars of stuff that had been in there for three months, mold on top. God-awful. And then those stories—it was as if, maybe if she could write about it, then in her own mind that's how it was."

As her family stories began to sell, to ever increasing popularity and at ever increasing prices over the years, many friends automatically assumed they were potboilers, turned out for a quick buck. They did make money, and Stanley and Shirley always needed money. But there was more to it than that.

At the same time, Stanley—though he enjoyed the family tales—considered her other writing her serious work, and as usual Shirley dutifully took her cue from him. She had been trying since college to write novels, with little success—most of them sputtered out long before the finish line. Somehow, in the relative peace of Bennington, she was finally able to launch what would be her first complete long work, *The Road Through the Wall*.

Here, at last, she was able to use all the memories of Burlingame she had nurtured for so long, to depict delicately and damningly the hypocrisy and evil that had been just below the bland suburban setting. She worked on it diligently, giving it to Stanley bit by bit. Stanley knew he himself could never write fiction but he had a real genius for shaping and polishing the thing once it was on the page.

"She was very much in certain ways Stanley's creation," said Walter

Bernstein, who had been allowed back in the fold soon after the move to Bennington. "I remember Stanley saying to me that a lot of things Shirley wrote she had no real idea what the hell they meant. It was the closest thing to automatic writing. She would go to him for explanations— what does this really mean?"

Shirley's writing process fascinated Bernstein. "Whatever came into her head came right out onto the page." He never forgot seeing her sitting at a table in the living room, typing away, while children ran in and out.

Their new friends at Bennington were amazed at Shirley's energy—it seemed to have no limits. Both she and Stanley were able to stay up later than anyone, drink more, play more games, yet still get more work done. And Shirley was also running a house, cooking, cleaning, entertaining, handling the kids, and scurrying around to serve Stanley. *"Shirley!"* he would bellow from his study. "I have *no ink* in my *pen!*" And if someone else was there, she might raise an eyebrow or give a ladylike snort, but nevertheless, in under a minute Stanley would have a working pen.

And yet all the time she was writing. "Whatever happened to her, she'd begin writing the story of it in her mind," said Kit Foster. One night the Fosters were over at the house playing Monopoly, when suddenly Shirley began to sell off her property, highly unusual for her, since she was an avid, competitive player. She excused herself, went into Stanley's study, and sat down at the typewriter. A short time later, she emerged with a story and read it aloud. They all voiced their opinions, particularly Stanley. Shirley listened carefully, went back into the study, made a few revisions and brought it back out for another reading. The manuscript was in an envelope and ready to go out by midnight.

The story, "The Intoxicated," dealt with a conversation in a kitchen during a cocktail party, between a drunken man and a young girl—a very odd young girl, who is matter-of-factly awaiting the end of the world. "It isn't as though we didn't know about it in advance," she assures him. "Somehow I think of the churches as going first . . . and then all the big apartment houses down by the river, slipping down slowly into the water with the people inside." A neat domestic setting, a sudden glimpse of utter destruction—vintage Shirley. "Maybe something in the conversation made her think of it," said Kit Foster. "Maybe she'd been brooding— she was a broody person, very high-strung. But she made something out of it."

The oddest element in the story, however, was the identity of the girl. There is no doubt in anyone's mind that the girl was a dead ringer for Sally, Shirley's third child. There was only one problem: at the time the story was written, Sally was yet to be born.

The Hymans entertained often—big parties and smaller get-togethers, many of which involved bridge. Shirley, an expert player since college, taught Stanley how to play, but despaired of ever making him a truly great player—she felt his logic, his mistrust of intuitive leaps would always hold him back. The Brockways remember Stanley's telling them, in awe, that Shirley never made a mistake in bridge.

But Stanley's true game obsession was poker, and along with a group of like-minded men—Burke, Feeley, Lionel Nowak, George Finckel, local garageman Danny Fager—he helped launch a ritual that would last for years: a weekly Rabelaisian orgy of card-playing. The group would eventually include Howard Nemerov, Fred Burkhardt, Dr. Oliver Durand, and one or two other regulars. Held alternately at various houses, usually on Thursday nights, the game would grow to assume mythic proportions, appearing directly in Nemerov's poetry, indirectly in Nowak's music and Feeley's canvases. A boys'-night-out with a vengeance, the poker game often lasted straight through to morning—Nemerov remembers "small children passing through on their way to bed and then later, on their way to school"; it involved drunken revelry, torrents of abuse, large amounts of cash, and even, in one case, a near stabbing (by Stanley, of Burkhardt, via sword-cane). More than money changed hands—since no one was rich, there was a hectic commerce in property. A great deal of Feeley's oeuvre, for instance, ended up hanging in the homes of other players. "A mild obsession," Nemerov called it, and certainly the college has never forgotten it.

"More hard drinking than high thinking," said poet and faculty member Ben Belitt, who was not a member of the group. "They meant to play hard poker, spend a lot of money, do extravagant things. It was boyish, boastful, naive. That was their release: they played into the morning and then went out in the mountains skinny-dipping."

There were people, Nemerov remembered with amusement, who thought the group gathered to discuss college policy. "Of course, if anyone had said anything about the college the reaction would have been, 'Shut up, deal the cards.' "

At the larger parties, too, the arguments and liquor flowed—and flowed—just as they had in New York. Stanley truly loved an argument—"he loved to tell you how wrong you were," said Brockway—and with Kenneth Burke, Paul Feeley, and shortly Fred Burkhardt and Howard Nemerov around, there was never a lack of players for his favorite game. One of Stanley's persistent crusades was an attempt to prove to everyone that Jesus Christ had never existed historically. "He had a dandy time with that thesis," Kit Foster said.

Liquor was always an integral part of the evening. Tom Brockway remembers one night at the Hymans' when a terrible discovery was made at midnight: there was no more alcohol in the house, and it was too late to buy another bottle. Consternation reigned; brilliant minds convened to discuss the best method of dealing with the problem. At last Kenneth Burke, a recognized genius, came up with the solution. Waving a pitcher, he led the group throughout the house, marching up and down stairs, covering every inch of the three stories by foot. Whenever a glass was found, the remaining dregs were poured into the pitcher. At the end of the journey, back in the living room, a rousing cheer went up—enough fuel had been salvaged to sustain the party for another hour. Stanley, at least, could not have failed to recognize the odd resemblance to the miracle of Hanukkah, when one can of oil miraculously burned for eight days.

In the meantime, between revel and routine, Shirley worked on her novel and various short stories, while Stanley concentrated on writing his seemingly endless tome (which would eventually become *The Armed Vision*) and doing various work for *The New Yorker,* including weekly pieces for "Talk of the Town." His rates had gone up: Helen Feeley was visiting Shirley one day when Stanley yelled out of the study, proudly, "Hey, I just wrote a hundred-dollar paragraph—wanna hear it?" After a year of teaching, he had taken time off to write—some say a wrangle with Lewis Jones precipitated the break—but not long after Burkhardt took over the presidency in 1947, Stanley was once again back on the hill. He and Burkhardt, a New York City boy himself, clicked at once, although it wasn't immediately obvious to onlookers.

"We first met at the Brockways' house, and we scared them to death with our repartee," said Burkhardt. "Jean Brockway had never heard people talk to each other that way before." The air was blue with insults as the two native urbanites squared off in a verbal street-fight; Burkhardt immediately started referring to Stanley as Kaplan (after the hero of Leo Rosten's *The Education of Hyman Kaplan*); Stanley for his part called the new president a Kraut—and worse. "We got on well right away, but it wasn't a normal way," Burkhardt laughed.

Burkhardt was determined to get the best for the college, and he realized right away that Shirley would be a great addition. "I thought, Here we've got this talent right here, we need it badly." Shirley begged off. Burkhardt was persistent, but to no avail. A few years later, in 1949, when a faculty member abruptly left in mid-semester, he managed to persuade her to take over two short courses—one on the short story, the other called "Fantasy and Order"—for the duration of the term, which was three weeks. But that was the only teaching Burkhardt or Bennington ever managed to extract from Shirley, though occasionally she would give a reading. The college was Stanley's department. Ben Belitt remembered getting the definite message from her about academia: "That's what you boys do, not me."

What she did was write fiction. *The Road Through the Wall* was nearing completion. "shirley has finished five-sixths of her first novel ever to get past the halfway mark, and will finish this one, for sure. it is red hot," Stanley wrote Jay Williams excitedly in November 1946. By luck, Tom Foster had recently become a scout for the brand-new publishers Farrar, Straus & Company. In fact, Kit Foster had stayed with the Hymans while her husband took an extended trip to England to sign up new talent. When Foster heard of the book, he urged Shirley to have her agent send it to Farrar, Straus, and he would pave the way. (Shirley had been using Rae Everett, an agent with MCA, to market her short stories.) Both John Farrar and Roger Straus liked what they read and decided to publish it—her advance (half on acceptance, half on publication) was $500.

The Road had its moments but suffered from an unwieldy framework—there were far too many characters roaming around in Shirley's suburban neighborhood, diffusing the effect. It was a mistake she would never make again. Two adolescent girls, friends, were more or less in center stage—one fat and awkward, the other skinny and Jewish, both distinct outsiders, both with marked similarities to Shirley herself. In one scene, the girls write their deepest hopes down on paper and bury the papers in the ground; they're found later by another outsider, a young boy. One says: "In ten years I will be a beautiful charming lovely lady writer without any husband or children but lots of lovers and everyone will read the books I write and want to marry me but I will never marry any of them. I will have lots of money and jewels too." The other, simply: "I will be a famous actress or maybe a painter and everyone will be afraid of me and do what I say." Typically, Shirley gave no indication which girl held which hope—most likely, she herself had held them both.

While Harriet, the awkward fat girl, seems on the surface more like Shirley's own adolescent mirror, it is to Marilyn, the skinny Jewish girl, that she gives one of her wistful adolescent visions, a memory of another life, lived centuries ago at the time of the commedia dell'arte: "There's a very very *very* blue sky, and the hills and grass are so green they almost hurt your eyes . . . and there are flowers and trees and everything is so *soft-looking,* and far away beyond the hill you can see where the road leads into a little town. . . .There's a little covered wagon that comes down the road and inside they're all talking and laughing and singing . . . there's Pantaloon and Rhodomont and Scaramouche, and Pierrot . . . and Harlequin."

In many of the books to come, Shirley would again split herself into two or more characters, each representing a distinct side of her personality. It was a process that obviously fascinated her, this splitting, and in *The Bird's Nest* she would deal with it directly, in the story of a girl with four separate personalities. In other books, the split was more subtle. Her last complete work, *We Have Always Lived in the Castle,* would reflect the final refinement of the process: two women characters, one an explorer, a challenger, the other a contented, domestic homebody—the yin and yang of Shirley's own inner self. Oddly, or perhaps not so oddly, the characters would also represent the personalities of her two daughters.

There is no question that Shirley saw her first novel as an exploration of wickedness; although it was perhaps the most naturalistic book she ever wrote, the one most grounded in reality, she herself felt it arose directly from her own conscious awareness of much darker forces.

"I have had for many years a consuming interest in magic and the supernatural," she wrote after *The Road* was published. "I think this is because I find there so convenient a shorthand statement of the possibilities of human adjustment to what seems to be at best an inhuman world." Another consuming interest, not unrelated, was eighteenth-century novels, which she loved for "the preservation of and insistence on a pattern superimposed precariously on the chaos of human development.

"I think it is the combination of these two that forms the background of everything I write—the sense which I feel, of a human and not very rational order struggling inadequately to keep in check forces of great destruction, which may be the devil and may be intellectual enlightenment." *The Road Through the Wall,* she said, "stated this in miniature, in the factual account of the affairs and concerns of a middle-class neighborhood where the individuals attempting to progress according to their own limited visions, were destroyed by their own wickedness." The recurring theme in all she wrote, she said, was "an insistence on the uncontrolled, unobserved wickedness of human behavior."

But there was another reason she had written the novel, and years later she told her daughter Sally what it was. "The first book is the book you have to write to get back at your parents; the book you always had in you. Once you get that out of your way, you can start writing books," she said.

Sally agreed she had fulfilled the task. "That book kicked ass," she commented. "I don't think they [Shirley's parents] even read another one after that; they were too scared."

Shirley's first novel was published early in 1948, to favorable reviews but no particular acclaim, though a great deal of personal satisfaction. The dedication read simply, "To Stanley, a critic." Farrar, Straus held a small wine and cheese party in her honor, at which Roger Straus presented her with a check for $250—the balance of her advance. "Well, what are you going to do with the money?" he asked paternally.

"I'm going to have my teeth fixed," said Shirley, smiling sweetly.

"Here was someone who really didn't have a dime," Straus recalled. Shirley to him was "a rather haunted woman. She was a very strange lady and she had all kinds of very strange ideas. She lived with a lot of bad dreams, I suppose is the best way to put it. She had all kinds of chips on her shoulder about life and about people and about things."

The blurb on the book jacket described her as being "perhaps the only contemporary writer who is a practicing amateur witch, specializing in small-scale black magic and fortune telling with a tarot deck." They were Stanley's words, and undoubtedly it was Stanley's idea to use the description; at the time, since the book sold only modestly, it did no harm.

Up in Bennington life continued unchanged; the earth did not move, wealth and fame did not descend from the skies. Shirley carefully put together a scrapbook of releases and reviews—one, a favorite, noted the book's "sense of latent evil." Seeing a number of blank pages, she padded the book with reviews of her own: typewritten raves from George Sand, Samuel Richardson, and Henry Fielding. "I wish I could have written this book," they claimed. As for the rest, she wrote a funny, caustic piece, "Fame," about a wildly disjointed interview with a local columnist, an interview she fondly hoped had at least some connection with her new book—until she saw the paragraph that later appeared in the newspaper. Tersely, it informed readers that "Mrs. Stanley Hyman has moved into the old Thatcher place on Prospect Street. She and her family are visiting Mr. and Mrs. Farrarstraus of New York City this week."

Had she but known, perhaps she would have relished it: her last taste of anonymity before the deluge. For in a few months, the spotlight of fame, even notoriety, would be turned on her searingly. And nothing would ever be the same.

CHAPTER
·12·

On a bright morning in the late spring of 1948, Shirley, pregnant with her third child, descended Prospect Street to do her daily errands. She pushed little Joanne in her stroller; Laurie was away at kindergarten until noon. As often on these trips, she let her thoughts wander in various odd directions. A recent book Stanley had brought home on the ancient rites of human sacrifice had stuck in her mind. The book discussed tribal units in which each member was willing to stand up for the others. How, she wondered, would such a rite work today, in this village? The sons of one prominent village merchant hadn't spoken to each other in years, for instance. What would happen if one of them were forced to "stand up" for the other? Open rebellion? Or would the law of the tribe prove too strong?

An hour or so later she walked slowly back up the long hill home, pushing the stroller with its additional load of newspapers, mail, and groceries. The germ of a story idea had started to fester in her head. She set the two-year-old in the playpen, put the food away, and went right to the typewriter. Quickly, effortlessly, as if everything in her life so far had been leading to this, she wrote the masterpiece that would be linked to her name forever, possibly the most chilling horror tale of all time: "The Lottery."

"Perhaps the effort of that last fifty yards up the hill put an edge to the story," she later said, teasingly. "It was a warm morning, and the hill was steep." The result of her work came to barely nine pages, and was under five thousand words in length. It had poured out of her in less than two hours; she was done by the time Laurie came home for lunch.

"Writing the story, I found that it went quickly and easily, moving from beginning to end without pause . . . except for one or two minor corrections, it needed no changes, and the story I finally typed up and sent off to my agent the next day was almost word for word the original draft. This, as any writer can tell you, is not a usual thing." It was not that the story seemed perfect to her, just that "I felt very strongly that I didn't want to fuss with it." She was pleased with her day's work, but not particularly ecstatic; she had no sense of having written one of the few short stories of the twentieth century that seems destined to survive.

Simply, even sparely written, without one extraneous word, one false step, "The Lottery" tells of a traditional rite held annually in a small New England village: the townspeople gather together in spring to draw lots, as their ancestors have done for generations. Finally one woman, an average housewife, ends up holding the single piece of paper with a black spot on it. Swiftly, eagerly, yet in a dignified, deliberate manner, the other members of the village descend on her and stone her to death.

Stanley recognized the story for what it was at once. "Shirley has written a story that just astounds me," he told Ben Belitt. "She's written a real masterpiece, and I don't know where it came from."

"That was before the world came to confirm that," said Belitt. "He had an unerring sense."

And Belitt agreed with him. "It was the pure thing. She could be funny, she could be readable—but this came from somewhere else. I could see the wonderment in Stanley—here he had stumbled in his own household on the real, right immortal thing. It was incandescent, the mythic thing you find in Greek literature. With 'The Lottery,' she had made it. She did something unkillable, irreversible."

No one, not then, not ever, would be able to read the story without having a powerful reaction. Its quiet tones and everyday setting only contributed to the force of its final, shattering climax. Even *The New Yorker* must have sensed some of its potential for disturbance. The magazine bought it immediately, but fiction editor Gus Lobrano thought it prudent to call Shirley and ask if she had any explanation she would like to pass along. Editor Harold Ross, he said apologetically, was wondering—Ross had often said he would never publish a story he himself did not understand. Was there anything special she was trying to convey? Not really, said Shirley, who hated explaining her work, it was just a story. Well, said Lobrano, even more apologetically, did she think the story might be called an allegory which made its point by an ironic juxtaposition of ancient superstition and modern setting? Sure, said Shirley kindly (she had no use for that kind of fancy-pants academic drivel), that would be fine. Good, good, said Lobrano, that was what Ross thought it meant.

"The Lottery" came out in the June 26, 1948, issue of *The New Yorker,* and its effect was instant and cataclysmic. Nothing in the magazine before or since would provoke such an unprecedented outpouring of fury, horror, rage, disgust, and intense fascination. Any idea that this could be treated as an intellectual allegory, an armchair attempt at mythmaking, went out the window, and fast. This story was incendiary; readers acted as if a bomb had blown up in their faces, as indeed in a sense it had. Shirley struck a nerve in mid-twentieth-century America the way few writers have ever succeeded in doing, at any time. She had told people a painful truth about themselves—and the people were fighting mad. Letters begging for a simple explanation came in by the hundreds—and they were annoying enough. But a great many of the letters were also filled with abuse, with anger, with tearful horror. They insisted, these letter writers, that they did not understand the story; but their emotional reaction, raw and defensive, showed that on the deepest level they understood only too well.

"Tell Miss Jackson to stay out of Canada," roared one. "I expect a personal apology from the author," wrote another. A Massachusetts reader snapped: "I will never buy *The New Yorker* again. I resent being tricked into reading perverted stories like 'The Lottery.' " The letters rolled in, swamping the magazine offices; the name-calling reached a fever pitch. The story was "in incredibly bad taste," "nauseating," and "gruesome"; it represented "a new low in human viciousness." One man wrote to complain that it had upset his wife so badly she was still recovering several days later. Shirley Jackson herself, said letter writers, was either "gratuitously disagreeable" or "a perverted genius."

"Was the sole purpose just to give the reader a nasty impact?" whined one reader. Another wrote to say that since reading the story he had been unable even to open any issues of *The New Yorker,* for fear of another shock; he simply dropped them in the trashcan as they came, in their brown mailing paper, handling them as little as possible. "We would expect something like this in *Esquire,*" a woman remonstrated. "But NOT in *The New Yorker.*"

"There were three main themes which dominated the letters of the first summer," Shirley said later, in a lecture she gave at a writers' conference: "bewilderment, speculation and plain old-fashioned abuse." More than a few of the letter writers were not terribly concerned with the story's meaning at all, she said—what they wanted to know was where the lotteries were being held and if they could go watch. "Will you please tell me the locale and the year of the custom?" wrote one reader. "Are you describing a current custom?" wrote another. "If it is based on fact would you please tell me the date and place of its origin?" said a third.

Phone calls, too, poured into the magazine—canceling subscriptions, demanding explanations, venting fury. The fact that the story was not as readily understood as, say, a *Lone Ranger* episode—that, in fact, it might even require a few moments of thoughtful consideration—seemed to anger them most. Readers felt called upon to invent their own instant explanations, and they came up with some real beauties. "A friend darkly suspects you people of having turned a bright editorial red, and that is how he construed the story. Please give me something to go on when I next try to placate my friend, who is now certain that you are tools of Stalin," wrote one. Another was sure he had found the key: "In this story you show the perversion of democracy." Yet another was philosophical: "I suppose that about once every so often a magazine may decide to print something that hasn't any point just to get people talking."

The letters were eventually sent to Shirley, who saved them, although, "if they could be considered to give any accurate cross section of the reading public, or the reading public of *The New Yorker,* or even the reading public of one issue of *The New Yorker,* I would stop writing now." The onslaught eventually died down, though never completely— to the end of her life, Shirley was receiving letters demanding explanation of "The Lottery." By then, though, the tone of the letters had changed to respect; the story had been anthologized innumerable times and translated into hundreds of languages; it had appeared as a radio show, a one-act play, a television drama, an opera, and even a ballet, and was well on its way to becoming a classic.

Even in Shirley's own circle, there was disagreement about the meaning and origin of "The Lottery." Many of Stanley's colleagues, closer to him than to her, were certain that he had been instrumental, that at the very least he had fed her generous helpings of anthropological myth and ritual over the years, and in return she had spilled out the story almost automatically. In fact, he did make one concrete contribution: the jingle that appears in the story, "Lottery in June, corn be heavy soon," was his.

Others believed she had written it, all right—she just didn't understand it. Walter Bernstein, for one, says Stanley himself was convinced Shirley never understood "The Lottery." And perhaps he was right. But Stanley also later insisted that Shirley had written the story during a bridge party— she had been dummy, he said, wandering around aimlessly, and he told her to go write a story while they played out the hand; she came back twenty minutes later with "The Lottery." Stanley may not have been able to write fiction, but oral fiction was another matter. In the village itself, another myth grew over the years—that Shirley had been stoned by local children while pushing the stroller and had returned home to write the story.

Shirley herself gave varying clues to friends. She told Helen Feeley the story was based on anti-Semitism and grew out of her encounters with one particularly prejudiced shopkeeper; she told another friend that all the characters had come directly out of North Bennington and she proceeded to reel off their names. When an old professor of hers from Syracuse, H. W. Herrington, wrote to congratulate her, she wrote back saying that it had all originated in his folklore course.

In truth, "The Lottery" originated with Shirley, and nowhere else. It was the purest, most direct expression she would ever give to that knowledge of human evil she had carried within her since childhood. The tale used the trappings of anthropological myth; it used the character of the village she lived in; it used the painful awareness of anti-Semitism she had acquired over the years. Yet the raw materials were really no more than layers, a series of veils for the reader to pass through on the way to the truth. And that truth was so bitter, so ugly, so hard to bear, it was no surprise readers raged, cursing her and the magazine that had printed the story. This was a time, after all, only three years after the war, when the United States was determinedly doing its best to forget all about evil. It would be twenty years before books analyzing the Holocaust would begin to appear. Then, of course, there would be a flood of them, many articulate, moving, thorough. Yet not one of them was ever able to say more—or say it better—or see more clearly into the very heart of human evil itself than Shirley Jackson did in one nine-page story. Her political knowledge was almost nonexistent, her world almost entirely private and personal, but Shirley understood the Holocaust. Writing only what she had seen, she managed to cast a beam of light which in its own way illuminated an entire century.

And now the light was turned on her. People wanted to know more about this young woman who had made them, in the words of one letter writer, "want to put my head under water and end it all." A columnist from the *San Francisco Chronicle*, Joseph Henry Jackson (no relation), turned his column over to a discussion of the story for several weeks running. Finally, he sent Shirley a letter: "No one writes a story in a vacuum. Something pulled the trigger that set 'The Lottery' off in your mind—what was it?"

Shirley responded in a general way: "I suppose I hoped, by setting a particularly brutal rite in the present and in my own village, to shock the readers with a graphic dramatization of the pointless violence and general inhumanity of their own lives." She felt that reader response showed she had "pretty well accomplished" that aim, though "I gather that in some cases the mind just rebels. The number of people who expected Mrs. Hutchinson to win a Bendix washer at the end would amaze you."

Shirley reacted to the publicity with ambivalence. She liked the idea of affecting a large number of people, gaining readers, broadening her power base; she was delighted to find that her stories were now in demand, and could bring a better price. "womb's home companion is currently threatening to buy one for eleven hundred smacks," Stanley informed

Jay Williams."you and i should be plumbers, bud." Yet the idea of people talking about her, judging her, not just her work, made her extremely anxious. Shirley liked her privacy. She wanted to live anonymously in a small town, sending out her fearful, disturbing messages to the rest of the world, without consequences. Power appealed to her; fame itself was threatening.

Her publishers, Farrar, Straus, had no such ambivalences to deal with. They were frankly delighted and moved quickly to capitalize on the sudden attention, making plans to issue a collection of Shirley's stories early in 1949. "The Lottery," of course, would double as title and featured presentation.

Shirley's productivity continued. Pregnancy, as usual, seemed to unleash even more energy. Barely a month after "The Lottery" appeared *Mademoiselle* published her wickedly funny family story, "Charles," about Laurie's experiences in kindergarten—a story which also used a shock ending, though of a very different sort, and which would eventually find its way into almost as many anthologies as "The Lottery."

In the story, Laurie—the fictional Laurie—takes to kindergarten right away, talking nonstop about the various terrible activities of a classmate, Charles, who kicks people, throws crayons, and gives vent to a number of off-color oaths. After a month, his mother, who has been worrying nervously about possible bad influences, finally meets the teacher. "You must have your hands full in that kindergarten, with Charles," she commiserates.

"Charles?" says the teacher."We don't have any Charles in the kindergarten." (The tale, of course, was fiction, but according to many of Shirley's friends, not all that far from truth; Laurie could be an aggressive little boy. The odd thing was that Shirley *was* always worrying about bad influences on Laurie—while at the same time, as the story clearly shows, she knew her kid.)

Several other stories followed, appearing in various places. She also wrote "The Summer People," a tale of vacationers who come up against the brutal justice of a small New England town, which impressed Stanley—"not only seems scarier than lottery but is probably better," he wrote Williams, in August—but no one else, at least then: it was rejected by several magazines. (Stanley, as usual, had the better eye—three years later June Mirken, who was then fiction editor of *Charm* magazine, spotted it on a visit and grabbed it fast. It made *The Best American Short Stories, 1951.*)

Stanley, too, was finally nearing the end of his book. He had been trying for some time to get out of his contract with Alfred Knopf; in fact, he and Shirley had managed to work up quite a head of steam against the publisher. Mischievously, as they both later described it, Shirley decided to see what she could do with her witchcraft skills. When she heard that Knopf had gone on a skiing trip to Vermont, she made a small voodoo doll out of matchsticks and broke its leg. Knopf, she later insisted to everybody, immediately fell down a slope and broke his own. She had had to wait until he entered Vermont before making the doll, she said gaily; she couldn't practice witchcraft across state lines. (Knopf himself, in answer to a query about the incident, wrote tersely that he had "never published Shirley Jackson," which left the question somewhat up in the air; he has since died.)

At any rate, Stanley was finally able to break his contract—he bragged to Jay Williams that Knopf had released him from his options "as a result of my sending him a phony manuscript." His book, *The Armed Vision,* a study in the methods of modern literary criticism, was published by Greenwood and received a good deal of respectable attention, though not, of course, the "Lottery" kind. The book was clearly Stanley's attempt to stake his claim to the territory; with considerable chutzpah, he took on venerable critic Edmund Wilson and attempted to pummel him to the ground, which horrified a number of his friends at *The New Yorker.* His anti-Wilson blast was conspicuously absent from later editions of the book; Stanley, when teased about this, maintained a stony silence. "I'd say, It's inconceivable that you could have changed your mind, so what gives?" said Burkhardt. "He wouldn't say anything."

For all his humor and party antics, Stanley had always had a tendency to be pompous—he took his work very seriously indeed. When June, who did the index for *The Armed Vision,* stuck in a number of stray references to their pal Frank Orenstein, just for the hell of it (he was not, of course, mentioned in the book), Stanley was furious—especially when they ended up in print. They weren't in college anymore—this was the real world. June apologized handsomely, privately rolling her eyes.

With all the brisk marketing going on, the Hymans were still far from solvent. "In the midst of life, we are in debt," Stanley sighed to Williams, whom he borrowed from freely, as he did from most of his friends. "You inquire about our financial circumstances (How come so broke, you say crudely)." It was no secret, he went on—he did not make enough from *The New Yorker* to live on; they had to be dependent on checks for Shirley's stories. "When those do not come, we run into debt." The minute they came, of course, they were gone. "I doubt that we will ever be ahead, with money in the bank like other people. . . . Still, life is very pleasant, and think how many people and institutions have a stake in my continued health and productivity, not to speak of Shirley's psyche."

The truth was, the Hymans did not particularly enjoy having money in the bank—money was meant to be spent, for food, parties, liquor, books, and toys. Sure, it could pay off debts too, but wasn't it a lot more fun to use it to buy an ice-making machine or a television set or a lithograph, or any one of a million appealing items? And wasn't it nice that, through the medium of charge cards, you could buy a lot of those items without having any money at all? Helen Feeley remembered clearly her first visit to the house with the pillars—the living room had nothing special in the way of furniture, but it did have an enormous, ugly, spanking-new television set.

Both Stanley and Shirley were lusty, unabashed consumers. Not selfish ones, to be sure—their generosity, in the gifts they gave, the parties they threw, was legendary even then. But ferocious all the same: their bills at New York stores (Gimbels, F.A.O. Schwarz, Hammacher Schlemmer) were astronomical, and both of them had a distinctly cavalier attitude about paying them off. In fact, bills of any kind tended to get lost in the Hyman household. Years later, after both Shirley and Stanley had died, and a new family, the Aldriches, had moved into their house, they suddenly realized after several months that they had never been billed for their newspapers. David Aldrich went to the news store to inquire about it and was greeted with surprise: "Stanley never paid," he was told. Neighbors remembered seeing Geraldine Jackson on several visits, perfectly coiffed as always, dressed to the nines, descending the hill to stop in at every store and pay off accounts. "In their own way," said their youngest son, "they were rebellious little shits."

The lack of money was an irritant but rarely a major deterrent—there was too much else going on, especially now. "Everyone always says the third baby is the easiest one to have, and now I know why. It's the easiest because it's the funniest, because you've been there twice and you know," Shirley would write later in one of her best family stories, later incorporated into *Life Among the Savages*. Sarah Geraldine Hyman took her time arriving—"for the last two weeks before I went to the hospital almost everyone I know called me almost once a day and said 'Haven't you gone YET?' "—and needed a bit of a push—"I finally made the doctor give me dope to bring on the pains, since I felt I couldn't wait any longer, and he gave me a combination of quinine and castor oil that tasted awful but did the trick," she wrote her parents. But she finally made it, on October 30, 1948.

Almost from the start, this one was different. Sarah Geraldine (Sarah after Stanley's late grandmother, to please his father), known as Sally, was a tiny, engaging sprite who, it soon became clear, did not just march to another drummer—she was out to lead the entire band. Magical, intuitive, forceful, blazingly intelligent—this was, in a way, the child Shirley had been looking for all along. "She felt Sarah was her, Shirley, before Geraldine poisoned her," said her sister, Joanne. "We all knew Sarah was the one most like Shirley." (Today, Sally is called Sarah.) Sally too was a born disturber of the universe, a child whose mind moved in odd directions, a challenger, a continual tester of the status quo. And her imagination was all but limitless. She was, as her sister says, "burning with a blue flame when she was a little kid."

In the years to come, Shirley would go to a great deal of effort to nourish that flame. She was always fiercely protective of all her children in their dealings with others outside the house, but with Sally the protectiveness would amount almost to a perpetual armed campaign. "She didn't want the environment acting on her in ways that would kill her, reduce her, stifle her spirit," said Joanne. At the same time, though, there was an uneasy by-product to all this: who wanted a wild thing running around the house? Certainly not the mother of a large family who was simultaneously pursuing a very busy career and catering to a demanding husband. And so the seesaw teetered back and forth, the scales juggled, the double messages flew. "Sally was the golden girl, Sally could do no wrong," said one friend, and many, many concurred. Yet the golden girl could drive Shirley around the bend faster than any other kid in the house—and once went an entire year without seeing the end of a meal because she was sent to her room long before dessert every single night.

But this was all down the road. Sally's birth peaked what had been a banner year for the Hymans. "I have a story in the October Mademoiselle, and one in the November Harper's, and one in the December Hudson Review and one coming up in the February Woman's Home Companion. . . . Also my book of stories is due about February fifteenth," Shirley crowed ecstatically to her parents. Leslie Jackson had formally retired, and he and Geraldine had returned to the San Francisco area; Shirley had begun to write them the long cozy letters that she would continue to write the rest of her life—letters of a mature, well-organized, serene housewife and mother and hostess who handled every contingency with a minimum of fuss and just happened, on the side, to have a flourishing career.

"Her letters were her revenge," said her youngest son. "They were sort of: 'I'm going through the vicissitudes of raising children without becoming a sterile negative old bitch, and I'm still alive and have a sense of humor.' Yet at the same time it was also: 'Dear Mom, how are you, here's the good news.' I don't mean to say she didn't love her mother, or that her mother didn't love her too." It was just that her feelings for Geraldine, and to a slightly lesser degree Leslie, were so hopelessly scrambled, the good with the bad, that sorting them out was next to impossible. What she wanted was their approval, and being Shirley, she wanted it with an intensity that did not fade with time. Unfortunately, it was the one thing she could not get.

And so the letters, in part revenge, in part a vain attempt to bridge the unbridgeable—the gap between her parents' life and her own. Funny, warm, confident, they offered a rose-colored glimpse of her life. Joanne was in nursery school and "very happy and very good natured and very smart"; Sally was "such a good baby . . . so pretty . . . the best of the three . . . cries hardly at all, sleeps until seven in the morning"; all three children "get along beautifully together." She herself had "lost twenty-five pounds and no longer liked candy" (the former undoubtedly due to the recent birth of Sally; the latter either an outright fib or a very short-lived truth). The people at Farrar, Straus were "the nicest . . . in the world," and on a recent trip to New York Stanley's father had given her such an extravagant birthday party, with champagne and presents, that "she felt like a movie star being feted."

Luckily Shirley had too good a sense of humor to be able to turn out this kind of syrup unabated. "I must go feed Sally, since what I said just now about her not crying seems not to be true," she interjected dryly at one point.

She generally kept her comments on her work to a bare minimum in the letters. But her fury at Farrar, Straus's proposed handling of her upcoming book of short stories was so violent it spilled out:

"My book of stories is all wrong; they set it up in type all mixed up. . . . They put through the copy for the jacket blurbs without consulting me, and made two serious errors and a number of embarrassing statements about me . . . and their advertising campaign is so excruciating that I will never show my face out of Vermont again. They are playing up *Lottery* as the most terrifying piece of literature ever printed, which is bad enough, and they have a long statement from Christopher Morley saying that *Lottery* scared him to death and will give ulcers to anyone who reads it and they are working on things that say, 'do you DARE read this book?' And except for *Lottery* it's a harmless little book of short stories. I feel like a fool." (Overreaction was certainly Shirley's usual response to a whole range of occurrences, but as a matter of fact, she was not exaggerating about Morley's statement: he warned that "if you don't feel the tweak of the ulcers, you haven't really read this story"— hardly an appealing invitation.)

In general, though, she preferred to deal in her letters with happenings in the home—holidays, for instance, particularly Christmas. Christmas was Shirley's special holiday, a day of lavish magic. She planned for months beforehand, typing up lists of gifts, ordering everything well ahead from New York. June, Frank, Arthur, and Bunny were almost always in attendance, and Shirley made sure not only that each had a special, unique gift, but also that each received a separate gift from every single Hyman— Stanley, Laurie, Joanne, Sally, and after he came, Barry too. Even Stanley was drawn into the preparations, finding gifts, wrapping the Christmas-light wire with tire tape every year, Stanley, the avowed atheist who was determined to keep even the slightest breath of religion far away from his house. God could be dispensed with. But nobody was going to take Christmas away from Shirley.

"Even in the beginning, they'd go in hock up to here, for Christmas," said Arthur Hyman.

"Christmas was her thing, oh God, was it," said Bunny Hyman. "She'd call up and absolutely buy out Macy's and Gimbels. She'd have two Christmas trees and ornaments, from the time she was a little girl. The kids could decorate but they couldn't handle those decorations, they were very fragile.

"Then the kids were shipped off to bed very early and we'd go in and lay out all the toys, put everything out in the room, and she'd slide the two doors shut to the living room and tape them so the kids couldn't come down in the night—they'd get killed. And in the morning, after they ate something, she'd untape the doors, and oh my God, the screaming and yowling, each kid sitting by his piles—'I got it, I got it.' And every Christmas my father-in-law would send a photographer to take pictures of the whole bunch." He had come a long way, Moe Hyman, from the time when he had sat shivah to mourn his son's marriage to a non-Jew.

Shirley had a simple aim every Christmas: to gratify everyone's dearest wish. The presents the Hymans gave to family and friends were invariably unique, imaginative, personal, and very expensive. Rare books, African masks, Japanese swords, Egyptian scarab necklaces. All this, plus Shirley's special imagination.

"She'd raffle the turkey off—everybody had to buy tickets. Everyone would end up eating it, but it was Joanne's turkey, or whoever's. It was spontaneous—she'd take a routine and suddenly turn on the lights," said June, fondly.

Christmas 1948 was typically spectacular, Shirley reported. "Jannie [Joanne] had the stove and the refrigerator and pantry table and a broom and dust mop and dustpan and sets of dishes. . . . Laurie had a set of bricks . . . an elaborate erector set . . . a wonderful little set for moulding trains out of plaster of paris" and "a wealth of clothes and books and more books and records and more blocks." The baby got "fifty pink sweaters and a teddy bear and an elephant and bath toys and a silver cup." So what if they had overspent wildly (a few paragraphs later Shirley thanked her parents heartily for sending two checks to bail them out), Christmas was important.

The "Lottery" letters continued to arrive, in batches, from *The New Yorker*, but things had calmed down considerably by the end of the year, somewhat to Shirley's relief. By now the story had reached several foreign shores, leading to at least one banning, in South Africa, which made her quite pleased. ("She always felt," Stanley noted years later, "that they at least understood the story.") Despite her anxieties about the jacket cover, blurbs, and so on, she looked forward to seeing her collection of short stories published, knowing it was unlikely to be ignored the way *The Road Through the Wall* was, if only because of the notorious title story.

Most of the stories had been published before in various magazines but taken together they made an impressive, well-integrated, disturbing whole. Woven in and out, elusively, was the specter of the Daemon Lover, which she had first contemplated years before—alluring, evil, unobtainable, though those words seem somehow much too solid and opaque to apply to Shirley's flickering phantom, whom she named James Harris, after a figure in an English ballad. The stories dealt with evil, with prejudice; they teetered on the brink of other realities—they were truly unclassifiable, unlike anything anyone had ever written before. Reading them was not an entirely pleasant experience, but Shirley was not trying to give her readers simple pleasure. She was out for bigger game.

The collection, published in April 1949 (with the dedication "For my mother and my father"; one wonders what they made of that), made quite a splash, not surprisingly—"The Lottery" was still very much on everyone's mind. Success was heady, and for once Shirley allowed herself to be swept away.

"I am so excited about my book that I've got to tell you about that even before anything else!" she told her parents exultantly. "They've already sold more than they did of the novel and are talking seriously about passing any records so far for short story sales. . . . An associated press review says I am author of the week and that Lottery is a work of genius and the publishing event of the year!"

Stanley, too, was caught up in the excitement. "The book went into a second printing before publication, about six thousand altogether, and seems to be selling them at a furious rate, with favorable reviews and interviews all over. The army, bless us, bought two thousand," he bragged to Williams. What with the book and her consistent magazine sales, Shirley was obviously out to make his fortune, he noted. "She follows me around saying, 'You look shabby, boy. Here, go buy yourself a suit.' "

Now critics were determined to find out more about her, and Farrar, Straus was happy to oblige; first the house rediscovered Stanley's blurb for *The Road,* which had featured the memorable line "perhaps the only contemporary writer who is a practicing amateur witch," a phrase guaranteed to make journalists' hearts beat faster. This time around, Shirley too had contributed some biographical notes that could hardly have failed to pique interest: "My children and I all believe wholeheartedly in magic. We do not any of us subscribe to the pat cause-and-effect rules which so many other people seem to use, and which work so ineffectually and unreliably. I have a fine library of magic and witchcraft and when I have nothing else to do I practice incantations."

In the notes she made for her biography, she expressed herself even more thoroughly: "I am tired of writing dainty little biographical things that pretend I am a trim little housewife in a mother hubbard stirring up appetizing messes over a wood stove.

"I live in a dank old place with a ghost that storms around in the attic . . . the first thing I did when we moved in was make charms in black crayon on all the door sills and window ledges to keep out demons and was successful in the main . . . there are a number of marble mantels which have an unexplained habit of falling down onto the heads of the neighbors' children . . . my most interesting case so far is a young woman who offended me and who subsequently fell down an elevator shaft and broke all the bones in her body, except one and I didn't know that was there." All a giant lark, naturally—except it was all true, as well. Shirley, of course, had always had more layers than an onion. She liked to pretend she was a witch; she liked to make people believe it; at the same time she liked to poke fun at the entire business, and at the very people who believed her so literally. And behind that? Well, there lay the real mystery. In one sense it was all true—she did consider herself an expert in magic; certainly she had made the crayon charms and the voodoo dolls, just as she said. And in another sense every layer held the truth. She was simultaneously believer and debunker, psychic traveler and removed, amused onlooker. It was the same duality that made it easy for her to move between humor and fear in her work. She would not cut any of her options; she would not be cubbyholed, no matter how much easier it would make things for others.

Rare was the interviewer who could resist asking her about black magic. And at first, rather naively, she answered the questions honestly. Then she began to see the results—the ever-so-slight elbow nudging that surrounded her answers when they appeared in print.

"She says all that is needed is 'clarity of thought,' evidently a kind of concentration, an unshakable conviction," wrote AP reporter W. G. Rogers, with a barely suppressed sneer. "Thus she says she can break a man's leg and throw a girl down an elevator shaft. Such things have happened, she says. She insists, 'It's hard to explain so it makes sense.' Miss Jackson tells you all this with a smile but she is not joking; she owns a library of 200 books.

"Magic, she is convinced, is better than science. Most people are tired of a world which eternally goes on the assumption that one and one make two, a world which places no credence on anything that can't be seen or touched. She thinks we would all be happier with 'a different rationale.' We lost 'our notion of human dignity' when we lost the devil and the soul and she wants it and them back again." Rogers was also responsible for the rather unwieldy observation that "Miss Jackson writes not with a pen but with a broomstick," which would follow her to the grave.

Interviews like this horrified Shirley. Not only did she feel violated, and very very sorry she had spoken so freely, she had an immediate, sinking terror that Geraldine might read them. It was bad enough she had married a Jew; she did not want her parents to know how serious her interest in witchcraft was. Swiftly, she wrote them, to counteract any possible effect, to make it all seem breezily normal:

"[I was] interviewed by a very nice man from the associated press, who said that he understood I was a specialist in black magic and would I please tell him all about it. Fortunately he had just bought me two drinks, so I was able to tell him, very fluently indeed, about black magic and incantations and the practical application of witchcraft to everyday life, most of which I remembered out of various mystery stories."

But the problem didn't stop there. To enhance her reputation as a witch, which seemed to be bringing in as much attention as the short stories, one Farrar, Straus publicity hound began to circulate the story that she had broken Alfred Knopf's leg, by voodoo—the story she herself had told quite proudly less than a year before.

Shirley wrote quickly to Geraldine again, to head this one off at the pass. It was all a silly joke, of course, she said several times, and not even a good one; hearing it repeated felt "exactly as though I had a very bad hangover and everyone was telling me the screamingly funny things I had done the night before." A very reasonable explanation, suitable for the Stonewall Jacksons—but most of her friends are positive that Shirley most certainly did think she had broken Knopf's leg using magic (and more than a few are not too sure she didn't, either).

After the AP interview, Shirley was much more careful: she admitted to writer Harvey Breit, in an interview for *The New York Times Book Review*, that she believed in magic but she also said that it was "a silly thing to talk about." And that was all she would say on the subject.

Breit's piece reflected another theme that would become popular in dealing with Shirley: her amazingly wholesome, motherly demeanor. "Looks not only wholesome but very much on the dayside. She is neat, detached and impersonally warm. She subtly radiates an atmosphere of coziness and comfort, and appears to be of a tranquil disposition." (If after one round of martinis Shirley could come off as a knowledgeable practitioner of black magic, God knows how many rounds it would have taken to make her appear "tranquil.")

"Writing in general, she says, short stories in particular, are perhaps nearest and dearest to her heart," Breit continued. "But it is as a mother—and not as a witch—that she approaches the heart of the matter.

"I can't persuade myself . . . that writing is honest work," he quoted her. "It is a very personal reaction, but fifty percent of my life is spent washing and dressing the children, cooking, washing dishes and clothes and mending. After I get it all to bed, I turn around to my typewriter and try to—well, to create concrete things again. It's great fun, and I love it. But it doesn't tie any shoes."

Writing, she said, was "relaxing. . . . For one thing it's the only way I get to sit down. . . . I like thinking about it, turning it around, thinking of ways to use a situation in order to get a haunting note. I think of what other things it will go with while I'm washing the dishes. But I do it because it's fun, because I like it."

At least one faithful reader found this cheerful-Marmee gambit too much to stomach—Stanley. "dear neat detached miss jackson," he wrote evilly, in a note. "writin? taint nothin but fun!!! neatly tucking a wisp of gray hair in place . . . d'ruther be raisin my passel of kids but since they laid henry off at the mill . . . flouring her apron with careworn hands . . . n'poppin blueberry pies in the oven . . . neatly detaching her goddamn head . . . shucks . . . yessir yessirree yessirreeindeedee!"

Shirley appreciated it, and stuck it in her "Lottery" scrapbook, along with another of his notes—a "Chart, with visual aids," a handy pocket guide to the economics of book buying: "Out of every 100 readers of the Lottery, 98 walk out without buying, two spend $1.50 at $.75 a copy, of which Farrar Straus takes $1.45, the agent takes $.10 and the author owes $.05."

Shirley did, as she told Breit, spend time on innumerable chores; she also hired an endless stream of housekeepers, local girls, mother's helpers, in a vain attempt to find the one perfect jewel who would make it all run smoothly. Along the way, she ran into various problems—one girl had a sudden breakdown, another stole, a third had a prominent religious bent that made Stanley, especially, very nervous—but part of the problem was of her own making. Shirley, like Stanley, tended to blow hot and cold, with both people and places.

And lately both were beginning to feel a little unhappy with Bennington—even though in her biographical notes, written only a few short months before, she claimed brightly that "it's a nice town for children to grow up in and I'm on the Entertainment Committee for the PTA and write the programs for the Home Talent Show." Rather abruptly, they began making plans to move nearer to New York City, ostensibly so Stanley would have an easier time commuting to *The New Yorker*. "His college teaching was interfering with his work," said Tom Brockway.

But Helen Feeley believed there was another reason for the move. "As I understood it, it was the anti-Semitism she felt in the town, that was why they moved," she said. "Whether Stanley felt it I don't know. He could have hardly felt the college was anti-Semitic—in those days it seems to me at least half the faculty was Jewish. But Shirley made a big thing out of it. It was the town. She didn't talk about it all that much, but it bothered her enormously. Stanley always passed things off as a joke— in a way he was what you might call a professional Jew, he made a big thing about being Jewish, made a lot of jokes. But Shirley—her disturbance showed more."

So once again the Hymans began the process of relocation, looking for a house in the Westport, Connecticut, area, "a nice fancy rich arty community," as Shirley described it to her mother.

CHAPTER
·13·

Helen Feeley may have been aware of darker reasons for the move, but to her parents, of course, Shirley relayed only the more superficial ones— North Bennington seemed to have "fewer advantages than ever before" lately, now that both she and Stanley constantly had to go to New York to meet with publishers, agents, interviewers, and the like; the idea of living in a town with movie theaters and restaurants and shops and more than one television channel was terribly appealing. Laurie was bored in school and "seemed to have no competition at all . . . the old story of the fairly bright child looking brighter because he is in with a number of stupid children."

Actually, Laurie's schooling and, more important, the sort of children he was spending time with did genuinely concern her—Shirley wanted her children to mingle with the locals, but not to the point of becoming indistinguishable from them. "Laurie looks like a typical North Bennington subnormal farmer," she complained to her parents. "His Vermont accent is so flat and nasal he could pass for Calvin Coolidge." There was no question that Shirley, who wrote so knowledgeably about prejudice, harbored a great deal of it herself—she looked down her nose at most of the people in town with a sense of superiority that was as aristocratic as it was intellectual. Helen Feeley heard her refer to the locals as "peasants" more than once and was bothered by it—it seemed to her the tensions between town and college were bad enough without name-calling. But Shirley felt her children came from better stock, and didn't care who knew it. It was in fact very much the way Geraldine had felt about her own children, many years before.

Moving now seemed eminently desirable, but money posed a problem.

Rents in Connecticut were far above those in North Bennington; the Hymans had been paying only fifty dollars a month for the fourteen-room house with the pillars; a comparable house in Westport, they realized, could easily cost them three times as much. They agonized over the difference, but by now Shirley was absolutely committed to the move: "We are no longer fond of the town," she told her parents flatly. Laurie, she had decided, "is getting rough and vulgar from spending all his time with kids who are not what you might call cultured . . . fighting and quarrelling all the time . . . really ought to be gotten out of this town unless we want him to be a farmer when he grows up." Joanne, age four, was "beginning to talk and act like the disagreeable little girls around here." Sally, at one, was presumably so far uncontaminated.

They had found a house they liked in Saugatuck, on Indian Hill Road, just outside of Westport, "the same sort of rambling Victorian mansion like the one we have now . . . fifty years old and very solid and nice," with five bedrooms, two bathrooms, a large porch, and a whopping price tag: $175 a month. There seemed to be no way to swing it, but at the last moment Shirley's agent, Rae Everitt, came through with a contract arrangement with *Good Housekeeping*—the magazine would put her on a drawing account of $6,000 a year against sales of stories; in return she would agree to send them at least eight a year. "The best news of our lives," Shirley wrote delightedly, not realizing the arrangement would later come back to haunt her. She signed the contract at once, and Stanley called the real estate agent in Westport to say they were taking the house.

The summer had been filled with a good deal of fun and not much work—guests had come nearly every weekend; she and Stanley had made several trips with friends to the Saratoga racetrack, which Shirley loved; both of them had given lectures at nearby writers' conferences. Then, too, there had been a number of trips to New York City, where Stanley's parents seemed always able to scrounge up last-minute Dodgers tickets. (Stanley told friends that one of the Dodgers' managers was an old boyfriend of Lulu's.) Most of the fall was taken up by the move to Westport— the planning, the financial finagling, the final move itself, in early December.

Yet somehow, in and around the various activities, and in the throes of "the worst hay fever I've ever had," Shirley managed to keep at least one hand on the typewriter. She was turning out a number of family stories, now—they sold fast and brought in nice checks. She was aware that she was using her children as copy and was scrupulously careful to make sure each of them got a cut of the profits. Whenever a story sold, she took Laurie and Joanne out for "story presents."

The family stories came easily to her and were beginning to attract a following from a very different kind of reader. Shirley was now getting letters from young mothers, pleading with her for advice—she seemed to do it all so easily. Most of the time she replied crisply that if she knew enough to give advice, her children would be better behaved. She had no interest in other women's problems; there was little of the social worker in Shirley. She had a definite disdain for the sort of young mother who would read her work in *Good Housekeeping* or *Woman's Home Companion* and think she had found a soulmate, and it led her to have a certain disdain for the family stories themselves. When her parents criticized them, she replied airily:

"I quite agree with you. . . . They are written simply for money and the reason they sound so bad is that those magazines won't buy good ones, but deliberately seek out bad stuff because they say their audiences want it. I simply figure that at a thousand bucks a story, I can't afford to try to change the state of popular fiction today. . . . I won't write love stories and junk about gay young married couples, and they won't take ordinary children stories, and this sort of thing is a compromise between their notions and mine . . . and is unusual enough so that I am the only person I know of who is doing it." The criticism hurt, though, and she permitted herself one small spiteful dart—"the stories you repudiate are selling at a furious rate abroad, two in England, one in Sweden."

They were not, however, what she considered her real work, and once the move had been made in December 1949, she plunged into the novel she had been planning for some time—*Hangsaman*. In many ways this would be the most revealing, complex, and difficult book she would ever write. Later books would be better written, perhaps, more skillful, more critically esteemed—this was the one that went the deepest. *Hangsaman* was an exploration of adolescence, Shirley's adolescence, a look at the turbulent, lonely, half-real, half-mad inner life of a brilliant, sensitive young girl, Natalie Waite, as she moved from her parents' world to that of a small women's college, from shaky integration to disintegration, then back, to a kind of shaky whole. It was an erratic book, not perfectly formed, a book that seemed often on the verge of splintering, like Natalie herself. But it was a book of almost terrifying insight and talent.

Perhaps Shirley had always planned to write about adolescence, but it seems likely that a tragedy that occurred at Bennington in 1946 had a strong effect on her, unleashing her memories. During Stanley's first year at the college, a young student, Paula Welden, disappeared on a mountain hike without a trace. For weeks, even months, police and rescue workers searched for clues, while both college and townspeople agonized over the mystery, the girl, and the entire hidden country of adolescence itself.

The girl was never found, but Shirley was pushed back into memories of her own time in that awkward, lonely place, late adolescence; her half-stab at suicide, her moods, her confusions. The book was a mixture of her past and present lives: the college bore a close resemblance to Bennington; Natalie's father was a blend of her father and Stanley. A popular English teacher, also showing distinct signs of Stanley, appeared in the book, along with his drunken wife, a woman at odds with the college environment, who in turn resembled Shirley. But the vast part of Shirley was in Natalie—more of her than she had ever invested in a character before, more perhaps than she would ever invest again.

A strange girl, Natalie; lonely and alienated, she is prone to soaring flights of self-love and fantasies of power. Walking through the dark campus at night she sees herself looming giantlike over the buildings, capable of lifting them, one by one, crunching the walls and the people inside, "chewing ruthlessly on the boards and the small sweet bones." There is madness here, but somehow it is a familiar madness, forcing the reader to an uncomfortable question: How far away are any of us from madness during those early years? " 'Hangsaman' was the book I most identified with," said her friend June. "It reflected an experience we sort of shared at the same age."

Hangsaman also included one of the few sexual episodes that would ever appear in Shirley's work—and the incident is vague, elusive, and as Frank Orenstein points out, "between chapters." In fact, the scene is not truly written at all—only inferred. Natalie and an older man start a conversation at one of her parents' garden parties. They walk away from the group to a small clump of trees. "The danger is here, in *here*," Natalie thinks. The man tells her to sit down:

> "Tell me what you thought was so wonderful about yourself," the man said; his voice was muted.
> Oh my dear God sweet Christ, Natalie thought, so sickened she nearly said it aloud, is he going to *touch* me?

And this is all. The next morning, Natalie wakes up, buries her head in the pillow, saying, "No, please no.

> "I will not think about it, it doesn't matter," she told herself, and her mind repeated idiotically. It doesn't matter, it doesn't matter, it doesn't matter, it doesn't matter, until, desperately, she said aloud, "I don't remember, nothing happened, nothing that I remember happened."

The scene in the garden is never mentioned again. But the incident throws up a dark shadow that hangs over the rest of the story. Such an episode, even in a strongly autobiographical work, is not necessarily telling, of course. But if Shirley did encounter sexual abuse as a teenager, one feels the memory would have floated back in just this form—elusive, denied, half unconscious.

She was able to descend to a deeper level in her writing than ever before. Find a safe place and do your work, one great philosopher said— and Shirley had found it. Her place was her family, loud, boisterous, demanding, secure. The move to Westport certainly had not slowed the Hymans' social life—now friends came up from New York even more often (it was an easy drive, after all), as well as down from Bennington; in addition, there were new friends, bridge-playing friends like the Olsons, writer friends like Peter De Vries and his wife, Katinka, J. D. Salinger, and others (Westport was crawling with writers). Their old friends Jay and Bobbie Williams lived only one town over, in Redding, and visited often. As ever, the Hymans were terrific hosts, providing generous helpings of liquor, food, and talk.

Yet there was a part of Shirley, always, that she kept utterly private, locked away from everyone. She could heartily enjoy the incessant socializing, especially when it was with old friends; she could get into the spirit fully, laughing, singing, and serving mountains of food. But a part of her was completely at home only when she was writing, spilling out stories from that strange land she alone had access to, her mind. It could not have been easy, despite her amazing energy, despite her flair for assuming different roles, to write a few pages, then whip up lunch for Stanley, write another few pages, then take the baby out for a stroll, play a few rounds of baseball with the older children, prepare a dinner party— not easy, particularly when the subject was as close to the bone as *Hangsaman*. Yet in some ways this was what she needed most, the lifeline that allowed her to descend so far into the well of her own tangled memories. This was her safe place.

Still, no balance is perfect. Shirley had always been tense, prone to innumerable ailments, and the steady regime of burning the candle at both ends—nightly carousals, daily hard work—was already beginning to take its toll. For several years now she had suffered from headaches and taken large prescription doses of codeine to alleviate them. Her teeth had always been bad, the endless cigarettes, coffee, and candy doing them no good whatsoever, and this necessitated hours of dental work, which she feared and hated even more than most people. Her weight problem had gotten worse with each pregnancy, which bothered her more than many people realized. It was not that she ate huge amounts, particularly—no one, not close friends, not her children, ever remembers Shirley as having an enormous appetite. It was more a matter of what she ate—she loved toast with huge slabs of butter; she could eat her way through a plate of chocolate very quickly; and then there was, of course, the matter of alcohol. Drinking was a nightly custom with the Hymans, and the drinking was often heavy. "I want you to put me on a diet," she told Dr. Oliver Durand once. "Eight hundred calories of alcohol a night—now what can I eat?"

Fancy Westport had its share of fancy doctors, of course, and it wasn't long before Shirley met up with one. She had gone mainly because she wanted a refill of her codeine prescription; Shirley usually liked to stay as far away from doctors as she could. But this doctor was keen on dieting too, it turned out, and very understanding as well. He knew, he said, that people found it hard to give up food like bread and potatoes, and certainly no one felt like doing without their nightly drinks, but he had a plan that would make all that abstinence unnecessary. All it involved was a series of shots and pills, perfectly safe—the weight would come off like magic.

Shirley was wary but agreed to try his plan. Amazingly enough, she found she did lose weight, and very quickly; furthermore, she did not feel tired or even particularly hungry. "My magic pills," she called them, very pleased with their effect. And so, somewhat earlier than the rest of the country, Shirley at age thirty-three became acquainted for the first time with the potent charms of amphetamines—and it was to be a lifelong friendship. Not long after, she began to use tranquilizers, too, turning to them whenever her anxiety level was high, which was often. At the same time, her alcohol use continued unabated. The common wisdom in the fifties was that these pills were completely safe, and a great boon to mankind. Shirley had no reason to doubt the common wisdom.

The children were quite used to the constant parade of guests, the feverish socializing that went on at the house. Not that they attended any of the dinner parties or late-night revels then—Shirley and Stanley were firm believers in separation between adults and children at those times. The kids were fed early and, if at all possible, tucked away before party guests arrived. But the daytime was another matter—on weekends there would often be a baseball game on the lawn, with everyone from Sally on up participating. It would be many years before Laurence would appreciate how rare it was to live in the kind of home where the guy pitching the ball to you might well be J. D. Salinger and the man yelling out the window for you to pipe down so he could work was often Ralph Ellison.

Shirley's housekeeping in Westport was as cavalier as ever. She hired helpers when she could, but often they were more trouble than they were worth. One she was fond of had a psychotic episode at four in the morning, and Shirley had no interest in taking her back after her hospitalization. Geraldine came for a brief visit and was horrified at the state of things, as usual; she launched a private search for a housekeeper for her messy daughter. She met a woman on a train ride who seemed suitable, and persuaded Shirley to hire her for a time.

Despite her general disinterest in household niceties, Shirley did have occasional enthusiasms: Helen Feeley was astounded to see colored sheets on the beds when she came for a visit. They had just come out on the market, Shirley said proudly, and she had snapped them up at once.

Messy as it was, the Hyman household ran smoothly, which often impressed visitors; it was obvious Shirley was the one responsible for all the meshing gears. "Most organized woman I ever saw," composer Lionel Nowak told his wife after he and the rest of the poker crew descended on the Hymans one weekend. "Why can't you be like that?"

Shirley and Stanley went into New York frequently, for business, baseball games, and parties. Stanley's old friend Red Sdolsky and another friend, Louis Scher, an older man who helped operate a book-finding business, The Seven Bookhunters—and who probably could have subsisted on Stanley's business alone—often picked them up for a night in Queens, attending prizefights, which Shirley loved.

Other evenings were less successful, and one suburban dinner party in particular aroused her scorn. "Everyone there was a rich writer and had written a best-seller," Shirley wrote her parents. "They were all surprised to find we had not been in Florida this winter. . . . They all also commute to Hollywood. Stanley said it was the most awful evening he has ever spent in his life, and I think he was right." (The only comparable evening, she said, was one they spent in Binghamton, New York, with four of Stanley's aunts.) The writers were "all very generous and pleasant but just the same . . . very dull and too shrimp newburg-y for us. No chips on the china, napkins for everybody and so on." Still, she had learned something, she noted wryly: "There's no doubt but what there's money in writing, if you work it right."

Shirley's critical eye was rarely on hold, except with a very few treasured friends. As a child she had resolved one New Year's that in the future she would "look for the good, rather than explore for the evil," but it was not a resolution she was ever able to keep for long, any more than she had been able to fulfill her resolve to "be healthy (thin)" or to stop spending money. She made lightning-fast judgments about other people, and used her wit—always a powerful force—to nail them home.

Even when there was no particularly noticeable fault to discern, Shirley could often find something to latch onto. After spending an afternoon with Katinka De Vries, she wrote that she had had a terrible headache and "found it difficult, on top of the headache, to spend the day with someone named Katinka, even though she is very nice." Friends often arrived with "badly behaved children," she would note, proceeding to list their shortcomings—her own children generally coming off quite mature and reasonable in these tales. In the case of the Feeleys, whom she really cared for, they had come with "their well behaved daughters and their badly behaved dogs."

Their first summer in Westport, Shirley and Stanley arranged, rather uncharacteristically, to host two disadvantaged city children for two weeks, as participants in the Fresh Air Fund. Shirley found the boys pathetic, but nonetheless had them labeled, damningly, within moments—both were "rather dull," one "fat and cowardly," the other "thin and sly." It was almost a knee-jerk reflex, this sort of instant cubbyholing, and obviously one she found serviceable. If nothing else, it was a good way to cut people down to manageable size, something Shirley seemed to need to do, even if she no longer, like Natalie, envisioned chewing on their "small sweet bones."

The first year in Westport was a full one for Shirley. She worked on *Hangsaman,* wrote several stories, entertained innumerable guests, and ran through a series of maids, all of whom initially seemed perfect but revealed themselves almost immediately to be considerably less than that, and soon afterward unthinkable. But something else happened to Shirley in 1950 that affected her deeply, far below the surface. This was the year she met the man who fitted her conception of the Daemon Lover almost completely: Dylan Thomas.

Their encounter was brief, by all accounts, and undoubtedly made little mark on Thomas himself. The wild Welsh poet, as known for his drunken revels as for his genius, had come to New York on a lecture tour in February; John Brinnin, who lived in Westport and had the job of squiring him around, took him to a party at the Hymans'. Some say he had voiced a particular interest in meeting Shirley, whose stories had impressed him.

Late in the evening, an evening clouded as usual by liquor and smoke and endless rhetoric, Shirley and Thomas met alone outside on the enormous porch that wound around the house. Precisely what happened between them is not known, but they were alone together long enough for various stories to spring up—and since there were plenty of storytellers around, they did.

Stanley turned it into farce, of course, immediately. What happened, he told Brendan Gill soon after (Gill later printed the version in his book *Here at The New Yorker*) was that Thomas, very drunk, had started pursuing Shirley, also drunk, and that the two rather large figures had raced clumsily through the house, Thomas in pursuit, Shirley in retreat, going through the living room, out the door, around the back, up the porch, and back through the house again, each time passing in front of Stanley, who was trying to watch a ballgame on TV. At the third go-round, utterly fed up, he had grabbed Thomas by the belt buckle and brought him down, giving Shirley her chance to escape.

John Brinnin had a straighter version, which appears in Paul Ferris's biography of Thomas. According to his account, Thomas and Shirley did go outside for a while, and there was a certain amount of "fooling around in the snow," but Thomas told him later that the cold air had been too much for him; nothing had happened.

And Shirley too had a version that she told Helen Feeley years later. "She confided to me that, yes, she was one of those women Dylan Thomas screwed on the back porch." Helen was a little shocked—not because of the statement, people were always saying outrageous things in their group, but because Shirley had made it; she never discussed sexual matters with anyone. "It was almost like name-dropping to impress me." Helen was not sure whether to believe her or not.

Whether or not anything truly occurred, the incident did have an effect on Shirley—she dwelled on it and made at least three attempts to write about it, each story moving further away from the actual occurrence into the realm of private myth. After her death, Stanley republished her final attempt, originally published in 1952 in *New World Writing*, under the title "The Lovely House." In the collection of her work he issued in 1968, Stanley returned the story to its original title, "The Visit," and restored its dedication, to Dylan Thomas.

It was a strange, magical tale set in an English country house, full of inexplicable happenings, movements back and forth through time, a phantom lover, a chief figure named Margaret, and a recurring allusion to another long-dead Margaret, "who died for love." In all three stories, Shirley used the name Margaret—the name she had first used years before, when writing of the Daemon Lover.

Her second attempt to write about Thomas, "Weep for Adonais," never published, was made after his death, a few years later; it was an icy little tale that effectively skewered the self-serving academic types who had surrounded him in his last days, watching his antics with amused contempt, from the safety of their bell tower. The Margaret in this story was the wife of one academic.

Only her first attempt, also unpublished, hovered around the actual encounter. In this story the Margaret figure, here a wife, mother, and hostess, is at a party in her home, growing increasingly bored and alienated from the party chatter, the constant arguments. She slips out to the porch—where he is sitting alone. They exchange a few words; he puts his arms around her. "I'm not even afraid," she says. "Can you cross a borderline as easily as that?" "Easily," he says. "And never go back? And never never be afraid?" Going back inside, she encounters a woman guest. "There ought to be a name," she tells her abruptly, "for a woman who has to find someone to mind her children when she wants to be unfaithful to her husband." The woman narrows her eyes, shocked. "We are the good artist and the bad artist, you and I," says Margaret. "I shall conceive heroes." Returning to the living room, she sits down. "I have a secret, she was thinking, sitting in her chair looking unafraid at the people around; I have a brave brave secret locked in with me."

The secret, which would be locked inside her forever, was her brief time alone with Dylan Thomas—whatever effect it had on him, to Shirley it was not a minor, casual occurrence. Thomas himself was too much of a mythic character in his own right—the prototype of the wild, self-destructive artist—not to have affected Shirley strongly. She was fiercely proud of their moments together; they had been hers alone. Dumpy, overweight, unbeautiful, she had still attracted the attention of the foremost poet of the era for a night. It was a tiny personal triumph which was hers alone.

On the surface, life continued unchanged. "I am writing because of news. A most amazing thing. A really most amazing thing. I want you to brace yourselves," she told her parents. She and Stanley had bought a car from friends, a 1940 Buick, and she was in the process of learning to drive. Stanley had tried once or twice over the years, with terrifying results, especially in reverse; no one was eager to see him try again. But it had gradually become clear to the Hymans that someone ought to be able to do it, especially if they were going to live away from the city, and Shirley was obviously the more reasonable choice.

The learning process was not without problems. "Naturally there have been small difficulties. For instance, my attempting our driveway without estimating my speed and crashing into the stone wall, while Eric [the instructor] screamed 'second, second' and I said, 'What? What?' and the little girls sat on the front porch and laughed their heads off and wanted me to do it again." But within a couple of weeks, Shirley had gotten her license, although she had yet, she said, to make a left-hand turn. Initially a bit fearful, in an amazingly short time she was tearing around the streets like a pro, doing errands, taking the kids to the beach, planning small trips with Stanley. Learning to drive was like mastering a game, and Shirley loved games. She quickly became a zestful, speedy driver, completely at home behind the wheel. In short order, too, she had turned out a hilarious piece about her learning experience, which sold at once and was later incorporated into *Life Among the Savages*.

They visited Bennington occasionally that summer of 1950, to see friends, but had no urge to return. "It was awful, seeing Bennington again. . . . I don't ever want to go near that place again," Shirley wrote, with her usual adamance (in less than two years they would be back for good). In August, they again lectured at a few writers' conferences, as they had the summer before. Shirley reported happily that she had read a story at the Marlboro School of Writing that had reduced everybody to tears, including her publisher, John Farrar—everybody, that is, except Stanley, "who is the only critic I trust." He had, however, told her the story was good.

The Westport community was not perfect either, Shirley had discovered by now—too suburban for her taste, too many picnics and Cub Scout outings, a few too many self-conscious artists around. The elementary school itself could be annoyingly casual, she thought—at the slightest excuse (hurricane warnings, for instance) the children were sent home. And even here, far from North Bennington's influence, Laurie had managed to meet a number of unruly types. But the Hymans were relatively content with the area—until October.

In October 1950, two days before his eighth birthday, Laurie rode his bike out of the driveway and was hit front-on by a car. "It was a bloody mess. They thought I was dead," he said. He was, in fact, unconscious for two days and in the hospital for two weeks; he had suffered a severe concussion and injuries to the shoulder, thumb, and hand.

Later, Shirley would turn it all into high comedy—"I had under my wavering care this active patient . . . who was not, under doctor's orders, to excite himself, to move his arm; who was not, most particularly, to raise his head or try to turn over; and who was not, it was clearly evident, going to pay any attention to anything the doctor said." At the time, of course, it was anything but comedy, and several days passed before the Hymans knew whether or not their son had sustained irreparable injury to the brain.

"It was completely his own fault," Shirley wrote her parents. "He came down the driveway on his bike without stopping at the road, and the poor old lady tried to stop fast and skidded into the bike." This view would change rather soon; Shirley and Stanley eventually sued the "poor old lady" for a large amount; the case was settled out of court, in their favor.

"It was my fault, but the point is, the woman should have been more careful; she was driving absentmindedly. It was a country road with a lot of perpendicular blind driveways, and a lot of kids around," Laurence pointed out. The accident, and the subsequent lawsuit, turned Shirley against Westport for good. "She was irrational about some things, and would develop a like or dislike for something completely apart from the facts. I think it was just that the whole experience was so distasteful, she was in a hurry to get out of there after that," said her older son.

Laurie came out of his coma in time to commiserate with Stanley on the absence of his beloved Dodgers from the World Series. His parents were impressed with his stoicism: "Very mature and quiet . . . he has not cried or whined once while we were there, unlike most of the other kids," Shirley told her parents. Their close friends, like June and Frank, called nearly every day for news; even not-so-close friends, like William Shawn, editor of *The New Yorker,* were concerned. "He and his wife are both in constant fear of some horrible thing happening to their own children, and he was so afraid to ask about Laurie that when he heard the news he made someone else call first to ask how he was before he could call himself . . . very touching and very silly," Shirley commented.

The most distraught person of all, other than Stanley and Shirley, was Moe Hyman, who had a very strong attachment to his oldest grandchild, as well as a harrowing memory of an accident Stanley had had as a child. "He had been hit by a car on a snowy night and lay in the street for several hours before he was found. . . . When [Moe] heard about Laurie it sort of fused together in his mind and made the shock twice as bad for him," she wrote her parents. "The poor old man wanted us to get a day and night nurse and we had to stop him from sending a brain specialist up from New York; I really believe if he could he'd fly Laurie to the Mayo Clinic tonight, and of course he's really worrying about the two of them at once and half the time says Stanley when he means Laurie."

To keep Laurie amused during his long convalescence, Stanley started working with him on a coin collection. Moe and Arthur Hyman, at the paper company, dealt in cash to a large extent; they now began saving coins for Laurie and shipping them up. Laurie would lose interest eventually, but Stanley would not—the coin collection would grow over the years to include gold, Greek, Roman, and Byzantine coins and come to be worth an estimated $100,000.

Late in the year Shirley finished *Hangsaman*—Laurie's accident had delayed her by a month. The contract with *Good Housekeeping* was already making her uneasy; the arrangement had been murky to begin with and the magazine now seemed to think she owed them money, not just stories. Shirley wanted out. She was also now thoroughly disgusted with her agent, Rae Everitt, for embroiling her in the first place—even though, of course, at the time the contract had been made she had hailed it as "the best news of our lives."

She was ready to break off the relationship with Everitt, and in typical Shirley fashion, did it abruptly, with one swift cat scratch.

"She wrote me a letter," said Everitt. "It said something like: My association with you is mixed up with what went wrong and I have to quit." Everitt had always known Shirley was "mercurial," and she knew the *Good Housekeeping* bind was upsetting her, but the letter came as a true shock; Shirley had given her no hint that she was about to dump her. "I tried to reach her by phone, many times, but I was never able to," she said. "It had been an intense relationship, a friendship. I still don't know what I did wrong." The two women never spoke to each other again.

Shirley was ready for a new agent, and found one—Bernice Baumgarten, of the Brandt & Brandt agency, wife of the reclusive writer James

Gould Cozzens, and widely rumored to be the toughest and best in the business.

The switch was successful. Bernice really was tough as nails, it turned out, and Shirley respected and appreciated her. "My old agent used to quit on any deal when it looked like she couldn't get as much as she wanted, and anyone could scare her, and she spent more time taking people out to lunch and asking me for news about the children than she ever did making money; but I don't think Bernice has ever taken anyone out to lunch in her life and she has certainly never said two words to me about anything but business, and she isn't at all fond of children and there is nothing she likes better than getting someone by the throat. I wouldn't like to have her for a sister, but I do love doing business with her," she told her parents. And unlike so many of Shirley's laser-fast judgments, this one would not change.

Under Bernice's astute management, Shirley's career would become more lucrative than ever before. One of her first acts was to involve Shirley in a possible moviemaking deal; actor Franchot Tone and a few other Hollywood types had decided for some unknown reason that she was the perfect person to write a movie script about dancer Isadora Duncan. There were a number of New York meetings with Tone before the whole thing petered out, though Shirley did get a fee for writing a treatment. It was all rather silly, but exciting and fun while it lasted. Bernice also tried to move Shirley toward a more public profile, but there Shirley dug her feet in—she hated interviews, radio appearances, and the like. One request, to be on a panel to discuss the tragedy of alcoholism, she turned down at once—"I am rather more in favor of alcoholism than against it," she said judiciously.

Hangsaman came out in April 1951 to generally high praise but relatively unimpressive sales; Farrar, Straus ended up scrapping initial plans for a second printing, and a brief flurry about movie rights came to nothing. Reviews praised Shirley's "almost macabre honesty" but seemed a little puzzled by certain sections of the book. "Parts are subtle, witty, shrewd, rich with sudden insight but other parts are as strange and obscure as nightmares of a mad psychoanalyst," said Orville Prescott in *The New York Times*. Shirley, he felt, had "erred in trying to fuse realistic psychology and symbolic fantasy." As a writer she was "unfairly brilliant," a strange criticism, and one not likely to send readers flocking to their nearest bookstore. Bernice saw the way the wind was blowing and immediately began making plans for Shirley to collect her family stories into a book—that, she knew, would be a seller.

Shirley herself had last-minute doubts about *Hangsaman:* "It's coming out, even though no one likes it anymore, including me," she told her parents—oddly, since Roger Straus had written her that it was a "brilliant job" and his company intended to "hit it hard" with advertising. Part of the problem had to do with the last section of the book, in which Natalie takes up with a strange friend, who is, one finally realizes, a fantasy. At least it seems fairly clear that Shirley meant her to be a fantasy—but she emerges all too realistically on the page, and many readers had trouble figuring out whether she was, in fact, flesh and blood or not. Even Jay Williams, her old friend, fellow writer, and onetime black-mass impresario, was unsure. "I was puzzled by the Trib's saying Tony [the other girl] was purely imaginary—is this my own coarse perception?" he wrote. If someone like Williams could have trouble discerning the fantasy, anyone could, and many did.

But many readers were dazzled by Shirley's exploration of adolescence. "It's such a perceptive book, I kept thinking, 'What a difficult thing to be Shirley Jackson's daughter!' " said one reviewer in the Louisville *Courier-Journal*. A few wrote to praise her understanding. "How wonderful for your children, having a mother who understands; it will make it so much easier for them," said one. In fact, Shirley had dedicated the book to her children, so perhaps she was thinking along those lines herself. She was mercifully several years away from learning that even the most brilliant perception in the world does not make it any easier to deal with adolescents.

But for now there were no teenagers in the Hyman household to teach anyone unsettling lessons, and pleased with her brood, now aged eight, five, and two, Shirley decided to go to the well one more time "to balance the table," as she told friends. Stanley had no objection; he rather enjoyed being sovereign over a large family, and since it had turned out that Shirley did a good ninety to one hundred percent of the child-rearing chores, there was no problem. So far, all the kids had been born three years apart, within weeks, which surprised no one—it was the sort of carefully orchestrated symmetry Stanley was noted for.

Barry Edgar Hyman, however, came within a hairbreadth of spoiling the arrangement. Shirley's babies had always been late, but Barry beat them all; in addition, the doctor could not decide whether he was due in September, October, November, or December, enough to drive any pregnant woman up the wall. Since Laurie's accident, the Hymans had been eager to leave Westport; when Fred Burkhardt offered Stanley his old post back, Bennington suddenly seemed desirable again. "All the reasons for leaving Vermont in the first place are still there, but we'd rather the kids grow up in a less artist-colony sort of town," Shirley said. But no one wanted to move with a baby due at any moment. And the problem was, that moment stretched over nearly four months.

"The children are by now openly skeptical," Shirley reported to her parents, as September slid into October with no baby in view. Having decided to move back to Bennington, they suddenly found the schools in Westport looking worse every day: "I hate these progressive nursery schools where hitting another child over the head with a block is regarded as a sign of extroversion." Laurie at nine was vacillating between "maniac behavior and lovely solid maturity"; the former having caused him to be grounded for a week, after which she lifted the ban, despite the lack of improvement, for the traditional reason: "We couldn't stand having him home and unoccupied for another week."

As October gave way to November, Shirley and Stanley became increasingly edgy. Finally Stanley urged Ralph Ellison to move in with them for a few days, so he and his station wagon would be available to drive Shirley to the hospital when the baby came, which was certainly going to be any minute now. A generous man, Ellison agreed.

Feeling more secure having Ellison near, the Hymans decided to go to New York for a party, at which, as Ellison put it, "we all had enough to drink, but only I was capable of driving home." With both Shirley and Stanley sleeping in the backseat, he headed out to Westport; he had reached Greenwich when he ran out of gas. It was five in the morning and the future National Book Award–winner was stranded on a highway with two sleeping passengers, one of whom might decide to have her baby at any second. It was a time, if ever, when he could have used some of Shirley's magic—and incredibly, he got it. Out of the night came a car filled with Hispanics, none of whom could speak a word of English, but who understood the international language of car problems. "They stopped, got out, siphoned a couple of gallons from their car into mine, without exchanging a word, got back into their car, and shot off," said Ellison. Gratefully, he drove on.

But the vigil was far from over—the "few days" turned into a week, then another week. "The damn baby wouldn't show up," Ellison said. Finally the doctor gave Shirley a directive—she was to take a bottle of castor oil, mix it with something she didn't like, since she'd never be able to drink it again (she chose cream soda), swallow it all, give herself an enema, and go to sleep. The baby should be there by dawn. Ellison even turned his car around in the driveway so it would be facing the street, ready for the late dash to the hospital.

She managed to down the dose, with Stanley and Ellison urging her on, complied with the rest of the instructions, and went to bed. She woke up the next day feeling fine, with no aftereffects. And no baby, either.

Eventually, after another week, Stanley and Ellison took matters into their own hands. They deposited Shirley in the hospital, bought a big box of maple creams and a quart of whiskey, and crowded into the room with her. "We spent the night there drinking and eating candy. The next morning, Barry was in this world." Ellison and his wife were named godparents, which seemed, considering everything, no more than fitting.

Because of the long wait for Barry (his birthday was November 21), the Hymans decided to put off their return to Bennington until spring—it was too hard to move their "books and books and children and junk" in the middle of winter, not to mention the coin collection, which was growing heavier by the day. One set of coins Stanley ordered had come in the same package as a set of counterfeit coins—unfortunately the boxes were damaged in the mail, leaving the two sets freely intermingled and Stanley nearly inconsolable. Shirley, of course, was tickled; she couldn't wait to slip it into her next family story. Much as she revered Stanley, he did take himself awfully seriously; she always got a kick out of his comeuppances and usually wrote about them too—probably another reason why Stanley was ambivalent about what he called her "potboilers."

By April 1952, the Hymans were back in Vermont; they had been gone only a little over two years. They moved temporarily to a house in the Orchard on campus; they still planned to live in town, and wanted to take some time to look for a house. This time, they wanted to buy.

CHAPTER
·14·

The Orchard was an easy place to spend the summer. The Feeleys were only a stone's throw away, and the socializing was relaxed and casual. But Shirley was not entirely thrilled to be immersed in the college community; she liked to stay a bit removed, to retain her privacy. With other women in and out of the house during the day, comparisons were inevitable. None of the other faculty wives had anything remotely resembling a career, even though Lionel Nowak's wife, Laura, did give piano lessons. Their energy was poured directly into their homes, and it showed: their floors were cleaner, their kids better groomed. Shirley couldn't help but feel she was being judged by these women and was coming up wanting, and this was something she was acutely sensitive about.

One week she and Stanley went out of town to a writers' conference and farmed each of the children out to a different family, leaving Barry with a baby-sitter. Helen Feeley got Joanne, and another neighbor Sally. Without premeditation, each woman, in response to an irrepressible urge, immediately grabbed the little girl left with her, and dumped her into the bathtub to wash her hair. "I don't think their hair had ever been combed," said Helen. "Joanne told me not to cut any snarls because she'd never had her hair cut in her life and her father didn't allow her to have it cut. So I did the best I could and she did look one hundred percent better."

On her return home, Shirley was greeted with the spectacle of not one but two daughters with shining-clean hair. Her response was immediate— she blew up. "She was so angry," Helen Feeley remembered. " 'The nerve of you,' she said, 'what are you trying to do, show me up?' I said it had never occurred to me, I just thought, Gee, the kid needs a shampoo. But she took it very personally. She said, 'You two got together and ganged up'—she thought we'd done it after a discussion, to show her up, as a commentary."

There had been no collusion, but Shirley wasn't entirely wrong either—it was a commentary of sorts, and she had realized it at once. What sort of mother lets her daughters' hair get in such a mess? A mother, of course, who is trying to do other work at the same time she is raising children. But in 1952 there were no other mothers like that, certainly not in the Orchard. Once again Shirley was being seen as different, strange, outlandish. And on one level she gloried in it: these women couldn't do what she did, not for a minute; she was brilliant, talented, unique. Yet that didn't stop the judgment from hurting. The truth was that Shirley wanted their approval, she wanted—with the desperation of a fat little girl who had never pleased her mother—to be able to pass for one of them.

Gradually Helen realized it. One day Shirley approached her almost timidly. She had been asked, she said, to give a luncheon speech to a women's group in a small town just outside Albany; would Helen mind coming with her? Only she must dress very respectably, Shirley said; this was important.

"So I put on my suburban-lady's suit, and she put on her one good dress, which was black and very unbecoming, but respectable, highly respectable," Helen said. And they drove to the town.

"She was terrified. She was so scared she could hardly eat lunch. It was important to her to come across the way the housewives in her stories did. If any of them had walked into her house, of course, the image would have been spoiled." It was almost funny, the idea of Shirley dressing up and insisting she do it too, just so she could appear at a women's luncheon in mufti and pass for one of them. Except it wasn't funny; Shirley had been dead serious. "I just remember her fear," said Helen.

Shirley may have felt uncomfortable in the Orchard, surrounded by eagle-eyed housewives, but her letters to her parents, as usual, reflected nothing but sunshine. "So much pleasanter than Westport, we all feel we were right to come back," she wrote. They were playing bridge almost every night; Joanne had a new best friend; Laurie had been hanging out at the local stables, where a horse had stepped on his foot; and she and Stanley were finally learning to enjoy shrimp, "the greatest innovation in our life in years." Somehow, in her letters, her work—which she did every day, day in and day out—was reduced to the level of minor hobby, something far less engrossing than house-hunting, for instance, and certainly less important than her last bridge hand, which she often recounted in detail.

It was hardly surprising. Shirley always knew how to gear herself to an audience, even an audience of two. Though proud of her fame, Geraldine and Leslie had no interest in her work habits and, furthermore, were not always wholeheartedly thrilled with her finished books, either. Geraldine in particular saw nothing wrong with putting in her two cents from time to time: "You have too many demented girls in your books," she scolded. Her lifelong inability to understand her daughter was clearly reflected in her letters: "How are the books and stories coming along? I keep thinking of you with a perfectly normal childhood with nothing unusual happening, then having you people your childhood with such odd characters and experiences."

Even the upbeat family stories came in for their share of criticism— her mother was not at all sure they showed her in the most proper light: "Read your story in the Companion. Dear, you are getting in a rut. Your stories are getting a little repetitious and why oh why do you dwell on your complete lack of system and order in your household? I don't think you should write about it too much. You know we are proud of you but please don't spoil your wonderful gift for writing by writing any more about your helter skelter way of living. The same thing over and over. We love getting your letters and like them better than your stories."

Generally, though, Geraldine confined herself to what had always been her strong suit—nagging about personal habits. "Hope you are being good about housekeeping. You haven't been before and when you are renting someone else's place you really have to take care of it," she fussed when Shirley moved back to Bennington. Comments about weight dotted her letters like flyspecks: "Glad you're dieting." "Excess weight is hard on the heart." "You should get down to normal weight. Try non-fat milk." Her opinion of the Hyman menagerie, with its full complement of kids, dogs, and cats, was one of barely concealed disgust. "I wish you would calm down and get rid of a few cats and dogs and take things easier. You can't get rid of them [the children] but the cats and dogs could go," she urged hopefully. When little Barry had an asthma attack she was sympathetic but couldn't resist a pointed dig: "Poor little fellow, do you think he is allergic to dog dandruff or house dust or any of the things like that that bring asthma?"

Still, real concern and love came through: "Are you really all right? I worry about you. You have so much to do and so many responsibilities and keep taking on more," Geraldine wrote. Shirley read her mother's letters, gritted her teeth at some of the comments, snorted at others, replied to none of them, and continued—as always—to live her life according to her lights.

The work she referred to so rarely was going strong, as always. She had started on what would be one of her best books: *The Bird's Nest,* a story of a girl with multiple personalities. It was the first time she had undertaken anything that required actual research. Her point of departure was a case that had occurred in 1906, handled by a Dr. Morton Prince, who had written it up under the title "The Dissociation of a Personality" (most of her friends are sure Stanley dug it up for her initially), and she was being given background briefing by one of the college psychologists. The doctor had used hypnosis as a means of achieving contact with the various personalities, a technique that fascinated Shirley, as did any means of mind exploration.

The subject of multiple personality attracted her in a very personal way—Shirley knew that she too, in a sense, had several different personalities, all jostling against each other in uneasy truce. There was the warm, engaging hostess, opening her doors to hordes of company—and the intensely private woman who revealed herself to no one; the conventional homemaker, experimenting with pie crusts—and the artist of the terrible, searing vision; the dutiful daughter of the letters—and the unforgiving, still seething, rejected adolescent. On top of this there was the caustic wit, the haughty dowager, the psychic, the witch, the loving and engaged mother, the frumpy slattern. And none of the parts were buried; all were flourishing strands of a complicated, if at times dissonant, whole. It was no wonder that she saw herself as a traveler between alternate realities. Her world was composed of them, and each reality demanded another persona. In the world of her fiction she was an artisan of fear, of shifting realities; in the home she was peacemaker, harmonizer, font of all comfort. A weaker person would have discarded some of the options, buried a few parts. Shirley insisted on giving them all free rein, despite the risk—a substantial one—that the center might not hold forever.

The world outside had a harder time accepting her various parts; to others, she often appeared to be a mass of deeply puzzling contradictions. How could a woman who wore no makeup, rarely combed her hair, and gave the clear impression she had put all personal physical vanity far behind her spend days trying to track down an expensive pair of alligator shoes she had spotted in an ad? How could someone so terrified of electricity that she hardly dared plug in a cord stand outside in a thunderstorm, thrilled by the lightning?

How could a woman who was manifestly obese write gleefully to her slim mother regarding a photo of her even slimmer brother that "I can't believe how fat he's gotten! My brother looks like a pig!" Above all, how could the author of "The Lottery" write the warm, delightful tales that would later be collected into *Life Among the Savages*?

Was it all simply willful blindness, or something more unusual—something in fact much closer to the phenomenon of multiple personality that fascinated her so?

Multiple personality is a rare syndrome about which little is understood.

Outfitted within an inch of
their lives, Shirley and Barry
Jackson stand rigidly in front
of their San Francisco
apartment, 1922.
(Courtesy Barry Jackson)

Shirley's uncle, Clifford Bugbee, lounges with Dorothy Ayling, an unidentified
neighborhood girl, and Shirley, on the lawn at Burlingame, about 1930.
(Courtesy Dorothy Ayling Gielow)

Dorothy Ayling, Shirley's closest childhood friend, with her in Burlingame in 1932, shortly before the move to Rochester. *(Courtesy Dorothy Ayling Gielow)*

Shirley and her college friend Jeanou in front of the Jackson home in Rochester, 1935. "What a miserable picture!" Shirley scrawled in a note on the back to Dorothy Ayling. "J's socks are bright red and I am not really that tall!" *(Courtesy Dorothy Ayling Gielow)*

Barry and Shirley the way their
mother liked to see them
dressed. Rochester, 1936.
(Courtesy Barry Jackson)

A rare mother-daughter outing, in Rochester, about 1935. Geraldine keeps a
firm eye on Shirley, who looks ready to bolt. *(Courtesy Barry Jackson)*

Shirley as she was when Stanley first met her in 1938—young, vibrant, intensely alive. *(Courtesy June Mirken Mintz)*

June Mirken, in front of her
cottage at Syracuse University
in winter 1937, just before
she met Shirley.
(Courtesy June Mirken Mintz)

The most visible effect of Shirley's
falling in love with Stanley was a
dramatic weight loss. Unfortunately,
it was not to last.

(Courtesy Peggy Kraft)

Arthur and Bunny at their wedding in April 1946. It was a day of high drama
that also included the first meeting in six years between Stanley and his father.
(Courtesy Arthur and Bunny Hyman)

Shirley mugs for the camera at Arthur and Bunny's wedding party, while
Stanley engages in his favorite sport: intense conversation.
(Courtesy Arthur and Bunny Hyman)

Only his beloved grandson Laurie could have persuaded Moe Hyman to assume such an undignified position—late 1946, not long after the family rift was mended, in front of the house with the pillars.
(Courtesy Sarah H. Stewart)

Shirley at work in the claustrophobic confines of Stanley's study, around 1947, in their first North Bennington house. Some friends believed the Hymans' library held as many as 100,000 books.
(Courtesy Sarah H. Stewart)

Barry, Sally, Joanne, and Laurence, aged one, four, seven, and ten, in an outtake from the photo session for *Life Among the Savages,* in 1952. Sally refused to follow the photographer's instructions and instead confronted the camera head-on—chin set, eyes blazing—as she did most things in life.
(Courtesy Lloyd Studio)

Christmas 1953. Moe Hyman avoided the holiday scrupulously but sent a photographer every year to capture the event. On the couch, left to right: Stanley, Bunny and Scott Hyman, Laurence, Shirley, Arthur Hyman. On the rug are Joanne, Barry, Sally, and Toby the dog.
(Courtesy Arthur and Bunny Hyman)

Shirley, Joanne, and Barry in a 1954 portrait of cozy togetherness. Posed as it is, the picture does reflect reality—Shirley read to her children nightly for years, although almost never from her own books. *(Courtesy Joanne Holly)*

A comfortable, noticeably paunchy Stanley relaxes in his study, New Year's Day 1959.
(Courtesy Laurence Hyman)

Joanne, Sally, Laurence, and Barry in an impromptu session, about 1959.
Laurence was already working as a trumpet player; Barry would later play
guitar professionally. *(Courtesy the Brockways)*

A pensive Ralph Ellison behind Stanley's bar, a permanent fixture in the living room
of the Main Street house in North Bennington.
(Courtesy the Brockways)

The true center of the Hyman house was the dining room table, where discussion, argument, music, jokes, food, and wine flowed freely. Here, in 1961, are (clockwise, from lower right) Tom Brockway, Barry Hyman, Jean Brockway, Stanley, Joanne, a family friend, and Laurence, on bass.
(Courtesy the Brockways)

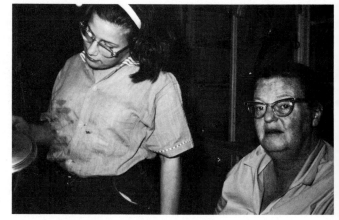

Sally and Shirley, about 1961, when Shirley's problems were becoming more and more evident.
(Courtesy the Brockways)

Three generations in an all-too-unusual embrace: Joanne,
Shirley, Geraldine, and Sally, in front of Laurence and
Corinne's home in North Bennington, 1963.
(Courtesy Sarah H. Stewart)

Geraldine and Leslie Jackson enjoying their pursuit of leisure living. The years
after Leslie's retirement were filled with cruises and banquets.
(Courtesy Sarah H. Stewart)

One of the last pictures ever taken of Shirley is this haunting study
by her son Laurence. *(Courtesy Laurence Hyman)*

But certain facts are known—that it nearly always has its roots in early sexual abuse; that it is found almost exclusively in extremely gifted, creative people; and that it carries with it certain abilities called, for want of a better phrase, paranormal—telepathy, heightened energy, a psychic sense—all qualities Shirley possessed.

"I contain multitudes," said the poet; Shirley would have understood. Whatever the reason, she gloried in every one of her separate parts and, not improbably, in the concept of multiple personality itself. It was not a subject she had chosen lightly.

She had also begun to do something Walt Whitman could never do—she was now finding and identifying some of those various antithetical parts in her children as well. It was almost as if her own personality had been filtered by a prism into four separate rays—Laurence and Sally were the independent challengers; Sally was intuitive, highly psychic; Joanne was a homebody, drawn to the conventional; Barry was steady, a "dogged little foot soldier," as Shirley once described him. She saw them as individuals, but she saw them as mirrors as well, reflecting her various parts. With time, this would be refined into only two rays—Joanne and Sally, her daughters.

For now, though, it was Elizabeth Richmond who concerned her—or more specifically Lizzie, Beth, Betsy, and Bess. The idea of a person whose various personalities were completely separate and distinct, locked off from each other—a truly splintered entity—compelled her.

The Bird's Nest was different from her first two novels. Since this was a story that did not grow quite as directly out of her own experience, she was freer to mold it. Then, too, Shirley's mastery, her ease at the wheel, was now unmistakable; with this book, she was truly hitting her stride. She was at last comfortable enough to use her wit even in what was essentially a serious work; her characters—the tough old aunt, the Edwardian doctor, the four-in-one girl—were light-years ahead in texture and appeal from her earlier creations.

Yet there are signs of Natalie in Elizabeth—her mad, fond notes to herself, for instance. And again, there is a reference to an early, disturbing sexual incident. This time the reference is even less noticeable than in *Hangsaman*—in fact, the episode is interwoven so subtly into the book that a careless reader might easily miss it. Betsy, the most childlike of all the personalities (she believes herself to be sixteen, the age she was when her mother died), runs away to find her mother, in actuality seven years dead. In a long stream-of-consciousness interval during this odyssey, she refers to her mother's lover, Robin, in passing—she had been fiercely jealous of their relationship but managed finally, she brags, to get rid of him.

Then, many pages later, there is this disconnected bit of dialogue:

"But then why did Robin run away?" he asked [an older man she has met during her flight].

"Because I said I'd tell my mother what we did." She looked up, dumfounded, fork in hand; "no," she whispered, staring fearfully, "no."

It probably pained Shirley to be that specific, even once, but she had no choice, she said later. Her research had convinced her that a multiple personality needed to have an act of sexual abuse as its cornerstone. Yet Shirley did not place the episode in childhood, where it would have made more psychological sense. Once again, as in *Hangsaman*, the abuse occurs in her character's teenage years.

To the clinical eye Lizzie (et al.), like Natalie, is mad. But the madness itself is a far from miserable state; both young women experience a heady rush of delight, exultation, a pure sense of power in its sway. It is actually the reintegration into "sanity" which somehow feels like a loss—of potential, of possibility, of self. It is hard not to believe that Shirley, who took such pride in the strange quirks and turns of her own mind, was expressing her own feeling that a certain sort of madness had its appeal, at least up to a point.

Of course, there is a downside. Her women also experience terror, alienation, and loneliness, as if in payment for those leaps of joy. Interestingly, the leaps and plunges also bear a distinct similarity to the creative process itself, at least the way Shirley experienced it: the soaring pride in her own mastery, the desolate, inevitable undertow.

Such a vision might seem to be ripe for feminist interpretation, and on the surface Shirley's work does adapt well to that lens. Her protagonists are invariably women, and strangers in a land not theirs. Their position, teetering on the brink of reality, seems a brave, even noble reaction to their presence in a world they never made—and do not accept. When both Natalie and Elizabeth settle in the end for integration, the result is diminishment.

But Shirley was no feminist. Her vision was personal, not political, and she would have strenuously resisted any effort to view her work in that way, even if she had survived into an era in which the personal had become the political. The movement itself would not have appealed to her at all, for many reasons. Her conventional Geraldine side would have been appalled; her fierce pride in her own uniqueness would have made her disdainful. Certainly she had little admiration for its early rustlings in the sixties, and said so.

Shirley had no patience with the idea of victimization or passivity. Her later works would show this clearly. Eleanor in *The Haunting of Hill House* kills herself rather than accept a lesser, saner reality. Merricat in

We Have Always Lived in the Castle—the boldest heroine Shirley ever created—erects her own new world. True, it is a fortress, with only one other beloved person in it, but it is an act of triumph nonetheless. Shirley did not need a political movement to tell her that women were capable of exercising power.

In an odd coincidence—one of those coincidences that Shirley relished—now that she was immersed in psychology, the Hymans found themselves renting a house owned by famed psychoanalyst Erich Fromm, who was currently living in Mexico. It was a modern house, a short distance out of North Bennington; not their cup of tea, exactly (neither, of course, was Fromm—Stanley was a devout Freudian, Fromm was distinctly New Era), but a place to stay while they looked for a house to buy. They had had to leave the Orchard in August since the house had been available only for the summer—besides, by then Shirley was quite ready to go.

The Fromm house was smaller than they were used to, but it had compensations—a large, completely soundproof office, for instance, which came with a huge couch. "What kind of psychoanalyst uses a double bed couch, do you think?" Shirley asked teasingly. The usual stream of house-guests continued; when Ellison came for a visit, Stanley gleefully took him down to the basement to show him their odd discovery—thousands of used safety razors, in carefully wrapped packages, lining the walls. "You can always count on something weird," said Ellison, who was no more impressed with Fromm's work than Stanley was. "It didn't hurt his reputation with me," he noted dryly.

As part of the house-hunting process Stanley went to call on one of the village patrons, an extremely dignified older gentleman who owned a number of houses in town. He took Laurie, who grew increasingly restless as the two men talked on. Finally, even Stanley noticed the fidgeting and interrupted himself to deliver what may have been one of the strangest ultimatums of all time. "Stop that!" he snapped at his son. "If you don't behave, Mr. McCullough will eat you." The older man was stunned speechless; the visit ended soon after, without real estate transactions. "The Hyman father technique, I guess," said Fred Burkhardt, who heard the story from McCullough. The town would soon see another example of it.

In the home both Shirley and Stanley could be sharp disciplinarians, brooking no nonsense from their children, who were high-spirited and individualistic and who, certainly in the case of Laurence and Sally, often needed a good deal of reining in. Yet faced with threats from the outside about those same children, they could be fiercely protective—at times, militantly so—even when those threats were of the mildest nature conceivable. When Laurie came home one day complaining that three of his friends had ganged up on him, Shirley and Stanley sprang into action at once.

The other children—Jennifer Feeley, Ross Burkhardt, and Willie Wohnus—were all Laurie's age, around eleven; the four had played together for years. Their parents were not only part of the college community but good friends of the Hymans' as well; Helen Feeley and Peg Wohnus were particularly close to Shirley. It made no difference—the Hymans had been attacked, and their reaction was immediate and total. Stanley grabbed his beloved sword-cane, and he and Shirley rushed out, ready for battle.

"It was a Sunday afternoon," said Helen Feeley. "Most uncharacteristically, the Feeley family was sitting around the fireplace, listening to the New York Philharmonic and I think even drinking tea. There was a bang at the door."

Without waiting for a response, Stanley and Shirley burst into the house, Stanley waving his sword-cane ominously. Looking neither right nor left, he pointed the implement straight at Jennifer and began to roar. "He yelled about how awful she had been, beating up on Laurie, waving this cane, scaring her absolutely to death. Shirley just stood there behind him, shaking. I was assuming Jennifer had done something terrible—I went over and put my arm around Shirley, to show her I knew she was upset. But she didn't say a word."

Jennifer Feeley remembers Stanley's words well: "He said, 'Jumping Jehoshaphat! How dare you do that to my son!' "

With a final thrust—"I hope your father beats the living bejesus out of you!"—Stanley whirled out of the room, Shirley close behind. Neither of them had said a word to the rest of the family. There was a moment of silence, then Jennifer burst into tears. Nothing that bad had happened, she insisted, sobbing.

It took a good while to calm her down, but once Helen had succeeded, she went to call the Wohnuses, since Jennifer said that Willie, too, had been at the scene. "I had hardly gotten my name out when Fred Wohnus said, 'My God, do you know what just happened?' " They had, he told her, been sitting by the fire drinking tea, listening to the Philharmonic, when Stanley and Shirley had burst in the door, Stanley waving his sword-cane and roaring. Helen could hear Willie howling in the background.

Fred Burkhardt was out of town that day, but he heard the story the minute he returned. "My secretary called me and said, 'Stanley Hyman is in a terrible state about this thing; he claimed your son and Willie and Jennifer ganged up on Laurie.' He and Shirley had appeared at all three houses, absolutely hysterical."

Exactly what had happened between the children that day to set Shirley and Stanley on the warpath is unclear. Jennifer Feeley remembers only that "somehow or other we all got into a squabble and Laurie was at the center of it. My memory is, he either fell off his bike or somebody, God forbid, pushed him—I have this vision of him lying on the dirt road, near his bicycle, and we were all really angry at him. That was the incident.

"I remember being very angry at Laurie for lying to his parents. What had he told them? Why had he done this to us? And he would not look at me in school the next day. I think he must have felt scared of what he stirred up."

Laurence himself does not remember the fight at all and finds it hard to believe, "since I could have eaten Willie Wohnus for lunch." Indeed, no one in the community had ever pictured him as the kind of kid who needed much protection.

The children patched up their fight within days. Shirley and Stanley's reaction was not so easily forgiven. For several months, the Hymans were completely estranged from all three families. Stanley continued to play poker every week with Burkhardt and Feeley—he just didn't talk to them. Finally Helen Feeley decided enough was enough. "It went on nine or ten months; finally we were all at some party together, and I thought, This has gone on too long, and went up to them and started talking." The incident itself was never brought up, however, and there was no apology.

"Somehow or other, during a poker game, Stanley broke the ice," Burkhardt remembered. "I learned later he asked somebody what he should do—he realized he had made an ass of himself." And so, tentatively, all three families resumed their friendship with the Hymans.

Burkhardt, for one, is convinced that the overreaction came out of Stanley and Shirley's sensitivity to anything that smacked—no matter how remotely—of anti-Semitism. "He indicated to Wohnus or somebody that it was the idea of two Kraut kids and an Irish kid ganging up on his son—he more or less accused him of being an anti-Semite. I think he was very touchy about it. He didn't talk about it much, but if you knew him well you could see—and she obviously had the same kind of feeling, of being an isolate, a victim."

At the time of the incident, Helen had assumed that Shirley was shaking in horror over Stanley's behavior, that she had gone along in hopes of stopping him. After all, he was behaving completely irrationally. Who waves a sword at a kid? But later she was not so sure at all. And nothing Shirley did or said afterward ever gave the impression that she and Stanley had not been totally unified in their brief crusade.

In the community at large, a certain message had been received—it was wise to be a little wary around the Hymans, especially where their kids were concerned. You just didn't know what they might do. These were not typical parents. And as time went on, this wariness focused on Shirley—after all, she was the one connected with the community, the PTA member, the involved parent; Stanley was much less visible. She was seen as "fiercely parental," as one resident put it, "like a lion with her cubs."

CHAPTER
·15·

Yet just when this was going on—the explosive confrontation, the subsequent estrangement from three sets of friends, and of course, the simultaneous work on *The Bird's Nest*—Shirley was busily collecting her warm, cheerful family stories into the book that would be *Life Among the Savages,* one of the most delightful books ever written about family life. The book began with their move from New York to Vermont and closed with Barry's birth. It gave the impression that the Hymans had lived in the house with the pillars for all that time—the move to Westport and back was eliminated, along with a number of other actual events. One of the points in writing about her family in the first place was to erase whatever she wanted, to make it all work smoothly this time around. And Shirley was a master at it.

There was a great deal of truth in *Savages.* Her first three children emerged in full color on the page, their separate personalities amazingly real and convincing—Laurie the independent, Joanne the romantic dreamer, Sally the wildly imaginative. Stanley—referred to only as "my husband"—at work in his den amid the chaos; she, Shirley, the amused, sardonic, at times bemused, slightly overwhelmed, but always appreciative witness. All true, all accurately reflective of one kind of truth about her life, the most pleasant, palatable kind. The town they live in is warm and inviting; local people are kindly; friends are close and supportive.

Not that the book is remotely syrupy—Shirley's sense of humor is in high form; no one since Ring Lardner has ever been able to wring more hilarity from family life. But, as befitted the genre, and just as in her letters, all was sunny and peaceful—there was no dark side. Four years later, when she would again collect her family stories into another book,

Raising Demons, the result would not be quite as smooth—some of the edges were beginning to fray, even on paper. But with *Savages,* Shirley hit the perfect note. It was a book close friends like June and Frank would turn to for memories again and again over the years; a book her daughters would read aloud to their own children, at times wondering which of their own childhood memories were accurate, which came out of Shirley's typewriter. Only her older son would avoid it completely.

The stories had been popular enough, but stories in magazines are transitory. *Savages,* published in June 1953, put the Hymans on the map, in a modest way. The book climbed to "the lowest level" of the *New York Times* best-seller list, and thousands of readers now felt they knew the family intimately, particularly "Laurie and Jannie and Sally and Barry." The back jacket carried an engaging picture of all four, blond, wholesome, all-American, irresistible—the very model of family togetherness.

Readers across the country responded to the book, and the picture. Shirley had done her job only too well, managing to paint her world in colors they recognized at once. Here was a wife and mother just like them, readers felt, facing the same typical problems, raising the same typical kids, with wry humor. It was hard to believe this was the author of "The Lottery," *Hangsaman,* and the soon-to-be-published *Bird's Nest.* Luckily, many of these readers had never seen her other work; it would have confused them a great deal.

Years later, one Midwest ladies' club shanghaied Barry Hyman into a speaking engagement because "they said my mother was just like Erma Bombeck." He snorted, remembering. "My mother was not like Erma Bombeck." But there is no denying that *Savages* tapped directly into what would later become the Bombeck market.

By the time *Savages* was published, the Hymans had found their house— an enormous twenty-room white elephant sitting halfway up Main Street in North Bennington. It had a large lawn, a barn in back, a long row of hedges setting it off from the street, and two gateposts, one straight, one crooked, which pleased Shirley even more than the pillars had—she liked the sense of something awry.

The house had been broken up into four separate apartments; there was enough room for each child to have an actual suite, and plenty of space. Downstairs was a large kitchen, where Shirley kept her witchcraft books; a dining room, where Stanley put his curio cabinet (much like the one Freud had kept, filled with oddities) and blues records; and a living room, where they set up a permanent bar. Stanley's study—it would always be called Stanley's study, no matter how many books Shirley wrote in it—was off to the side of the living room. Much of the coin collection was kept in a glass-top table in the living room. Other collections—Asian hand puppets, witchcraft curios (a human skull, amulets), Shirley's collection of cats (glass, ceramic, and actual)—were scattered throughout the house.

All Hyman collections—coins, cats, children, whatever—paled next to the biggest amalgamation of all: books. Bookshelves crammed to bursting lined the house, blocking doors, crowding hallways, screening windows. And still there were not enough. A few years later, when Laurie began to show a flair for carpentry work, he was put in sole charge of making the family's bookshelves, nearly a full job in itself.

For years Stanley had bought books in mass quantities; on occasion, he had given book-finders like Louis Scher orders for a thousand at a clip. In addition, both he and Shirley often reviewed books, taking their compensation in the form of more books. Over the years, the books kept piling up; eventually, estimates of their library ran to thirty or forty thousand and up—according to some, possibly more than the entire stock of the Bennington Free Library and the Bennington College Library combined at that time. Probably nobody knew for sure how many there were except Stanley—he not only knew the number, but knew exactly where every single book in his house was kept.

When he was at the college, he often called home to ask Shirley to find a book for him. His instructions on such occasions were faultless: "On the second floor, to the left of the bathroom door, third row up, sixth book over." Once Shirley had dutifully retrieved it, he would tell her the page—and often the paragraph—that he needed checked. Needless to say, the book then had to be returned to precisely the same spot: that was one of the matters he was inflexible about.

Since their return to Bennington, Stanley had blossomed as a teacher; while he continued to write for *The New Yorker* and keep up his outside connections, he had settled into a comfortable niche at the college and was enjoying thoroughly his position as one of the Great Men on Campus, whose course "Myth and Ritual" was the most popular. Never ill at ease in the face of reverence, Stanley took the slavish adoration of his students as his rightful due. And at an all-girls school, slavish adoration was the order of the day.

With Stanley a confirmed fixture on campus, Shirley found herself in yet another role, and not one she had picked for herself: she was now a faculty wife, with everything that implied, which was plenty, all of it negative. Faculty wives were expected to stick to the sidelines, stay away from parties (except perhaps the occasional graduate tea), and do nothing to interrupt the hallowed relationship between teacher and student. Now and then they might be allowed to serve brunch, perhaps, if they were discreet enough to leave the room immediately. The fact that this was Bennington in the unliberated early fifties only underscored the problem.

"Faculty wives during that period didn't have a very happy time of it," said Anna Schlabach, who taught history at the college. "Their husbands were terribly engrossed in the college and had wonderful teaching opportunities. . . . It was a lively kind of place. Most of the wives felt a lot of their husbands' best energies were being used up—there were a lot of frustrated women in the midst of a basically very happy faculty. And the students had their eyes on the male faculty—they weren't interested in any of their wives."

"It was not a good place for wives, Bennington," Ben Belitt put it succinctly. "Crushes all over the place—middle-aged boredom sets in and plays havoc."

The most mild-mannered, secure woman in the world chafed at the role of faculty wife. Helen Feeley once painted a picture of faculty wives without faces "because that's how I saw us." Shirley, who was emotional, fitful, and about as relaxed as a coiled spring, despised it. She hated students on principle—she knew perfectly well they were fantasizing about her husband and wishing, in a vague, romantic way, that she would fall down a manhole somewhere. And she also knew, of course, that Stanley didn't mind this in the slightest. But usually, just as she had years before, she directed her anger away from him, toward the students.

There were exceptions. Each year there would be a few students who appealed to Shirley's mothering instinct, which was strong. "Stanley would find them and take them home, and if they evoked maternalistic protectionistic feelings from Shirley, they'd be gathered in and fed and housed and given hot chicken soup," said June. Often these would be the lost ones, the ones on the brink of nervous breakdowns—the Natalies. To them she was kind, compassionate, and generous.

But this was not the general rule. In most cases, the students who congregated at the house "were there for Stanley. They cared nothing about her life. A lot of spoiled little princesses, many of them quite illiterate," June said. Arthur Hyman put it another way: "A rich snotty bunch of Japs." Not surprisingly, Shirley didn't like them for beans—and for the most part, they returned her feelings.

With no other males around to divert their interest, the students focused their energetic attentions directly on the male faculty—often with explosive results. Ralph Ellison saw the students' crushes as a sort of "innocent evil. It's a part of growing up. The kids could be quite forward." With someone like Howard Nemerov, who was handsome as well as brilliant, the hysteria could reach a fever pitch: "I remember Howard walking by and the girls just fainting," Ellison said.

But even Stanley, who was brilliant but not at all handsome, had plenty of fans. "They were very pushy," said Bunny Hyman. "They hung around Stanley all the time because they obviously adored him, and Shirley would get very jealous. Every once in a while she'd get real mad and clean out the house, just throw them all out."

Perhaps only at a small women's college like Bennington would Stanley Hyman have been able to enjoy the status of matinee idol. And there was no question but that it was an intoxicating phenomenon. "It's easy to see why it's difficult for them to resist," said June. "This was their fantasy from age sixteen, when no girl would have anything to do with them, and there it is in living flesh—these gorgeous young things."

And inevitably, Stanley did not resist, not all the time. Certainly he told his friends he did not. "He did have sexual relations with a number of students," said June. "Shirley never knew about it specifically. I knew about some of them. No way any of them were substitutes for Shirley, his relationship with Shirley was so unique." He did not make passes at students while they were his students, though. "One of his little ethical things," June said.

Frank, too, heard the stories. And when Stanley remarried, a year after Shirley's death, he presented his new wife, Phoebe Pettingell, with a full confession of his former peccadilloes. "He felt so bad he had never told anybody the whole story, I got the whole works," she said. "He was certainly an enormous philanderer during periods of that marriage."

"Stanley had quite a reputation," said Helen Feeley. "The minute you'd give him a couple of drinks, Stanley would be chasing the girls."

Undoubtedly there were incidents; but undoubtedly, too, there were far fewer than many people thought. Stanley loved a good story more than life itself; he had always enjoyed presenting himself to the world as a rakish wild man. "He liked to give people the impression that any woman who came across his path was in his bed," said Frank. When Stanley said that a gorgeous blonde had attacked him, bango, in the middle of her first tutorial; or that a student had seduced him on a bet at a party; or that a girl had sneaked into his study at home to perform various ministrations—and he did say all those things—it was always wise to take it all with several grains of salt.

Certainly he was far from being a wily seducer—his passes, when he made them, were apparently more in the nature of mindless grabs, the sort of frontal attack which, as James Thurber once said, often resulted only in "hysterical laughter on the part of the love object." Helen Feeley remembered one try:

"The poker game was at our house, and I was upstairs in bed. All of a sudden I realized someone was in bed with me. It was Stanley and he had his shoes on. Clothes too. I kicked him out on the floor with a big crash, saying 'Get out' at the top of my voice. But I think he did this kind of thing all the time."

But real or not, truth or braggadocio, for Shirley, it was all very painful. The pattern of accusation and denial that had been set in Syracuse years before continued; she was aware of Stanley's reputation, and having no specifics on which to base her fears did not make them any easier to bear. Jealousy rode her constantly, digging its spurs into her sides. Shirley accused, Stanley denied, and there the balance hung. She was not the sort of person who could cultivate a philosophical attitude toward such things. Helen Freeley could be amused, sardonically, by the student who refused to baby-sit for her "because I have a tutorial with Mr. Feeley tomorrow and I have to wash my hair." Shirley could not; she saw these girls as a threat—to her home, her marriage, her survival—and she hated them with a passion. Even when she wrote about being a faculty wife, sitting at her typewriter, the one place she was completely at ease, at the throttle, controlling the world the way she wanted, even then her humor was cut through with acid. It was not, and never would be, a laughing matter.

Her jealousy did not stop with students; it could still spill out at any time, especially with women she did not know well enough to trust. When Walter Bernstein visited in 1953, bringing a young, attractive companion, Shirley's hackles went up at once. "She seemed very threatened," he said. "It culminated when she was in the kitchen, preparing dinner. She had baked a pie and was taking it out of the oven when it slipped and spilled all over. She turned on this woman and accused her of pushing her! I tried to kid her out of it, but she didn't want to be kidded out of it. She turned very sullen; Stanley had to try to pacify her. It was very uncomfortable. My friend just said later, 'What was the matter with her?'

"She was very jealous of other women, because of Stanley—she didn't want to compete with them."

One of Stanley's students in the early fifties, Uli Beigel, remembers attending student gatherings at the Hymans', presided over by a jovial Stanley and a patently unjovial Shirley. "They used to have students over every few weeks for little get-togethers. I had the feeling he enjoyed it and she didn't.

"She used to drink a lot and be extremely sarcastic. Sarcasm was her big thing. They used to fight a lot at these parties. She didn't like his immense interest in all these girls. She would get drunk or he would get drunk. I didn't know too much of what was going on—they were adults, we were kids—but I think it had to do with her being in a foul mood because he insisted on having these idiotic gatherings. It was almost as if he was trying to run a salon."

Savages had just come out, and Beigel, who wanted to be a writer, was impressed with Shirley's talent, her status as a famous author, but was wary of her in person. "I was very aware of her hostility. My memory is of her making faces at whatever Stanley said, staring into the fire while everyone else was talking and laughing, telling Stanley to shut up and leave her alone. She'd drink a lot and not respond to anyone talking to her. Or she would say something suddenly, drop these pearls of wisdom, and then turn away."

Later, when Beigel had graduated and moved back to New York, Stanley and Shirley helped her publish her first book, a collection of short stories, using Shirley's agent, Brandt & Brandt; gratefully, she dedicated the book to them both. She was less grateful when Stanley took her out to dinner on one of his trips to the city and made a pass.

"I knew it was going to happen; other people had told me. He didn't sleep with students, he waited until they graduated, and then immediately made passes at them." She declined, which he accepted with a fair show of grace. "It wasn't unfriendly, but it wasn't friendly either."

Yet she felt relaxed enough to go up to Bennington with her boyfriend, not long after, and stay with the Hymans. "It's amazing what you can do when you're young and attractive and think the world loves you," she said, sighing. At the time, she considered Shirley, in her thirties, to be long past her prime. "I thought it was too late for anybody that age. She was very heavy, and her hair was stringy and dirty. But you could see she had a pretty face. He didn't look attractive, but he looked better than she did—roly-poly, losing his hair."

Other students, too, took a dim view of Shirley, who was never at her best, seen from the faculty-wife perspective. "She was fat, she drank, she was a hash-slinger," said another former student of Stanley's, Elena Delbanco, dismissively. As reluctant hostess at Stanley's student soirées, Shirley had seemed to her to be mulish, removed, at times downright hostile. Stanley, on the other hand, was "the most popular teacher ever."

"He loved lusty girls, spacy girls. He always hand-picked his counselees [every student at Bennington was appointed to a faculty adviser]. And they were always the blonde girls, wacky, voluptuous. This was a school where girls were called Aza—and he always managed to get the Debbies and Muffys. Counseling sessions were for his own amusement."

"It was all fantasy—he couldn't even drive!" In fact, Shirley chauffeured him daily, dropping him off in the morning and picking him up later in the day. The suspicions, the occasional extramarital forays had not eroded the deep basic strength of the marriage, which continued to flourish. After all, this was a side of Stanley that had been there all along, part of the package from the start. It did not affect—and Shirley knew this—his loyalty, his commitment, his immense pride in her, now greater than ever. "My earnings pay the bar bill and that's it," he told Frank, and it was not a complaint.

In its nineteenth year the relationship was as intense as ever, and as mutually important. "Symbiotic," Walter Bernstein called it. "I suppose all good relationships are." He was still her mentor, her teacher, "the only critic I trust"; she was still the most unusual finding in all his collections. "Your mother was the one who taught me that a woman could have a brain," he told his children grandly. To them, the parents presented a united front, which never wavered.

Yet there were faculty members too—the ones who knew her slightly, who saw her only at the larger college bashes—who had much the same view of Shirley as many of Stanley's students.

"I wasn't part of the Hymans' inner circle," said Ben Belitt. "And there was an inner circle, very inner, partial to late hours, hard drinking, carousal. I was usually there at large parties given for speakers, parties where the whole literature division was invited." Shirley at these occasions "did this kind of bourgeois thing of being a faculty wife, unobtrusive; loading tables, staying in the kitchen, cooking, using the kitchen as a kind of refuge. When she finally did appear, late in the evening, she usually had a glass in her hand and was pretty well along."

She rarely joined in the conversation at those times and seemed to have a low tolerance for the sort of intense intellectual exchange so prized by faculty members, particularly those in the literature division. Now and then she would "slam out her views—this writer was good, that one was bad. Just quick, intuitive judgments, without any kind of discussion." She struck Belitt as energetic, restless and more than a little impatient with the academic atmosphere.

"Generally it was assumed that Stanley was the great man, the distinguished member of the household. That was the sense of it, in Bennington. He was the event, he was the mind.

"And yet somehow this wife we caught glimpses of was writing—to our surprise, increasingly internationally successful novels. And she was good. She was no Dinesen. But she was damn good. And for one story at least, she was as good as Borges."

The Shirley who could be sullen, biting, removed and hostile was a woman close friends saw rarely, if ever. The person they knew was warm, generous, full of life and humor; someone who took immense pleasure in her daily life, her children, her marriage, her competence. June was dazzled at how easily she seemed to handle everything, zipping through chores, corralling the kids, and of course, waiting on Stanley constantly. June herself, she confessed to Shirley, had a hard time even mastering the art of washing silverware—whenever she held a spoon under the faucet, it spurted water in her eye. For God's sake, said Shirley, pulling June over to the sink to demonstrate, the idea was to turn the spoon over. See?

Her housekeeping might be cursory, or worse, but her concern for her kids went deep. "She was very warm, very outgoing—she reached out, embraced them, she was very demonstrative, very affectionate, totally involved in terms of stories and talking and wanting to know what they were like," said June. "A great mother. Ideal, marvelous. Even strong enough that Stanley was pulled into being a father."

She was the core, the heart of the family, the one who held it together and made it work. And she was as proud of that as she was of her writing—this too was creativity, a way of forming your own world.

Her children's imagination fascinated her; she encouraged it, nurtured it, rejoiced in it. Joanne's imaginary adopted daughters were important, as were Laurence's occasional tall tales—much more worthy of attention than waxed floors or fresh laundry. But Sally was the one—Sally with the strange private world that only she could visit, which she would occasionally describe to them. "I saw her sometimes as wandering perpetually in a misty odd world, where familiar shapes merged and changed as she passed . . . a form-fitting fairyland," Shirley wrote.

She wanted them to be bold and avidly encouraged their fearlessness. Standing on the porch when a lightning storm hit, her hair blowing back from her face, Shirley would howl back at the thunder, urging her children to do the same. Yet they knew, too, that she herself had unusual fears. Moving a toaster from one counter to another, she would lift it up gingerly, holding the cord high above her head, so any stray electricity would be kept as far away from her body as possible. If it struck them as odd, they knew, too, even from an early age, that the odd was often more highly prized than the common in their family.

"She had boundless energy," Frank Orenstein recalled. "I can remember when I'd visit, I'd be in a chair slumped and exhausted and she'd be rolling over the floor with a couple of kids, with the dog getting in the act—an outsize dog to match the outsize house—and the cats trying to stay out of it. And then she'd get up and go make dinner, jauntily. That's how she always walked, with a spring.

"She did everything. She was a hearty-meal cooker—macaroni and cheese, roasts, chicken. Plain food. I thought it was great.

"Despite this wild place and the constant streams of people and alcohol—much too much—it was never alcoholic. When it looked as if it was getting out of hand, they laid down the firm rule: nothing before five—and that was it, it stayed that way for years. So there was discipline in the chaos."

Arthur and Bunny Hyman came up often, with their son, Scott, born a few months before Barry. The minute they walked into the house, Stanley would hand each of them a bottle. Years later, Bunny had a hard time remembering whether or not Shirley was a good cook: "I think she was marvelous, but by the time you got to the meal, with all the drinking, who knew?"

But there were always plenty of activities involving the kids, too—picnics, baseball games, taffy pulls, swimming trips to the local pond. Sally, already at five the boldest, was constantly trying riskier feats. It scared Bunny, but Shirley seemed to take it in stride. "I finally realized, nothing's going to drown this kid," Bunny said. In the morning, after breakfast, Shirley and Bunny sat over coffee, talking for hours, just girl talk, never about Shirley's work. Her work was private. When she left her typewriter and came out of the study, she left it behind completely, Bunny felt.

To close friends and family, she and Stanley seemed almost perfectly attuned to each other. "It was a kooky relationship—but it worked," said Arthur. At parties Helen Feeley used to watch them in awe. They could tell stories together, do comic bits so perfectly timed you felt as if you were watching a professional vaudeville act. At home, too, they seemed to complement each other with almost eerie precision. Of course, Stanley had long ago divided up responsibilities into his and hers, even if it may have seemed to others that her department—all cooking, shopping, chauffeuring, cleaning, child and pet care—was ludicrously over-weighted.

Bunny was visiting the day Shirley discovered that Laurie had suddenly broken out in spots—she grabbed him and shrieked for Stanley. He emerged from his study, glanced at his son briefly, gave her a stern, meaningful look, and promptly went back to his work. Childhood diseases were her business. After a moment, Shirley called the doctor. It's hard, of course, to believe she didn't feel a deep satisfaction when she found out that Laurie had chicken pox and that everyone in the house, including Stanley, would have to be quarantined at once.

On the other hand, Stanley was available for help in certain situations. One time, eating a salad of home-grown lettuce at the Brockways', Shirley dropped her fork and shrieked imperiously for Stanley—she had discovered a spider nested in the leaves. After a brief discussion, Stanley removed her plate and took it out to the kitchen. Spiders, apparently, were his domain.

"Stanley lived in his own world," said his brother. "The house is the woman's responsibility. If the furnace went out, he'd do something. But no kids, no house, no dogs, no cats—that was someone else's responsibility."

"And Shirley never answered back," said Bunny. "Traditionally, at least in the Jewish home, you answer back. But my mother-in-law never answered back either. Shirley adored Stanley, absolutely adored him."

She may not have answered back, but Shirley had her own methods of dealing with Stanley. "He was the czar, but she was the real ruler," said Frank Orenstein. "It was her house, her rule." Generally, wry humor worked best. "Stanley was probably smarter than anybody, but he didn't have this quick wit—and I think that was part of what evened up the balance.

"She wasn't really submissive, even though she waited on Stanley hand and foot and he never lifted a dish." One scene in particular underscored this seeming paradox in Frank's mind. The house on Main Street was filled with cats, more than ever before, at least ten, often more. And all the cats were Shirley's. Stanley would have been glad to do without any; he hated them. From time to time Stanley would deliver pronouncements on the cat situation. "The cats must go," he would announce, loudly and decisively, usually after he had found one clawing through his favorite leather chair. "This house will have no more than two cats."

Once, immediately after he had said this, the clock on the wall struck the hour, emitting a sharp, clear series of cuckoos. With perfect timing, Shirley waited a second, then turned to her husband. "How about nine?" she drawled.

"So she wasn't submissive, not really," Frank said.

Only one time did Stanley seem so infuriated about the cats that Shirley actually got nervous. Arthur and Bunny were visiting, and everyone had just sat down at the table for dinner, when suddenly Stanley went pale. "Shirley!" he bellowed. "*The cat has just peed on my leg.* By noon tomorrow the cats must go."

"When Stanley spoke in that tone of voice, the rafters shook," said Bunny. "I nearly spit up, trying not to laugh, but Shirley was really upset. Later she said to me, 'What am I going to do, he really means it.' She'd really taken it seriously. And I said, 'Forget it. Forget all about it.' And she did, and nothing ever happened—his pants dried, he forgot about the whole thing. But she really agonized about that, she couldn't live without her cats."

She spent time with them, talking in a low voice no one else could hear, and every night she called them for supper, singing out either "Cats-cats-cats-cats-cats," or a chanted combination of their names—"Faun mal*kin* applegate harlequin *blue,*" clapping her hands and pitching her voice to a weird tone that instantly flushed out every cat in the area, resident and stranger alike. She was not about to give them up, even if it meant a certain amount of subterfuge—like making sure they were all one color so Stanley wouldn't know how many there were and feeding them when he was out of the room. Cats were truly important to Shirley, and with the truly important things, she usually managed to have her way.

CHAPTER
·16·

Since the Hymans' return from Westport, some of the North Bennington locals were at least a bit more approachable than before. "It was because they came back," said Dr. Oliver Durand, who became their family doctor. "We gave them a bad time, but they came back. People were more receptive, much, much more." The Hymans had passed their first test. Several of the people Shirley dealt with in town every day—like the Powerses, the grocery-store owners, and the Perceys, who owned the news store—began to move toward a kind of acceptance.

To a large number of villagers, however, the Hymans were different, and not acceptable at all. And more than a little of this grew out of Stanley's stand against religion.

"We were the town atheists," said Sally. "Everyone in my class went to church from childhood through high school. We were raised to atheism. My father was a rabid atheist." Often on Sunday morning Stanley would take his children on a long walk through town, being careful to pass by churches so the pious could get a glimpse through the stained-glass windows of the godless Hymans en masse (except, of course, Shirley, who would have died before accompanying them). With his beard, cape, and sword-cane, leading his minions, he presented an unforgettable tableau—certainly the village had never seen anything like it. The kids loved the walks—Stanley was a born teacher, who knew how to make even architectural history lively and memorable—but when they passed by churches, they would cringe in unison.

Stanley was a dedicated atheist. There would be no God in his house, by God. His personal deity, if any, was Freud, and he enjoyed aping a certain number of the master's traits and habits—the beard, the curio cabinet, even at times, with students, a faintly European manner. As usual, Shirley went along with his pronouncement—God was hardly as important to her as her cats were—yet it was Stanley's disbelief, not her own. Both her daughters at different times were able to worm out of her the shy admission that, yes, she thought perhaps there might be, well, something out there. Sally, who was always trying to rout out the truth about her parents (even to the point of going through their garbage occasionally), was thrilled—"I just clutched it to myself like a hot little secret for days." But Joanne just felt bad. Imagine actually believing, and having to listen to Stanley scoff at that belief every day of your life!

But to the village at large they were the godless Hymans. "The town scuttlebutt was that we had a statue of Jesus with a beer can on his head in our front hall," said Sally. "In fact, it was a naked lady from Greece holding a lamp, a classical statue at the bottom of the bannister. But the kids would look in the front door and then run away—you know, Let's go look at the atheists."

And that was not all that set them apart. " 'The Lottery' painted North Bennington to the world as a bunch of savages, and a lot of people didn't like that," said Barry Hyman. "They were only dimly aware of it, but they still didn't like it. They hadn't read it, but they knew the reputation. It was, 'That Shirley Jackson's a witch, married that Jew from New York. That nigger comes visit them once in a while, he teaches at the Commie place up the hill, where the girls are.' That sort of thing.

"My parents were among the first to move down the hill, and they dealt with a lot of prejudice."

"We were always perceived as outsiders," said Laurence, looking back. "Particularly because we were all the combinations of strange things. From the city, my father was Jewish, my mother wrote strange books. Their friends came up from New York, even Negroes, for God's sake. These were people who had never even seen a Negro, and my parents would be driving around with Ralph Ellison—people would say taunting things. There were no black people in Vermont, and damn few Jewish people."

Ellison remembers at least one visit when he had a moment's queasiness himself. "There was a party going on, and I was asked to drive some of the students to get Italian food. We drove to a place, and there were a lot of young Vermonters around the bar. One of the girls—it was Miriam Marx, Groucho's daughter—was trying to rile them, acting overly friendly to me. I wanted to kick her butt. I thought I was going to have to fight my way out. It was potential dynamite—I was the only Negro in the place, with three or four of these little Bennington gals." Wisely, Ellison led the students into another room, away from the bar crowd, to wait for the order; peace was maintained.

The college, of course, was a very different environment—enlightened, intellectual, avowedly colorblind (though there were few black faces on campus). "But North Bennington was a much more primitive place," said Laurence. "Very primitive, a somewhat ingrown and inbred community, very low intelligence, very low education. A small-minded, little people. There was almost no crossover between the college and the community. The college was considered very suspect by the local community. They thought there were a lot of Communists, that any college that would devote itself to teaching women had to be weird anyway. It's an old Vermont saying: What do women need from college?

"My parents were among the few who wanted to live in town—they were idealistic and believed they could win out in this difficult situation."

Stanley and Shirley had set themselves quite a challenge, however, one that would perhaps have been ultimately unwinnable even in the best of circumstances. Pleasant as some aspects of life in North Bennington were— "a Huck Finn kind of life," Laurence called it—a number of nasty incidents occurred over the years.

For months a little old lady walked carefully past the Hyman house once a week in order to dump her trash in their hedge. "A local lady who thought my mother was a witch," said Barry. "She would bring her two paper bags of garbage. You'd see her walking along, and then she'd come up at the other end of the hedge with no garbage. It would take days to get it out, we could never get it all out. We never caught her."

At times there was hate mail. "Shirley used to get letters from people in the town: 'Why don't you stop writing this witch stuff and go away, you Jew,' " said Sally.

Then there were the neighborhood boys who soaped swastikas on the Hymans' windows or climbed up on a shed near the house to yell anti-Semitic curses. "We got the whole treatment," said Laurence. " 'Jews, go away.' They'd heard it from their parents." Until finally Stanley took after them with an air rifle. "He took particular joy not in hitting them but in scaring the hell out of them. Which he did do."

As a youngster, Barry was attacked on the playground more than once by rowdies yelling anti-Semitic epithets. "I'd think, What do you mean, a Jew? Do you mean my Jewish grandfather?" he said. Sally, who was fiercely protective and never shrank from a fight, often did battle for him.

"I was never taunted and harassed that I can remember," said Laurence. "But Barry was always running from greasers, the local townies. To this day he carries a stick in his car."

Inevitably, it was Shirley, much more than Stanley, who had to deal directly with the town's prejudice. She was the one who did the errands, the shopping, the carpooling and made the PTA appearances. The town rarely saw Stanley; he was insulated by the college. Shirley was, as Laurence says, "the representative of the family, the eyes, the ears, the mobility." And it was she who was most sensitive to the townspeople's opinion.

Outright incidents were not that common, of course. "It wasn't a war zone, it wasn't Nazi Germany. They were always treated respectfully to their faces," said Laurence. "Of course, you're always vaguely aware. My mother would walk into the post office and all conversation would stop." Even with the shop owners she knew best "it could be a double-edged kind of thing. They would be polite to you and even like you—but the minute you were out of the store, they might say something. It was like the South in a way, this old-boy bench full of people sitting there, with nothing better to do than collect stories about those strange people who live in that big house on the hill."

And yet, there were still qualities about the basic character of the village that Shirley truly admired—and continued to admire. "She liked New England, she liked Yankee humor," Barry insisted. "There was an element of her that enjoyed the banter of the grocery store; she knew if she adopted a certain tone she could stand there and talk about the weather with these old codgers. And the fact that they'll sit there and talk to you about the corn is sort of an acceptance.

"There was a certain timelessness in Vermont Yankee farmers she really admired. The fact that they'd seen many seasons and many lotteries come and go, and things were still pretty much the same. Solidity in the face of—all the crap."

And there was something else innate to the region that she envied and wanted for herself—a true understanding of and respect for privacy. "In New England Yankee tradition, every little city-state is independent. Every clan has its plot of land and that's the border. You don't ask questions. You might meet them in town on market day, but you don't really ask questions about what goes on in their land, their house, their clan," said Barry. "That's sort of why she wanted to live there.

"She figured she could be anonymous and just write and be happy and sit out back in the sun with the dogs and the cats."

But the problem was that neither Shirley nor Stanley was capable of looking anonymous, not for a minute. Stanley had the cape, the cane, the beard, and an unmistakable Brooklyn accent; Shirley by now weighed over 200 pounds and liked to drape herself in large flowing gowns of red and purple. "She would think she was perfectly inconspicuous when she was dressed like a perfect clown," said Barry. "They didn't really try to fit in. They tried to advertise what they were and still be invisible. You can't do that."

But Shirley's difficulties with the townspeople went deeper than that. The real problem was that she didn't truly want to be accepted as equal at all—she wanted to be accepted as superior. A lady of noble birth who descended daily to move among the commoners in a dignified manner, making pleasant conversation, then returned to her grand house on the hill in a cloud of glory. Better yet, a queen. Shirley enjoyed envisioning herself that way; as a young girl, Sally often inscribed her artistic offerings "To our Mommy the Queen."

"She had all those European aristocratic class things that were supposedly washed out by the twentieth century but weren't really washed out at all," said Barry.

The fact that she regarded the townspeople as peasants, for the most part, and held them in contempt made their rejection of her even harder to bear—and probably went a ways toward fueling it, as well. They were locked in a struggle for dominance, she and the village, a struggle not unlike that between two strong, stubborn individuals; each was determined to bend the other to his will. Eventually the balance had to tip one way or the other; that much was clear.

But in early 1954 Shirley was feeling both balanced and buoyant. "I think this has been the best year we've ever known," she wrote her parents. "I think it's the house that makes it so wonderful, actually, because we've never had a place of our own before, and never lived anywhere we liked so well."

She was aware of the townspeople's opinion of them—Shirley was never not aware of what people thought—but she was capable, at least for the moment, of taking the good with the bad. After all, Shirley was no stranger to the practice of holding two or more opposing views in her head at the same time. She had always been comfortable with duality; perhaps in a way she even preferred it. Only a few months before, in fact, she had written a story which was almost a parable of duality.

"One Ordinary Day With Peanuts" was later to become one of her most famous and most anthologized tales, though it languished for several months unsold and was finally bought by *Fantasy and Science Fiction* for an amount roughly equivalent to the last word in the title—fifty-four dollars. The chief character, Mr. Johnson, spends a day wandering around the city doing various good deeds: he baby-sits for a small child, arranges a date between a boy and girl, helps a man find an apartment. Tired, he goes home to his wife, "a comfortable woman," who tells him about her day. Nothing out of the ordinary: she sent several dogs to the pound, brought a waitress to tears, and managed to get a bus conductor fired. Casually, they decide they will switch off the following day.

The story would eventually be chosen for *The Best American Short Stories, 1956* (the same way her earlier story, "The Summer People," was first ignored, then honored). Years later her younger son would use it as a litmus test for prospective girlfriends. "I would meet some girl, make her read that, and see if she understood it, see if she was smart enough," he said. "If you can understand contradiction, if you can understand the Zen of everyday life, then you've passed the first test."

Shirley, who had written it, understood it better than anyone. This was how she saw the world, and this was how she saw the town she lived in as well. North Bennington was the village of "The Lottery" and the village of *Life Among the Savages,* simultaneously, all in one. A kindly neighbor could be a stone-thrower, but a stone-thrower could also be a kindly neighbor.

"I've kind of learned what she knew," said Barry. "To take it and see the humor, the humor of the horror of the humor." Of course, it took a certain amount of detachment to maintain this view—and Shirley's detachment would not stay invincible forever.

But in 1954 what Shirley felt toward the town was more wry amusement than anything else. She had other things on her mind. She was winding up *The Bird's Nest* at breakneck speed, making her usual mad dash to the finish line—twenty pages one night, ten the following morning. "I read it to a literary seminar at the college and it scared them to death— I'm so pleased," she wrote her parents. The publishers were advertising it as a psychological horror story. "It's really more like *Moby Dick,* penetrating to the depth of the human heart, and whatnot," she explained airily. "But I bet you won't like it."

The new house delighted them, but that wasn't all the Hymans were happy about. Thanks to the popularity of *Savages,* for practically the first time in their lives they were solvent, and glorying in it, though of course the money was being plowed right back into the mainstream almost as fast as it came out, toward a new car, new dishwasher, new washing machine, and various other needed and not-so-needed sundries. Christmas had been a very merry one, even by Hyman standards—new Erector Sets, dolls, stilts, Pogo sticks, toy steamrollers, coins, books, paintings, jewelry all around.

And why not? It looked as if the golden eggs were going to keep on coming. The completion of *The Bird's Nest* meant more money, and maybe even movie rights; and Shirley's agent, Bernice Baumgarten, always on the lookout for the next project, had already lined up another contract, this one for a children's book on the Salem witchcraft trials, for the Random House Landmark series. Professionally and financially, Shirley was flying high. In fact, the only cloud on the horizon was the arrangement she had made several years before with *Good Housekeeping*.

At the time, it *had* enabled the Hymans to secure the house they wanted in Westport; she had signed the contract gaily. Rather quickly, though, it had turned into an albatross. Without thinking much about it, Shirley took it to mean that the magazine would give her a retainer in return for first look at her stories. *Good Housekeeping* was not buying this interpretation; within a year they had begun to press for payment, pointing to the fine print.

Now editor Herbert Mayes had gotten into the act, taking it on as a personal pet cause, and was making louder and louder noises. He refused to let her use her stories to discharge her debt; in fact, he had formed a positive distaste for them. The way he saw it, the magazine had given her a fat sum of money, and he wanted it back. Now. Cash in full. What's more, he was threatening legal action.

Shirley had initially switched to Bernice because of the *Good Housekeeping* fiasco, but Bernice was having a hard time holding Mayes in check. When Shirley suggested that she write to him herself, Bernice was wary. "I think Mr. Mayes is beyond being placated by a nice note," she said. "I think he's determined to get his money back."

But Shirley knew she was capable of something a lot more powerful than just a nice note. In a short time, using all her verbal wiles, she conjured up a lengthy, heavily persuasive plea. She was, she assured him fulsomely, "deeply and constantly aware of my debt to your organization and have not for a minute felt that anything less than full repayment was required," although she admitted she had been hoping to pay him back in stories.

"Nothing would make me happier than to be able to pay this obligation in full," she assured him; his assumption that she was indifferent and his subsequent decision to take legal action were "extremely disturbing . . . unkind." The fault, she hastened to add, lay entirely with her old agent, who was "responsible for the whole thing . . . but I have no idea of where she is or what she is doing." Mr. Mayes, on the other hand, had been "most generous and patient." She knew he had done her "an extraordinarily great favor [which] required any return in my power." Not, of course, a lump-sum return, but perhaps a few stories and an occasional payment.

When Shirley turned the combined force of both her personality and her talent on someone, the result could be devastating. Even Bernice, who rarely gushed, was awed: "Your letter to Mr. Mayes was really wonderful," she told Shirley. As an additional sop, she said she would send Mayes a check from the agency, saying she had deducted it from Shirley's last payment, as she had requested (she hadn't, of course). The two-pronged effort paid off; Mayes backed down, although he continued to refuse to print Shirley's stories. It wasn't until after his retirement, in 1958, that *Good Housekeeping* once again became a market for her.

Mayes was not the first to become the target of a verbal onslaught from Shirley, nor would he be the last. Shirley knew she possessed powerful and effective weaponry and did not hesitate to use it; throughout her life she called on it whenever she felt the need to persuade, convince, blister, and on occasion skewer various officials, creditors, publishers, and lesser lights who had somehow managed to get in her way. The letter to Mayes was persuasive, with just the right air of aggrieved gentlewomanhood—the sort of letter Jane Austen, perhaps, might have written in a similar unhappy circumstance. But with others—creditors, for instance—Shirley could singe the page:

"I have received the enclosed surprising pink slip and I am returning it at once to enable you to correct your books and make your apologies without delay," she wrote crisply to one. "I have considerable reputation as a writer, and a thoroughly respectable credit standing. If your foolish mistakes have done anything whatsoever to damage my position in either area I shall not hesitate to take legal action."

To an acquaintance who had interrupted her work, by dropping by unannounced, she smashed out a letter that was as close to a nuclear device as a letter could be: "I am afraid that I must ask that in future you telephone us before stopping off at our house, so that we can avoid further interruptions of our working days. I regard the six hours you spent with us yesterday as a wholly unreasonable intrusion, and I would prefer not to have it happen again. Our house is not a hotel, a public telephone booth or a country club, and I resent having it treated as such. I suggest that if you cannot find anyone in Bennington with time as free as your own, you make your local headquarters in some professional establishment better equipped to cater to transients."

She felt more at ease doing this sort of thing behind the typewriter, but she could do it in person too, when the need arose. Bunny was visiting one Christmas when Shirley took on a department store, and won hands down. It was a side of her sister-in-law Bunny had never seen before.

"She had ordered something for Sally from Gimbels, and it didn't come. She got on the phone, the day before Christmas, putting on a haughty voice—'I don't want to talk to an assistant, I don't want to talk to a manager. Put me through to Mr. Gimbel.' Then, 'I've been a customer of your store for years'—owed them a considerable balance too. 'If you ever want me to pay my bill, you'd better get that up here and not ruin my child's Christmas.' "

Bunny was floored. "It was another Shirley. She was never assertive. Whatever Stanley said, she shook. We used to think, What kind of dope is she? She's the one making the money, and so brilliant, and she's saying, 'Yes, Stanley,' and shivering over everything he said—which he enjoyed tremendously, he was king of the hill there.

"And here all of a sudden this different Shirley came out of a box and was talking to Gimbels. And they actually sent a messenger. This little man arrived at the door with a rocking horse late that night. Unbelievable."

It was a lesson Bunny never forgot. "I knew how to deal with department stores after that. Even today, Arthur will say, 'Put on your Shirley voice.' And it works. Believe me, it works."

It is quite a knack, the ability to unleash a force that will bend others to your will, and Shirley relished it. In a way, it was not all that far removed from witchcraft.

For witchcraft, too, continued to be important to Shirley. She had a collection of more than five hundred books devoted to the subject by now, some of them hundreds of years old, plus a considerable array of objects—charms, amulets, even a human skull. She continued to dabble in Tarot readings and made two appearances at college carnivals in the early fifties as a fortune-teller, a turban wound around her head; on occasion she still made matchstick voodoo dolls of people who had offended her, or manufactured good-luck spells for specific events—a friend's marriage, for instance.

But it was the powers of the mind that fascinated her the most. Once when Howard Nemerov was criticizing an unpublished piece of Stanley's, Shirley ordered him out of the house. He was hexing it, she said, and Stanley would never be able to sell it. She was completely serious, and Nemerov left a little uneasily.

She shared her interest with her children in different ways. She taught Joanne to turn pillows on guest beds to be facing, so that the couple would dream of each other. With Barry, she tried the ESP cards developed at Duke University. Sally, however, was the most interested of all her children.

"Did Shirley do magic with Sarah?" Joanne asked rhetorically. "I just don't know. She told me, 'Don't let me find you messing with this—because you don't know what you're doing.' It was said with enough impact. She knew I knew the difference between playing with Ouija and trying to find serious stuff, and she told me not to. I'm sure she told Sarah too, but that would have probably started her. That's our nature."

Even as a young child, Sally was drawn to magic, occasionally trying spells. Bunny Hyman was convinced—only half humorously—that she was a witch. "She stopped the elevator in our apartment building in Brooklyn in mid-flight, she hexed the refrigerator so it went on the blink," she said. "She made a ring for me and wanted to put a spell on it before she put it on my finger—and I wouldn't let her."

Today, Sally is silent on the subject of her own forays, and a bit cynical about her mother's. "She wanted very much to find provable magic," she said. "And I think by the time I met her she'd gotten to the kind of point where she pretended she already had, and she wouldn't talk about it, because her mystique would be blown. We'd say, 'Mommy, is magic real?' And she'd say, 'Of course.' And if we bugged her enough, she'd say, 'Why don't you take out the garbage?' "

The human skull in Shirley's collection of magic objects fascinated Sally. "I'd say, 'Whose skull is that?' And she'd say, 'Mine, it's my skull.' And I'd creep up behind her and feel her head to see if it was soft. I'd say, 'Come on, Mommy, it's not your skull.' But she'd never admit it when I was little."

There was a playful, sunny aspect to Shirley's interest. The one trick Joanne remembered best had to do not with dark spells but with kitchenware. All the small kitchen tools—the peelers, can openers, knives, and so on—were crammed into one drawer on top of each other. Whenever Shirley wanted one, she would slam the drawer hard, call out the name of the tool, and open the drawer. The desired implement would always be on top.

Perhaps the real truth was that magic, to Shirley, was not an arcane, exotic pursuit at all, despite her collection of learned books on the subject. It was something she had domesticated, reinterpreted, and integrated into her home; it was part of her very nature.

"What should I do with this dime?" Laurence asked her one day when he was around nine.

"Oh, why don't you give it to the old oak tree out back and ask it for ten cents' worth of wind," Shirley said casually.

In a few minutes he returned, mission accomplished. It was the sort of idea any child would have responded to, the kind of imaginative suggestion Shirley often made. Yet neither of them was surprised, an hour later, when a storm hit.

"She would allude to witchcraft," said Harriet Fels, wife of Bill Fels, who became president of Bennington in 1957. "She acted as if she believed in it on the one hand, but it was a game on the other hand. She wasn't above sticking pins in dolls, it was a real thing—but she treated it in conversation as a game."

Shirley enjoyed her reputation as a witch. "She liked to hoodwink stupid people on a superficial level," said Barry. "At the same time, she didn't just believe, she knew there were other things going on."

Her Tarot readings were reputed to be amazingly accurate. One Bennington student—so a popular story went—was shocked when Shirley told her that her mother was about to die. At the time, so far as she knew, her mother was completely healthy. A week later, she was dead. Whether the tale was apocryphal or not, Helen Feeley was not the only one of Shirley's friends who refused to let her tell her fortune. Not necessarily because she thought that it would be fake, either; but because she felt, a bit nervously, that it might not be.

Once Sally and a friend sat at the dining room table watching Shirley study the cards. "How did you learn to read Tarot?" they asked her.

Shirley hesitated. "You won't believe me," she said.

"Yes, we will," they insisted.

She looked up at them, her pale eyes unfathomable. "I was born knowing," she said.

Eventually, Barry feels sure, Shirley's magic went beyond the crystal-ball stage. "She realized that the only tools the magician needs are in the head. You make the world, you decide what your name is, your role, decide what people are going to think of you by your own force of will. And that's real magic in the real world." Again, not unlike writing itself.

CHAPTER
·17·

The Bird's Nest, once again a work dedicated to Stanley, came out in June 1954 to nearly unanimous praise. "Once more Shirley Jackson the housewife and mother has yielded to Shirley Jackson the literary necromancer who writes novels not much like any others since the form was invented," said Dan Wickenden in the *New York Herald Tribune Book Review.* He was quick to note that, this time around, Shirley had not ignored her comic sense, even in a serious novel. "The drama repeatedly turns into farcical comedy, and under the comedy lies pathos." The book as a whole was "superlative entertainment."

William Peden, in the *Saturday Review,* went even further: "Miss Jackson has done much more than produce just another perceptive clinical study of emotional deterioration," he wrote. "She has created a kind of twentieth-century morality play in which the familiar medieval conflict between good and evil has been replaced by the struggle for domination between Elizabeth, Beth, Betsy and Bess."

The sudden cessation of creative frenzy depleted her; Shirley's mood plunged downward. For many years she had worked steadily, one project overlapping another. But with *The Bird's Nest* she had focused all her energy in one direction. Reaching that finish line meant a sharp change in pressure. She reeled, unmoored, a woman without a subject. She spent most of the summer feeling "very tired and depressed," without "energy or spirit," she told her parents. A natural reaction, she quickly assured them, to her "wild writing schedule last winter." She had asked their family doctor, Dr. Durand, about it, and he said he thought her depression and tension were due to overwork, and that she should try to get more sleep. So she was hanging around the house, sleeping more than usual.

To make things worse, her oldest cat, Shax, had disappeared, a hard blow, even though a new kitten had turned up a few days later, as if in compensation.

She had also slipped and fallen on her elbow, bruising it badly, and was exercising it, she said, by lifting a glass to her mouth several times a day as fast as she could. But a bout of flu had kept her away from alcohol for a few weeks. Stanley, too, had stopped drinking briefly, in sympathy, and their friend Paul Feeley had been deeply shaken on dropping in one day around cocktail hour to find them both drinking tea at the kitchen table and Stanley apparently engrossed in knitting. Actually, he was untangling a string for Barry, but Paul, horrified at the cozy tableau, backed out the door.

Their old friend Ben Zimmerman was staying for a time in the back apartment of the house, with his wife and newborn baby girl, which provided some diversion. "We are all so grateful to Ben and Marge for providing the kids with a new toy," Shirley commented. A few jaunts to the Saratoga racetrack and lectures at writers' conferences took up the slack. By fall, Shirley was still feeling so aimless she even briefly considered working as a nursery aide at Barry's school. It might be nice to have "an honest job," she told her parents, a bit wistfully.

In the wake of *The Bird's Nest* publicity, Bernice was hard at work marketing every unsold story in Shirley's file, so the money was still flowing in, even with the hiatus. It was hard to get started again on any real writing, once she had stepped off the merry-go-round. She managed to grind out the Salem witchcraft book, somewhat halfheartedly; straight, unadorned history had never been her métier, even if the subject was witches.

Stanley might have been a devout Freudian, but when faced with an emotional problem in his own home his gut instincts were all behavior mod. He ordered dozens of new books for Shirley in an attempt to pique her interest and insisted she start singing lessons—anything to get her up and doing again. Meanwhile, Bernice kept pleading for her to send more stories; the time was ripe, she could sell just about anything Shirley wrote right now, she urged her.

Bit by bit, Shirley got back into harness. The kids were all busy, involved in projects—Laurence had taken up the trumpet, the girls were taking piano lessons; friends were in and out; meals were chaotic and boisterous; the demands on Shirley were constant and imperative. The Hyman household in 1955 was an environment capable of jump-starting almost anyone, particularly its chief engineer. Shirley came out of her funk.

A trip to New York early in the year helped too. Bernice had managed to wangle a movie deal for *The Bird's Nest* with producer Ray Stark, who was quite enthusiastic. "Nothing will give me more pleasure than to show all of these Hollywood dimwits how stupid they were to have passed this up," he wrote Shirley.

Unfortunately, the movie, *Lizzie,* would not come out until 1957, when it would be met head on by *The Three Faces of Eve,* another, much more skillful movie about a multiple personality. *Eve* starred Joanne Woodward in a stunning, Academy Award–winning performance and won high praise; *Lizzie* was almost completely overshadowed. The book *The Three Faces of Eve,* a nonfiction study of a case, did not come out until after the movie had been made, but the movie's vast popularity ensured that this would be the book people thought of when they thought of multiple personality, not Shirley's fictional work. Which meant nothing except for those, like Shirley, who appreciated irony.

The main reason behind the trip to New York was to attend the huge golden-wedding celebration for Stanley's aunt and uncle, Anna and Harry Hyman. Not Shirley's favorite sort of activity, being surrounded by wall-to-wall Hymans, but the kids behaved well and she managed to enjoy it, after a fashion. She and Stanley also took Laurence to a Golden Gloves fight, a much more enjoyable event.

The publication of *The Bird's Nest* meant a flurry of interview requests, all of which she was able to dodge; she had learned her lesson. "I have made it a rule—officially on file at my agents and my publishers—that I will involve myself in absolutely no personal publicity under any circumstances, which includes everything from interviews and photographs to that cute biographical information (she writes with a turkey feather dipped in rainwater) everyone is so crazy about. I just refer everyone to Who's Who in America, with great satisfaction," she wrote her parents. The book had also flushed out at least one crank—a woman who was positive Shirley had used her name for the chief character and kept writing to ask why. Bernice told her to ignore it.

The manuscript for the witchcraft book had been sent in—a straightforward, unadorned account, with an air of having been written on automatic pilot, definitely a lesser work. But Random House was pleased, although publication was being held until 1956. Bernice, realizing Shirley was unlikely to write a novel this year, was prodding her to start thinking ahead to another collection of family stories.

The movie sale of *The Bird's Nest* impressed the kids. "Everyone around here was very excited for about a day, and then of course lost interest when it turned out that there was no amazing amount of money involved and no one was going to have to fly to Hollywood and no movie stars were going to be hanging around upper Main Street in North Bennington," Shirley wrote her parents. The screenplay, which she had had no hand in whatsoever, sounded like "Ma and Pa Kettle, or Abbott and

Costello meet a multiple personality. The college psychologist, who lent me books and gave me much good advice for the book, says he is going to shoot himself."

Shirley may have been doing less work than usual, but the Hymans' social life was as vigorous as ever. Louis Scher, Stanley's chief book-finder, who was a sort of self-appointed honorary uncle, came up often, bearing gifts for all, including carloads of delicatessen food. Ralph Ellison visited often. Their Bennington friends—the Fosters, Brockways, Feeleys, Wohnuses, Burkes, Nemerov—were often at the house. "Two things they never ran out of—booze and friends," said Arthur Hyman. As always, the liquor consumption was prodigious, although Stanley's rule stayed fixed: no drinking until sundown. But confining it to certain hours did not seem to affect the amount downed. Shirley "could put away more in two hours than anyone I ever saw," marveled one friend.

"It was a wonderful time, it really was," said Helen Feeley. "I think what was so great about it was that the conversation was always fascinating. People talked about ideas. It was great to listen to. I can remember sitting on the couch and listening to Lionel, Paul, Howard, and Stanley go on till two or three in the morning. They were never stupid or boring. They had many faults, but they were never dull. Looking back, I realize it was sort of a rare life."

The poker games continued too, of course, a riotous weekly macho melee that the wives tolerated as well as they could. At one point the wives attempted to start a poker game of their own as well, but after a few games interest flagged and they gave it up. But the men's game flourished unabated, despite occasional fiery confrontations involving Stanley and his infamous, ever ready sword-cane.

The sums that crossed the table were often large enough to affect family budgets, too. "The excitement [of social life in Bennington] was always tempered by the harsh reality of having lost three hundred dollars the night before," Helen remembered a little grimly. "You would be seething with rage." One time she had made her children snowsuits, just to save money, spending thirty dollars on material; that night Paul lost thirty dollars playing poker. "I was so mad. But now I can sort of think, Gee, I wish I were there again."

Stanley and Shirley's New York friends, like Ellison and Scher, enjoyed the Bennington social circle. But at least one, June Mirken, was less than thrilled with it. "The whole scene at Bennington was so incestuous," she said. "You had the feeling everyone was either screwing everyone else or thinking about it or thinking about stopping or switching or whatever. There would be stag things, almost like the Rotary Club—a night out to play poker. A lot of that man stuff and woman stuff."

Shirley's daily schedule now included a nap between one and three, which she sorely needed. "I don't think she would have been able to function at all without it," said June. "After lunch, that was her nap time. She'd go upstairs and she'd sleep.

"She not only ran the damn house and did everything else and brought up her kids and waited on Stanley and then had dinner parties at night and on weekends, but she wrote. If she hadn't had that nap she probably would have physically fallen apart."

Bernice wanted the sequel to *Life Among the Savages* by early 1957, so Shirley was again concentrating on turning out family stories. Certainly there was no lack of copy. In the spring of 1955, Laurence joined the local Little League, giving Shirley and Stanley a whole new activity (and Shirley, naturally, another story). Shirley and Peg Wohnus, whose son Willie also played, formed an enthusiastic cheering section. Even Stanley was willing to leave his beloved study for the games. Larry Powers, son of the owner of Powers' Market, remembered Stanley exhorting Laurie loudly from the stands to "stick it in his ear!" "A little Brooklyn started coming out there," Powers remembered, chuckling.

The Little League was a cooperative effort between the town and the college, one of the few ever attempted, and certainly the most successful in anyone's memory. It was so successful, in fact, that Shirley was filled with optimism about the relationship between the two factions. Could baseball succeed where all else had failed? For a while, it looked that way. College contributions paid for half the field; both town and college offspring were represented on the team. Shirley was ecstatic:

"It's amazing how the whole town has reacted . . . as though they've been waiting for it. Everyone turns out for the games. It's done what nothing else so far has been able to do completely, which is finally break up the old feud between the college and the town. . . . We've been yelling for a long time about how the college people ought to come down off the hill and meet the townspeople." Some of the college people, she added, had even refused to let their kids play with townspeople—"but now they're all mixed up and it's wonderful."

So it was, briefly, although the warm glow of unity cast by Little League never spread very far beyond the field. Shirley did want her children to mingle with the local children, up to a point. Yet she wanted them to stay aware of their roots, of their superiority; to remain untainted, unchanged.

It was a difficult requirement to make of children. She and Stanley had purposely chosen to live outside of the college, in the diaspora—they wanted the fruits of assimilation with the town. But not, God forbid, assimilation itself. A hard trick to pull off, hard enough when the rules have been set for centuries, as in many Jewish households; almost impossible when the rules are being set on the spot, day by day, always inferred, never directly expressed. Over the years, it had a different effect on each of her children.

"Our parents raised us separate from the town we lived in," said Sally. "We were like the Vatican in Rome, but the other way around in some ways. We were kind of aliens in our hometown. We were disliked, each of us in our own way."

Sally was a fighter, adept at playground squabbles. Always aware of tensions, with an intuitive grasp like her mother's, she handled them in her own way, which was to challenge, to attempt to bring things to a head. "My father has a bar in the living room," she would announce brightly at school. Or worse, "My mother doesn't like Catholics," this to a class almost entirely filled with them. Not surprisingly, this would lead to a rapid escalation in tension throughout the whole village, as what Barry called "the latest Sally scandal" made the rounds. And once again, Shirley would try to explain how certain things should stay in the house, how you had to try to live with people even if it meant not being entirely honest—try, in other words, to explain what to someone like Sally was inexplicable.

Joanne was in many ways the most conventional. She had all of Shirley's basic yearnings to fit in, without any of her just as basic urge to be unique. Joanne did have local friends, friends whom Shirley would make jokes about, reducing them to parody, cruelly, hilariously, making Joanne laugh so hard her stomach hurt, yet at the same time filling her with a terrible hollow anguish: These are my friends, you're making me betray my friends, she would think, even while she laughed.

It was not until adolescence that Laurence began to comprehend their odd position in the town. He was active, a doer, a kid with a thousand projects going at once. "Jai [Joanne] and Barry were more the watchers, Laurence and I were more the doers," Sally said. Independent, off on his own, Laurence had an easier time escaping the yoke of Shirley's rules. And Barry in some ways benefited by being the last of four; he was an easygoing child anyway. It was the girls who were most affected by Shirley's requirements—just as, in her own family, Shirley had been the one most affected by Geraldine's.

The Hyman children were certainly not the only ones affected by the sharp split between town and college. Anna Fels, daughter of Bill and Harriet Fels, remembers it clearly: "You got the message as a child that you were different from everyone else in the town, which you were. You felt like a transient. There was that feeling of being different." Faculty children were exposed to classical music, to dance classes, to foreign films, to the entire cultural smorgasbord available at Bennington College. Inevitably, they developed an intellectual sophistication that widened the gap between them and the town children. Their world did not end at the village limits; it was open-ended.

Yet Anna Fels also feels it was worse for the Hymans. "They lived in town. All the other faculty kids lived on campus, in the Orchard. I think it was hard on them. They weren't part of the college crowd, and they certainly weren't part of the town crowd."

Partly as a protective device against the town's anti-intellectual atmosphere—but more, undoubtedly, because it came naturally to them, Shirley and Stanley turned their own house into a private glass bell, a place that in some ways resembled nothing so much as an intensive educational laboratory. The children were exposed, constantly and consciously, to reams of information—history, psychology, literature, folklore, criticism. "We've all been running on it for years," said Joanne dryly.

Dinners were often structured quite intentionally as ongoing seminars, where anything and everything might be brought up—English royalty, grammar, biology—and almost anything could be said, provided you had your facts straight.

"Most of what I learned in my childhood I learned from them at dinner," said Sally. "For a year or two they read the Bible, two chapters at night. Then for a year they wrote everything on the blackboard in Greek letters—we all knew the Greek alphabet. Whatever they read they shared with us. They shared intellectual things with us, though they kept their private lives very private.

"She [Shirley] loved the Tudors. She told stories. From childhood on, she told us stories. Her favorite areas of history would get opened up, mostly these romantic English eras."

"Anything could be discussed, if you had the balls to discuss it," said Barry. "You could make any kind of claim, bring up any kind of unmentionable thing, as long as you could back it up. You couldn't say 'shit' because you dropped something, but if you wanted to bring up the etymylogical background of the word 'shit' . . .

"Stanley was always having projects. Like reading the Bible at dinner. We'd all be scratching and twitching, wanting to get away. But it was interesting, because he could answer any question you had about it; he would stop at the slightest excuse and explain things in wonderfully lucid detail. So it came alive to some extent.

"And they were always bringing out Fowler or the big dictionary on wheels to discuss some word or other."

"Rarely have I been at tables with conversations as interesting as those," said Laurence. "My parents would really get going and insist that all the children participate in the discussion. My father was the dominant voice, but they had an interesting relationship: in many areas my mother had the dominant voice and he would willingly recede and take the backseat. They were big fans of each other."

When Shirley talked, she would gesture with whatever she was holding in her hand—a chicken leg, a cigarette, a cup of coffee. When Stanley had the floor—a common occurrence—she sat back, attentive, appreciative. No one had ever heard her throw even the faintest sort of critical, belittling comment in his direction. (When Sally was sixteen, she was absolutely floored when her mother confessed, late one night, "You know, sometimes I think your father is a little—weird." "Mom!" she burst out excitedly. "You noticed!") Yet often when she sat at the table, listening to him expound, there was a faint gleam of amusement in her eyes.

But it was not dry, it was not stuffy, ever, around the long table; both Stanley and Shirley liked to laugh too much for that. Some nights they held joke-telling contests. "Falling off your chair with laughter, rolling under the table, was acceptable behavior," said Barry. "Making a bad joke or saying something stupid, that was not. It was interesting, when I got older, to contrast my upbringing with that of other people, to realize how peculiar it was, what was permissible, what wasn't."

"Both of them were total suckers for anything slapstick. I remember big laughs—they knew they were the funniest people on earth. They'd get you laughing, let you breathe, then nail you again," said Joanne. Stanley was the raconteur, the storyteller—but Shirley was the one with the lightning flashes. One night at dinner she did an impression of a drunken goldfish that had everyone on the floor. Do it again, do it again, they begged, but she refused. Shirley hated to repeat herself.

She had a taste for inspired silliness. Once, at a cocktail party in a lawyer's house, a large tome caught her eye—*The Law of Cadavers,* by Jackson. "I can't stand that you don't have this autographed," she squealed; opening the book, she signed it at once.

There was a roguishness about her humor, too. Sitting in an airport bar with friends, she demanded suddenly that one of them "bring a plane in for me." When a plane appeared in the sky, she insisted he "talk it down."

As all children do, the younger Hymans spent a good deal of time sizing up their parents. The differences between them were striking. Both had strong, complex personalities, but Stanley was saner, more stable, less changeable. He had a mighty temper, which could make the rafters ring, he could be horrendously inflexible in many instances, but he was generally a cheerful, even jolly person who stayed on an even keel; there were no mood swings with him. He was the bedrock, the stabilizer they all depended on.

It was true that he managed to avoid most of the nitty-gritty duties of parenthood, the cooking, washing, carpooling, the school activities. But each child found a way to seek him out. Laurence realized very early that you had to wait till after nine, when Stanley was finished working. If you slipped into the study around then, he would be just about ready to put his papers aside, stretch out in his leather chair, and put on a blues record. He would be, in other words, available.

The fact that Stanley was almost always in his study when he wasn't at the college made him easy to find. Sally often did her homework in there, content just to sit near him, now and then throwing a question at him—Stanley could never ignore a request for intellectual enlightenment. Joanne would often take a book in to read, quietly. In this way, each one of them was able to make contact with their father.

They needed it. Not just because they needed a father; they needed him for balance. Stanley's strength, his logic, his rational, steady nature were the perfect antidote—perhaps the only antidote—to Shirley.

Shirley was many things to her children. She was warm, physically affectionate, playful, funny. Understanding, imaginative, magical, intuitive. She was deeply involved with them, the way Stanley could never be; in many ways a near perfect, archetypal mother. A mother who would read to them for hours, or tell wonderful stories about everything from history to kitchen appliances; a mother who kept a stack of hidden gifts in the house for each child, so she always had one on hand to present when she thought the occasion warranted it.

But of course, that was not the whole picture. She was also emotional and erratic, and this too spilled over into her parenting. Her moods and her anxieties colored the children's days; her demands, both surface and subterranean, often confused and upset them. No one could be more loving; no one could be meaner. She could applaud their fierceness, delight in their mischief on one day—and then sulk for hours over a similar episode two days later. "A champion sulker," Sally called her. What did Shirley want, what did she want? It was something her children did not always understand and, even when they did, were not always able to comply with.

"She got mad if I betrayed her in ways I didn't even understand," said Sally. "I'd be honor-bound to be good in some fashion, when we went somewhere or when my grandparents came, and later she'd say—she was a blackballer beyond belief—'I really thought I was dealing with good Sally here. I really thought I could trust you.' She could do more with one finger of guilt than I've been able to do with all my rationalizations with my children.

"It was my ambition in life to please my mother all day. Not to blow it. And I would sometimes go till after dinner. Usually I'd blow it at dinner by arguing, or asking her something that would make her mad."

One problem was that Shirley's rules often seemed as changeable as her moods, making obedience impossibly complicated. "She'd feed us sweets seven times a day," said Sally. "And then she'd bitch if we went in there during unauthorized hours. When she gave you a cookie it was everything love can be—but when she busted you stealing cookies an hour later, it was as if you had betrayed your mother."

Sally was the one most like her, so naturally Sally was the one who infuriated her the most. There was no question she could be difficult, with her wildness, her arguments, her maverick ways. Yet these were the very things that made Shirley identify so strongly with her. It was terribly confusing, and Sally, sent to bed for a misdemeanor, would often creep back down the stairs "just for the pleasure of listening to her be funny about the terrible crimes I'd committed during the day."

All the children were aware, well aware, of Shirley's emotional volatility. Sally said: "The game she played was: 'I'm terribly delicate emotionally. Don't do anything to shake up my shaky calm here, my shaky cool.'" At certain times, nearly anything—a dropped knife, a spilled glass—was enough to splinter her into near hysteria.

"I must have been six or seven when I had that thing about wanting to please her all day. And I finally told her, because I had made it to bedtime without once getting her angry. She came to my bed and I asked some question she didn't like and she got mad. I said, 'Mom, I've been trying so hard,' bursting into tears . . . and she was really sympathetic. She held me close, called me her little Sallicat, it was so nice.

"But I knew the next day I might see her watching me appraisingly. It was schizophrenic. She was the one you confided in, and the one who would later get you for it."

Shirley's moods hung over the house, filling every room. Coming home from school, her children could tell at once what sort of day it had been—the emotional atmosphere was palpable, like heavy smoke; the house exuded it. Often, her moods were linked to her work.

"If things were going well, there would be flowers on the table and little rolls, and she'd perk around serving peas, and she and Stanley would talk about what to do about chapter four," said Sally. But if things were going badly, in any way, "you'd come in the door and just feel danger.

"She formed my emotional moods all through childhood. She was the core of the house, the throbbing heart of it. By far. None of us kids could approach her in emotionality. She just radiated the stuff."

She reflected, somberly: "I know all my life I worried about her. When she was mad at me, I could be mad at her, but when somebody else picked on her—if my father yelled at her—it was like I wanted to kill him. We were all like that. It was—'Mom! Mom's in trouble! Let's go!'

"She was our baby."

Sally's relationship with her mother was in some ways the closest; she was the child who probably spent the most time trying to figure her out. But even from the perspective of many years, she is not at all sure she was ever able to do it.

"Her books were funny about stuff I didn't know she thought was funny—I thought she wanted to kill me at the time. When I heard her at parties, being funny about something I had done, I felt relief. But now I realize she was just trying to impress her husband's colleagues, and it wasn't the real her.

"The books weren't the real her. And the parties weren't the real her. Her letters to her parents sure weren't the real her. So . . . where's the real her at?"

Shirley liked to be in control. "She could radiate disapproval from five miles away," Joanne said. "To her, wicked and stupid were the same. And she'd let you know."

Joanne was aware, from a very young age, that "I was not the daughter she wanted. She and I were very unsympathetic, we were not close, ever. We didn't get along. I didn't suit her, she didn't suit me. I was too conventional. I didn't have that thing that would have been exciting for her to see—a certain fierce boldness. Laurence and Sarah were the obvious major favorites. We all knew Sarah was the one most like her.

"It's not that I was unhappy, just that I never felt any real connection. I don't remember that shining feeling."

And yet oddly, or maybe not so oddly, this very fact—that Joanne, like Shirley years before, was not the daughter her mother wanted—gave them a kind of bond. And there would come a time when Shirley would lean on her, in a way she was never able to do with her other children.

Joanne was aware of disappointing Shirley on another level as well. "I think she would have liked to have really beautiful little daughters," she said. "And very soon we grew into little big-nosed bitches. I think she probably got dumped a lot of Geraldine shit that she came from a beautiful line, and she was the Polack on this beautiful family tree. So she secretly wanted us to come up princesses. She told us we were beautiful. I woke up when I was eighteen and said, Okay, joke's over. But I think she wanted it."

CHAPTER
·18·

Shirley wasn't the only one in the family with idealized notions. Most children have a fairly conservative idea of how parents should look and behave, and the Hyman kids were no exceptions. From an early age, they were aware that Shirley was not a typical mother. In North Bennington in the fifties there were town mothers and faculty-wife mothers—and then there was Shirley, who fit no mold whatsoever. It wasn't always easy.

"It was an effort for us to deal with a mother who was demonstrably smarter than our friends' mothers," said Sally. "Way hipper, way into liberal ideas for those times. Always reading. It made us uptight.

"My mother was also the only really fat parent. When she used to come to school once or twice a year when we were kids, I was horribly embarrassed. She never had her hair done. She was just so different."

There was no way to avoid the fact that Shirley looked utterly different from most other mothers in town. Seen in a room full of slim, impeccably groomed faculty wives, she almost seemed to represent another species altogether. She was fat, she wore no makeup, and her hair, by now a colorless light brown, was held straight back from her face with a rubber band. The face itself, with its square jaw and heavy jowls, was severe, almost masculine in its lines. Her pale eyes stared steadily from behind glasses, missing nothing. It was an arresting face, a face that radiated intelligence, but it was not a pretty one, and patently not that of the average mother.

"I wished she would be like other moms," Laurence admitted, wistfully. He knew, of course, that she was a writer, but for a child that meant little—"I wasn't impressed at all with this book-writing business."

Jennifer Feeley, who knew Laurence well throughout childhood, did not realize until many years later "the tremendous embarrassment he felt about his mother . . . her looks. She was such a dynamite woman, it never would have occurred to me then that he had these other feelings."

Besides her looks, there was also the fact of her career to contend with. "There was not another wife or mommy around who did anything," Joanne remembered. "She was the only mother in the entire school who had a real career, a serious job."

Other mothers poured their energies into housekeeping. Shirley had always confined her efforts in that area to a lick and a promise, and often a half-lick and a skipped promise at that.

"She'd be compulsive about some stuff, forget about other stuff completely," said Sally. "She'd make [my sister] and me clean our room on Sundays, but when we came to the fancy dinner we'd see dust under the table. There were actually years when I didn't brush my teeth, and Shirley didn't notice. She could be very unaware."

Bunny Hyman concurred. "She'd never wash their hair, she didn't believe in it. And her housekeeping—she'd buy all this food and pile it into the refrigerator, everything piled on top of everything else, no way to find a damn thing. I'd say, 'Shirley, you've got two girls here, you've got to train them a little better.' But that was her way and that was the way she did it."

"She didn't know how to sew on a button. We'd save our mending for Lulu," said Joanne. "If you wanted laundry, there was a very short list of what she was willing to do, because it cut into her important work. Writing came first, Stanley came second, I think we came after that. I don't think either of them ever thought being a parent was something you do on purpose, that you work at. I sometimes think that's why I'm so obsessed with being a good parent."

There was no denying that it meant a certain bonus in terms of freedom and independence, having a mother whose entire focus was not on her kids. For years, Shirley sent her children to bed in a pattern—Barry first, Sally ten minutes later, Joanne ten minutes after that, then Laurence. Workable enough in theory, but success depended on attention, and Shirley's was often somewhere else. If she wasn't writing, she was entertaining friends. The kids learned very quickly that after the first call, the time between calls could expand indefinitely. If you lay low and didn't draw attention to yourself, you could pretty much stay up as late as you wanted.

And there was freedom in other ways as well. Scott Hyman, Shirley's nephew, remembers the feelings of exhilaration and nervousness he had when he visited his cousins. The adults were busy socializing, leaving the kids free—to stay up, to sneak out after dark, to get into trouble. It was wonderful, but at the same time a little scary, like being in a car when the brakes go out. Shouldn't someone be stopping us? he would think.

Yet in many ways Shirley hewed closely to the traditional line. She could be adamant about dinnertime, for instance. Despite Scott's feelings when he visited, she generally kept a firm rein over her children, wanting to know where each was throughout the day. Both she and Stanley were careful to oversee their reading: mysteries and science fiction were off limits until they reached a certain age. Sally worked her way around that one by sneaking mysteries off the shelves and replacing them with books that had jackets of the same color.

"I used to go over to the house a lot when we were little," said Jennifer Feeley. "Dinner was always a family sit-down affair. And Shirley always told stories at night or read out of one of the Oz books. She'd sit them down at bedtime, get out the book, and everyone would listen. I thought it was wonderful. My family didn't do that."

Yet Jennifer was also aware, even as a child, of certain odd discrepancies in the "perfect little family on Main Street" picture.

"On the one hand, there was this regulated atmosphere, dinner on time, everybody at the table—it was important, she cared about it. But on the other hand, there was this bizarre side of her, which didn't jibe at all. . . . How could she be so attentive to having dinner on time, getting them up in the morning, and yet let the girls' hair mat to such a degree that they couldn't comb it anymore and went to school that way?" It was a discrepancy that puzzled many people.

Shirley also divided chores and expectations in a rigidly conventional manner. The boys handled the typically manly duties—mowing the lawn, raking leaves, taking out the garbage. The girls set the table, helped with cooking, washed the dishes.

"The girls were servants," said Joanne. "Laurence's chair was back to the refrigerator, but Shirley would say, Get the milk, to me, even if he was the one who wanted it."

"She bullied us in a lot of ways about sex roles," said Sally. "I was made to wear a shirt all the time, I might at some point grow breasts. It was, You're a girl, that's all. Manners, you know."

Many of the rules and proprieties she taught her daughters were the exact ones she had been taught by Geraldine years before: "My childhood was filled with the phrases 'a lady always' and 'a lady never,' " said Joanne. "Half the sentences she said to Sarah and me started that way. She was teaching us so we'd know when we needed it, like a grammarian."

At the same time, she left them in no doubt as to how she felt about her own mother: "She tried to raise us to a standard better than the one she'd been raised to. I know she hated Geraldine and thought she was a wicked and cruel mother. The stories she told—I could never care for [Geraldine] again."

In one area, Shirley was very careful not to make the same mistake Geraldine had made. It was her cardinal rule never to violate her children's privacy. All of them knew that one of the reasons she hated her mother so much was that Geraldine had repeatedly searched Shirley's room.

"My parents would never go into our privacy at all," said Sally. "We were able to hide all kinds of things from them. They were very honorable. They wanted us to be honorable. We were often able to persuade them that we were."

Both Stanley and Shirley were in complete agreement on this matter. Once Stanley accidentally opened a letter meant for his older daughter. He not only wrote an extensive apology on the envelope but followed it up with an oral one. Both were heartfelt.

Respect for privacy, in fact, was one of the basic tenets of the Hyman household. The angriest Sally and Joanne ever saw their father was the time they sneaked down during a party to tape-record him doing one of his wilder songs. "It was very dramatic," said Joanne. "He dragged us out, took the tape and flung it. It was a point of honor. The lesson wasn't 'Don't mess with your parents'; it was 'You invaded my civil freedom.' "

Yet at the same time, Shirley was violating her family's privacy all along, in one way—by writing about them. Perhaps because she sensed this, she often involved her daughters in the writing process, particularly when she was planning a family story. She would sit on her stool in the corner of the large kitchen, by the stove, her ashtray filled with Pall Mall butts, her giant coffee cup or her glass next to her on the counter, occasionally stirring a pot, and run ideas by them. She listened carefully to their suggestions, often incorporating them. As a result, they have a certain fondness for these stories that is not shared by their brothers. But even Joanne has some ambivalence:

"Do you have any idea what it's like being nine years old and not knowing what you remember, what you were told, and what you read? I had no trouble disassociating myself from the stuff that wasn't about us. But the stuff about us—I sort of knew it wasn't the official family version and sort of knew some of that wasn't what I actually remembered.

"It turned on an automatic narrative voice in my head that I haven't gotten rid of yet."

When it came to matters of discipline, Shirley and Stanley presented their children with a solidly united front. Decisions were arrived at behind closed doors and announced unilaterally. All four were aware of the strong bonds between their parents, their admiration for each other, their fascination with each other's work. Shirley might seem to be the parent who was running the household, but Stanley "was the one who gave her strength," said Sally. When he was away on a trip to New York, Shirley would cuddle with them on the couch. "I don't like it when your father isn't here," she would say.

"They were very into controlling us. 'Go to your room' is what they'd say all the time. And you had to go right away, there wasn't any foolishness—or my father would stand up! He never hit us. She did the spanking when we were little and the scaring when we were bigger. But he sure could be dangerous," said Sally. "I've never been able to figure out which one was really dominating things."

More consciously than in most families, certain roles were assigned to each child. "They divided up the world, like Spain and Portugal," said Sally. Laurence was the carpenter, the musician, and later, the photographer; Joanne was the homemaker, encouraged to sew on buttons and to learn womanly pursuits; Sally was the child who was being groomed to be a writer and (courtesy of her father) the first white blues singer; Barry for a long time was the baby, the "dogged little foot soldier bringing up the rear," and later the one with the scientific bent. There was an ongoing attempt, more conscious than in most homes, to make the Hyman household a fully operative, self-contained organism, complete unto itself. A small world, with its own rules and rituals, provided by Shirley and Stanley.

In other homes, religion provides ritual; Stanley himself had grown up under strict Orthodox requirements, all of which he had tossed out when he left his parents' house. Yet a certain need apparently remained. Shirley and Stanley found their rituals in the world of magic, of folklore, of their own—especially Shirley's—imagination. Holidays like Christmas, Thanksgiving, birthdays were filled with special customs. Joanne and Sally, for instance, were trained to be singing waitresses; they performed at every dinner party for years, singing old English ballads, obscure medieval chants.

Shirley continued to identify most closely with Laurence and Sally, respecting their spirit, even when the authority they were challenging was her own. "Tell your brother to come in for dinner," she said to Joanne once, who dutifully conveyed that message and, minutes later, Laurence's response: "Tell her I'll be in when I'm goddamn good and ready," which broke at least three ironclad rules (the ones against swearing, refusing to obey, and referring to his mother as "her"). The fur flew—Shirley did not take this sort of thing lying down. Yet at the same time she understood the impulse.

Joanne, with the spirit of a born peacemaker, had a hard time understanding her brother and sister. Once Shirley took all four of them into

Bennington to shop for fall clothes. Instantly Laurence and Sally spotted a popcorn stand and started clamoring for a snack. Shirley snapped at them to be quiet, but they kept on, making her more and more angry. Joanne was amazed. Couldn't they stop bugging her? Didn't they know that if they stopped whining and let her calm down she would decide on her own to buy them popcorn, and then everyone would be happy? It was so simple, to her. Couldn't they see it?

She tried, sotto voce, to warn them, but without success; both of them continued to plague Shirley until finally, at the end of her rope, she threw all four back in the car and went home. Such a waste, Joanne thought sadly—now none of them had what they wanted.

But of course that wasn't quite true, since both Laurence and Sally had been interested in something larger than popcorn. This was a matter of muscle-flexing, an exercise in kiddie power. The fact that the effect achieved was, strictly speaking, a negative one mattered not a jot. Anyway, how negative was it? What kid really enjoys going shopping with his mother? They had pitched battle and won, and Shirley, every bit as infuriated as Geraldine was years before with her own mulish daughter, took them home. Only, unlike Geraldine, Shirley at least recognized what was going on.

In the home, Shirley brooked no nonsense—she was a sharp, firm disciplinarian who meted out justice with a swift, at times stinging hand. She never worried about possible misuses of her own power; she was no anti-authoritarian as far as parenthood was concerned. But the threat of discipline, or even disapproval, from outside the house was another matter. It was okay for her to cuff them around occasionally—they were hers. It was not okay for anyone else. When little Scott got into a scuffle with Sally—more than two years older than he—Shirley was instantly incensed. It was Scott's fault, he had bitten her, she maintained to Bunny and Arthur, who rolled their eyes and decided to forget it.

"Sally was the golden girl, Sally could do no wrong," Dr. Oliver Durand said. And the same was true, to a great degree, of Laurence—outside the house. Unfortunately, Shirley's reputation for standing by her younger daughter, no matter what, would come back to haunt her the one time Sally truly needed a defender.

Shirley busied herself turning out family stories for the new collection, keeping her eye out for any experience that could be incorporated into a tale. Nearly anything would do—a birthday party for her daughter, Laurie's trumpet lessons, Sally's experiments with magic, and even, on one occasion, a lost sneaker. She would have a minor car accident, rush home and tear off a new story by the end of the day. When a tax man showed up to audit them, she didn't even wait until he left—she sat down with her typewriter at the dining room table while he was closeted with

Stanley, and had nearly completed the story before the two men emerged from the study. It always pleased her to take one of life's irritants, run it through the typewriter, and emerge with salable copy.

The *Raising Demons* manuscript was ready by spring 1956; publication was scheduled for early 1957. She was basically happy with the outcome, although the jacket annoyed her: "A mess," she told her parents. "They made the house a beautifully landscaped Connecticut type, all fieldstone and fancy outdoor equipment. . . . The artist clearly lives in suburban Connecticut and thought this was a good picture of 'country life.' " Even worse, he had put five children in the picture and had to be persuaded to take one out.

Sometime earlier she had written an article on being a faculty wife, which ran in the Bennington alumnae magazine, with Helen Feeley's illustrations. That spring she was infuriated to learn that the college had carefully hidden all copies of the magazine during commencement week, so that no parents would see the piece. Not because of its anti-student overtones, which were quite apparent, but because it portrayed students drinking alcoholic punch at a party—this, the admissions director explained, would horrify parents and lead to bad publicity for the college.

Absolutely disgusted, echoes of Syracuse censorship ringing in her ears, Shirley immediately sold the article to *Mademoiselle* and made plans to incorporate it into *Raising Demons* too. Stanley told her she was being a little spiteful, but for once she ignored him.

With the publication first of *The Witchcraft of Salem Village*, her second family collection a few months later, then the opening of *Lizzie*, the *Bird's Nest* movie, the publicity mill geared up yet again; once more Shirley was kept busy turning down requests for interviews. The kids were put out when she said no to Edward R. Murrow, she told her parents, but there was no way she was going to change her mind: she hated interviews. Even publicity photos were traumatic. A few years later, when Laurence began learning photography, she announced that henceforward he would take any pictures needed of her (although, he admitted ruefully, she was none too happy with the ones he took either).

Raising Demons was reviewed genially and quickly began what looked like a brisk climb up the sales chart, though actually it would fall far short of *Life Among the Savages*. The tales had "a fine lemon flavor, nothing of the chocolate cream," said the *New York Herald Tribune* approvingly. "Tart and tangy" echoed the *Chicago Tribune*. Though funny and enjoyable, the book as a whole did not come off as well as *Savages*—the tone was more harried, at times even irritable, with more than a few rough edges. Occasionally a harsher reality broke through; Shirley's jealousy of Stanley, for instance, cropped up in no less than three episodes.

There was another reason the tales in *Demons* were not as successful as those in *Savages,* one Shirley herself was quite aware of: her children were getting older. What she had prized most in them was beginning to fade.

"I began writing stories about my children because, more than any other single thing in the world, children possess a kind of magic which makes much of what they do so oddly logical and yet so incredible to the grown-up mind," she wrote in notes for a lecture. "Now that my children are old enough to read and have become more aware of themselves, I find it almost impossible to write about them without sounding artificial, because they are doing things with that unfortunate adult reasoning which takes away all the magic." And without that magic, which had been so important to her, some of her connection to her children faded just a little.

But the reviewers didn't seem to notice or mind, with a couple of exceptions. "Two bad reviews of *Demons* came in, both from Texas, where they apparently don't like me (and I don't like them, come to think of it). And in spite of the fact that they are the only bad reviews out of about thirty I've seen, they still make me mad," she wrote her parents. Oddly enough, the witchcraft book too had received a negative review in Texas. "What do they do down there, tear books up to feed the pigs?"

As always, the publicity and the new books resulted in a new rush of fan mail, which ranged from the sublime to the ridiculous. A small publishing firm, Julian Messner, Inc., decided the time was ripe to lure her away from Farrar, Straus; aggressively, they pitched woo. A small firm was better equipped to handle her, the editor in chief wrote: witness what his company had done to publicize its recent best-seller, Grace Metalious's *Peyton Place*. As a matter of fact, when Metalious's husband had been fired from his job as school principal, Messner, Inc., had been able to turn it into publicity hay almost instantly, the editor bragged.

It is unfortunate that Shirley's reply has been lost; it must have been a beauty. A few days later the editor wrote again, a stiff note saying he was sorry she had taken the *Peyton Place* story personally and that the company had had nothing to do with the firing of Mrs. Metalious's husband, despite her implication. Shirley had obviously flattened him against the wall, and Messner, Inc., did not bother her again.

Much of the fan mail was plain silly: "I was reading your story in a magazine in the doctor's office and someone had removed the last page. Could you please tell me what happens?" Others wrote for inside information on how to get published. "Should I write double space or single space?" asked one eager amateur. And still, nine full years after its publication, the letters came begging her to explain "The Lottery." "Our class spent an entire day trying to figure it out. We finally decided to write to you," was a typical plaint.

Shirley had become royally sick of "Lottery" questions by now; even when someone she knew well, Jennifer Feeley, who was away at boarding school in California, wrote to ask her if she could "elaborate on the ending," Shirley's response was terse. "It really kind of crushed me," Jennifer confessed. "Her answer was, It's there, I'm not going to comment any further, you either get it or you don't, that's it. I was taken aback."

Often Shirley ignored readers' letters completely. But occasionally—"when there was a gleam of sanity," Sally said—she would answer. One letter she received was too agonized to dismiss. A woman with three children, a large home, a sociable husband, and a busy schedule beseeched her: "Shirley, how do you do it?" When she tried to write at night, she ended up in a TB sanatorium for a year, she said; later she developed high blood pressure. She sent a list of yes-or-no questions, which Shirley checked off and returned.

It was a reasonable query, one anyone following her career might have asked: How did she do it? Shirley's energy was unusual, prodigious—yet even her energy had its limits. So what was the answer? Unfortunately, at least part of it may have lain in her increasing reliance on stimulants. Dexedrine, which she had first taken in Westport, was more than a magic diet pill, she had discovered; it was a way to boost her energy artificially. Gradually, over the years, it became a household staple; both she and Stanley fell into the habit of taking it nearly every day. The amphetamines charged her up, making her even more high-strung, so she took tranquilizers and alcohol to combat them: Thorazine, Miltown, phenobarbital, bourbon.

This regime continued for the rest of her life. Whether it made her more productive is impossible to know. What is undeniable is that it greatly affected her life, and probably helped shorten it by a good many years. Only a basically strong constitution could have allowed her to survive even as long as she did. But the effects were apparent long before her death. The pills intensified her mood swings, her irritability, her emotional outbursts. As time went on, they worsened her anxieties and panics and heightened her fears. It is possible they even caused hallucinations toward the end of her life. No one can say for sure what other side effects the pills caused, but one thing is certain—at the time she was taking them, daily, casually, it never occurred to her, nor did anyone think to tell her, that there were any harmful effects at all. They were, after all, prescription drugs.

Although Shirley had come to detest interviews with a passion, she had discovered she did enjoy giving occasional lectures at writers' conferences.

When a newly formed group, the Suffield Writers' Conference, in Suffield, Connecticut, directed by Paul Sanderson, invited her to join them for a week in the summer of 1956, she accepted. It turned out to be a small congenial conference which included Louis Untermeyer, Irish poet Padraic Colum, and her old black-magic compatriot turned children's writer, Jay Williams. Somewhat to her surprise, she loved it so much that she returned year after year.

"Her feeling about coming was sheer exuberance," said Jeanne Krochalis, one of the conference planners, who quickly became a good friend. "It was something she looked forward to for the entire year. Stanley often said it was amazing—as a teacher she had so many things that would have been against her. She was overweight, inexperienced in public speaking, had never had teaching experience. Yet each was an asset. He said she talked all year about what she was going to do that one week."

The Suffield Conference gave Shirley a chance to do something she did nowhere else—talk about the experience of writing itself. "I personally love writing," she said in one talk. "It is a logical extension of the adolescent daydream . . . most clearly a way of making daily life into a wonderfully unusual thing instead of a grind."

"I tell myself stories all day long," she confided another time. "I have managed to weave a fairy-tale of infinite complexity around the inanimate objects in my house, so much so that no one in my family is surprised to find me putting the waffle iron away on a different shelf because in my story it has quarreled with the toaster. . . . It looks kind of crazy, of course. But it does take the edge off cold reality. And sometimes it turns into real stories."

And another time, revealingly: "The very nicest thing about being a writer is that you can afford to indulge yourself endlessly with oddness, and nobody can really do anything about it, so long as you keep writing and kind of using it up, as it were. All you have to do—and watch this carefully, please—is keep writing. So long as you write it away regularly nothing can really hurt you." It could almost have been a manifesto; certainly it was one of her most deeply held beliefs.

She did some reading in her seminars but spent more time discussing the process of creating itself. She wrote only on yellow legal pads, she told her students, and always kept one under the bed. For typing she used yellow paper. Every writer had her own particular devices and favorite tools, and these individual quirks should be respected. It always gave her a shock to see her books in galleys—for one thing, the pages weren't yellow anymore.

She spoke often about the relationship between experience and fiction. "The only way to turn something that really happened into something that happens on paper is to attack it in the beginning the way a puppy attacks an old shoe," she said. "Shake it, snarl at it, sneak up on it from various angles."

Shirley indicated to her students that her own writing tended to flow out almost automatically, without much conscious planning. Once, after reading several pages of a work in progress, she stopped suddenly. "I can't tell you what happens next because I haven't gone any further," she said.

For a private person like Shirley, Suffield was a wonderful release. Other than Stanley and one or two friends, like Howard Nemerov, she had never shared her views on writing with anyone. And writing was the single most important element of her life. In an odd way, even though it was only one week out of fifty-two, the Suffield Conference was a support group, a safe place where she could feel entirely comfortable being herself. When darkness began closing in on her a few years later, she wrote letters to each one of the people she had known well at Suffield, explaining her troubles as much as she could. She felt they knew her well enough to understand.

When the movie *Lizzie* finally opened, in early 1957, Shirley managed to avoid going to New York for the premiere, ostensibly because Barry had chicken pox, more likely because she had no great urge to view it in the middle of a crowd. The distributors arranged a private showing for her at the Bennington movie theater a few weeks later, at ten in the morning. The kids enjoyed it all thoroughly—Barry (who was five) mainly because of the MGM lion, she said later—but she herself was too unnerved to watch the movie with any critical acuity. Stanley did, however, and pronounced it "horrible." She was more amused at the simultaneous release of *The Three Faces of Eve* than anything else—the college psychologist strongly suspected that case of being a phony, she told her parents.

The oddest part of the experience, she later wrote, was hearing her words come off the screen. "Ever since I can remember, the act of writing has been a private one for me"; seeing her characters brought to life was "like being hit on the head with a rock." She could not throw off the sense that "these were real people and I had stolen them for my book." Their words were both familiar and foreign—she rarely remembered anything she had written. "I can read my own books in print the way I read and reread old books from my childhood; I can remember more passages from 'Jane Eyre' than I can from any of my books."

In retrospect, she came to share Stanley's view of the movie. "They made her into a lunatic, which she can't be, by definition, and the doctor cures her with a very interesting combination of Freudian analysis, pre-Freudian hypnosis, Jungian word-association and Rorshak inkblots. Not one of these systems gets along with any of the others in real life. I should think every analyst in the country would shoot himself, which of course might be a good idea too, except that then all the Bennington students who are being analyzed would have to find something else to do," she wrote tartly. On the whole, she was glad to have the whole thing over with.

She soon had something else to concern her, which was much more immediate. It would take up her entire attention, and have extremely far-reaching results.

Sally, who was eight years old, had been acting strange and sickly for several months, eating and sleeping poorly, overreacting emotionally in a way that was unusual for her. Her schoolwork had been bad, yet when Shirley tried to question her about it she answered only that she "couldn't think." Her behavior puzzled Shirley, who finally took her in for a checkup, which showed nothing. It was not until the first week of April 1957 that another mother called her, having finally gotten the story from her own son.

Sally, it turned out, was one of several children who were being victimized regularly by the third-grade teacher at the North Bennington school. The abuse had been going on all year, and involved physical and emotional assault. Sally and four or five others in the class had been slapped in the face, hit with a yardstick, forced to stand with clothespins fastened to their ears, and continually humiliated before the class. One little boy had even been shoved headfirst into an iron pipe. All had been threatened with even worse punishment if they were to tell.

Horrified, furious, Shirley swung into action. She and Stanley persuaded Sally to tell them what had been happening, promising the terrified child that no more harm would come to her. Then Shirley and the other mothers involved organized a lobby to have the teacher fired, meeting first with the principal, then the school board.

The abuse stories multiplied. "We kept hearing more that we did not know," Shirley wrote in an unsent letter to her parents. "She has been telling the kids nightmare stories (one about a mother murdering three little babies) to frighten them, and she keeps a baseball bat beside her desk to enforce order. Most of these parents had the same story—the children were irritable, and unable to eat and sleep, and yet had nothing physically wrong, and here these poor little kids have been going along for months absolutely defenseless, afraid to tell." She obviously had second thoughts about this letter, realizing its tone was distinctly at odds with the usual brisk, cheery reports she sent her parents; the one she finally sent mentioned the subject only briefly.

Several other parents were involved in the campaign to oust the teacher, but Shirley was the one who spearheaded the crusade. She was also the angriest. This was, after all, the child she had most wanted to protect from the forces of the outside world, the one most like her, whose spirit must not be crushed. Her reaction was not sorrow or depression, as it might have been in another parent—it was simple, explosive rage. To her this was a stark example of injustice, something to be exposed and eliminated at once.

"They were angry. Not just because the teacher had done it, but because she had succeeded in shutting up so many witnesses. There was a great sense that Sarah was in peril," said Joanne. "These were the things Shirley had always been trying to guard, protect, make everybody leave alone about Sarah; to protect what had not been protected in herself."

Shirley was tough, but she came up against something even tougher—solid New England rock. The teacher had been at the school for years and had taught several generations of North Bennington villagers. Almost instantly, there was a backlash in the town. Who was this stranger—the Hymans had been back in town only five years—to tell them what to do with one of their own? How bad could it have been, anyway, if nearly everyone in town had survived it? Meetings to protest the protest, meetings at which respected townspeople rose to affirm the teacher's good character, were held. The local newspaper handled the matter as if it were a tempest in a teapot, the natterings of a few overanxious parents; they too championed the teacher.

The upshot was that all the town's innate suspicion and prejudice rose up against Shirley. She did manage to make enough waves so that the teacher was eventually transferred, but she also effectively destroyed forever any chance she ever had of fitting in, of becoming an accepted member of the village. The townspeople swiftly forgot the facts of the case, the ins and outs, rights and wrongs—but they would never forget that Shirley had set herself up against them.

"She made no friends in the community over that," said Laurence. "Whole generations had gone through that teacher and been similarly abused and gone on to become pillars of the community. So the public reaction was against my parents: Why were they making waves? In Vermont, you're not considered a local until you've lived there forty years. We hadn't made our bones at all. You don't tell the school what to do. That was the perception in the community: Here [are] these city people, Jewish at that, telling us how to run our operation."

It was not that the town did not know that this particular teacher was occasionally brutal. "It was something everyone else thought was a part of life," said Joanne, who herself had gone through the same class with the teacher, although without being hit. To Shirley it was simple—justice versus injustice, right versus wrong. But to the town it was tradition versus change, local versus stranger, and thus no contest at all.

As the dust settled and time passed, and the incident seeped into legend, even some of the college community remembered only that Shirley had taken on the school for a "minor incident." Discussing it thirty years later, one faculty wife, Laura Nowak, recalled, "I had a child in that class. . . . Someone called me and said it was steamrolling. The teacher was an unmarried woman, they called her before the board. I really liked her a lot. . . . It seemed unfair."

"Shirley accused the teacher of putting a clothespin on Sally's ear," Willie Finckel, wife of cellist George Finckel, remembered. "It was hard to believe."

"Sally was always the most mischievous one," said Nowak.

Shirley's reaction was intense, and she undoubtedly did little to disguise her contempt for the teacher and the townspeople who rallied around her. She had known all along that the teacher was "a stupid and illiterate woman," she noted in a description she wrote of the incident. Early in the year Sally had asked her if it was okay to correct her teacher's grammar; Shirley had told her not to be rude but to watch her own. If her opinion of the teacher was low, her opinion of those who had hired her— and allowed her to teach their children—was not much higher. Undoubtedly she stepped on toes during her crusade; undoubtedly she led it in her most imperious, high-handed, Geraldine-like manner. The subtle art of political diplomacy was not her forte, and would never be.

But she was not overreacting, and she was not wrong. It seems certain that abuses did occur, if for no other reason than that Sally and the other victims uniformly exhibited a pattern of behavior uniquely common to abused children. Right and justice were on Shirley's side—not that it made any difference. Forced to choose between the known and the unknown, most of the town went straight for the known, quickly deciding that it was the teacher herself who was being victimized by Shirley, not the other way around. Everyone knew Sally was a little devil. The teacher had probably had her hands full; what was wrong with a little swat?

The scandal quieted down with the end of the school year, but the damage had been done; Shirley's position in North Bennington would never be the same. Before, she had been a stranger in town, an oddity, to be viewed with amusement and curiosity. True, some townspeople had hated her on principle for her lack of religion, her witch reputation, her Jewish husband, even the fact that she wrote. But others at least had taken a watchful-waiting approach.

Her campaign, though, left a residue of bitterness that reverberated through the village. She was still a stranger, but now she was a stranger who had gone against time-honored notions of the way things were done. She was a stranger who had overstepped her bounds, who could not be trusted. A stranger, in other words, who looked more like an enemy.

CHAPTER
·19·

The experience left its mark on Shirley. In the next few years her feelings of isolation and rejection would intensify, growing to alarming proportions. More than any other specific incident, the battle over the teacher tipped the delicate balance she had achieved with the town of North Bennington, cutting through her carefully constructed detachment. Gradually the sense of being surrounded on all sides by hostility would wear her down, finally leaving her helpless, nearly paralyzed, and close to madness. Always acutely sensitive to emotional atmosphere, and especially to rejection, she felt the town's opinion of her as an oppressive weight, which grew heavier every day. It was a slow process, barely discernible at first, but it started here.

Her first reaction, though, was to attempt to handle it through her writing. She had begun a new novel, finally, and poured into it all the feelings that had been stirred up by her battle with the town. Not surprisingly, *The Sundial* was a distinctly sour book, filled with almost as many unpleasant characters as *The Road Through the Wall* had been nearly ten years before (though this time there was humor as well, something that had been entirely lacking in her first novel). It was a book that, perhaps partly because of its large cast, did not quite jell. But it was a book she needed to write. Writing it allowed her to vent some of her rage, and to indulge her fantasies of power and vengeance as never before.

The Sundial concerns a small group of people, mostly related, who live in a huge, ornate mansion far above a town. The setup is strikingly reminiscent of the ultrarich Newcastle estate that loomed high above Shirley's neighborhood in Burlingame, a place that had fascinated her as a child so much that at times she and her friend Dorothy Ayling would sneak up, fearfully, to get a closer look, even though it was well-known in the neighborhood that any trespassers would be shot on sight.

Shirley's own entourage is rich, powerful, blatantly eccentric. The house seethes with backbiting, infighting, rivalry, greed, and a great deal of silliness. The book begins with one character's vision of an oncoming apocalypse, which will mean death by fire for everyone not living in the house. It ends, perhaps, with exactly that—there is no way to know for sure. Still, it must have pleased Shirley a great deal not only to become, for a time, as rich and powerful as she had always wanted to be, placing herself high above the town, but also to toy with the possibility of finishing off the entire world in one mighty swoop. The Natalie in *Hangsaman* who saw herself grabbing tiny houses and crunching on "the small sweet bones" of the people within would have understood completely.

"She put it all in the writing," said Barbara Karmiller, a student of Stanley's in the fifties who was one of the few to become Shirley's friend as well. "Her writing was very much from the unconscious. I think it didn't even go through the conscious part of her mind." Once Shirley gave one of her books in progress to Barbara and Jean Brockway to read; Barbara noticed immediately that the book had a scene that was word for word like a scene in an earlier book. "It was the 'Come out of the gate, be lost' scene, I don't remember which book it was. I didn't dare to say anything about it, but Jean Brockway mentioned it. She took it out eventually."

In *The Sundial,* for the first time in any of her books, the house itself took on importance, developing a palpable character of its own. The architectural genes of the Bugbees were at last catching up with her, although it was the essence of a house that intrigued her, more than its structural elements. The Halloran mansion in *The Sundial* is seedy, or-nate, dark—a presence more venerable than any of the characters.

The interchange between house and character fascinated Shirley. Even in *The Bird's Nest* she had drawn a corollary—brief but memorable—between her chief character and the museum she worked in. ("It is not proven that Elizabeth's personal equilibrium was set off balance by the set of the office floor, nor could it be proven that it was Elizabeth who pushed the building off its foundations, but it is undeniable that they began to slip at about the same time.") With *The Sundial,* the house itself began to move toward center stage, giving a foretaste of her next novel, in which a house would all but take over the entire work.

Shirley's skill was evident throughout *The Sundial,* but the book, pub-lished early in 1958, somehow missed the mark, a fact noted by many reviewers, several of whom complained vaguely that it "didn't quite come off." "Seems a highly unprofitable scatter-gunning of all the craftsmanship Miss Jackson so notably has," said *The New York Times,* with some aspersion. William Peden, who had waxed so complimentary over *The Bird's Nest,* was also a bit disturbed. "For all its wry humor, the novel seems to be primarily a bleak inquiry into what can only be called the idiocy of mankind," he complained in the *Saturday Review.*

Harvey Swados, in *The New Republic,* was even sterner: "While Miss Jackson is an intelligent and clever writer, there rises from her pages the cold fishy gleam of a calculated and carefully expressed contempt for the human race," he admonished. Considering her state of mind when she wrote it, he may have hit the nail right on the head. Not that Shirley had ever been the human race's greatest fan.

Still, despite various cavils, most reviewers agreed it was an interesting, well-written book, so Shirley was not particularly unhappy with the reception. Few failed to mention how disturbing it was, which of course pleased her mightily; she took as much pride in her talent to disturb as others took in their ability to amuse or entertain. She was especially delighted with the reaction of one Catholic magazine:

"We got a furious review . . . saying that the Halloran house was actually heaven and Mrs. Halloran was the anti-Christ and the other characters were dissenting Protestant sects and true Catholics everywhere should rise to defend themselves against this defamation," she wrote her parents. "Considering that my information about the Catholic church is extremely slight, I am very pleased to know that I managed to get so much of it in."

The publication of *The Sundial* was followed by two major changes in her professional life, which occurred simultaneously. After years of little recognition, Bernice Baumgarten's husband, novelist James Gould Cozzens, had finally hit best-seller pay dirt with his novel *By Love Possessed,* and Bernice decided the time was right for her to retire. As a parting gift, she broke off Shirley's contract with Farrar, Straus and signed her to a much more profitable one with Viking Press for her next three books, the money to be doled out over three years.

The change in publishers was "something she [Bernice] had been promising me for a long time," Shirley wrote her parents. "I keep getting sad little letters from people around Farrar Straus saying how they are so sorry I am leaving them . . . and I write sad little letters back which read like Lee's farewell to his troops although actually I am delighted to be leaving them and I bet they are just as happy to see me go, since we have been fighting for fifteen years." It was an exaggeration, of course; for the most part the relationship had been fairly smooth, and Shirley in fact felt a great deal of affection for senior partner John Farrar in particular. But more recently she had been rather irritated with them; she felt *Raising Demons* had not been given the advertising campaign it needed.

Bernice handled the breakup with her usual cool skill; she was a master at this sort of maneuvering. She first asked Farrar, Straus for money for Shirley and was turned down, as she expected to be. She then asked for money as an advance on a new book and was again turned down. Finally she asked if she could have an advance if Shirley wrote an outline and agreed to a specific deadline—and again was told no. At this point she calmly pointed out the small print in the contract that said if the publisher refused this sort of arrangement the contract was officially broken. She immediately called Viking, which had been sniffing around hopefully for years; by the end of the day, Shirley had her new contract.

The switch meant Shirley would also be dealing with a new editor. At Farrar, Straus her editor had been Robert Giroux, though "in her case 'edit' had little meaning," he said. "I merely put [her books] through the press. In her writing, she was a perfectionist and it showed. By the time she delivered her manuscripts, they were as nearly letter-perfect as possible—an ideal author." At Viking, she came under the kind, fatherly hand of Pat Covici, who was very much a gentleman of the old school of publishing. Covici understood instinctively what Shirley needed most— unconditional, unequivocable approval—and delivered it.

At the agency, Bernice handed Shirley over to Carol Brandt, the widow of the head of the agency. Brandt struck her initially as "one of those terribly well-dressed, self-possessed women I always seem to tangle with in New York." But that relationship too worked out extremely well and eventually grew to be one of mutual respect and affection. Brandt felt a great deal of protectiveness toward Shirley. She was not, however, terribly impressed with Stanley—for reasons that had nothing to do with literature.

"She would come to New York with him and we'd go to lunch, maybe four or five times a year. And he—for reasons of professional jealousy or whatever—he would encourage her to eat, urge food on her. Thick cream pies. She was very fat, maybe two hundred fifty pounds. I had to watch him stuffing her like a goose," Brandt said, shuddering.

Carol Brandt was not the only one to notice, of course. It was hard to miss the fact that Stanley and Shirley were heroic indulgers. They liked their food and drink and cigarettes in ample amounts and always had. Shirley cooked solid, all-American food, heavy on the cholesterol, with plenty of desserts. Potato pudding was one of her specialties. Kenneth Burke chuckled, remembering the way Stanley, at the college dining room, would disdain everything put on his plate but the meat and potatoes; Burke, who liked vegetables, would trade with him. "And you see how that worked out," he said (Burke is still healthy at ninety). Visiting the Hymans' house, he and his wife were always amazed at the amount of food cramming the refrigerator; in every room there was a snack.

"Later they got into the whole gourmet thing, fancy French cooking, fatty meats, lots of butter, salt, everything cooked too long, vegetables boiled in butter for two hours, everything you're not supposed to do," said Barry. "They were never willing to give an inch in terms of cutting back; they never made any effort to slow it down. It was all party, party, party."

Even in a much less health-conscious age, the Hymans' habits were noticeable. "I felt they didn't take care of themselves," said Ralph Ellison. "But there was a lot about them I didn't understand. Both Stanley and Shirley didn't expect to live long. They used to say it. In some ways, it was expected—they talked about living short lives."

Many of their friends concur; Stanley and Shirley not only seemed to assume they would die young but joked about having their ashes side by side on the mantel. "I don't know if one anticipates one's own mortality," June said. "Stanley certainly did. He had a heart murmur when he was a child, and I think he always assumed he was going to die around fifty. And I think Shirley may have had something like that too. She wanted to get as much done as quickly as possible."

Shirley did attempt to curb her habits off and on—her notebooks are filled with calorie lists—and occasionally she even tried to cut down on the drinking, or at least tried to try. "She told me she was drinking too much—I guess we all were," said Helen Feeley. "She said it would be impossible to give up by herself, but that if I would promise not to have a drink, she wouldn't either."

Helen agreed. "I had gotten sort of accustomed to my evening drink, so I'd call her up about six and say, Are you doing okay? I'm out in the kitchen getting dinner, wishing I had a drink in my hand but I don't. And she would promise me that she didn't either.

"It turned out later that she'd had her drink every night. I was griped, but she didn't do it to be mean. I don't think she had any control when it came to blinding herself to facts."

Stanley, too, had grown quite corpulent over the years, but it was Shirley's weight that attracted the most attention. People who had read her books and met her for the first time could hardly control their shock. This was not the way they expected an author to look.

"I was absolutely stunned," admitted Harriet Fels, "I had read her funny book and 'The Lottery,' and I wasn't picturing her that way. She had written in one place about going to the hospital to have a baby and bringing lace nightgowns, something like that. And here was this woman who took up literally half the sofa. With lank hair hanging down. Oh, boy. It wasn't at all what I had pictured. I think I was prepared to be a little scared, but then I was stunned—by this monster.

"But when she opened her mouth, everything changed. You forgot all that. Because she was witty, brilliant, and she knew it and used it. Used it to overcome all this. It made you forget it. Once someone had slighted her and she said, 'Oh, they will never know the brilliance of the corridors of my mind.' She knew she had that, in spite of the physical appearance.

"They smoked and they ate and they drank—and they both said, 'We want to live this way.' Their doctor implored them to lose weight. They just said, 'We know we're going to die at the age of fifty—and we're going to live this way.' "

But their habits and their weight were finally no more than quirks—it was the force of their personalities that people responded to.

"I have always thought of them as giants," said Barbara Karmiller. "Not physically. They just had more life than most people do."

"You got impressions of immense personal power from both of them," said Howard Nemerov. "Enormous confidence. I don't know that it was misplaced confidence at all. They just felt it about themselves. She had a lot of energy. If she were a smaller woman you would describe her as pert . . . if you can imagine pert on a grand scale.

"A cheerful, melancholy lady. Aristotle said wit and melancholy go together."

And the melancholy was most likely to appear after she had finished a book. The abrupt end of the creative rush often left Shirley with her moods and energies at low ebb. But not this time. Perhaps *The Sundial* had been a little unsatisfactory, even for her; perhaps the new contract with Viking served as a spur. For whatever reason, instead of the usual postpartum depression, she was full of energy and plans.

With the three younger children safely stashed at camp, and Laurence playing his trumpet at a music inn (the trumpet had become much more than a hobby; within a few months, in fact, at fifteen, he was able to get a union card), she and Stanley spent the summer of 1957 lecturing at a series of writers' conferences, even making an appearance—the first since graduation—at Syracuse University, where they spent time with their old mentor, Leonard Brown, and Shirley had the unnerving experience of lecturing in a room where she had once failed a Spanish final. Once again, she spent a week at Suffield.

When the new Bennington president, Bill Fels, asked her to teach a course in the fall, she turned him down, but she did agree for the first time to help counsel some of the students. "I can steal their plots," she wrote her parents, gaily. She also took over the job of chairman of the Faculty Wives Committee. This was more involvement with the college than she had ever had, but as she pointed out, college social life beat that of North Bennington. What she didn't say was that, since the teacher fiasco, she had been doing her best to turn her back on the town.

Her creative energy was flowing in a number of directions at once. She wrote several short stories; she prepared a complicated birthday present for Stanley—the script of a bridge game in which every rule was broken, to be tape-recorded by several of his friends (tailor-made to drive logical Stanley up the wall). She also turned out, without much ado, a one-act play for children called *The Bad Children,* a variation on *Hansel and Gretel* written because Joanne needed a play for school.

She had always, she said, "resented violently the fact that Hansel and Gretel eat the witch's house and never get punished for it." Her Hansel and Gretel were whiny brats whose beleaguered parents were delighted to have the witch take them off their hands. "I had a wonderful time writing it," she said later. "Every time I thought of something my children do that I can't stand—and there's a lot—I put it in for Hansel and Gretel."

Naturally, the kids adored it and completely brushed aside the moral lesson Shirley was trying dutifully to insert à la Miss Piggle-Wiggle. They thought the bad children were wonderful, the parents were ridiculous. They were also completely charmed by the witch, whose primary aim in life was to go on a game show and make millions of dollars, and the enchanter, a character Shirley added as a kind of a witch's gigolo. "Not proper parent figures at all," she noted—and thus, of course, irresistible.

"I did make one attempt to rescue the play—I quickly wrote an ending in which by means of magic Hansel and Gretel are transformed into sweet dear good kind little kiddies, but the children threw it right out again. Hansel and Gretel stay horrible to the end."

Laurie, who was becoming quite a blues expert, wrote a "Mean Wizard Blues" for the enchanter to sing, which began with the ringing declaration, "I want a rich witch, baby"; other songs were also incorporated. Area high schools got word of the play and began clamoring for the chance to produce it. Shirley had the whole thing copyrighted and gave it to her kids. "It belongs to them," she said. It had become, under their interpretation, "a defiant statement by a pack of children about their world and their acceptance of it."

Shirley enjoyed these sideline pursuits, they added zest. But by far the greatest part of her attention was taken up with her latest book project. The subject was one that excited her more than anything had since *The Bird's Nest;* this would be a book she had in a way been leading up to for a long time. After years of fascination with the supernatural, Shirley was writing a ghost story.

She had always been intrigued by haunted houses; for years she had been ready at a moment's notice to grab her kids and drive out to the countryside to investigate a reported ghost sighting. Even Stanley, who did not like the idea of actual supernatural happenings at all, had once written a formal statement, in old English script, attesting to the fact that their own house was haunted (Shirley, amused, stuck it into *Savages,* in the appendix).

The possibility of ghosts had never made Shirley uneasy in the slightest. But then, why should it have? She had always been at home with the supernatural. From childhood on she had been accustomed to thinking of herself as a lightning rod for strange occurrences, inexplicable by logic. And so did her family. "The children have a saying that everything is either true, not true, or one of mother's delusions," she joked. But in fact the children and Stanley, too, were well aware of Shirley's connection to the occult—and aware that it was genuine. "Not shuck and jive," Laurence put it. She didn't just believe, she knew such things were real. Even if she wasn't positive where they came from.

"Is the quote supernatural unquote ghosts of dead people, or another way of verbalizing other sides of the mind, other sides of emotion?" asked Barry. "If you see a ghost walk across the room, have you seen a ghost or are you hallucinating?

"There's no way to tell. And as with a lot of things where there's no way to tell, it makes absolutely no difference. It's equally real, whether it exists in your head or in the room. The effects it has on the sphere are identical. So there is no difference between unknown parts of the human mind and the supernatural. There's a lot of the mind people don't know about and don't know how to use—or aren't aware they are using."

Shirley's interest in the supernatural was at one with her interest in the powers of the mind. "She was fascinated at the notion that there were chambers in the mind you could lock and unlock and get access to," said Laurence.

Magic, of course, had always been one of the tools she used. Her involvement with magic had never been a secret; anyone visiting the Hyman house could see the evidence at once. Shirley's magic collections, books, devices, amulets, memorabilia, were everywhere. Yet Shirley was always very close-mouthed, even to her children, on the question of whether or not she actually practiced magic. "When she was asked, she would say nothing about whether she did or didn't," said Laurence. She could joke—or seem to joke—about being a witch, she could allude to certain spells and charms in passing, but the actual practice of magic was very private and real to her, something she felt strongly should be hidden from the outside world. "I wouldn't want to violate any secrets," Laurence said.

"She definitely did have a powerful aura," said Jennifer Feeley. "It was part of her, something very mystical, even scary. If you were unin-itiated to it, you were not allowed to know too much. Part of her power was in your not knowing. But at the same time, it was a presence; there was just something mystical about her, in her voice, in her presence."

Over the years she had tried out various charms, spells, and curses. The ancient art was one more door into the supernatural, into the unknown powers of the mind—and Shirley was interested in every door.

Old houses represented yet another passageway. "She was fascinated by the past in an old house, by the fact that it's still going on, that you can get a glimpse every now and then, through psychic awareness, into what used to happen there," said Laurence.

The Hymans had always lived "in old strange houses, with lots of rooms, with attics that were cobwebby and strange. My mother particularly always wanted us to live in old houses," he pointed out, the sort of houses that could be haunted. And in fact, there were a number of incidents over the years.

"Bizarre occurrences," Laurence said. "It was always an atmosphere in which things like poltergeists were very possible." An old music box Shirley had inherited from Geraldine occasionally turned itself on in the middle of the night. On one on his visits Scott Hyman saw something odd run past the bedroom window—a window two stories above the ground. "It had a human form," he said. "And there was nothing outside the window, no balcony, no ledge. I wouldn't be surprised if the house were haunted. There was a real Halloween atmosphere there, all the time."

Bunny Hyman was sitting over a late breakfast with Shirley one morning when both women suddenly noticed a thin line of blood slowly oozing out of a kitchen cabinet. The cabinet door was closed, and neither woman had the slightest urge to open it; they moved their chairs slightly away from the wall and continued to sip their coffee, determined not to scream. When Laurence came into the room half an hour later, Shirley asked him, tensely, to open the cabinet. A bottle of red wine had been knocked on its side.

Nowhere else, Bunny realized later, would you assume that a trickle of red liquid had to be blood. At Shirley's house, you not only assumed—you almost expected it. There was an aura of possibility in the air; the boundaries of cold logistical reality were just a bit blurred.

"Some of the dreams I have to this day are related to their houses," said Jennifer Feeley. "There was an aura, an atmosphere. I find myself roving around in the upper levels, down corridors and into rooms, on the rickety old wood. You had the feeling you had to keep your head down; it was very closed and slightly scary and claustrophobic. The houses were like the family—full of secrets and dust and mystery."

A friend of Joanne's, Linda Gould, remembered going to dinner at the Hyman house for the first time. A gray cat leapt up onto Shirley's shoulder and whispered in her ear as she sat attentively. The cat had told her a poem, Shirley announced, and proceeded to repeat it aloud. It all seemed so natural, so believable, that Linda left wondering how many times her own cats had tried to talk to her. . . . Was she just not listening right? Later, Joanne told her quite matter-of-factly that her mother was a witch.

Bennington College, in those years, filled as it was with artistic, intellectual, creative types, had a reputation itself as a breeding ground for forays into stranger territories. Stories abounded of mysterious happenings, of witches' covens in the woods, of a Hungarian warlock—and many of those stories became attached over time to Shirley, who was, after all, a self-professed witch.

Nor were all the tales apocryphal. Writer Hal Crowther, who graduated from nearby Williams College, remembered dropping by Bennington one evening in 1962 with his roommate, John Nesvig, and walking into a nightmare.

"We were very young, eighteen years old, about as green as you could get. A few girls came over and said, 'Would you guys like to do us a favor?' And we of course were willing to do anything to get their attention, so we said, 'Whatever you like, sure.' "

The boys were taken down the road to where a group of young women were standing in the trees, dressed in dark robes. The women had heavy medieval candleholders, which they asked the boys to carry for them. They then blindfolded both boys and led them into the woods, removing the blinds when they emerged at a small clearing around a pond, only a little larger than a well, backed by a small stone wall.

"There was some chanting, not in any language I knew—and I had studied Latin. Then one woman got up on the wall, took off her robe and dived into the pond. As if it were very deep. And here's the strangest part: she didn't come up."

As the minutes ticked by, the two boys became more and more agitated. Finally they tried to reach into the pool, but the women stopped them. "We were going crazy. We were sure we were a part of some horrible crime or mystery and this girl was dead and we were going to be found by the police. We were shaking with fear."

The women blindfolded them again and took them back to the cottage. They drove back to Williams College, where they spent a petrified week waiting for the police to knock on the door. Nothing happened. At last they decided to return to Bennington and search for the one who had dived into oblivion. They found her on their second trip. "We didn't have the nerve to confront her, but at least we knew she was alive," he said. They did their best to forget all about it.

Later, he heard other tales of witchery, and heard them linked to Shirley—although at the time of his own experience he had never heard her name.

Crowther's story, of course, needs to be taken with the knowledge that freaking out buttoned-down Williams students was one of Bennington's favorite sports. Still, it does seem a relatively complex prank, and undoubtedly strange things did go on in the woods off campus. But it is hard to picture Shirley being directly involved, Shirley with her strong devotion to privacy, and her even stronger aversion to Bennington students en masse. She made a lifelong pursuit of other realms, other possibilities—but she made it alone.

Now that Shirley had decided, finally, to write a real, bloodcurdling ghost story of her own, she plunged into research enthusiastically. She plowed through architecture books and magazines, looking for a house that radiated exactly the right sense of evil and malevolence. She wrote asking her parents to send her information and pictures on any "big old California gingerbread houses.

"The reason for this is my new book; it is to be about a haunted house and I can't seem to find anything around here; all the old New England houses are the kind of square, classical type which wouldn't be haunted in a million years. . . . Perhaps mother might have somewhere some of my grandfather's old books?"

It is unlikely Geraldine was able to dig up any old pictures, but Shirley obviously was tickled at the idea of using for her purposes a house one of the Bugbees had built. In a later lecture at Suffield, she swore that during her search she had come upon a picture of a California house that exuded disease and decay, and that when she wrote to ask her mother about it she had been told that her great-grandfather had built it. "It had finally caught fire and it was generally believed that that was because the people of the town got together one night and burned it down."

As part of her preparation, she also immersed herself in ghost stories, "volume after volume of luminous figures glimpsed floating down the garden path, or mysterious moanings in attics; every now and then I had to go and read 'Little Women' again to get back in perspective." In the book, she knew, she would be confronting the nature of reality itself, as she had in so many of her short stories. "No one can get into a novel about a haunted house without hitting the subject of reality head-on; either I have to believe in ghosts, which I do, or I have to write another kind of novel altogether."

Her preparations had an effect on her. "More than ever before I am wandering in a kind of fairytale world," she said. Shirley had always sleepwalked occasionally, and now she began to find rather disturbing notes she had written to herself while in that state—"Dead Dead" was one. Feeling more than a little driven, she put her research aside and launched into writing her book.

The result, *The Haunting of Hill House,* has been called by no less an authority than Stephen King one of the greatest horror novels of all time. King, in fact, dedicated one of his books, *Firestarter,* "to Shirley Jackson, who never had to raise her voice." *Hill House* is eerie, subtle, infinitely chilling. "I have always loved to use fear," she said—and she rarely used it better.

During her research, she had asked a number of people what they thought of ghosts, and discovered there was "one common factor—most people have never seen a ghost, and never want or expect to, but almost everyone will admit that sometimes they have a sneaking feeling that they just possibly could meet a ghost if they weren't careful—if they were to turn a corner too suddenly, perhaps, or open their eyes too soon when they wake up at night, or go into a dark room without hesitating first." And it was this feeling of fearful half-expectancy that Shirley played on. The effects in *Hill House* are offstage, indirect, unexplained, elusive; not just the characters but the readers too are not sure what they have or have not actually experienced. Quite a feat to pull off in cold print.

The story is about a group of people brought together by a psychic researcher to investigate a particular house; all are supposed to have some sensitivity to supernatural forces. The dark energies of what Shirley called "Hill House, not sane" are aroused by the main character, Eleanor, an odd, lonely girl who feels her first sense of happiness and pleasure when at the house. Whether the ghostly effects are caused by the house itself or by the unconscious workings of Eleanor's mind or by some strange combination of the two is never known. (As Barry says, What difference would it make?) But at the house, Eleanor experiences a sense of belonging for the first time, even amid the horror, and she refuses to give up what is hers. When forced to leave, she smashes her car into a tree, killing herself, triumphantly. For it is not a defeat, far from it—in the moment she makes her decision to merge with the dark powers, Eleanor is more blazingly alive than she has ever been in her life.

The book, brought out in fall 1959, met with almost unmitigated praise. "A goose pimple horror story, and a good one," said the *New York Herald Tribune.* "Miss Jackson can summon up stark terror, make your blood chill and your scalp prickle," approved *The New York Times,* calling her "the finest master currently practicing in the genre of the cryptic, haunted tale."

"We have here what we ought always to have in ghost stories but so rarely get," said the *Times Literary Supplement.* "A breeding claustrophobic atmosphere which thickens overpoweringly as we go along. A novel which has distinctiveness and genuine power."

Nor were the critics the only fans. The book was immensely popular, became a modest best-seller, and earned, with reprint rights and a $67,000 movie sale, a tidy fortune. It was a memorable book; next to "The Lottery," it would become the one work readers most identified with her name. And like "The Lottery," it appealed to a variety of fans.

Not long after its publication, Shirley heard about one of them from the Burkhardts. Friends of theirs had vacationed in a tiny upstate farm far from Bennington. While they were there, a man who had become a respected member of the community was revealed to be a fugitive—a bank robber who was on the FBI's Ten Most Wanted list. Someone had spotted his photo on the post office wall and turned him in. On his bedside table, it was reported, was a copy of *Hill House,* a marker at the halfway point. Shirley was quite taken with the story; she instantly sent a copy of her book to the Georgia penitentiary where her fan now resided, with a warm note.

On quite a different end of the spectrum, she also received a flattering note from novelist Isaac Bashevis Singer. The book had impressed him a great deal; he could see, he said, that they shared some very similar notions about writing. (Later, in an interview, Singer reflected views very close to Shirley's: "The supernatural expresses the subconscious better than any other events a writer can write about," he said; he himself was "always reminding people that there are powers in the world that we don't know, that the supernatural is here, among us.")

She had written the book she had always wanted to write, and it was a total success; her triumph was as total, and as smashing, as Eleanor's.

And maybe, in some ways, as lethal.

CHAPTER
·20·

The dramatic success of *Hill House* was a high point. It was followed by a long undertow. Over the next few years a series of shifts occurred in Shirley's life, some subtle, some distinct. But each tore another hole in her safety net.

Change was in the air. Her children were getting older, taller, less controllable. The spirit of adolescence had been loosed in the house, charging the atmosphere. She could still joke: "Actually, if you're a writer, the only good thing about adolescent children is that they are so easily offended. You can drive one of them out of the room with any kind of cross word or personal remark—like why don't you pick up your room—and get a little peace to write in." But the tensions left their mark. Stanley was being pulled into parental duty more than ever. "Shirley takes care of them until they're adolescents," he told a friend. "Then she gets scared and hands them over to me."

Laurence's trumpet had launched him precociously into a state of semi-adulthood; by age fifteen he was playing on weekends at clubs throughout New England, earning quite a respectable sum of money, most of which Stanley insisted he bank. ("I became quite adept at misrepresenting my earnings," he admitted.)

Many of their Bennington friends were shocked at the amount of freedom Stanley and Shirley allowed their oldest. "Shirley must have found part of it appealing," said Jennifer Feeley, who often accompanied Laurence on his gigs. "Yet on the other hand, here was this kid drinking himself into stupors, getting into trouble. And she knew about it."

He had almost no interest in school, and this did worry them. At one point they packed him off to a nearby prep school, but it was too late for such measures. He was much too used to freedom to fit into such a regulated atmosphere and was back home in three weeks. It wasn't until the following year, when he was allowed as a high school senior to take a class at the college, that he began to develop an interest in learning. "It was Kit Foster who did it," Laurence said. "Her course opened me up." She was able to do what all of Shirley and Stanley's influence had not done: awaken an interest in literature in their son.

There may have been blowups at home, but outside the home Shirley continued to maintain a fiercely defensive position about anything Laurence might do. "I remember Laurie driving the kids home from skiing one time, and my kids were saying he went over the yellow line and passed cars and took risks," said Harriet Fels. "Shirley was so furious at me when I brought it up—no child of hers could possibly do anything that wrong. No way. She defended her children under indefensible circumstances."

Shirley worried about Laurence, but was horrified at Joanne. "Helen Feeley says Jennifer was even worse at her age, but I don't believe it," she wrote her parents. She seemed, in the manner of thirteen-year-old girls everywhere, to have nothing on her mind but clothes, records, and boys. This was not an adolescent who moved precariously between different worlds, as Shirley had, brilliant, creative, erratic, strange—this was a fairly typical teenager, as different from Shirley as she herself had been from her mother. In fact, wasn't Joanne really the sort of adolescent Geraldine had wanted so much, years ago?

It was not a new thought. Joanne had had the feeling she was being groomed for Geraldine for many years. "I think my whole life was a rehearsal to meet her mother," she said. She knew Shirley had always regarded her as the conventional one, the gentle homebody type, the one child who could be dangled in front of Geraldine if the need arose.

So it came as no surprise when Shirley announced to her that she alone would go to visit Geraldine in California, in the summer of 1959—a trip none of the other children had ever made. She knew it was important, that she was somehow carrying her mother's honor with her. Geraldine needed to be shown: that Shirley had succeeded where she had failed? that she at least had produced a conventional daughter? It wasn't clear in Joanne's mind, but she knew it was important. Sally was the fighter, but this battle was hers.

And yet afterward she wondered if it wasn't also that Shirley simply needed to have her understand certain things about her parents and had chosen this way of making sure she did—as a sort of preparation, as if she knew that someday soon she would be needing Joanne's understanding.

"I didn't know consciously how she felt about her mother then, when

I was thirteen, but by the time I got back, I was a lot more ready to be sympathetic. I was out there for a month. Geraldine made me feel awful. You weren't allowed to read in bed in the mornings. I know when I got there I realized how unprepared I was.

"It wasn't that Geraldine was unkind. I had my nose so deeply into books, what I did realize I didn't know for a year. I don't think I looked up at the expressions on their faces."

But something had come across, all the same, and Shirley was not disappointed. Perhaps what she had wanted most was a witness, someone who would travel back in time to her parents' house and understand what it had been like for her, growing up in that tight, prim, suburban household. After Joanne's trip, Shirley was able to discuss her parents with her daughter in a way she never had before.

"She made me feel her mother hated her and feared her and wished her ill—that she would go through her things to see if she could manipulate circumstances so that Shirley would look bad, feel bad, or be bad. That's the message I got. Very clear. She was still so tight-jawed angry."

And it wasn't only Geraldine she wanted Joanne to see clearly; it was Leslie too. "I commented when I came home that Leslie seemed like a really nice guy, and she said had I noticed he was the one who made the unpopular decisions and made Geraldine carry them out? I looked, and by gum, it was right. He was the jolly one, making her do the dirty work.

"She had been a daddy's girl, Shirley, but it wasn't enough."

On the surface, of course, everything was genteel. Shirley made sure Joanne wrote a proper thank-you note, and she herself was extravagantly grateful. "Joanne seems to have had the most wonderful trip of her life," she assured them. Below the surface, at least on one level, she was grimly satisfied. She had engineered the campaign, brought the troops together, and the result was at least a partial victory, a gain for her side. It was the satisfaction that comes to every good general. But on another level there was a weary sadness. Her anger with her parents was not something that could be put to rest, ever; after all the years, it still beat on, unchanged.

Nothing in the town had changed either, but in the sudden stillness that descended on her after the completion of *Hill House,* Shirley was more acutely aware of the atmosphere around her. Even aside from the villagers' animosity, North Bennington was a peculiarly difficult place to live, particularly during winter.

"We are such an odd community," Shirley wrote in an unsent letter to Jeanne Krochalis, her Suffield friend, early in 1960. "If you can imagine it, try; we live in an isolated valley with no way of leaving, since we have no trains and busses are unreliable and nasty; driving anywhere in this weather is foolhardy. Our entire faculty community numbers one hundred and twenty-three persons, of whom about fifty are staff, librarians, secretaries or generally second-class citizens; we do not meet them socially. Consequently our circle of friends is an iron-bound seventy, which includes husbands and wives, and of whom we ordinarily see only thirty."

The year was composed of four seasons—fall term, winter vacation, spring term, and summer vacation, she said; each vacation was two and a half months long. "When winter comes we go underground and simply do not see anybody." Now, however, winter vacation had ended, heralding the start of the social season. "Campus, which has been pure and smooth under the snow, is now full of dirty little girls in skin-tight pants carrying books and screaming at one another, driving foreign sports cars and eating all the time. . . . Laurie is in an ecstasy of delight, of course." Despite the humor, her tone was weary; a sense of the town's almost suffocating atmosphere rose sharply from the page. The letter broke off abruptly, as if she had suddenly realized how dismal she sounded.

She was having trouble getting a good start on her next book, which was unusual for her. Stanley thought the sudden windfall from *Hill House* was the problem; maybe she was feeling too prosperous to write? After all, money had always been an effective prod. But she knew that wasn't the real problem; the real problem was the subject she had chosen.

Shirley wanted to write about her experience with the village. She wanted to set down her feelings of isolation and rejection, her sense of herself as a pariah, set apart from the rest of the town. The project would in some ways be closer to the bone than any she had tried before; she would be going deeper into her own fears, and perhaps something in her wanted to discourage the journey, sensing perhaps, that it could be dangerous.

At any rate, she found it hard to get a grip on *We Have Always Lived in the Castle* (although the title, at least, she was sure of from the beginning) and made a number of false starts. In a long, unsent letter to Howard Nemerov, a writer who knew about blocks, she tried to convey some of the problems she was having. "This starts funny," she began. Partly as a joke, Stanley had ordered a book for her from England called *Sex Variant Women in Literature,* and flipping through it late at night, she had found her own name in the index. Indignant, she woke Stanley, who told her groggily to wake him again if she found out what she had done that was variant, and went back to sleep. The reference, she discovered, was to *Hangsaman;* the author had called it an "eerie novel about lesbians."

Her first reaction was fury. "I happen to know what Hangsaman is about. I wrote it. And damnit it is about what I say it is about and not some dirty old lady at Oxford," she fumed. "Because (let me whisper) I don't really know anything about stuff like that. And I don't want to know. Yes yes . . . I know, I read Freud. But there has got to be a point where I dig in my heels and decide who is going to be the master, me or the word.

"Anyway, this has completely disintegrated 'Castle.' Stanley can't see it. Says write about what you want to write about and the hell with what dirty old ladies say but of course I can't."

The problem was that *Castle,* like *Hangsaman* (and *The Bird's Nest* too, of course), was a book about separate personalities—separate women—who are actually one. The two main characters, Merricat and Constance, are "two halves of the same person." One, Merricat, "wants to see the world, with always one foot on base at home"; the other, Constance, "never wants to leave home. . . . Together they are one identity, safe and eventually hidden."

And of course, that one identity was Shirley herself, just as Tony and Natalie had been, just as Lizzie, Beth, Betsy, and Bess were, too. The relations among these splintered parts, familiar, affectionate, cozy, intimate, were meant to be the relations among parts of one single mind—and to have that misread as lesbianism horrified her. At this point, the letter stopped being addressed to anyone but herself.

"If the alliance [between the two women] is unholy then my book is unholy and I am writing something terrible, in my own terms, because my own identity is gone and the word is only something that means something else.

"No. I am writing about ambivalence but it is an ambivalence of the spirit, or the mind, not the sex. My poor devils have enough to contend with without being sex deviates along with being moral and romantic deviates." Her women "are not bitches, they are not witches, they are most emphatically not switches."

And yet—"I did want that sense of illicit excitement [with Natalie]. But not that. There it is not a he or a she but the demon in the mind, and that demon finds guilts where it can and uses them and runs mad with laughing when it triumphs; it is the demon which is fear and we are afraid of words.

"We are afraid of being someone else and doing the things someone else wants us to do and of being taken and used by someone else, some other guilt-ridden conscience that lives on and on in our minds, something we build ourselves and never recognize, but this is fear, not a named sin. Then it is fear itself, fear of self that I am writing about . . . fear and guilt and their destruction of identity. . . . Why am I so afraid?

"So here I am. I am frightened by a word. I am frightened by a word because it tells me I am frightened. But I have always loved to use fear, to take it and comprehend it and make it work and consolidate a situation where I was afraid and take it whole and work from there. . . . I delight in what I fear. Then 'Castle' is not about two women. . . . It is about my being afraid and afraid to say so, so much afraid that a name in a book can turn me inside out? Why why?"

Fear. It had always been a part of her life, from the beginning; she had been afraid of practically everything. People, buildings, planes, electricity, machinery, public speaking, private comments. And rather than run from it, cowering, she had done her valiant best to use it, control it, even conduct it, letting it pass through her—a lightning rod, again—into her writing. But *Castle* involved a more direct confrontation with her own personal fears. Before, she had managed to draw some kind of curtain—time was always a good one—between herself and her subject. She was in her thirties before she allowed herself to write about her adolescence.

Now, though, she was writing about her experience with the town while she was still living through it. In *Castle,* two sisters, young women, live in complete isolation on the edge of a village; all the rest of the family have been killed off in an unfortunate incident involving arsenic (it's rather clear, by the first page, who the murderer was). When the younger sister, Merricat, goes into town to do errands, people shrink back from her, taunt her, even occasionally throw stones.

Later Shirley admitted to the people closest to her that in *Castle* she had written the truth of what it was like for her in North Bennington. "She said that was pretty much how it was," said Howard Nemerov.

"In the beginning of *Castle* there's a vivid description of what it was for her. . . . That's what was going on every day, when she had to walk down the street to the grocery store and was taunted by the villagers," said Barry.

None of this made it an easy book to write. In addition, she was quite consciously splitting herself into the two characters, Merricat and Constance, and at the same time modeling them directly after her daughters.

"She told me that's what Constance and Merricat are about," said Joanne. "They are the same person, both Shirley. The Constance part is me, the Merricat part is Sarah. She told us. I would not want to be the Merricat part. Sarah would not want to be the Constance. Shirley, really, did not want to be both, I think."

Constance, the older, is all warmth, the complete homebody, a loving, motherly, almost Victorian gentlewoman. She mirrors the side of Shirley her older daughter called "the queen of charm," the woman who "made comfort" for people, fluffing the pillows, serving hot cocoa, buttering toast better than anyone else in the world. ("I've been disappointed a lot in the world, because of her odd little perfectionisms," Sally said.)

Merricat mirrors the other side. She is uncivilized, bold and fierce, incapable of compromise. A champion disturber; the essence of the untamed artist. Unfailingly true to her own nature, she insists on expressing herself with complete honesty—even if that means (as in fact it does) committing mass murder.

Merricat nails her colors to the flag from the start: "My name is Mary Katherine Blackwood. I am eighteen years old, and I live with my sister Constance. I have often thought that with any luck at all I could have been born a werewolf, because the two middle fingers on both my hands are the same length, but I have had to be content with what I had. I dislike washing myself, and dogs, and noise. I like my sister Constance, and Richard Plantagenet, and Amanita phalloides, the death-cup mushroom. Everyone else in my family is dead."

Merricat is the pure thing, the strongest character Shirley would ever invent, although "invent" doesn't seem quite the right word. Merricat was not so much invented as let loose on the page. She was, after all, somebody Shirley knew very well; she was Shirley, in part, and her daughter Sally, in full. In setting her down, Shirley was confirming her unique bond with her second daughter.

"Sarah was like the exorcist for Shirley," Joanne said. "I think maybe Sarah was born with a full valise and Shirley had to beat hers out of plowshares after Geraldine got done with her. I often thought Shirley felt Sarah hadn't paid her dues, in a way. She had powers Shirley had worked for—writing skills and magic." Powers of the mind.

There was no doubt that Sally's mind worked in unusual ways. Once, as children, she and Joanne played a game of Twenty Questions. Joanne became more and more irritated—she hated mysteries—and finally announced she was quitting. "I can't get the answer, it's impossible," she said.

Sally grinned, triumphantly. "That's because I change it with every question," she crowed. It was exactly the sort of fiendish, mischievous rearranging of reality that Shirley did so often in her fiction, and it came as naturally to Sally as breathing.

But Shirley had powers of her own. She put her daughters in the book and told them they were meant to stand for parts of herself as well. She shared her problems writing *Castle* with them, and encouraged both of them, but particularly Sally, to suggest changes and offer criticisms. Both girls were pulled in closer to her creative process than ever before and, flattered, they reveled in it.

But at the same time, it was their personalities, their very beings, that Shirley was using and defining, incorporating into her own, assigning to roles she had chosen. She was, after all, the stronger force. There was a certain ruthlessness to it; it was not unlike possession. She cast her net over them, and neither daughter would have an easy time throwing it off.

Castle was the hardest book she had ever written. There had always been a very direct link for Shirley between the book she was writing at any moment and the life she was then living. Writing the family stories, she had been more attentive to her children; writing *The Sundial,* she infused it with the rage that had been stirred up by the school fight. With *Castle* she was directly examining one of the central questions of her life—her own identity—and probing for a solution. No book had ever been closer to mirroring her own fears, and no book would ever be as ultimately damaging.

Together and alone, Merricat and Constance are complete, a world unto themselves, perfect, whole, seamless. The only threat comes from the outside, in the form of curious neighbors, a fortune-hunting cousin, evil and stupid townspeople. The answer, then, is obvious: the outside world must be closed off. Forever. It takes a dramatic series of events, and a fire, to do it, but in the end the girls decide to remain in their castle (all but destroyed), locked off completely from the rest of humanity, in safety, wholeness, and serenity, for the rest of their lives. They will no longer deal with the world, although they will allow certain members, those who have awakened finally to a sense of guilt, to bring them small offerings—covered casseroles, baked chickens—and leave them at the door.

Castle is almost a paean to the panic order known as agoraphobia, whose sufferers are unable to leave the house. Constance and Merricat end up entombed and blissfully content. Merricat is not a passive creation; if anything, she is a conquerer. Yet her final choice, made with a flourish of triumph, is to opt for a suspended state, a kind of death-in-life. Writing *Castle,* Shirley shuffled through her options and chose agoraphobia as the best answer for her characters—and, through them, for herself.

For as she struggled her way through the book over three long years, life and art became inextricably intertangled for Shirley and the line between the two worlds dissolved. In the end she discovered that she, too, could no longer leave her house. Not only was *Castle* a paean, it was a siren call as well.

Oddly, or perhaps not so oddly, early in the process of writing the book, she wrote a short story which explored a very different option. "Louisa, Please Come Home," which won the Edgar Allan Poe Award in 1961, is the tale of a young woman who leaves her home on the eve of her sister's wedding and begins a new life utterly unconnected to the old. Yearly her parents go on the radio to plead for her return. Finally, she does come back. But her parents do not recognize her; several other girls have shown up over the years, one or two of them much more convincing, they tell her. Stoic, resigned, she leaves for good.

Shirley, as she said to Nemerov in the letter she never sent, knew that at least part of her had a strong urge to wander. "Louisa" illustrates, with terrifying simplicity, the underlying fear that accompanied that urge: What if you left and they wouldn't let you come back?

In the end she didn't. She wrote *Castle* instead.

An amazing thing has happened, she wrote Jeanne Krochalis, with just a touch of amusement. "I have written myself into the house."

To her parents, she was brisker: "What 'ails' me, Pop, is what they used to call a nervous breakdown," she wrote tartly, obviously in response to his query. The description was apt, as far as it went. Shirley did have a breakdown, for a number of reasons, most of them completely out of her control.

But the form it took was something she did control; in fact, she had designed it herself. And *Castle* was the blueprint.

CHAPTER
·21·

She had always been plagued by a number of physical ailments—asthma, hay fever, a certain amount of arthritis, particularly in her fingers. Working on *Castle,* she began to suffer severe attacks of colitis as well. Her anxieties had always gone straight to her stomach; but now the colitis, intensifying, itself fueled the anxieties, in a vicious cycle: If she went out, would she be able to find a bathroom when she needed it? Attempting to combat it, she took more tranquilizers than ever before. She didn't even bother to keep them in a pillbox; they were in a heart-shaped ceramic candy box by her bed.

Her physical problems and the difficulties she was having with *Castle* were not all that was bothering her, though. There was something else— Stanley.

For years he had been her rock, the one solid, dependable, necessary element in her structure of survival. His flirtations, his occasional sexual adventures she had always known about or at least sensed. Painful as they were, none of them had ever truly threatened her; despite her jealousy, she was as sure of her uniqueness as she had been years before in college, and as sure of its ability to mesmerize him. Stanley, she knew, would never give that up.

But shortly after he turned forty, with a totally uncharacteristic lack of imagination, Stanley did something he had never done before in their marriage—did, in fact, just what thousands of lesser men did when they turned forty: he fell in love with another woman.

Had Shirley's success, particularly with her last book, finally gotten to him? Had the long, intense marriage taken a toll? Possibly. But more likely his reasons were not much different from those of any other middle-aged adult—a sudden grab at emotional magic, to stave off the coming night.

It had happened, however, at exactly the wrong time for Shirley. He did not tell her, of course, any more than he had told her about his lesser intrigues. In fact, he later swore to his second wife, Phoebe Pettingell, no one had ever known about the affair, except the principals. But of course, being Stanley, he was shading the truth. Actually, he had told June and Frank about it, and very likely a few others as well. Secrecy came hard to Stanley; even denying the facts to Shirley was difficult, though he did it steadfastly.

Still, denial or not, Shirley certainly knew. This was a woman many people were convinced could read minds; she had always been incredibly intuitive to moods and emotions around her. Furthermore, the woman involved was a friend of Shirley's, someone she had taken under her wing, as she did with women now and then. She could not know with absolute certainty, but the suspicion alone was enough to make her terribly upset, more than she ever had been before. This was not one of Stanley's snippy, aggressive students, or a stray literature groupie, and Shirley knew it. The woman Stanley had fallen for was an adult, serious, intelligent, and— most painful of all—very lovely.

"Shirley wasn't much for discussing her problems, but she was terribly distressed when she found he was having an affair," said June. "And this time was the worst. She was very proper, quite Victorian, in that she never wrote about sex, and couldn't talk about it either. But I think that she was very taken with sexuality, and resented it very deeply when she was being deprived.

"In a strange way, because she would not discuss it and would not deal with it openly, she was a very sexual woman."

The affair came at a time when she was at a low ebb, creatively; a time when she, too, was aware of her age, her decreasing energy. She was forty-three and her health was worsening; she was increasingly short of breath, burdened by her large body. She could see ahead both to meno- pause and to the end of her life as an active, engaged mother. Some women glide through these passages unscathed, but for Shirley, who felt so deeply the importance of both creativity and productivity, in all its forms, it would not be an easy trip.

She began, little by little, to fray. She had always kept her jealousy and suspicion of Stanley locked away from her children; both she and Stanley believed strongly in keeping adult problems strictly to themselves. "They did a masterful job of giving us a world as suitable for children," said Joanne. "Nothing to do with adults or the truth."

Now, though, her fears began to spill out in front of them, especially when she had been drinking. One cold, stark night, after a phone call from Stanley, she gave way completely in front of her three youngest children. Completely hysterical, she ran outside in her housecoat and slippers, a ridiculous, bulky figure slipping in the snow, desperate, trying to get to the car, screaming that she was going to go over to confront him and the woman.

Terrified, her children ran after her, the girls circling her, Barry, just eight, in his pajamas, sobbing with fear.

Joanne, reeling in "helpless horror and pity," somewhere found the strength to take control: she talked calmly and quietly to her mother, persuading her finally to go inside. Then she held little Barry in her arms and tried to soothe him. It took a long time.

"I was crying and screaming, saying, 'No, Mommy, don't go,' down to even being kind of aware: 'No, Daddy's not fooling around,' " he said. Even after Shirley had gone back into the house and up to her room, he continued to sob. "I don't want my mother to be crazy! I want my mother to be like everybody else! I don't want my mother to be crazy!" he cried.

Because by then they knew, all of them, that something was terribly wrong.

"A night of major drama," Joanne called it. "It went down in family folklore." She was sure Shirley's jealousy was groundless (even though Sally, three years younger, told her it probably wasn't); this assurance had helped her deal with her mother. "It takes a pure heart to talk somebody down like that." To her, it was inconceivable that her father would do such a thing, that another woman would do such a thing—to Shirley.

"I would crawl back in my cave before I would ever mess with Shirley's boyfriend. She'd turn you into a fucking toad. She was really a presence of force. You didn't know she could really turn you to stone, but you didn't know she couldn't," Joanne said.

But there was no doubt in her mind that Shirley herself had believed that Stanley was with another woman that night.

Stanley's affair ended after less than a year; it had never truly threatened the marriage. Nor did it cause Shirley's breakdown; too many other factors, past and present, were involved. But it hardly helped.

Shirley's terrors were intensifying; they were starting to incapacitate her. It was becoming more difficult to leave the house for the simplest of errands—going to the post office, shopping at Powers'. It was becoming difficult to leave the house at all.

Sally was aware even then that some of her mother's troubles had to do with the book she was writing. "She'd be at a point in her book where she couldn't stand to see anyone in North Bennington. What's fear of everybody but your own tribe called? A feeling that you're different, you're better, you're in danger . . . She took it to reality.

"She started saying, They're all talking about me. They wait till I go home. It was like . . . we were nursing her suddenly."

"She couldn't go to the post office, she couldn't go to a school play," said Joanne. Shirley, who had taken such pride for years in her competence, her ability to act as the eyes, ears, and mobility for Stanley and her family . . . Shirley, who had been for so long the lioness, protecting her cubs from danger . . . was becoming helpless.

Her closing-down did not happen all at once; it was a slow process of fits and starts. Despite everything, she had a solid core of strength that bobbed up repeatedly, in between bouts of terror. Part of it was simply confidence in her own worth or at least her talents. "Last week Gore Vidal lectured here and at the party afterward got very drunk and started cursing at me because I am a better writer than he is," she told her parents. "I did not find it very flattering, considering the language he used," she added.

But life was pressing in on her hard. The marriage may have been intact, however strained, but the family unit was beginning to crack. In fall 1960 Laurence entered Goddard, a Bennington-like school in upstate Vermont. The following summer Moe Hyman, the tyrant of their early years of marriage, died. To her he had always retained an aura of fearful invincibility; the death was a shock. Shirley went to New York with Stanley and the two oldest children, although she refused to go to the funeral ("I have a real terror of such things and will not go," she told her parents). Even more terrifying, though, was Stanley's reaction to Moe's death. "He sat in his chair and shook and lost twenty pounds in a night," Sally said. It was the first time anyone in the family had seen a sign of weakness in Stanley, and it upset them all.

In fall 1961, Joanne was sent away to private school, the Cambridge School in Weston, Massachusetts. Very few of the children of Bennington College faculty stayed at the local high school through graduation; the pressure to send them off to prep school was strong. But the sudden reduction in the number of children—from four to two—hit Shirley hard. For nearly twenty years, she had defined herself as supermother, bustling, caretaking, presiding over a large household. It was not easy to lose one of the roles she had prized the most.

She worried about Sally, precocious as ever, who at age thirteen was already showing signs of troubled adolescence. "Oh, well, someday she will be grown up and write books about her unhappy childhood," Shirley told her parents, a casual dismissal she was far from feeling. (Still, at the same time, it was a sly thrust as well—for wasn't that exactly what she had done herself? Not that she expected them to pick up on it.) Barry, on the other hand, had "none of Sally's rebelliousness," Shirley said, not altogether pleased.

Her increasing problems rarely showed up in her letters; she had long ago mastered the art of keeping them relentlessly upbeat at all costs. Even when she did describe a specific malady—her colitis, for instance— she was careful to tack on a happy ending. "The colitis induces a sudden attack of nausea, which causes an abrupt drop in blood pressure . . . which is exactly like getting kicked in the stomach, and I all but pass out. . . . Like most fainting spells, it is entirely a matter of suggestion: once I start thinking it might happen, then of course it all starts. I stay home as much as possible in the mornings, and so am making fine progress on my book; there's nothing like being scared to go outside to keep you writing."

A page or so later she thought better of writing even that much un- varnished truth: "Reading this over I feel that I have laid undue stress on my ailments. Please don't get the idea that there is anything serious about it; even the doctor doesn't take it very seriously." If there was one thing Shirley was never going to allow Geraldine and Leslie for a minute, it was the luxury of feeling sorry for her.

Stanley had been deeply involved in writing another tome, the most ambitious work he had done since *The Armed Vision.* This one, *The Tangled Bank: Darwin, Marx, Fraser and Freud as Imaginative Writers,* to be published by Atheneum in spring 1962, was a cool quarter-million words in length. "If nothing else, you can use it as a door stop," Shirley cracked. The index alone was 120 pages.

Money continued to roll in from the success of *The Haunting of Hill House,* and she was following the book's progress on the Hollywood front keenly; the movie was to be called *The Haunting,* directed by Robert Wise and starring Peter Ustinov, which pleased her, she said. (As it turned out, Ustinov did not star in the film.) Her letters were as brisk and cheerful as ever; there was no way for her parents to guess they were written by a woman who was retreating more and more from the outside world.

In the latter part of 1961, Shirley was finally getting toward the end of *Castle.* Pat Covici, her editor at Viking, had seen the first few chapters and was smitten; he sent letters beseeching her for more. The writing was going smoothly, at last, and Shirley was filled with hope—perhaps, when she was done with the book, the demons would be stuffed neatly back in the bottle; her problems would evaporate, her fears of going outside would fade, and she would be able to resume her life.

She ended her book on April 20, 1962. It had taken her three years, at least three times as long as anything else she had ever written. "I can hardly believe it's finished; it's exactly like having one of the kids leave home," she told her parents. "The desk is so empty without my folders of notes and the wall is bare; I usually make pages and pages of odd notes and tape them to the wall or the bookcase so they are right next to me while I work, and taking them down makes the room look funny."

Covici, to whom Shirley had dedicated the book, told her that not a word needed changing and that Marshall Best, editorial director of Viking, had cried when he read it. "Stanley says if the book can bring tears to those mean old publishing eyes it ought to make a million dollars; it's foolproof," she wrote her parents. On the other hand, Stanley had also told her that with taxes, another movie sale would finish them.

"Actually, I do not think this book will go far. It's short, for one thing, and Stanley and the publisher and the agent all agree that it is the best writing I have ever done, which is of course the kiss of death on any book, and then there is that batty heroine." ("Pop: the heroine of this one is really batty," she had warned.)

"As you can see, it is practically all I can think about. This is the worst time, when the baby has been sent out into the world, and you don't know how it's going to get along." Her colitis had vanished the minute the book was completed, too, she assured her parents, with vast bravado (it returned almost at once).

The months ahead looked hopeful: Laurence was planning to go on a European tour with his band; Sally would be attending the Cambridge School with Joanne in the fall; there would be the usual lectures and the Suffield conference. Shirley was truly relieved to have *Castle* done with at last; she looked forward to its publication and to an undemanding, uneventful summer.

She did not get it. In June Laurence announced that he and his girlfriend, Corinne Biggs, a local girl, needed to get married immediately, for the most age-old of reasons.

It was a hard blow, and Shirley reeled. This was not the route she had envisioned for her firstborn son. To get married at only nineteen, and to a local girl at that? Given Shirley's relationship to the town, this was not an easy thing to accept. Laurence's relationship with Corinne was comparatively recent, too; for years he had been attached to Jennifer Feeley, whom the Hymans knew and loved.

"Corinne was at an enormous disadvantage," said Barbara Karmiller. "She was from town, and coming into this incredible family which was very intellectually snobbish—not a lot of tolerance of stupidity or even the semblance of it. If you weren't verbal, agile and quick, out with you.

"She wasn't educated, she didn't have any experience, and she was very young. She was also beautiful, in an almost medieval kind of way. There was a temptation to think there was nothing there because of that."

In fact, there was a great deal. "Corinne turned out to be a genius," said Barry. Adopted as a baby by a family who had little regard for education, she had already completed two years at Bennington, almost unheard-of for a local girl. She eventually received advanced degrees in

Eastern philosophy and is currently studying at a Buddhist monastery outside Paris. But Shirley, with all her prescience, was unable to sense any of this. Her son was marrying a local, a breed for which she had little but contempt. No matter what her qualities, Corinne was a townie, and a bitter pill to swallow.

At the same time, both she and Stanley felt strongly that marriage was the only option at this point. It was a situation that brought out Shirley's conventional side, Jennifer Feeley felt—you have dinner on time, and if you get a girl pregnant you marry her. Others saw it in a darker light. "They let Laurie hang himself," said one woman. "He was nineteen— he had no business being a husband, much less a father."

Shirley struggled to put as good a face as possible on the events. "We are every bit as pleased and happy as I told you," she insisted to her parents. "I know it sounds awful and it was something of a bad shock to us at first, but actually we have been so accustomed to the idea of Laurie and Corinne getting married sooner or later that after the first gasp we decided that we were really delighted."

Geraldine's reply must have come as almost as great a shock. "We are not a bit surprised or shocked," she wrote breezily. "These things happen. With sex the topic of every movie and play and TV I can hardly see how the young people can avoid getting into scrapes." The one time Shirley was feeling most haughty and conventional, and would have welcomed a horrified reaction to match her own, her mother let her down flat.

It was a stressful time for everyone. Corinne's family was Catholic and wanted a church wedding, which, oddly, bothered Shirley even more than Stanley; arguments raged back and forth between families. ("I've said I'll never vote for Kennedy again," Shirley wrote her parents.) Relations within the Hyman household, too, were anything but calm. Stanley and Laurence had been at loggerheads for most of his adolescence anyway, in the time-honored tradition of fathers and firstborn sons, and the crisis did nothing to improve matters. "It should be a soap opera, *Laurie Faces Life the Hard Way*," Stanley joked nastily, his lack of sympathy plain.

"Stanley was vicious to Laurie when Laurie was a teenager," said Frank Orenstein. "If the father is a Freud expert and has read *The Golden Bough*—you have to get in there and keep the young prince from killing the king. Stanley did behave badly. He was very anti-Laurie and Shirley was very pro-Laurie; this was her child."

"He was harsh, really harsh," said June. "He accepted his kids, they were the children, but he was a harsh, disciplinarian father. He expected enormous things of them from the beginning. And Laurie always got a lot of the brunt."

Yet his love for his son was evident as well. When Shirley raged about the impossibility of a church wedding, he was quick to caution her. Anything was preferable to alienating parents from their children over a mixed marriage, he said. Didn't she remember what had happened with them?

As it turned out, no priest would marry them anyway, which solved that problem, at least. "So she is being married in sin, by a justice of the peace and her parents are sinning by coming at all," Shirley wrote her parents with satisfaction. "The good guys won." Actually, Corinne herself had sided with Shirley, against her own family.

The wedding was held at the college in an outdoor garden. During the short ceremony, Shirley began to cry quietly, surprising no one—all mothers cry at weddings. But her sobs became progressively worse. "Suddenly she was overcome with shaking and sobbing and had to be led away," said Frank. Later, she managed to pull herself together somehow; the rest of the day was without incident. But friends and family had been given a sudden piercing glimpse into her true emotional state, and the picture lingered, disturbingly, adding a grim note to the festivities.

"She got real shaky that summer," said Sally. "She was brave when Moe died, but then Laurence left the house and wasn't coming back, the woman was pregnant, they had a little house. . . . It was hard for her. She started contradicting herself. She started getting a little bit odd."

Yet she did her best to keep busy that summer, even flying to Michigan with Stanley for a lecture. But the thunderclouds were gathering; the storm was closing in. Even the fine reviews of *Castle,* published in late summer, did little to help. Shirley was beginning to realize she was in real trouble.

No one incident causes anyone to collapse emotionally; if anything, it is a slow increment of thousands of unknowable "incidents," beads on a long chain. Shirley was already hovering close to the danger line early that fall, when she received a blow which tore brutally into what was left of her shaky equilibrium. It may have had nothing to do with her final collapse, or it may have had a great deal. It came in the form of a letter from her oldest enemy.

Time magazine had run a picture of Shirley along with its flattering review of *Castle,* and Geraldine, seeing it, was aghast; she quickly wrote to her daughter. She ignored the review completely and concentrated her remarks solely on the photo. They were completely honest and utterly devastating. Her letter cracked straight through the genteel surface laid down so painstakingly over the years.

"Why oh why do you allow the magazines to print such awful pictures of you?" she beseeched in her large, sloppy handwriting. "I am sure your daughters at school are proud to show off your picture and say 'this is my mother.' I would sue them for libel. Your children love you for your achievements but they also want you to be worth looking at too. If you don't care what you look like or care about your appearance why don't you do something about it for your children's sake and your husband's.

"I do not know if the book review is good or not—and I have been so sad all morning about what you have allowed yourself to look like. We are proud of your works, but why do you have to have such a dreadful picture.

"I am sorry. I tried not to be sad. You have always resented any interference. You were and I guess still are a very wilful [*sic*] child and one who insisted on her own way in everything. Good or bad."

She went on to berate Shirley for not having let her know whether their wedding present (silverware) had arrived for Laurence and Corinne. "Pop and I spent quite a little money," she said huffily.

"Sorry about this," the letter ended, with a tag line that must have burned: "We love you very much and wish the very best for you—Mother."

Geraldine had always been a rather stupid woman, and certainly the letter reflected that, but it is hard to believe she was not at least partially conscious of her own viciousness. She had attacked her daughter in the one area where she held all the cards—personal appearance. And the attack was merciless. So what if you are smarter, write books, have more children, and lead an intellectual life, her letter seemed to say—in this arena, at least, you will never measure up.

Shirley's reply was filled with pain and pathetic dignity. The letter, she said, "upset me considerably, as you no doubt intended.

"I wish you would stop telling me that my husband and children are ashamed of me. If they are, they have concealed it very skillfully; perhaps they do not believe that personal appearance is the most important thing in the world."

Also, she said, she was "tired of being told that I am ungrateful and thoughtless. Naturally you would have heard from the children if the silver had arrived.

"Will you try to realize that I am grown up and fully capable of managing my affairs? I have a happy and productive life, I have many good friends, I have considerable stature in my profession, and if I decide to make any changes in my manner of living, it will not be because you have nagged me into it. You can say this is 'wilful' if you like, but surely at my age I have a right to live as I please, and I have just had enough of the unending comments on my appearance and my faults."

But the reply—which would have been the first direct confrontation with her mother she had allowed herself in years—was never sent. Instead, she waited a few weeks, then sent a letter that was as bland, cheerful, superficial, and dishonest as all the others she had written over the years. Oh, yes, she added casually at one point, the silver did arrive.

She had decided her interests lay in ignoring Geraldine's note completely, and she tried her best to do it. But the poison dart had found its mark. Shirley continued to crash downward, in an ever narrowing spiral.

"I have a happy and productive life," she had written, bravely. But it was a lie. By Thanksgiving 1962, she had almost no life at all. Her safety boundaries, which had grown tighter and tighter over the past months, had suddenly narrowed even further, down to almost nothing. She was unable to leave the house; she was unable, for much of the time, even to leave her bedroom.

"She became psychotic," her agent, Carol Brandt, remembered. "She wouldn't come out of her room. She huddled by her bed."

"I didn't really know what was going on," said Barry, who was the only child at home that fall. "At the worst time, it wasn't just that she couldn't leave the house, she couldn't leave her room. The smooth operations of the household were all screwed up. Something was all wrong and I didn't know what."

Sally, who was almost fourteen and away at school, worried about Shirley constantly. "I was shocked that my mother would send me away, especially when she was having troubles, but Stanley had taken me aside and said, 'Your mother's having troubles, and that's why she's sending you away.' It seemed like an explanation to him."

After a few months, upset and desperate, Sally managed, by dint of a little acting-out, to get kicked out of school. "I felt she needed me." Her mother, she discovered, was in bad shape, even worse than before.

"We had to take care of her, go down to the store and do the shopping. She wasn't doing well. Sometimes she would go out to the car and say, 'I really think I'm going to make it to the store today.' . . . Then she'd grip the steering wheel and start to cry. I'd take her back inside and she'd say, 'Don't tell your father. Just take me up to my room.'

"It's funny so many people have called her fear agoraphobia. I always saw it as claustrophobia. She could get in the car, she could drive around the countryside, drive to a writers' conference, even go in a strange store. It was more a fear of the people in the town. Agoraphobia and claustrophobia, those are kind of symptoms. The fear of people is a real thing."

Looking back, Sally felt that menopause played a role. "I think what actually happened was that the hormonal changes of menopause triggered whatever was lying dormant or latent in her—real primitive antisocial stuff. Her fear came out.

"She had been so competent. Shirley was one of those people who'd go right past a raging dog to get one of her babies out of a swimming pool. She'd never had a problem with fears . . . and all of a sudden . . ."

At times Sally wondered if there hadn't been some sort of neurological damage all along, even as far back as childhood, affecting Shirley. There was also the matter of her pill habit—certainly amphetamines have been shown since to be fully capable of causing paranoia, erratic mood changes, even psychotic breaks with reality. And Shirley used them daily.

But Sally sensed, still, that there was more to it than that. "I think she was made really nervous by the fact that she fought Stanley and she fought the world and fought her parents to be true to herself, and then it soured.

"She got the four kids and the big house and the smart husband and she went crazy anyway. And I think she felt really bad. She felt bad that the books weren't enough therapy, that writing a book every year or two didn't keep her sane. Because she put her guts into it. But it wasn't enough."

CHAPTER
·22·

Now came the bad time, the worst she had ever been through. Even during her months of depression years before in Rochester, she had never experienced anything like this hopelessness and fear. Then she had felt trapped by her parents, hounded by their expectations, unable to begin her own life. Yet there was always the underlying feeling that somehow she would throw off the shackles, somehow she would emerge, and prevail.

And she had, she had. She had emerged, with Stanley's help, a strange chrysalis, and unfurled in her own odd patterns; she had forged her way down unique corridors and carved her own new world, even while managing to hold onto some of the trappings of the old. It should have worked; in many ways, it had worked. Yet after all those years she was trapped again. Only this time the constrictions were even tighter; she was older; her body was huge, heavy; her breathing difficult, asthmatic. How could she free herself from a prison formed in part by her own body?

Barry Hyman paints a disturbing picture. "There she was, in this enormous body . . . and with chronic bronchitis, asthma, smoking two or three packs of unfiltered Pall Malls a day, smoked down to the short butt. . . . I remember hot, dusty, oppressive afternoons in the summer when she'd be lying in bed sweating and trying to take a nap, and the various pills would be having their up and down effect. . . . Maybe she realized that she wasn't going to turn the corner, that she'd gotten too old to stop drinking, stop smoking, stop eating a pound of butter a day."

As always, she turned to writing. The act of spilling words onto a page had always had a crucial importance to her. All her life she had depended on it, to give form to her world, to give vent to her power, to keep her sane. The words tumbled out, unchecked:

"since so much of my daily life seems to depend on what stanley does or says first think about stanley. . . . i do not want to quarrel with stanley because no matter what he thinks he is still fond of me and yet all my ailments seem to come from him why because i feel that he is always belittling me why because i am always belittling myself why because i feel that i am inferior why because i am inferior."

Abruptly, she brought herself up short: "now this bad typing and this bad sense is surely deliberate; i can do better. why inferior because he says so but i know the answer to that what i mean is why do i purposely assign myself an inferior position not because of anything except my own foolish head why oh why the hell . . ."

She tried her best to unleash her feelings of depression and unworthiness on the page: "i used to be able to write but no one even thinks of me any more when it is writing no one includes me no one talks kenneth [Burke] doesn't any more no one even the kids i am a writer i used to be a good writer and now no one even stanley says to students that i used to be." She tried to encourage herself: "and i feel sorry for myself and that is good because up to now i have not been able to feel even kind for myself."

But it came hard to her, this kind of thing. The habit of professionalism was too strong to break. "now. this is lunatic and of course save it for when you need a lunatic," she reprimanded herself sharply at the end of one page.

The truth was, she was not used to exploring her emotions directly in writing. She soon gave up the attempt. She had been accustomed too long to touching on them only indirectly, elusively, drawing on them for a higher purpose, her art. It was too late to change.

Instead, she made long lists. She had always been a list maker, and now, along with her lists of groceries ("ten lamb chops, six chicken breasts, 4 cartons Pall Malls, orange soda, frozen spinach"), she began to keep other lists as well, an abbreviated form of personal stock-taking: "no nap, pills (colitis), stammering, stayed up with Brockways, no home panic, thinking of work again," she itemized carefully.

And at times, at the bottom of a list, there would be a sudden realization: "Rereading stories. I was like this then only the writing handled it."

It could not continue; something had to be done. She had not been out of the house at all for nearly three months, since Thanksgiving. Even the birth that fall of her first grandson, Miles (named in honor of Moe), affected her very little; Corinne told a friend that Shirley rarely went near the baby and seemed almost unable to touch him. Not only had her paralysis brought her life to a halt, it was interfering with others' lives as well—particularly Stanley's. He was not callous, but he was an eminently practical man when it came to his own needs, and he had counted on Shirley to fill them for too long. The home machine had broken down; the carpooling-cooking-cleaning mechanism was on the blink. It needed to be fixed, and fast.

The obvious choice was psychotherapy, but Shirley feared and distrusted the idea. "I always felt it was a little bit like Christian Science," she commented. Despite the pain she was in, she was wary of outside intervention—she had spent her life entranced by the odd turnings of her mind and was not eager to let a stranger come in and start puttering with the works. Besides, it all sounded too much like a trip to the dentist, her own personal idea of hell.

Now, though, several people launched a campaign to persuade her to go—her husband, her doctor, a number of friends. It was a shame she was not back in New York, many said, where psychiatrists were falling out of the trees. However, even Bennington had its resident psychiatrist, a bluff, cheerful man, Dr. James Toolan.

"I was blunt about it," said Dr. Oliver Durand. "I said, Talk to this guy whether you like it or you don't. Don't expect any good to come of it for some time, but talk to him." Stanley was blunt as well; the Karmillers, Barbara and Murry, who had both spent some time in therapy, also joined the chorus. At last Shirley agreed to try.

She had her first appointment in February. "I was fortified with my usual tranquilizer and a sedative injection from Oliver, two stiff drinks and Stanley and Barbara, Barbara to drive and Stanley to get me from the car into the office," she wrote later (in an unsent letter to her parents). "I think getting out of the car in front of the office was the most terrifying minute of my life."

Dr. Toolan reassured her. "He said quite casually that of course this condition could be helped; why had I waited so long?" At home after her first appointment, she had a vision, a "sudden clear happy picture of what it might be like to be free again, and I told Stanley I was going to have the fastest analysis on record because I was in such a hurry to be well."

Toolan labeled her problems a "classic case of acute anxiety," and the simple fact of having her symptoms collected under a neat heading eased her somewhat. "Acute anxiety" sounded so much better than madness. She began, for the first time, to write letters, unemotional matter-of-fact letters—to friends, to her agent and her editor—telling them what had been happening to her. The responses were quick and sympathetic.

"I was moved and touched and saddened," wrote Pat Covici at Viking. "Anxiety fights dirty and dies hard. But oh, what a relief when it leaves you."

"Depend on Stanley. He is your rock," Paul Sanderson, her friend from the Suffield Conference, urged.

She also attempted to describe her problems in a letter to her parents. "It was literally impossible for me to go through the door; if I tried, I would start to shake and my legs would give way and everything would go around and around and I would begin to pass out, unless I got back inside fast. It was very strange and most unpleasant, and it kept getting worse, with all kinds of wild attacks of panic and nightmares and finally I could not even answer the phone. Oliver had me taking tranquilizers all day long but all they did was keep me kind of stupid but still frightened all the time."

Her first visits with Toolan had an immediate effect. "This morning she went inside the post office and got the mail and tomorrow she plans to drive herself to the doc (with me along in both cases)," Stanley wrote Sally on February 28 (she was back in boarding school, after four months at home). "She is much better."

A few days later, Shirley was able to drive to her appointment by herself; in a week, she braved the post office alone. Her gains delighted her. "I've moved with astonishing speed," she wrote her parents; there was a certain touching naiveté to her pride.

Writing them, Shirley initially tried for a tone of amused hindsight— yes, it had been bad, but she was well on the way to recovery. But it was much too early to sustain that pose; by the second page, reality broke through:

"Along with all of this has gone a kind of unbelievable confusion, walking the floor all night crying and feeling perfectly dreadful over something I can't even remember the next day, and the most horrible, perfectly obvious delusions. . . .

"It changes back and forth; one day I am fine, and the next depressed and desolate, with no cause at all." In the end, Shirley did not send the letter; she decided instead to tell her parents about her problems by phone, briefly. The letter had reflected her suffering too clearly. And yet something else showed up clearly too, in all the letters Shirley wrote around this time—unhappy as she was, she was also deeply fascinated with what was happening to her. For all the pain, it was still an adventure unfolding within her, and she watched its progress with sharp interest.

The psychiatric visits did help, particularly with her primary complaint, the inability to leave the house. "It was essentially agoraphobia that drove her in and that responded to treatment quickly," said Dr. Toolan. He found Shirley "an extremely honest person. Very very very very vocal."

"It's very rare to find someone urgently in need of psychiatric care who will have anything to do with it," said Dr. Durand. "I'd say only one patient in twenty who desperately needs it can be persuaded to do it with a club. Shirley not only went, they hit it off like a house afire, in the first interview. Toolan said he ought to pay her!"

It was not, of course, quite as quick or simple as all that, much as Shirley would have liked to pretend it was. "I backslide very often," she admitted in another letter to her parents written several months after starting therapy. "Also one result of this is a complete mental tumult, so that I cannot trust my own reactions or opinions; everything changes from day to day and there is no sense of proportion."

The "really surprising thing" about her breakdown, she added, was that "it started perhaps eight years ago, and has been getting worse ever since. Oliver points out that his records show that it was eight years ago when he first started giving me tranquilizers because I was so jumpy all the time."

Her use of tranquilizers continued, although Toolan maintains he was unaware of it. "I was not prescribing at all," he said. "I would never have prescribed for her. She was able to handle it without medication."

In actual fact, of course, she wasn't—or at any rate, didn't. Her use of tranquilizers continued unabated, along with her daily use of Dexedrine. Mood-altering pills were by this time almost as accepted a commodity in the Hyman household as aspirin is in others; both Shirley's daughters remember being offered a Dex by their parents at times during their adolescence, when they were feeling run-down, and an occasional tranquilizer, when they were having trouble sleeping.

"When I was in high school, if I said, Oh, I really have to stay up, could I get a Dex? they'd say, Sure, just take one. Finally I smartened up and started taking three," said Joanne.

At the same time, both Stanley and Shirley were appalled at the idea of illegal drug use, a phenomenon that was daily becoming more common around the Bennington campus. When they discovered that Laurence, who was finishing up college there as one of the school's first male students, had tried marijuana, they were furious.

The "perfectly obvious delusions" Shirley referred to in one of her letters could be strange indeed. Once, Laurence borrowed her car to go to his part-time job at a racetrack and parked it at the side of the road. He returned to find it demolished—it had obviously been hit. Shirley, terribly upset, called Bernard Malamud.

"She wanted to be sure he was aware of it," said Ann Malamud, "and that perhaps someone was after writers' cars. She told him to be careful. He found that very interesting."

The psychiatric honeymoon period faded; there would be no instant cure. The next months were dark ones for Shirley. Going out of the house remained difficult, though she pushed herself to do it. In addition, she was unable to launch herself on a new book; she was truly blocked for the first time in her life, and this above all made her miserable. When Sally was kicked out of boarding school for the second time, this one for smoking cigarettes, and returned home, she too began therapy with Toolan. "We were the two neurotics in the family," she said.

"The first time I had kind of wanted to go home, I felt Mom needed me. But this time, she was getting kind of weird. She was very dependent on me. I could almost always get Stanley to side with me now because we all knew Mom was neurotic, that she had a lot of problems. Sometimes she'd talk and I couldn't understand her, late at night."

Toolan was "a handsome man and he flattered her. He was impressed by her," Sally said. Others agree. "It was quite a feather in his cap, treating Shirley Jackson," said one friend.

"It had to be good for his ego," said Barry. "He had a famous client, Shirley Jackson, who wrote these famous books—and came to him to be pieced back together."

Stanley encouraged the wives Shirley knew to invite her to lunch, to get her out of the house. She went, but with obvious strain.

"I'd have to walk her back to her car, she was so terrified to be on the street," said Harriet Fels. "And of course she was taking pills; she'd take lots of them before she could leave the restaurant and go to the car."

Helen Feeley, too, met her for lunch at a restaurant in Bennington. She talked brightly, trying to disguise her shock at the way Shirley looked— "pear-shaped, in a stained blouse, her teeth like brown sticks. It was tragic. You just sort of felt she was losing her grip."

The Hymans cut back on their social life during the worst time of Shirley's problems—there were fewer parties, fewer overnight guests, less home entertaining. Yet even pared down, the Hyman social calendar was by no means empty. Very often now, they entertained not at home but at the Rainbarrel, a French restaurant that had opened, conveniently, at the bottom of Main Street. It was easier on Shirley that way. It became quite a common sight to see Stanley, weighted down with several bottles of wine, leading a group of friends down the hill to the restaurant.

There were new friends, too. A young couple, Mark and Kayla Zalk, had come to Bennington when he was appointed playwright in residence, and Stanley and Shirley took them under their wing. "She just decided I was family," said Kayla Zalk. "She was generous in all sorts of ways. She was like a big sister, a surrogate parent—warm and loving. That was my experience of her." After a miscarriage, Kayla woke up in her hospital room to the sight of Shirley sitting at the foot of the bed "with a mound of her best homemade brownies."

"What she sometimes did was adopt people," said Barbara Karmiller. "That's what she did with me and Kayla. Kayla really liked Shirley and wanted to know her. In other circumstances, that might have meant she would have encountered the sarcastic side of Shirley—but that didn't happen. You really didn't ever quite know why you were in the inner circle. When she accepted you, she was the ultimate in charm, but she was a master at keeping people away."

But even with the friends she felt comfortable with, Shirley never spoke of her own problems, even when they were at their peak. "She was not used to talking about personal things," said Barbara. "Very reserved. It amazes me how little we did talk."

"She could talk about things being hard with the kids, she could talk about pressures on Stanley, but her own problems, that was private," said Kayla. "As far as entering her own territory, she led the way, I never felt that I could intrude—she didn't articulate it."

"She wanted us to be friends on an ordinary, householdy level," said Harriet Fels, who had also learned that with Shirley there was "territory where you couldn't wander in."

Shirley worked to overcome her anxieties with a fierce will, making almost daily excursions into town, to stores, to the post office. It never became much easier, but as the months went by, it at least became somewhat more possible. Everyone knew she was seeing Toolan, but very few of their friends, even in that insular community, knew how hard a time she was having. Nor did she want them to. She had long ago perfected the art of projecting great competence and strength, of acting in a social setting in ways that, in Sally's words, "took people's attention away from the pain she was feeling."

"She never spoke of her fears," said Jean Brockway, who had known her since she first came to Bennington. She had the impression Shirley's phobias were "a minor aspect of herself," almost "little foibles," and her husband, Tom, agreed. "She was such a steady, solid sort of woman," he said; the fears seemed "incipient, surprising."

Ultimately, there was perhaps no one Shirley truly trusted outside her family, and even there she kept many things private, locked inside. But more and more she began to lean on Joanne—the child she had kept farthest away from her. She had considered her older daughter the most conventional of all her children and had treated her at times almost with contempt. Yet she knew Joanne above all of them had a talent for nurturance and compassion.

Joanne enrolled at Bennington in the fall of 1963. Shirley insisted she live on campus, but she came home often. Having Joanne along with her when she attempted to go on errands was a comfort, particularly if she lost her nerve at the last moment.

"She had her shopping planned so she could go into town, get everything done as quickly as possible, and get home," said Joanne.

The local Grand Union in Bennington was the only supermarket that had the good rye bread Stanley liked. "I remember one trip. She had decided she was going in to get this rye bread. It was a big store—and she made it down the first aisle, as far as the cabbage. But then she just turned around, put her hand on her forehead, and said she'd meet me in the car. I said, Don't worry, I'll get it.

"We didn't talk about it. It was—not normal, but accepted. I told her I thought it was great she had gone in and gotten that far."

Although she had managed to convince many outsiders that she was well on the way to health by mid-1964, Shirley's family knew the truth. In spring Stanley had a serious talk with Joanne. She would have to stay home over the summer and help care for her mother, he said—it was either that or send Shirley away.

"It was a contract with my father, basically," said Joanne. "He said, If you can't stay home this summer, your mother's going to have to go somewhere where they'll take care of her. I said, All right, I will."

That summer, for the first time, a real closeness grew up between Shirley and her older daughter. "I'd always been such a disappointment to her, a candy-ass—Sarah was the one who was such a pisser, the one who had all the talent; I was a total waste of time." Yet it was Joanne Shirley needed most now.

"We'd never been confidantes, ever, but that summer we talked about everything. It was great. I'm proud of it. She didn't really talk about being crazy because she was pushing for the end and desperate, and also she didn't want to burden me. It was bad enough it was there. But we had some great conversations."

One night Joanne returned home late from a date with a Williams boy and found Shirley in the study. Shirley poured her a drink and they sat, talking, far into the night. Shirley was relaxed and warm; for the first time, Joanne had the feeling she was trying to relate to her as a friend, not a mother.

"What about sex—you like it, don't you?" Shirley asked suddenly, a little shyly.

Joanne was shocked—her mother never spoke about sex. Moreover, her date that night had been something of a bust. A little embarrassed, she mumbled an affirmative.

"Good," said Shirley. "I just wanted to be sure that . . . you like it, you know how wonderful it can be."

"We started chatting, and she talked a little bit about her own history, about the size of the commemorative 4-H stamp," Joanne remembered.

"Then the word 'fuck' came up. She said she didn't know how to say that. We had another drink, and she said, 'How do you say it, anyway?'

"I said, Well, I just say—'Fuck.' And she said, 'Ffff . . . Uuck.' She kept trying to get it out. Every time she said it, we both thought it was funnier. She didn't ever make it. She got close, but she couldn't say it."

There were other times like that between them, golden moments. Shirley talked about her own parents more than she ever had before. She told her daughter how she had burned all her writings before she left for Syracuse, so that her mother would have nothing of her left. And she told her about the single most terrible thing Geraldine had ever done to her when she was a child: telling her she was a failed abortion.

"[Joanne] treats the things Shirley told her as dark information," said Laurence. The sort of stories a returning war vet could relate, remembered visions of hell. They were pieces of information she trusted to no one else.

"Maybe I was the one she had the least to lose with, since we'd been the least close," Joanne said thoughtfully. For whatever reason, they did finally connect that summer, and Joanne became the curator of some of Shirley's deepest secrets—a painful treasure, but one she is proud to have.

"I'm lucky I had that summer. Luckier than most of the daughters I know, still having it out with their mothers."

The time with her daughter seemed to help Shirley; the therapy, too, was having an effect. Toolan had encouraged her to accept lecture dates whenever possible, and late in the summer she went to lecture at Breadloaf, a writers' colony, driving up with Howard Nemerov. Nemerov had struggled often with his own writer's block, and he was sympathetic with Shirley's difficulties. "Why do you not write?" he asked her, and the question reverberated in her mind. Why do I not write, she asked herself, over the next several months.

Finally, she sat at the typewriter to try to answer the question. What emerged over the next months was a long series of pages, a journal in which she agonized and analyzed, her sight fixed longingly on a far shore where she would be healthy, obsession-free, newborn, and fully in possession of all her powers. Psychiatry had made its inevitable inroads; at times she was clearly reexamining herself from the perspective (and with the vocabulary) of the newly converted analysand.

But what she wrote was not as important as the fact that she was finally writing. And writing, alone at her typewriter, Shirley began the long journey of struggling up out of blackness into the light.

The writing was just for herself, but it was far from the kind of emotional outpouring she had tried before, with so little success. This time she tried to confront her condition straight on, coolly. It was clear she could not continue as she had before; that route had led finally to a dead end where she huddled, broken and shaking, in a closed room. Yet it had been the only route she knew. To launch herself on another path, after all this time—was it even possible? And how would that affect the most important part of her, her art?

"Insecure, uncontrolled, I wrote of neuroses and fear and I think all my books laid end to end would be one long documentation of anxiety," she wrote. "If I am cured and well and oh glorious alive then my books should be different. Who wants to write about anxiety from a place of safety? Although I suppose I would never be entirely safe since I cannot completely reconstruct my mind. But what conflict is there to write about then? I keep thinking vaguely of novels about husbands and wives . . . but I do not really think that this is my kind of thing. Perhaps a funny book. A happy book. There's room for it and I could do it. Plots will come flooding when I get the rubbish cleared away from my mind."

She made up her mind simply to sit at her typewriter for at least an hour when she could and write about whatever came into her head. Even if she never actually began another book, there would at least be a pile of pages to contemplate, and production of any kind always made her happier.

"I told the doc yesterday that the writing was happy, which of course it is. Writing itself is a happy act." She worried, though, about what Stanley would think of this sort of exercise: "I think he would regard me as a criminal waster of time, and self-indulgent besides."

Her odd obsessions continued, but she tried mightily to push them aside, refusing to write them down: "I don't think that this is a refusal to face it . . . but I do think that being unable to write about it is a clear statement by my literary conscience that I know the problem is not real, is imaginary."

The simple fact that she was sitting at her typewriter and writing anything at all, after such a long period away, was a positive one, she knew. "I have been thinking obsession-wise this morning. Not good. Writing is the way out writing is the way out writing is the way out," she repeated, like a mantra.

A few lines down, she had a flash of insight: "I know. I feel I am cheating Stanley because I should be writing stories for money."

The journal writing helped, soothing her. "I still do not entirely believe that I was not writing because my mind was so full of trouble and mishmash; I am sure that is part of it, but there is also the unwillingness to relax, to subside into the words and be carried along." Perhaps writing was a happiness she had not wanted to allow herself, during the sickness.

"I think about the glorious world of the future," she wrote a few days later. "Think about me think about me think about me. Not to be un-controlled, not to control. Alone. Safe."

And later: "Wanting is wanting; I have no world to go to. This is not a refuge, these pages, but a way through, a path not charted; I feel my way, but there is a way through. Not a refuge yet. On the other side somewhere there is a country, perhaps the glorious country of well-dom, perhaps a country of a story. Perhaps both, for a happy book."

The journal writing was "partly like writing my mother and partly like the writing I used to do when I was learning. Perhaps I am learning again; heaven knows I am learning enough about myself to develop a new style and I look forward every now and then to freedom and security (and I do mean security by myself) and that great golden world outside which I should be getting closer to every day."

As she continued, the writing became easier; her fingers felt more limber and natural at the keys. She wrote long descriptions of dreams, not so much as a springboard for self-analysis, as to just keep the flow going; it had been a long time. "What a tremendous relief this is, this writing, and why did I wait for so long before I tried it?" she asked.

She teased herself about her inability to talk about sex, even in these private pages, when it cropped up in her dreams. "I have already thought I will not be able to re-read this page without embarrassment and cringing because I wrote 'getting laid.' Surely this is unreasonable. Getting laid getting laid getting laid," she wrote, determinedly.

"Who is looking over my shoulder all the time?" she wondered. What could possibly be wrong with "a little wholesome vulgarity"? But "that thought of how my mother would read it comes at once," she admitted.

Her problems did not magically dissolve, of course. "Very depressed," she wrote on December 10. "Badly obsessed. Depression obsession ob-session depression . . . Make me undepressed, words." It was a heartfelt appeal. Although the journal reflects some of the lessons she had ob-viously learned in therapy—the emphasis on "health," on "controlling" or "not controlling," on standing alone—in the end, Shirley knew therapy alone would not bring her back, any more than pills or love; it was writing she must put her faith in. Writing alone could save her.

"I must do it alone; do I have the courage? I am shaking. One new symptom is a kind of sadness, almost a sense of loss; I am giving up something very precious and am withdrawing from something very im-portant. The new life is worth it, I do believe that. But I cannot always remember that what I am losing is cancerous. To be separate, to be alone, to stand and walk alone, not to be different and weak and helpless and degraded and shut out. My focus is gradually turning on myself, which is where it should be."

CHAPTER
·23·

She had asked the words to free her, and they did. Not long afterward, Shirley did what she had been unable to do for the past three years, what she had almost come to believe she would never do again: she started work on a new novel. Her anxieties had not completely disappeared, by any means; the shadow of depression still hovered over her. But the door to her creativity had been reopened—that barrier at least had been broken down, and it was the one Shirley cared most about.

Come Along with Me was markedly different from anything that had gone before. For the first time, her main character was exactly like herself— age and size both forty-four—a woman who was psychic, who "dabbled in the supernatural." She was a woman unencumbered by family, friends, and place, who was, in fact, "hungry for strangers"; a woman who creates herself on the spot, taking a new name and stepping into a new life as "Mrs. Angela Motorman, who never walked on earth before."

Come Along resounded with wit and energy and, yes, health; gone was the dark fortress of *Castle;* sunlight streamed through the pages. In place of lurking phobias and odd terrors, there was an almost homey relationship with the supernatural. Mrs. Motorman is a spiritualist who has always had the gift of sight, of communication with other worlds, but there is no sense of horror in her abilities—she is cheerful, sardonic, down-to-earth. Despite the distinct change in atmosphere, though, there is no doubt that it is Shirley Jackson at the wheel; the writing, pacing, and style all belong to her—moreover, to a Shirley working at peak performance, sure, able, masterful. Her talent had come through the fire unscathed.

"She had turned the corner. To my way of thinking, she made a great leap forward, between *Castle* and *Come Along*," said Barry. "She stopped being the victim and became the puppeteer. She had decided actively she was going to be the motorman—Angela Motorman—and operate the show from now on."

Actually the transition from *Castle* to *Come Along* is almost too perfect: a therapist's dream of health come to life, the final segment of a made-for-TV movie. Nothing was ever that simple with Shirley, in sickness or health. All her life she had lived in a world of layers, and veils, and truths hidden behind half-truths, and this was no different. Bolstered by two years of fairly intensive psychotherapy, Shirley was trying on a brand-new role—the role of emotional health. How deep it went is impossible to know; chances are, not quite as deep as it seemed on the surface. But therapeutically correct or not, the happiness reflected in the pages was real. Of course Shirley was happier—she was writing again.

Sally, the one who had inherited Shirley's powers of intuition, was wary of her mother's newly proclaimed stability. "She came out of it in a fake way. She was all full of triumphant statements—this sort of fake cheerfulness. It wasn't the same effect you'd get from someone who's really cured who would just like to forget that they'd been sick and start acting like nothing was wrong. When people are telling you that they're better, they're telling you that they're still bad."

Yet at the same time, she clearly was better than she had been, and they all knew it. She was working again, which was a deep joy, and her relationship with Stanley was closer than it had been for some time. "I think they bonded—I was clearly going to be as much trouble as Laurence, and I think it brought them together," said Sally, wryly.

For, in recovering, Shirley was not just currying her psychiatrist's favor, in the traditional manner, she was also seeking approval from the one person she had always wanted it from most—Stanley. There was no question he was proud of her gains. On a trip to New York early in 1965, he and Shirley met Fred Burkhardt, now living in the city, for dinner at Lüchow's. After a drink, Shirley excused herself to go to the ladies' room. Watching her wend her way around the tables, Stanley flung his arm out dramatically in the old way. "There goes a triumph of psychiatry," he announced.

"You mean, because she goes to the ladies' room by herself?" asked Burkhardt, sarcastically.

"You have no idea," said Stanley, in a quieter voice. Burkhardt had not lived in Bennington for several years. Stanley began to fill him in on Shirley's problems, his enthusiasm causing his voice to rise again. "It's absolutely the greatest success you've ever seen," he concluded. When Shirley returned to the table, he beamed at her, his eyes full of pride.

Toolan, too, was satisfied. "I think we did very well. I thought she had

262 • Judy Oppenheimer

done beautifully. She had started writing again, and she'd been ninety-eight percent blocked. My experience with writers has been that when they begin writing again you know you're home free. Her creative spark had come back.

"She was essentially a normal human being again. She had started working on *Come Along with Me,* and that, along with other things, showed me that she was the old Shirley. She was functioning well enough that she was pleased and I was pleased." The appointments began to grow fewer.

It was not just her writing that had launched her on a more outward trajectory than she had been on for the past three years. Late in the fall of 1964 Stanley had gotten sick, while on one of his frequent trips to New York. At first he was diagnosed as having flu, but when he came home, Dr. Durand took one look at him and stuck him in the hospital. His blood pressure was perilously high, and it began to look as if the so-called flu had actually been a bout of heart failure. The day of reckoning was at hand, Durand informed him sternly—it was time for a complete over-haul. Not only would he have to go on medication, he must clean up his bad habits as well—starting with a diet.

Shirley plunged into the world of low-cal cookery with all her old energy and verve. She hunted down new recipes tirelessly, and spent hours making laborious calorie lists. The difference between the two projects—writing a novel and spearheading a strict diet—could not have been greater, yet both gave her a very similar sort of satisfaction. She was once more a writer, and once more a necessary caretaker as well. Friends were amused—she seemed as thrilled with a new recipe she had found for mock potato pudding as she would have been with a rave review. (The recipe used cauliflower instead of potatoes, a sea change that rendered the dish, in the words of one guest, "quite horrible," but Shirley was delighted; at least Stanley would not be denied some version of his favorite food.)

The marriage was in many ways better than it had been for a long time. Unemotional as he was, Stanley was thrilled to have Shirley back to such a large degree, after the long hiatus. There were problems still, but the paralysis seemed to have lifted. She was even able at times to poke fun at him, as she had in the old days.

Stanley prided himself on his storytelling abilities, which were prodigious; but the Hymans had been socializing with many of the same people for a very long time, and inevitably, many of the stories were repeats. One night, when Stanley launched into an old favorite—the story of his first shattering viewing of the film *Freaks*—Shirley coolly interrupted him.

"You know, you've been telling that story for a long time," she said.

"And I never wanted to embarrass you. But really, Stanley, you should know—there is no such movie."

Stanley reacted with righteous fury. "What are you talking about?" he demanded. "I can show you a book that lists it." He left the living room and returned a few minutes later with a puzzled look on his face. The book was gone, he said. Shirley just shook her head sadly.

Stanley couldn't leave it at that. The following day he went to the library. To his amazement, there was no book that even mentioned the film. "I don't understand it," he told her.

"Stanley, I told you—there never was a movie like that. You made it up," Shirley said patiently.

It was not until nearly a year later that Stanley, looking through a closet, came upon a stack of film books hidden in the corner. Some were his, some belonged to the library; all mentioned *Freaks*. It had been an elaborate prank, one that made him doubt the workings of his own mind; it had been, in other words, pure Shirley.

Her journey through the dark woods, so like the one she had sent Natalie on in *Hangsaman* years before, had ended inconclusively, just as Natalie's had. She seemed to be out, but where was she exactly? What came next? Still, she had emerged for now, apparently.

The world outside had not stood still during her inner odyssey, naturally. Laurence and Corinne had moved to New York City, where they had a second child, Gretchen, in October 1964. Pat Covici, Shirley's editor at Viking, died that fall. Her daughters were now both heavily into the wilder, experimental stage of adolescence, Sally, precocious as ever at sixteen, doing her best to keep up with—or better—her older sister. Joanne was now calling herself "Jai," the name she would keep; Sally had gone first to "Geri" (her middle name was Geraldine), then "Sal"; "Sarah" would come much later. "Dear whatever-you-are-calling-yourselves-this-week," Shirley once wrote them, wearily.

Sally was managing to put her own unique stamp on the process of adolescence. As usual, when it came to rearranging reality, she had her mother's touch. She had met a wonderful boy in boarding school, she told her sister, showing her some of his letters, which were indeed impressively sophisticated. Richard was coming to see her, and bringing a friend for Joanne; they would have to sneak out of the house to meet them, late at night.

Joanne was wary but, like Charlie Brown every football season, finally agreed to go along with her. She and Sally slipped out of the house to the steps of the library, where they waited throughout the night. The boys never showed up. Sally was extremely upset, but not as upset as she was a few months later, when she heard Richard had been killed in a car accident—then her grief knew no bounds. It would be at least a decade before she let her sister know she had made the whole thing up—boyfriend, date, untimely end—out of whole cloth.

Shirley had little patience with a number of her daughters' activities, which ranged from self-destructive to silly, as befitted their age, but she did find herself interested in their emerging personalities. There were times now when she could sit around late at night with both of them, playing Scrabble, talking and giggling, in a way different from when they were younger. "She really enjoyed her children," said Jeanne Krochalis, who also had four. "And she understood that, despite all the problems of adolescence, it really does get better as they get older."

Shirley's interest in Sally's writing was sharper than ever. This was the child who had inherited her talent, after all, and she had no intention of allowing her to fritter it away. She insisted Sally write at least ten pages a night, although she could, of course, keep them private.

"I never showed her anything that wasn't finished," said Sally. "She'd be nice, but I could tell from the backbone in her voice that it wasn't quite what she hoped for. Stanley would be totally incisive—he'd say, it's very nice but you have seven grammatical errors and four illogical modes of thought. He'd tear it apart very kindly and artily.

"Between them I didn't stand a chance."

Still, one of her stories was good enough for Shirley to send to Carol Brandt, who sold it to *Gentleman's Quarterly*. "A weird little story about a girl who shoplifts," said Sally. She was sixteen when it was published. In a few short months her life would change forever, and one of the things that would go out of it would be the writing. She would never publish a story again.

Shirley's emotional health had improved, but her physical health had not. In January she came down with a virus, which worsened into pneumonia; she had to be hospitalized briefly. A few weeks later, when she went to see the Karmillers' newborn baby, Barbara was struck uneasily by how gray and even elderly Shirley looked. She leaned heavily on Joanne, who had to help her up the steps to the porch.

But she had spent too much time locked in her house over the past few years—now that she felt freer, she wanted to get out into the world. Over the next months she and Stanley took a number of short trips. In April they hit the lecture circuit with a vengeance, driving from Syracuse to Rochester to Akron to South Bend to Chicago. "Exhausting," she wrote her parents. An aberrant heat wave had kept the temperature in the nineties all the way; lecturing in Chicago, she "dripped all over" her notes. She was not at all impressed with the atmosphere at the University of Chicago; the students seemed very apathetic, and there was no sign of any sort of student rebellion. "No child of mine will ever go there," she announced.

Syracuse University, which had pointedly refrained from honoring Shirley or, indeed, taking very much notice of her at all over the past twenty-five years—the memory of *Spectre* had rankled a long time—had finally come around. Their old friend and mentor, Dr. Leonard Brown, had died in 1960, but a young teacher, Robert S. Phillips, had taken up Shirley's banner. He, along with one or two other literature professors, Dr. Donald Dike among them, managed to convince university officials they should bury the hatchet and award her the Arents Medal, Syracuse's highest honor. Shirley took the news in stride when she heard:

"Everyone [at the university] was very full of hints and suggestions, because although it is an official secret everyone knows that they are giving me an Arents Medal in June," she wrote her parents after going to Syracuse to give a reading. "I got the official announcement just before we left. They give three medals and it is the occasion of our class' twenty-fifth reunion. What they don't know is that I would have to be out of my mind to go and get it; I wouldn't go back to that reunion for anything. Also such an acknowledgment from Syracuse after all these years is not really as much a compliment as they seem to think it is. . . . I am writing to say no thanks."

And so she did, although she didn't put it as bluntly as that—she was sick, she told them, and her doctor had expressly ordered her not to travel. Since she was just making up a handy excuse, one of the replies to her letter must have given her pause: "I am not surprised. . . . Some of us thought you were pretty close to being a sick lady when you were here for the reading," Frank Piskor, the vice-president for academic affairs, commiserated. Since the Arents Medal could be awarded only in person, the matter was shelved, although Piskor did assure her he would be in touch the next year.

The urge to get out, to see new places and people, continued; she and Stanley began to make tentative plans for a trip to Europe in the fall, even though Shirley had repeatedly told people she would never go—"I'm not going anywhere where I can't get ice in my drinks," she had said. But she did have a yen to see historical London; the bloody history of the Tudors fascinated her, especially Anne Boleyn, to whom she'd always been drawn.

"She was now happy most of the time," said Sally, but there were still sudden dark moments. "She'd taken all the vague pain that had bothered her all the time she was phobic and concentrated it, so that sometimes she would just seem terrified and melancholy and horribly depressed." But she made a valiant effort to throw off such moods.

"None of my friends will let me go back to feeling young and alive," she wrote in one of her interior conversations, "because they all want me to join them in that kind of lonely mountain where you sit and turn around suddenly and look back on the long long way you've come and then realize that there's no place farther to go except down again and you don't dare turn and look down because there's nothing there.

"I read somewhere that the first sign of maturity was the realization that you could, actually could die. The feeling they want me to have now is that from here on it could happen any time. When I was twenty every year that went by was a triumph because it was getting me on toward growing up and really living, and now they want me to think every year that goes by is a horror, because each year brings me farther into an ever narrowing passageway of statistics; if I pass my fiftieth year the chances of my dying of measles are very small, but the chances of my dying of . . . no, this is depressing. This is the kind of thinking I promised myself I would never do again."

"She may have known she was going to die," Sally said. "She said things like 'I don't know how I'm going to end it. How would you end it?' "

June Mirken had some of the same feeling too—that Shirley, always prescient, foresaw her death. Over the years June had married a Yale professor, had two children and gotten divorced; she was back in New York City now, working and raising her son and daughter. Shirley rarely went to New York, and when she did she spent most of her time meeting with her agent and publishers; her visits with June were harried, strained. But early in the summer of 1965 she called unexpectedly. She was in town and wanted to come over, she said—she had a present for June's son, Eric.

"I was startled," said June. "It was so uncharacteristic. That she would come to New York, that she would be so calm, that she would bring Eric a present for no special reason when it wasn't his birthday or Christmas—it was almost as if she wanted to establish a connection to him. I knew she had always had the feeling that Eric was the continuity of her child-bearing—this was the child who came after Barry."

She had brought Eric an enormous box of Godiva chocolates. "He was absolutely entranced. Imagine giving a kid this huge box of grown-up candy, and it was his. We talked awhile, and she was—a different Shirley. Very calm and gentle. In retrospect, there was almost the feeling that she was anticipating . . . that she was pulling together all these loose ends. It was weird. But there were always those uncanny connections between her and me. She wouldn't have thought it was a coincidence either."

Stanley had recently published a book of collected critical reviews, *The Promised End,* which had received some nice attention. He was now planning a critical consideration of Flannery O'Connor, a writer both he and Shirley had immense respect for. In June they drove south to Georgia for a brief visit with O'Connor's mother and a look at the house where she had lived. As on all trips, Shirley drove.

Less than a month later, they were on the road again. This time they headed up to Canada, taking along Barry and his cousin Scott—the two boys had always been close. For once, it was a trip that did not include business; this was four days of pure vacation. The mood was high-spirited, relaxed; everyone sang songs, told bad jokes. Despite all the visits his family had made to Vermont, Scott had never really spent time alone with his aunt and uncle before; he had always been a little awed by their brilliance and somewhat fearful of Stanley's temper as well. Now, however, he was seeing a different side of them.

"There were no other children, no friends, nothing to upset them—it was a very different atmosphere. This was vacation. Just eat, drink, be merry," he remembered.

"It was a delightful time," Barry said. "No dark shadows intruded. We all really enjoyed each other. I was the least difficult of the kids at that time and Scott was completely harmless and nice and fun. It was all just perfectly idyllic."

Shirley knew only one word of French—*fermez*—but she used it to good effect. "*Fermez*, Stanley," she said repeatedly throughout the trip, infuriating him and delighting the boys. "Goddamn bilingual," he growled back at her.

In Quebec, adults and children split up during the day, Barry and Scott wandering around the streets of the city. Shirley and Stanley followed their own pursuits, which usually led to one of Quebec's restaurants—Stanley's diet was apparently on hold for the trip.

They had arrived around the time of Bastille Day, July 14, and the city was doing a flourishing business in black-market fireworks. It was irresistible to the two thirteen-year-olds, and on their last day they pooled their money and bought a huge supply. Late that night they crept out to a motel several blocks away from theirs and set off half of their stash. Minutes later, they heard sirens—the police had arrived. Terrified, they ran back to their motel room, panting.

Stanley and Shirley were waiting and very much awake; they too had heard the firecrackers and the sirens. "Was that you, setting those off?" they asked.

There was no use denying it. The boys nodded, abashed, and waited for the axe to fall.

Stanley and Shirley exchanged looks. Neither of them appeared at that moment very much like a parent to either boy. Middle-aged, overweight—somehow they both suddenly looked very young.

"Do you have any more?" asked Shirley eagerly.

So all four of them went out behind the motel, furtively, giggling, keeping an eye out for the cops, and Barry and Scott set off the rest of their fireworks—lighting them one after the other, as fast as they could, before anyone could show up to stop them. Huge cracks of sound burst on the night, flames of light shot up in the air, illuminating their faces, as both adults and children stood rapt, electrified.

And for a moment, for Shirley, it was like those nights years before when she had shown her children how to stand on the porch in a storm and face the thunder straight on—roaring back at it, gloriously, pitting your own strength against the sound-and-light show crashing across the skies.

The moment passed, the last firework sizzled out. Abruptly it was over, leaving only blackness and the cold distant stars.

On a hot stuffy Sunday afternoon several weeks later, Sally went upstairs to wake her mother from her nap, as she had done nearly every day that summer. Joanne, who had done it before, was in Rochester, working in summer stock theater. Shirley lay under a spread on her bed, her long hair loose on the pillow. She did not respond when her daughter touched her, at first lightly, then with increasing agitation. Sally paused; the room was still, with no sound of Shirley's heavy breathing. Panic clutched her.

"Dad!" she screamed suddenly. She ran to the top of the stairs calling him. Stanley came up swiftly, Barry behind him. He knelt at the bed, calling Shirley's name, trying to see if he could find a pulse in her wrist. Quickly, he asked Barry to bring him a mirror—he held it to her mouth and they waited, watching for a sign of breath. The emergency measure did not seem odd to his children—if it had a literary flavor, it was because that was the world Stanley knew best. The mirror looked slightly cloudy: Was it breath? Was she breathing?

"We didn't think she was dead," said Sally. "We thought she was alive and tried to wake her up for minutes and minutes."

Less than two weeks before, Sally had tried to commit suicide, taking all the tranquilizers she could find in the house, then lying down with a copy of *Hill House* open in front of her. "I thought, She'll be so sorry, she'll know who the best child was, either way, if I die or live. Either way I win. It didn't make much difference to me. But maybe deep down I knew it wouldn't kill me." Stanley and Shirley had rushed her to the hospital to have her stomach pumped. Later Shirley wrote a letter to Joanne mentioning it almost casually; she had not taken it very seriously, it was just one more of Sally's dramatic gestures.

But when Sally and Stanley saw Shirley lying still and unresponsive on the bed, their first thought was that she might be playing a strange game of revenge. "We assumed she had taken a bunch of pills to get even with me," Sally said. "We used to do that kind of mother-daughter stuff." Long minutes ticked by as they tried to rouse her.

Finally Stanley told Sally to call Dr. Durand. But he was out; very few doctors were home on a sunny Sunday in August. Her heart pounding, she called the only other doctor she knew, Dr. Toolan.

Dr. Toolan himself was taking a nap that afternoon; the phone call from the terrified girl woke him up. They were having trouble waking Shirley, she said—what should they do? The psychiatrist suggested she call Dr. Durand. She had tried, she said, but he was out. Then perhaps she ought to call an ambulance, he said. He hung up and went back to sleep.

"I wasn't fully aware," he said. "It came across as 'Mom's just sleeping.' After I woke up from my nap a half-hour later, I called." By then, it was all over.

Dr. Durand checked in for his calls and was told about Sally's frantic one. Soon after she called Dr. Toolan, Dr. Durand arrived at the house. He and Stanley went into the bedroom, while Sally and Barry waited downstairs on the porch. "We were shuffled out," Barry recalled.

"I examined her and pronounced her dead," Dr. Durand said, simply. The date was August 8, five days before her twenty-fifth wedding anniversary. Stanley's present to her, a beautiful amber necklace, lay on the bureau near the bed. She was forty-eight years old.

The cause of death was cardiac arrest, said Dr. Durand. "I think I put down 'arterial sclerotic heart disease.' I'm morally certain in my own mind that she had the common cause of sudden death, ventricular fibrillation. It's a very common cause of sudden death. I don't think there was any particular cause—she went to bed and went to sleep and this thing happened. I no longer have the files."

Moments after Dr. Durand's pronouncement, the children heard Stanley's tread on the stairs. It was heavier than they had ever remembered it being. "Your mother is dead," he said woodenly.

It seemed unreal. "I remember him coming down the stairs and saying, 'Your mother is dead,' like a scene from a movie," said Barry.

The rest of the day blurred for all of them. Barry sat on the porch with his guitar, strumming a single chord over and over, late into the night. Sally stood at the sink washing dishes, compulsively, with meticulous care. Every so often she would hurl one against the wall, screaming, "Mom!"

Stanley sat in his study making phone calls, one after the other. Each time, he repeated the same words: "Listen, prepare yourselves. Sit down. I have some bad news to tell you. Shirley has just died." Sally and Barry heard the words again and again, an endless tape loop. Each time they struck the same chord of horror and desolation.

At Laurence's small New York apartment, late in the afternoon, the phone was ringing. Laurence and Corinne had taken the kids to the zoo for the day and returned late. They heard the phone from the hall outside the apartment. Laurence struggled with the key, urging the phone to keep ringing long enough for him to get to it. He burst into the apartment, grabbed the receiver breathlessly. It was Stanley. In a low voice, barely audible, he told him his mother was dead.

Friends from Bennington began to gather at the Hyman house in the late afternoon. Stanley's poker group, the Feeleys, Barbara Karmiller. Dr. Toolan, too, came to the house. Awkwardly, many approached Sally. "Are you going to finish your mother's book now?" they asked her, patting her. "You'll have to be the writer in the family now." Each well-meaning comment stung like a whip lash.

Philip Hamburger, Stanley's old friend from *The New Yorker,* was in Vermont that day; he and his wife had driven up to visit their sons at a music camp near Bennington. They had decided not to call the Hymans too early. "They're so generous, they'll insist we come have lunch with them," said Hamburger, who didn't want to put them out. "We'll have lunch first so we can honestly say we've eaten." After lunch they called. "Shirley died about a half-hour ago," Stanley said. "She went upstairs to take a nap and she died in her sleep."

Joanne could not be reached; she had gone away from Rochester for the weekend. It was over a day before her family was able to contact her. "We left messages for a day and a half, and by the time she got home, she couldn't even see Shirley," said Sally. "She'd already been cooked." Both Shirley and Stanley had always been adamant about wanting cremation—neither of them wanted anything to do with funerals, burials, or gravesites.

The night Joanne finally came home, the four children gathered in the dining room, around the long table, staring at each other, listening to the echo of Stanley's footsteps as he climbed the stairs to the bedroom. "He won't last five years," said Laurence quietly. The words hung in the air; to the others they had the sound of absolute, implacable truth.

Two people received letters from Shirley in the days after her death. Bunny Hyman, her sister-in-law, got a long, chatty one. Arthur had recently had a minor heart attack and had been told to change his diet; Shirley's letter was full of advice and some of the low-calorie recipes she had been experimenting with. Try brisket, she urged Bunny, even though you have to cut it on the diagonal "and I never know what that means." She also told Bunny again what an enjoyable trip they'd had with Scott;

his company had been a real pleasure. She was feeling a little sick, she added; nothing much, just a stomach flu that kept hanging on.

The second letter, to Carol Brandt, was odder—so odd that Brandt mentioned it to Sally and sent it to her. It was a happy letter, full of energy. She was about to go on a wonderful voyage, she told her agent, where she would meet many new people. There were no details, but it was plain she was not talking about an ordinary trip. She was, she said, going alone.

"Maybe—I don't really believe this myself—but you couldn't argue with the theory that she really did kind of leave her body behind," said Barry, "that she took the trip consciously. It's possible. She had turned the corner, with *Come Along with Me,* sloughed off mental illness as a technique that didn't work for her anymore. Maybe, coming to that kind of wisdom on top of a body that was that shot through with holes, she just decided, Rather than spend the next twenty years trying to get healthy, I'll just die. Pass on to the next phase.

"Maybe she did consciously decide her mind had outgrown her body. And just—made that leap."

There was one more message from Shirley. In December, four months after her death, in the week that would have seen her forty-ninth birthday, *The Saturday Evening Post* published her last story. It was not the best she had ever written, but in some ways it was the most nakedly revealing. Certainly nothing she ever wrote came as close to defining her own conception of herself.

"The Possibility of Evil" was set in a small New England village. The main character was named Miss Strangeworth, a highly unusual, unsubtle choice—Shirley had never before used a name to denote characteristics. Miss Strangeworth lives on Pleasant Street, where her family has lived for generations; she is an elderly lady, exceedingly proper, respected by all the villagers.

Yet she has a secret. Every night she retires to her room, extracts a page of stationery from her desk, and writes letters, terrible letters. The letters deal with evil; they explore the town's deepest, most terrible secrets. One, to a young woman, tells her of her husband's affairs; another informs a store owner of a trusted employee's dishonesty. It is not known— nor does it truly matter to Miss Strangeworth—whether the letters are literally true or not. It is, as the title says, possible evil she is concerned with.

Daily she goes out to send her letters to the people she feels should have them. On her way back from the mailbox she smiles pleasantly, occasionally stopping to chat with villagers, friendly but not effusive, as befits a lady.

There is at last a discovery and a retribution; the story ends on a weak note. Not entirely successful, but significant all the same. For this was almost precisely the way Shirley wanted to see herself—a proper lady, sure of her place, who sent forth her terrible messages to the world yet remained anonymously secure. The letters she wrote were disturbing, even unpleasant at times; they dealt with subjects others would prefer to keep buried; they forced people to face the evil—the possibility of evil— always present in the human heart. Yet this was what she was meant to do in the world. A difficult task, not perhaps the sort likely to bring much appreciation. But a necessary one.

"There was so much evil in the world and only one Strangeworth to deal with it," she wrote, sensing—possibly even knowing—that soon there would be none.

CHAPTER
·24·

Shirley was dead. The heart of the home, the great throbbing core of it, was gone. Her family reeled, shattered and lost. But none of them was as lost as Stanley.

In the weeks after Shirley's death, Stanley acted disgracefully to nearly everyone. He made cold, pithy announcements: "A great writer lost to the world," he told Tom and Kit Foster. "Such a great writer to die so young." He chortled loudly at some of the awkward things people said, not always out of their earshot. To the Brockways, he even imitated the look of exaggerated fake sorrow he thought he had seen on one colleague's face.

When the sympathy cards began to pour in, Stanley attacked them with critical venom as if they were a pile of sloppy freshman themes, quoting the choicest clichés aloud to guests. He had written back to one person "Thank you for your heartfelt platitudes," he bragged to Harriet Fels, who recoiled in horror.

He got drunk, he harangued, he made wild passes at nearly everyone within reach, blindly, even making a half-grab for his own daughters in a taxi one particularly drunken night. ("We weren't offended. We just said, Come on, Dad, it's us," said Joanne; they took him home and half carried him up to his bed.) He blurted out sudden false confidences to unlikely people. "We only stayed together for the sex," he assured one very proper woman, shocking her terribly.

In short, he managed to antagonize nearly everyone. It wasn't until weeks later, when he finally allowed his brother and sister-in-law to visit, that he sat in the silent, empty bedroom, surrounded by Shirley's things, and wept. He was a man who disdained emotion—that had been her department—but in front of his family, he could not avoid facing the truth. He had lost the most important person in his life, forever.

Even the most minor chores defeated him. Stanley had never learned to take care of the practical exigencies of daily life; Shirley had always been there for that. Sally and Barry remembered his first, desperate attempts to make coffee; he tried, with growing despair, to assemble the coffeepot, finally throwing it across the room with a howl of anguish. It was low comedy, the ultimate cliché—he had literally never learned how to boil water. Yet seeing it come to life was not comic at all; it was deeply unsettling.

"I had always had to protect my mother, I had to protect my sister, I had to protect my little brother," said Sally. "I didn't know I had to protect Stanley. I thought he was all-powerful, until he showed his weakness."

His energy was focused on his own survival; there was little left over for his children. In the next months, he relied on a series of housekeepers and students to help him out, with varying results. There had always been sycophants at Bennington who adored him from afar—but afar was one matter, taking care of his kids and his house and his diverse needs another. Not many young women were ready to pay the price.

"He got some real rotten housekeepers," said Sally. "Nasty old broads who would cluck cluck cluck over the way my mother didn't polish anything or had drawers full of junk. One of them put all Barry's teddy bear collection in plastic bags, because they were dirty, and then burned them."

It was plain this disruption could not continue; Stanley needed a wife. He began dating, and in less than a year had married one of his students, Phoebe Pettingell, a very bright, attractive, somewhat old-fashioned young woman from an upper-middle-class Chicago family, with "a high piping voice and a high Anglican religion," according to Howard Nemerov.

Most of his friends understood. "I suppose I thought at the time, That old fool," said Tom Brockway. "But now, looking back . . ." Nemerov was sympathetic from the start: "Imagine this poor corpulent learned man who didn't know fuck-all about running a house and who never wanted to learn." The new marriage came as no surprise.

"It had been so hard to think of Stanley coping at all," said Barbara Karmiller. "And it wasn't just Shirley's practical skills he missed, it was her intellectual skills as well.

"You don't find two Shirleys in a lifetime. So he chose one, chose the intellectual area. It seemed to work out." Phoebe shared his interest in criticism, in editing; she deferred to him as a teacher and mentor. His old friends gulped—no decision Stanley made now, short of donning saffron robes and pledging himself to celibacy, would be completely acceptable, Frank Orenstein realized—and tried to accept.

For Stanley, the marriage was a tenuous lifeline; for his children, particularly the two youngest, it was a heavy blow. His new wife was only twenty years old; she had, in fact, been in Joanne's class at Bennington. She was a contemporary, a consort for Stanley, not someone they could turn to for their own needs. Acceptance was difficult; it would have been with anyone Stanley married. All of them were still reeling in their own pain, the pain of having lost their mother.

She had been the fixed center of the family solar system, the one who brought it all together; with her death, each of them spun out of orbit into a lonely, often erratic path. Sally and Barry, still at home, only sixteen and thirteen, were the hardest hit.

"After she died, I didn't do well," said Sally. "I couldn't sleep at night, I'd be up all night, I wouldn't sleep till dawn, then I'd have to get to school like a regular human being. If it hadn't been for Dexedrine, I wouldn't have kept going. For months after she died, if I saw anybody's picture in the paper, I'd start to scream, 'That's my mother, get it out of here.'

"After she died, not only did everybody say, 'Are you going to finish her book,' they'd come right up in my face. Stanley too . . . 'Well, Sarah, I guess you're going to have to finish the book.' I didn't write after that.

"It was just a very uncomfortable time. Here I was, the cripple of the family, the one everybody was supposed to feel sorry for—and then my mother dies. I figured I could really jerk off on the world because my mother was dead."

Over the next years, Stanley published two collections of Shirley's work—*The Magic of Shirley Jackson* in 1966, which included eleven stories and three novels, *The Bird's Nest, Life Among the Savages,* and *Raising Demons;* and *Come Along with Me* in 1968, which contained sixteen stories, three lectures, and her uncompleted novel. With the help of Barry, Sally, and Phoebe he bundled up the old papers she kept in the attic—scrapbooks, diaries, letters, and journals—and donated them to the Library of Congress. In her will, Shirley had named Stanley as her literary executor and, after him, Sally, "the only child I would trust with my papers," she once said. (Stanley, mindful of her wish, handed down the executorship to Sally in his will, stipulating only that Phoebe retain it until his daughter turned twenty-four.)

He felt a strong commitment to Shirley's work, which had been such an important part of her—and this, at least, was a commitment he was fully capable of handling. A short essay he wrote after her death reflected the total belief he had always had in her:

If the source of her images was personal or neurotic, she transformed those images into meaningful general symbols; if she used the resources of supernatural terror, it was to provide metaphors for the all-too-real terrors of the natural. . . .

For all her popularity, Shirley Jackson won surprisingly little recognition. She received no awards or prizes, grants or fellowships; her name was often omitted from lists on which it clearly belonged, or which it should have led. She saw these honors go to inferior writers, or to writers who were no writers, without bitterness, but with the wry amusement which was her habitual attitude toward her own life and career. . . .

I think that the future will find her powerful visions of suffering and inhumanity increasingly significant and meaningful, and that Shirley Jackson's work is among that small body of literature produced in our time that seems apt to survive. That thought, too, she would have found wryly amusing.

His commitment to his adolescent children was another matter. His sense of responsibility was strong, but child-rearing had never been his department, or his talent. In the end, Stanley opted out. Barry was sent to a private school in Chicago, near Phoebe's family; later he returned to live with Laurence and Corinne, who had moved back to Bennington. Stanley and Phoebe traveled throughout Europe; on their return, Stanley, with Phoebe's encouragement, took a post at the University of Buffalo. The Hyman family was effectively disbanded.

Shirley's children—particularly Joanne, Sally, and Barry—were caught up in the rushing current of the sixties. All of them experimented with drugs to a greater or lesser degree, with Sally eventually spending two years in Synanon to overcome her habit. Both girls married early; Sally strapped her firstborn daughter, Shiloh, on her back to explore India; Joanne moved to upstate Vermont to a semi-commune. Barry, who had been the least difficult of all the children, had trouble at school for the first time in his life. He later plunged into "a ten-year abyss" involving heavy drugs. Laurence, at twenty-two the most settled, and always the most ambitious, had an easier time. He moved back to Bennington to design and manage the newly created *Bennington Review*. When his marriage broke up a few years later, he moved to San Francisco.

Stanley's response to his children's various routes was generally testy and ineffective. He refused to bail Sally out of a Florida jail when she was arrested for marijuana possession; she spent nearly three months behind bars, finally convincing the authorities that prison was "a bad environment for my unborn child." Stanley changed his will a number of times, to demonstrate his ire—against Joanne, for taking up with a man he did not approve of; against Laurence, for leaving his family. Generally he changed it back fairly quickly. Joanne was shocked to find after his death that she had been reinstated. Laurence, though, had not yet been restored to favor, a painful blow. Stanley had bypassed his older son, leaving his share to his two children, Miles and Gretchen.

Miserable up in Buffalo, Stanley begged Bennington to take him back. The old house on Main Street had been rented out to a new family, the Aldriches; now Stanley made plans to sell it to them. (Sally would have liked to buy it, but she was unable to come up with the money.) "But what do we do with all the junk?" he was asked; one room off the kitchen, for example, was crammed floor to ceiling with broken, rusting appliances—all the appliances the Hymans had tossed away over the years.

"Throw it out," said Stanley. It took a large truck five separate trips to clear the single room. Among the debris the Aldriches noticed at least six broken toasters, four blenders, several coffeepots.

Stanley and Phoebe moved into the Orchard on campus. On July 29, 1970, they went to dinner at the Rainbarrel with Corinne and a friend of hers, writer Jesse Kornbluth. Stanley had stayed close to Corinne. Discussion at the dinner table—as always when Stanley was present—was brisk and animated. About to make a telling point, Stanley lifted a wineglass to his mouth. Suddenly he paled, dropped the glass, and slumped across the table, dead of cardiac arrest. He was fifty-one years old, and Laurence's prediction had been eerily correct—he had not survived Shirley five years; he had missed the fifth anniversary of her death by ten days. His wife gave birth to his last son, Malcolm, three months later.

Each of the Hyman children has struggled with a difficult legacy. It has not been easy to come to terms with extraordinary parents who died young, long before they could be seen in more human, manageable terms. The children's sense of anger and loss runs deep, but their loyalty and love run even deeper.

As young adults, they were scattered, alienated from each other; they squabbled often, even about such matters as the proper place for Shirley's ashes (they changed hands several times, finally settling with Barry, who "procured them by deceit and held onto them by force," he said proudly. It is probably a better place for them than with Sally, who once seriously considered selling them to admirers, grain by grain, through *Writer's Digest* magazine). Today, though, twenty-three years after their mother's death, they are all close, a strong protective unity.

Joanne, divorced, lived until recently in a small town in upstate Vermont, with her son, Max; she has relocated in Bennington. The other three children are in the San Francisco area. Laurence, who heads a successful publishing company, lives in a town house not far from Seal Rocks, with his wife, Cynthia, their three-year-old, Nathaniel, and the twelve-year-old son of his second marriage, Bodie; Barry, who teaches courses in acupressure and works as a professional musician, lives with his fiancée in Oakland. Sarah is in nearby Emeryville, with her husband, Lao. She has three children, Shiloh, Ethan, and Reuben, and one grand-daughter, Jamila.

Very few of Shirley's beloved objects remained with her children. Her witchcraft books, along with Stanley's books and collections, were in-herited by Phoebe Pettingell; other things have been scattered over the years. Laurence treasures the few items of hers that he owns—the pewter mask of Pan, the Harlequin painting, the music box. Joanne has the Tarot decks she used, wrapped carefully, and the amber necklace that was Shirley's last present from Stanley. Sally did have her gold wedding ring for a time but lost it—a seer told her it had fallen down a toilet in Vermont.

All four are very conscious of the deeper parts of their mother that live on in them. Sally puts it sardonically: "Jai got the asthma, I got the claustrophobia." According to Laurence, though, "We are all somewhat reclusive."

Laurence knows that part of his attraction to San Francisco was the urge to seek out his mother's roots. He alone of the children made an effort to have a relationship with Shirley's parents, who died only a few years ago, and her brother, Barry, who lives in Burlingame. Laurence's publishing company puts out magazines for the San Francisco Giants—which was, in another incarnation, his mother's favorite baseball team. Between baseball and literature, Laurence should be able to find work, his mother once said—and he has.

Barry is aware that his strong interest in holistic medicine stems in part from his parents' complete refusal to take care of their bodies—a refusal that still angers him, even while he tries to understand it. "They thought that being artists meant you had to suffer and die for it. I'm not willing to buy that premise. I resent the fact that they're not here now. I resent that they died on me," he admits candidly. "Why weren't you sensible? When you add it all up, it's still worth sticking around and laughing at."

Joanne, for her part, knows that some of her intense involvement in parenthood is a reaction to Shirley. "I inherited the housewife side," she says. Her home is modest but immensely warm and appealing, the sort of place people gravitate to; she has clearly inherited Shirley's art of "making comfort" around her.

Sally, the rebel, continues to rail against the status quo. A final inter-view had to be postponed so she could lead a group in protest songs during the pope's 1987 visit to San Francisco. She has carried with her all her life the heavy knowledge that she was Shirley's anointed inheritor. "As I tried to write like Shirley, I've tried to live like her," she said. "I've sung her songs, I've worn those big velvet dresses she wore. But most people don't want what Shirley is and I am. . . . They'd much rather have something that's easy-listening, light music."

She has tried for years to "unobsess" herself. Lately, she has done AIDS counseling. For a recent Christmas she invited a number of homeless men to come trim the tree. "Trying compassion," she said, flippantly—and a different route. These are things she knows Shirley would never have done, any more than Merricat.

She has never written again, since her mother's death. Nor has she ever again tried to commit suicide. Her boldness, which meant so much to Shirley, has survived. "I would hope nothing could ever kill Sarah's spirit," said her sister.

Shirley's eight grandchildren—and one great-grandchild—are an unusual bunch—highly intelligent, remarkably beautiful. Her first grandchild, Miles, is an artist, a photographer, and a singer; her second, Gretchen, recently wrote a screenplay based on *Sundial*. "You know, my father always believed all this stuff skips a generation," said Laurence, looking at his sons fondly. He finds the thought oddly comforting.

At one point, during the worst of his bad times, Barry had a clear dream—one of those dreams that almost seem to tell you, Pay attention, this one's important. He saw Shirley, dressed in a white flowing gown, walking back and forth along the sands of an endless seashore, obviously intent on some task.

Eagerly he approached her. Where have you been? he said. We thought you were dead. Why are you out here?

She had a mission to fulfill, she said, simply. She couldn't stop until she was done.

It seemed a terrible, lonely thing to him, being out there on the sands, but Shirley made light of it, the way she'd always been able to do. Well, she said, grinning, it was a long time out there between brandies, she had to admit . . . but this was something she had to do. It was work that was essential.

The dream stayed with him a long time afterward, like a benediction—the vision and, most important, her humor. "That was what made me feel better," he said. "The sense that what I'm doing might look totally pointless, but I don't really care, I'm being true to myself."

It was very like the last lines Shirley ever wrote in her journal, six months before she died:

I am shocked at how miserable I have been for so long. I know something about this obsession business. It isn't real. It is a huge cloud of looming nothingness triggered off by small events. But it is not real. It is divorced from anything real, dissociated. Laughter is possible.

I am the captain of my fate I am the captain of my fate I am the captain of my fate.

Laughter is possible laughter is possible laughter is possible.

NOTES

In researching this biography I relied primarily on my interviews and correspondence with Shirley Jackson's friends, family, and associates, and on the Library of Congress's extensive forty-two-box collection of Shirley Jackson's papers—published and unpublished manuscripts, scrapbooks, sketches, diaries, journals, college notebooks, shopping lists, and letters, including those she wrote to her parents over a seventeen-year period, from 1948 through 1965. I have naturally used her published work as a source as well, not only her books but also the innumerable short stories and articles she wrote for magazines during her life.

For the generosity of those I interviewed and the comprehensiveness of the collection I feel deeply grateful to Shirley Jackson herself—she saved everything and she made good friends. Her only flaw from a biographer's standpoint was that she rarely dated anything she wrote (she was quite aware of this, even joking in one letter of how difficult she was making it for future biographers). Because of this, some of the papers and letters I refer to have only approximate dates, and sometimes no date at all.

One small but persistent problem involved the names of Shirley's daughters. Joanne, the older, has used the name Jai since college; Sally is now Sarah. However, it was decided to use "Joanne" and "Sally" most of the time throughout. These were the names their mother called them, and it is, after all, her book.

Additional research was conducted at Syracuse University's Arents Library, Boston University's Mugar Memorial Library, and the Bennington Free Library. Roger Straus, of Farrar, Straus & Giroux, was kind enough to allow me access to those sections of his oral history, on file at Columbia University, which dealt with Shirley Jackson.

KEY TO ABBREVIATIONS IN NOTES

BUML-JW	*Boston University Mugar Memorial Library, Jay Williams collection*
JW	*Jay Williams*
LOC-SJ	*Library of Congress, Shirley Jackson collection*
SEH	*Stanley Edgar Hyman*
SJ	*Shirley Jackson*
SU	*Syracuse University*
SUAL	*Syracuse University Arents Library*

CHAPTER ONE 11–21

Information about SJ's ancestry came from interviews with her son Laurence Hyman and her brother, Barry Jackson; from articles published in the *San Francisco Chronicle* in 1949; and from the family tree researched by Laurence Hyman.

Shirley's brother, Barry, remembered Barry Jackson interview, January 18, 1987.

"Isn't contraception a wonderful thing" Letter from Geraldine Jackson to SJ, May 1962, LOC-SJ.

"You were always a wilful child" Letter from Geraldine Jackson to SJ, June 1962, LOC-SJ.

"She felt Geraldine had squashed her" (Jai) Joanne Hyman Holly interview, March 10, 1987.

"Who is looking over my shoulder all the time?" SJ journal, December 1964, LOC-SJ.

She saw the man who lived with his wife Information about SJ's neighborhood in Burlingame is from Dorothy Ayling Gielow, her childhood friend, interviewed January 15, 1987. Much of it appears, unchanged, in her first novel, *The Road Through the Wall*, which Mrs. Gielow has never read.

"Most of us have a lost paradise" Elizabeth Young Henry interview, February 16, 1987.

"I always thought one or the other" Barry Jackson interview.

"She could always find a four-leaf clover" Sarah (Sally) Hyman Stewart interview, January 16, 1987.

"I had learned that to put myself to sleep" Unpublished SJ essay, probably late 1950s, LOC-SJ.

CHAPTER TWO 22–30

"Shirley was always the instigator" Barry Jackson interview.

Shirley later said that the only correct answers Unpublished SJ essay, 1950s, LOC-SJ.

"Every day all the way home from school" Unpublished SJ piece written while at SU, 1937–1940, LOC-SJ.

One, titled "Written for Mother's Day" Collection of SJ childhood poetry, May 1928, LOC-SJ.

"We were poor" Dorothy Ayling Gielow interview.

Years later Shirley would regale The stories about Uncle Clifford come from interviews with Laurence Hyman and Barry Jackson.

"I've decided to write down" SJ's girlhood diaries, LOC-SJ.

"pleasant and swift and easygoing" Unpublished SJ essay, 1950s, LOC-SJ.

"My dear friend Dorothy and I" Early, unpublished draft of "The Clothespin Dolls" story, LOC-SJ. The story was later published as an article in *Woman's Day,* March 1953, and still later inserted into *Raising Demons*.

CHAPTER THREE 31–37

"It didn't bother me that much" Barry Jackson interview.

And the trip, oddly enough Recollections of the sea voyage are from Barry Jackson.

"Rochester is considered, still" Betty Lyddon interview, November 28, 1986.

Playwright Thomas Babe Quoted in the introduction to his play *A Prayer for My Daughter.* In *Best American Plays, Eighth Series* (ed. Clive Barnes). New York: Crown, 1983.

"I think that was a severe shock" Jean Rathgen Jackson interview, January 10, 1987.

"Doris was fat" Unpublished SJ piece

written while at SU, 1937–1940, LOC-SJ.

"Not to do:" Resolution, undated, LOC-SJ.

"He hasn't fallen for anyone" Letter from Dorothy Ayling to SJ, 1935, LOC-SJ.

"Secretly, lovingly, afraid" Unpublished SJ story written while at SU, 1937–1940, LOC-SJ.

Marion Morton spent the night Marion Morton Strobel interview, March 7, 1987.

"Do you experience it" Laurence Hyman interview, January 18, 1987.

CHAPTER FOUR 38–46

"Jeanou was a communist" Elizabeth Young Henry interview.

Her loneliness was just a stage Letters from Jeanne Marie (Jeanou) Bedel to SJ, LOC-SJ.

Her friend's reply was laconic Letters from Dorothy Ayling to SJ, 1935, LOC-SJ.

"To sleep rather than to live" SJ diary, winter 1935, LOC-SJ.

"Poor Jeanou must have a swell time" Letter from Dorothy Ayling to SJ, June 15, 1935, LOC-SJ.

"when i first used to write stories" Unpublished SJ essay written while at SU, 1937–1940, LOC-SJ.

"an odd one" Jean Rathgen Jackson interview.

"I became eccentric" Unpublished SJ essay written while at SU, 1937–1940, LOC-SJ.

"She was like her father" Betty Lyddon interview.

"I think she felt about her writing" Jai (Joanne) Hyman Holly interview.

"She had a great interest in me" Michael Palmer interview, November 24, 1986.

CHAPTER FIVE 47–54

"Someone should chain me" Al Parsell interview, November 25, 1986.

"It didn't matter what the target might be" Ibid.

"but all i remember" Unpublished SJ piece written while at SU, 1937–1940, LOC-SJ.

"She was pretty emotional" Kay Turk Truman interview, January 12, 1987.

"Kay took care of me" Unpublished SJ essay written while at SU, 1937–1940, LOC-SJ.

"Why on earth such unsuitable guys" Unsent SJ letter to Elizabeth Young written in a college notebook while at SU, fall 1937, LOC-SJ.

"You see? What did I tell you" Letter from Jeanne Marie (Jeanou) Bedel to SJ, 1937, LOC-SJ.

"He could never make them see" Essay by Al Parsell, fall 1937, LOC-SJ.

"We were both ardent young writers" Unpublished SJ piece written while at SU, 1937–1940, LOC-SJ.

"Perfectly harmless" Letter from Al Parsell to practical jokers, early 1938, LOC-SJ.

"Al today has gone off" Unsent SJ letter to Elizabeth Young written in college notebook while at SU, early 1938, LOC-SJ.

his own particular favorite Essay by Professor A. E. Johnson in *The Threshold,* March 1938, SUAL.

CHAPTER SIX 55–61

The Scene with SEH in the fraternity house was described by Ben Zimmerman, interviewed March 22, 1987. **Details about SEH's ancestors and early life** were supplied by his brother, Arthur Hyman, interviewed November 9, 1986.

He would later tell friends Phoebe Pettingell, SEH's second wife, interviewed October 22, 1986, heard the story from him and took it as the truth; attempts to verify it with SEH's brother and sister-in-law brought only chuckles.

Very early in the third-grade year June Mirken Mintz interview, November 8, 1986.

"I was afraid of bugs and snakes" Arthur Hyman interview.

"he was so advanced" Frank Orenstein interview, December 17, 1986.

Walter Bernstein was convinced Walter Bernstein interview, March 9, 1987.

But Stanley, too, had a couple of friends Frannie Woodward Bardacke interview, March 12, 1987.

CHAPTER SEVEN 62–74

"When she met Stanley" Elizabeth Young Henry interview.

"He introduced her to me" Walter Bernstein interview.

"Our first meetings were somewhat constrained" Frank Orenstein interview.

"Do you realize you are actually espousing" Michael Palmer interview.

"You go on home" Walter Bernstein interview.

"Dear Philip" Unsent SJ letter written in college notebook while at SU, 1938, LOC-SJ.

"I do not want to fall in love" Note in college notebook while at SU, 1938, LOC-SJ.

"We liked each other" June Mirken Mintz interview.

Stanley had talked up Jay Williams Information about JW comes from Walter Bernstein, Frank Orenstein, Bobbie Williams, and SJ's unpublished SU pieces. The scenes and quotes involving JW in this chapter are from unpublished autobiographical pieces SJ was writing then. These were the most directly factual pieces she ever wrote; whenever possible they have been checked with others for accuracy. The scene in which JW conjures up a vision was confirmed by Bernstein and Orenstein.

He took his problem to Felmus and Bardacke The saga of SEH and SJ's initial, cruelly aborted attempt at consummation is from the Frannie Woodward Bardacke interview. Their second, more successful venture was related by Jesse Lurie in an interview on March 31, 1987. Kay Turk Truman in her interview clearly described the letter she received and tore up immediately.

Her roommate at the cottage Scene taken from one of SJ's autobiographical sketches written while at SU, LOC-SJ.

One disturbing story Scene from another autobiographical sketch written at SU, LOC-SJ. This piece does, however, sound as if it may have been fictionalized a bit.

Frannie Woodward, who was also not Jewish Frannie Woodward Bardacke interview.

"She was very quiet" Dr. Robert Seidenberg interview, October 10, 1986.

When a male friend . . . asked her via a note The sharp exchange of notes between SJ and her hapless friend were in one of her SU college notebooks, 1937–1940, LOC-SJ.

CHAPTER EIGHT 75–86

An editorial in the October 1938 issue Back copies of *The Syracusan,* as well as *Spectre,* SUAL.

"Some of the English department ob-
jected" Frank Litto interview, October 11, 1986.

"A wild magazine which shocked the college" SEH's fond description of *Spectre* is in a draft of a biographical sketch he wrote for SJ, who needed one for her publisher, September 22, 1947, LOC-SJ.

"o my love is long and hard" Unpublished SJ poem, circa 1939, LOC-SJ.

"shirley is really sick like a dog" SEH letter to JW, undated, BUML-JW.

"i got fairly chummy with kenneth burke" Ibid.

Brown . . . spoke glowingly . . . Malcolm Cowley interview, March 1987.

During a dull lecture Exchange of notes in one of SJ's SU notebooks, 1937–1940, LOC-SJ.

"shoiley and i go on being happy" SEH letter to JW, undated, BUML-JW.

In a long rambling piece Unpublished autobiographical SJ sketch, LOC-SJ. The accuracy was attested to by June Mirken Mintz and by a letter from SEH to JW.

"my latest stupidity with shirley" SEH letter to JW, October 7, 1939, BUML-JW.

"I thought I was starting a relationship" Florence Shapiro Siegel interview, October 14, 1986.

"shirley and i, with light housekeeping looming" SEH letter to JW, BUML-JW.

"it is a very simple problem" Unpublished SJ autobiographical piece, written while at SU, 1937–1940, LOC-SJ.

"You are like filigree of some coarse stuff" Unpublished SJ poem written while at SU, 1937–1940, LOC-SJ.

CHAPTER NINE 87–94

"It was a bad Sunday afternoon" Red Stodlsky interview, March 15, 1987.

286 • *Judy Oppenheimer*

"**no great academic distinction**" SEH draft of SJ's biographical sketch, September 22, 1947, LOC-SJ.

"**What do I care**" Unpublished SJ poem written while at SU, 1937–1940, LOC-SJ.

Stanley insisted to friends Frank Orenstein interview.

"**economizing by using the same coffee grounds**" Unpublished SJ piece, LOC-SJ.

"**Ere they invented moveable type**" Unpublished SJ poem, LOC-SJ.

"**Song for all editors**" Unpublished SJ poem, LOC-SJ.

"**I am twenty three**" Unpublished SJ piece, LOC-SJ.

"**That's where everybody who had a degree**" Taissa Kellman Julia interview, March 9, 1987.

"**thus giving us every aspect and privilege**" SJ journal, LOC-SJ.

"**He got me drunk**" Florence Shapiro Siegel interview.

Both were shocked at the primitive conditions Arthur Hyman interview.

"**You can't refuse to talk**" Unpublished SJ piece, early 1942, LOC-SJ.

CHAPTER TEN 95–109

she drew viciously funny sketches SJ's sketches, simple, often hilarious line drawings done in pencil, are in LOC-SJ. SEH has curly hair and glasses and is invariably depicted with his feet up, behind a newspaper; she herself wears a long gown and has three wild hairs coming out of her head. Laurie, when included, is usually dangling, head down, from her arm.

Elsa Dorfman . . . remembers coming by Elsa Dorfman Rosenthal interview, March 24, 1987.

"**He'd put her to work**" Taissa Kellman Julian interview.

"**Stanley was quite extraordinary**" June Mirken Mintz interview.

Philip Hamburger remembered Philip Hamburger interview, November 7, 1986.

"**Shirley usually did her writing at night**" Bobbie Williams interview, March 4, 1987.

"**She had an exact picture**" Unpublished SJ piece, circa 1943, LOC-SJ.

"**My father, Stonewall Jackson**" Ralph Ellison interview, March 2, 1987.

"**After You, My Dear Alphonse**" and "**Come Dance with Me in Ireland**" were both originally published in *The New Yorker* in 1943 and later incorporated into her collection *The Lottery*.

Frank Orenstein ran into a little girl Frank Orenstein interview.

"**Pillar of Salt**" was originally published in *Mademoiselle* in 1948 and later incorporated into *The Lottery*. "**The Beautiful Stranger**," written in 1946, was published in *Come Along with Me*.

"**Stanley was helping Edwin Seaver**" Ralph Ellison interview.

"**She lent it**" Walter Bernstein interview.

One friend from *The New Yorker* Jesse Lurie interview.

Ellison was so appalled Ralph Ellison interview.

"**I don't like her**" Frank Orenstein interview.

"**A virtual hermitress**" Elsa Dorfman Rosenthal interview.

"**Mrs. Van Corn had not been out**" Unpublished draft of an SJ story, circa 1943, LOC-SJ.

CHAPTER ELEVEN 110–126

"**mountains and children playing**"*Life Among the Savages*.

Ben Zimmerman remembers the discussions Ben Zimmerman interview.

Nemerov, who had written Howard

Nemerov interview, December 17, 1979.

Kenneth Burke remembered Kenneth Burke interview, March 15, 1987.

"Stanley said it didn't matter" Jean Brockway interview, July 3 and 10, 1986.

"You had to keep stoking it" Tom Brockway interview, July 3 and 10, 1986.

Nanci Payne . . . was surprised Nanci Payne Coonz interview, December 18, 1986.

Once Stanley told Junior Junior Percey interview, December 19, 1986.

One such trip gave a neighbor a clear glimpse Fred Welling interview, December 19, 1986.

"Whenever I am very very mad" Jeanne Krochalis interview, December 10, 1986.

"I've been doing it for years" Nicholas Delbanco interview, July 11, 1986.

Arthur took her to meet his grandmother Arthur and Bunny Hyman interviews, November 9, 1986.

"eat up, there are starving children" Kayla Zalk interview, April 1, 1986.

"to see them through a flattering veil of fiction" SJ lecture on writing fiction, published in *Come Along with Me.*

These writers "give no sense of being hurried" Draft of SJ autobiographical sketch written for her publisher, 1949, LOC-SJ.

"She was far too honest" SEH, "In Memoriam" for SJ, published in *The Saturday Evening Post,* December 1965, and again as preface to *The Magic of Shirley Jackson.*

"In those stories, everybody was so neat" Helen Feeley Wheelwright interview, January 14, 1987.

"She was very much . . . Stanley's creation" Walter Bernstein interview.

"I have *no ink*" Bunny Hyman interview.

"Whatever happened to her" Kit Foster interview, July 2, 1986.

"The Intoxicated" was published in the *Lottery* collection.

"More hard drinking than high thinking" Ben Belitt interview, July 8, 1986.

"We first met at the Brockways' " Fred Burkhardt interview, December 20, 1986.

"shirley has finished five-sixths" SEH letter to JW, BUML-JW.

he urged Shirley to have her agent Tom Foster interview, July 2, 1986.

"I have had for many years" Unpublished statement by SJ of her intent, for publisher's publicity use, 1948, LOC-SJ.

"The first book is the book you have to write" Sarah Hyman Stewart interview.

"Well, what are you going to do with the money?" Roger Straus's oral history, Columbia University.

she padded the book with reviews SJ's scrapbooks for each book are in LOC-SJ.

"Fame" was published in *The Writer,* August 1948.

CHAPTER TWELVE 127–142

On a bright morning in the late spring of 1948 Notes and drafts for SJ lecture on "The Lottery" given at writers' conferences, LOC-SJ.

"Perhaps the effort of that last fifty yards" SJ lecture on "The Lottery," published in *Come Along with Me.*

"Writing the story, I found" Ibid.

"Shirley has written a story" Ben Belitt interview.

fiction editor Gus Lobrano thought it prudent SJ letter to James Thurber, published in *The Years with Ross,* Thurber's memoir of *The New Yorker*'s founding editor (Boston: Little, Brown & Co., 1958).

"Tell Miss Jackson to stay out of Canada" *The New Yorker* sent most of the letters it received about the story on to SJ, who saved them in a scrapbook, now in LOC-SJ.

"There were three main themes" SJ lecture on "The Lottery," published in *Come Along with Me*.

In fact, he did make one concrete contribution Phoebe Pettingell interview.

Shirley responded in a general way Joseph Henry Jackson, *San Francisco Chronicle,* 1949.

"womb's home companion" SEH letter to JW, June 15, 1948, BUML-JW.

"Charles" was published in *Mademoiselle,* July 1948, and incorporated into *Life Among the Savages.*

he bragged to Jay Williams that Knopf had released him SEH letter to JW, BUML-JW.

"I'd say, It's inconceivable" Fred Burkhardt interview.

When June, who did the index June Mirken Mintz interview.

"In the midst of life" SEH letter to JW, BUML-JW.

Years later . . . the Aldriches . . . realized Jean Aldrich interview, July 11, 1986.

"Everyone always says the third baby" "Third Baby's the Easiest," *Harper's,* May 1949, later incorporated into *Life Among the Savages.*

"for the last two weeks before I went" SJ letter to parents, October 1948, LOC-SJ.

"She felt Sarah was her" Jai (Joanne) Hyman Holly interview.

"I have a story in the October Mademoiselle" SJ letter to parents, November 1948, LOC-SJ.

"Her letters were her revenge" Barry Hyman interview, January 17, 1987.

Joanne was in nursery school SJ letter to parents, January 1949, LOC-SJ.

"My book of stories is all wrong" SJ letter to parents, February 1949, LOC-SJ.

"Even in the beginning, they'd go into hock" Arthur Hyman interview.

"Christmas was her thing" Bunny Hyman interview.

"Jannie [Joanne] had the stove" SJ letter to parents, January 1949, LOC-SJ.

"She always felt . . . that they at least understood" SEH, "In Memoriam."

"I am so excited about my book" SJ letter to parents, June 1949, LOC-SJ.

"The book went into a second printing" SEH letter to JW, BUML-JW.

"She says all that is needed" W. G. Rogers, Associated Press, June 1949.

"[I was] interviewed by a very nice man" SJ letter to parents, June 1949, LOC-SJ.

She admitted to writer Harvey Breit "Talk with Miss Jackson," *The New York Times Book Review,* June 26, 1949.

"dear neat detached miss jackson" SEH note in the *Lottery* scrapbook, LOC-SJ.

"it's a nice town for children to grow up in" Notes for SJ autobiographical sketch written for her publisher, 1949, LOC-SJ.

"His college teaching was interfering" Tom Brockway interview.

"it was the anti-Semitism" Helen Feeley Wheelwright interview.

CHAPTER THIRTEEN   143–158

"fewer advantages than ever before" SJ letter to parents, fall 1949, LOC-SJ.

"We are no longer fond of the town" Ibid.

"I quite agree with you" Ibid.

a tragedy that occurred at Bennington Information on Paula Welden's disappearance came from 1946 issues of

The Bennington Banner, now on microfilm at the Bennington Free Library.

"I want you to put me on a diet" Dr. Oliver Durand interview, December 18, 1986.

But this doctor was keen on dieting SJ letter to parents, summer 1950, LOC-SJ.

"Most organized woman I ever saw" Laura Nowak interview, December 18, 1986.

"Everyone there was a rich writer" SJ letter to parents, spring 1950, LOC-SJ.

"found it difficult, on top of the headache" Ibid.

Friends often arrived with "badly behaved children" Ibid.

In the case of the Feeleys SJ letter to parents, summer 1950, LOC-SJ.

both were "rather dull" Ibid.

"I am writing because of news" Ibid.

"It was awful, seeing Bennington" Ibid.

"It was a bloody mess" Laurence Hyman interview.

"It was completely his own fault" SJ letter to parents, October 1950, LOC-SJ.

"She wrote me a letter" Rae Everitt interview, February 23, 1988.

"My old agent used to quit" SJ letter to parents, winter 1950, LOC-SJ.

"I am rather more in favor of alcoholism" SJ letter to parents, spring 1951, LOC-SJ.

"All the reasons for leaving Vermont" SJ letter to parents, summer 1951, LOC-SJ.

"we all had enough to drink" Ralph Ellison interview.

CHAPTER FOURTEEN 159–168

Helen Feeley got Joanne Helen Feeley Wheelwright interview.

"So much pleasanter than Westport" SJ letter to parents, summer 1952, LOC-SJ.

Her lifelong inability to understand her daughter Geraldine Jackson's letters to her daughter are in LOC-SJ.

Multiple personality is a rare syndrome A fascinating exploration of multiple personality is in the recent book *When Rabbit Howls* (New York: E. P. Dutton, 1987), written by the ninety-two personalities that inhabit one woman, Truddi Chase.

Certainly she had little admiration Dr. Robert Seidenberg interview.

"What kind of psychoanalyst" SJ letter to parents, fall 1952, LOC-SJ.

when Ellison came for a visit Ralph Ellison interview.

Stanley went to call Fred Burkhardt interview.

When Laurie came home one day Shirley and Stanley's cavalry charge was described by Helen Feeley Wheelwright, Jennifer Feeley (interviewed September 18, 1987), and Fred Burkhardt.

Laurence himself does not remember Laurence Hyman interview.

CHAPTER FIFTEEN 169–179

The book climbed to "the lowest level" of the . . . best-seller list SJ letter to parents, summer 1953, LOC-SJ.

Years later, one Midwest ladies' club shanghaied Barry Hyman. Barry Hyman interview.

When he was at the college, he often called Sarah (Sally) Hyman Stewart interview.

"Faculty wives during that period" Anna Schlabach interview, December 21, 1986.

"It was not a good place for wives" Ben Belitt interview.

"Stanley would find them" June Mirken Mintz interview.

"A rich snotty bunch of Japs" Arthur Hyman interview.

Ralph Ellison saw the students' crushes Ralph Ellison interview.

"They were very pushy" Bunny Hyman interview.

"He felt so bad that he had never told anybody" Phoebe Pettingell interview.

"He liked to give people the impression" Frank Orenstein interview.

"She seemed very threatened" Walter Bernstein interview.

Uli Beigel remembers Uli Beigel Monaco interview, October 20, 1986.

"She was fat, she drank" Elena Delbanco interview, July 11, 1986.

"My earnings pay the bar bill" Frank Orenstein interview.

"Your mother was the one" Sarah (Sally) Hyman Stewart interview.

June was dazzled June Mirken Mintz interview.

"I saw her sometimes as wandering" *Life Among the Savages.*

CHAPTER SIXTEEN 180–190

"It was because they came back" Dr. Oliver Durand interview.

"We were the town atheists" Sarah (Sally) Hyman Stewart interview.

" 'The Lottery' painted North Bennington to the world" Barry Hyman interview.

"We were always perceived as outsiders" Laurence Hyman interview.

"There was a party going on" Ralph Ellison interview.

"I think this has been the best year" SJ letter to parents, early 1954, LOC-SJ.

"One Ordinary Day With Peanuts" was published in January 1955 in *Fantasy and Science Fiction.* Bernice Baumgarten's letters (LOC-SJ) reveal how difficult the story was to market originally—and how little it brought in.

"I read it to a literary seminar" SJ letter to parents, early 1954, LOC-SJ.

Now editor Herbert Mayes had gotten into the act Mayes's letters demanding payment, Bernice's attempt to calm him down, and her reports to SJ on the situation, as well as SJ's direct letter to Mayes, are in LOC-SJ.

"I have received the enclosed" Copy of SJ's letter to creditor, LOC-SJ.

"I am afraid that I must ask" Several drafts of this letter are in LOC-SJ.

"She had ordered something for Sally" Bunny Hyman interview.

Once when Howard Nemerov was criticizing an unpublished piece Howard Nemerov interview.

"Did Shirley do magic with Sarah?" Jai (Joanne) Hyman Holly interview.

"She would allude to witchcraft" Harriet Fels Price interview, December 4, 1986.

Once Sarah and a friend sat . . . watching Shirley The scene was recalled by the friend in a note she wrote Sarah after SJ's death.

CHAPTER SEVENTEEN 191–201

"Once more Shirley Jackson the housewife and mother" Dan Wickenden, *New York Herald Tribune Book Review,* June 20, 1954.

"Miss Jackson has done more" William Peden, *Saturday Review,* July 17, 1954.

"very tired and depressed" SJ letter to parents, October 1954, LOC-SJ.

"We are all so grateful to Ben and Marge" Ibid.

"I have made it a rule" SJ letter to parents, March 1955, LOC-SJ.

"Everyone around here was very ex-

cited" SJ letter to parents, June 12, 1955, LOC-SJ.

Larry Powers . . . remembered Stanley Larry Powers interview, December 18, 1986.

"It's amazing how the whole town" SJ letter to parents, August 1955, LOC-SJ.

"You got the message as a child" Anna Fels interview, November 2, 1986.

Once, at a cocktail party Jeanne Krochalis interview.

Sitting in an airport bar Ibid.

CHAPTER EIGHTEEN 202–215

"the tremendous embarrassment he felt" Jennifer Feeley interview.

Scott Hyman . . . remembers Scott Hyman interview, March 17, 1987.

"Sally was the golden girl" Dr. Oliver Durand interview.

the jacket annoyed her: "A mess" SJ letter to parents, August 1956, LOC-SJ.

The kids were put out when she said no to Edward R. Murrow SJ letter to parents, October 1956, LOC-SJ.

"a fine lemon flavor" Lewis Gannett, *New York Herald Tribune Book Review,* January 6, 1957.

"Tart and tangy" Edmund Fuller, *Chicago Tribune,* January 6, 1957.

"I began writing stories about my children" SJ draft for a writers' conference lecture, circa 1957, LOC-SJ.

"Two bad reviews of *Demons*" SJ letter to parents, January 11, 1957, LOC-SJ.

A small publishing firm Letters from editor at Julian Messner, Inc., to SJ, LOC-SJ.

Much of the fan mail was plain silly SJ rarely answered her readers' letters, but she saved many of them, which are now in LOC-SJ.

Dexedrine . . . Thorazine, Miltown, phenobarbital, bourbon The information about SJ's pill-taking comes from interviews with her four children.

"Her feeling about coming" Jeanne Krochalis interview.

"I personally love writing" SJ draft for a writers' conference lecture, undated, LOC-SJ.

"I tell myself stories all day long" SJ draft for a writers' conference lecture, undated, LOC-SJ.

"The very nicest thing about being a writer" SJ draft for a writers' conference lecture, undated, LOC-SJ.

"The only way to turn something" "Experience and Fiction," lecture published in *Come Along with Me.*

"I can't tell you what happens next" Jeanne Krochalis interview.

"Ever since I can remember" Unpublished SJ essay, undated, LOC-SJ.

"They made her into a lunatic" SJ letter to parents, January 11, 1957, LOC-SJ.

"We kept hearing more" Unsent SJ letter to parents, April 1957, LOC-SJ.

"I had a child in that class" Laura Nowak interview.

"Shirley accused the teacher" Willie Finckel interview, December 18, 1986.

"a stupid and illiterate woman" Unpublished SJ description of the situation, May 1957, LOC-SJ.

CHAPTER NINETEEN 216–228

"She put it all in the writing" Barbara Karmiller interview, July 9, 1986.

"Seems a highly unprofitable scattergunning" A. S. Morris, *The New York Times Book Review,* February 23, 1958.

William Peden . . . was also a bit dis-

turbed *Saturday Review,* March 8, 1958.

Harvey Swados . . . was even sterner *The New Republic,* March 3, 1958.

"We got a furious review" SJ letter to parents, April 10, 1958, LOC-SJ.

"something she [Bernice] had been promising" SJ letter to parents, February 14, 1958, LOC-SJ.

"in her case, 'edit' had little meaning" Letter from Robert Giroux to Judy Oppenheimer, April 7, 1987.

"one of those terribly well-dressed" SJ letter to parents, February 14, 1958, LOC-SJ.

"She would come to New York" Carol Brandt interview, September 1979.

Stanley . . . would disdain everything Kenneth Burke interview.

"I can steal their plots" SJ letter to parents, June 16, 1958, LOC-SJ.

She had always . . . "resented violently" SJ draft for a lecture on writing, 1958, unpublished, LOC-SJ.

"The children have a saying" SJ draft for a lecture on writing, unpublished, LOC-SJ.

Scott Hyman on one of his visits saw something Scott Hyman interview.

Bunny Hyman was sitting over a late breakfast Bunny Hyman interview.

Linda Gould remembered going to dinner Linda Gould Abtalion interview, September 15, 1987.

Hal Crowther . . . remembered dropping by Hal Crowther interview, September 15, 1987.

"big old California gingerbread houses" SJ letter to parents, 1958, LOC-SJ.

"volume after volume of luminous figures" SJ draft for a lecture on writing, 1959, LOC-SJ.

"I have always loved to use fear" Unsent SJ letter to Howard Nemerov, circa 1960, LOC-SJ.

"one common factor" "Experience and Fiction."

"A goose pimple horror story" *New York Herald Tribune Book Review,* October 25, 1959.

"Miss Jackson can summon up stark terror" *The New York Times Book Review,* October 18, 1959.

"We have here what we ought always to have" *Times Literary Supplement* (London), September 16, 1960.

Later, in an interview, Singer reflected views *Conversations with Isaac Bashevis Singer* (New York: Doubleday, 1985).

CHAPTER TWENTY 229–237

"Actually, if you're a writer" SJ draft for lecture on writing, unpublished, LOC-SJ.

"Shirley takes care of them" Kayla Zalk interview.

"Shirley must have found part of it appealing" Jennifer Feeley interview.

"I remember Laurie driving" Harriet Fels Price interview.

"Helen Feeley says Jennifer was even worse" SJ letter to parents, May 1959, LOC-SJ.

"Joanne seems to have had" SJ letter to parents, August 1959, LOC-SJ.

"We are such an odd community" Unsent SJ letter to Jeanne Krochalis, LOC-SJ.

In a long, unsent letter to Howard Nemerov Circa 1960, LOC-SJ.

"I have written myself into the house" Jeanne Krochalis interview.

"What 'ails' me, Pop" SJ letter to parents, January 2, 1963, LOC-SJ.

CHAPTER TWENTY-ONE
238–248

"Shirley wasn't much for discussing" June Mirken Mintz interview.

"Last week Gore Vidal lectured" SJ letter to parents, April 9, 1960, LOC-SJ.

"I have a real terror" SJ letter to parents, September 1961, LOC-SJ.

"Oh well, someday she will be grown up" SJ letter to parents, November 1961, LOC-SJ.

"The colitis induces" Ibid.

"I can hardly believe" SJ letter to parents, May 1962, LOC-SJ.

"We are every bit as pleased" SJ letter to parents, June 1962, LOC-SJ.

"upset me considerably" Unsent SJ letter to Geraldine Jackson, LOC-SJ.

"She became psychotic" Carol Brandt interview.

CHAPTER TWENTY-TWO
249–259

Barry Hyman paints Barry Hyman interview.

"since so much of my daily life" Unpublished SJ writing, undated, LOC-SJ.

Instead, she made long lists SJ used small white pads of paper for these lists; many of the pads were saved and donated to LOC along with her other papers. These notes to herself were always in pencil: "They were pencil people," Sally said.

"I always felt" SJ letter to parents, January 2, 1963, LOC-SJ.

"I was blunt about it" Dr. Oliver Durand interview.

"I was moved" and "Depend on Stanley" Covici and Sanderson's letters of commiseration are in LOC-SJ.

"It was literally impossible" Unsent SJ letter to parents, circa February 1963, LOC-SJ.

"This morning she went inside" SEH letter to Sally, February 1963.

"I've moved with astonishing speed" and "Along with all of this" Unsent SJ letter to parents, February 1963, LOC-SJ.

"It was essentially agoraphobia" Dr. James Toolan interview, February 24, 1987.

"I backslide very often" SJ letter to parents, September 1963, LOC-SJ.

"She wanted to be sure" Ann Malamud interview, December 1, 1986.

"I'd have to walk her back" Harriet Fels Price interview.

"pear-shaped, in a stained blouse" Helen Feeley Wheelwright interview.

"She just decided I was family" Kayla Zalk interview.

"What she sometimes did" Barbara Karmiller interview.

"Insecure, uncontrolled" SJ's last journal, LOC-SJ.

CHAPTER TWENTY-THREE
260–272

"There goes a triumph" Fred Burkhardt interview.

One night, when Stanley launched Phoebe Pettingell interview.

In April they hit the lecture circuit SJ letter to parents, May 1965, LOC-SJ.

"Everyone [at the university] was very full of hints" Ibid.

"I'm not going anywhere" Jeanne Krochalis interview.

"None of my friends will let" One of SJ's last pieces of writing, unfinished, unpublished, LOC-SJ.

June Mirken had some of the same feeling June Mirken Mintz interview.

"There were no other children" Scott Hyman interview.

Late that night they crept out The fireworks story was told by Scott Hyman and confirmed by Barry Hyman.

Dr. Toolan himself was taking a nap Dr. James Toolan interview.

Philip Hamburger . . . was in Vermont Philip Hamburger interview.

"He won't last five years" Barry Hyman interview.

Bunny . . . got a long, chatty one Bunny Hyman interview (letter shown).

The second letter, to Carol Brandt Sarah Hyman Stewart interview.

CHAPTER TWENTY-FOUR
273–280

"A great writer lost to the world" Kit Foster interview.

"Thank you for your heartfelt platitudes" Harriet Fels Price interview.

"We only stayed together" Elsa Dorfman Rosenthal interview.

"If the source of her images" SEH, "In Memoriam."

Shirley's children—particularly Joanne, Sally, and Barry Information about the Hyman children comes from interviews with each.

He refused to bail Sally out Sarah Hyman Stewart interview, September 17, 1987.

"But what do we do with all the junk?" Jean Aldrich interview.

PUBLISHED WORKS BY
SHIRLEY JACKSON

The Road Through the Wall. New York: Farrar, Straus & Company, 1948.

The Lottery, or The Adventures of James Harris. New York: Farrar, Straus & Company, 1949.

Hangsaman. New York: Farrar, Straus & Company, 1951.

Life Among the Savages. New York: Farrar, Straus & Company, 1953.

The Bird's Nest. New York: Farrar, Straus & Young, 1954.

The Witchcraft of Salem Village. New York: Random House, 1956.

Raising Demons. New York: Farrar, Straus & Company, 1957.

The Sundial. New York: Farrar, Straus & Company, 1958.

The Bad Children (play). Chicago: Dramatic Publishing Company, 1958.

The Haunting of Hill House. New York: Viking Press, 1959.

We Have Always Lived in the Castle. New York: Viking Press, 1962.

Nine Magic Wishes (children's book). New York: Crowell-Collier Press, 1963.

The Magic of Shirley Jackson (ed. Stanley Edgar Hyman). New York: Farrar, Straus & Giroux, 1966.

Come Along with Me (ed. Stanley Edgar Hyman). New York: Viking Press, 1968.

INDEX

ABOUT THE AUTHOR

Judy Oppenheimer has been a reporter at *The Washington Post*, movie critic at the *Philadelphia Daily News*, contributing editor at *Washingtonian Magazine*, and associate editor of the *Montgomery Sentinel*. Her writing has appeared in *Ms.*, *The Village Voice*, and the *Manchester Guardian*. She lives in Chevy Chase, Md., with her husband and two sons.

Fawcett Columbine Literary Biographies You Will Enjoy

Jane Austen: Her Life by Park Honan
"The best biography Jane Austen has ever received."
Newsweek

Willa Cather: The Emerging Voice by Sharon O'Brien
"Reading this book is like coming upon Willa Cather for the first time. It proves to be a remarkable discovery. . . . O'Brian greatly widens our understanding and appreciation."
The Philadelphia Inquirer

Chaucer: His Life, His Works, His World by Donald R. Howard
"A triumph of imagination . . . rich and multifarious. . . . A dazzling and impressive performance."
The Washington Post Book World

Chekhov by Henri Troyat
"The biographer brings us closer than we ever have been to the charactor of Anton Chekhov."
The New York Times

Fyodor Dostoyevsky: A Writer's Life by Geir Kjetsaa
"A readable and provocative biography that contributes a fresh viewpoint to our understanding of a difficult writer."
The New York Times Book Review

Dashiell Hammett: A Life by Diane Johnson
"A legend . . . one of the few writers fit to share a pedestal with Hemingway."
Chicago Tribune

Hemingway by Kenneth S. Lynn
"Monumental." *The Washington Post Book World*
Winner of the *Los Angeles Times* Book Award

Private Demons: The Life of Shirley Jackson by Judy Oppenheimer
"Lively but harrowing . . . fascinating."
The New York Times

Nora: A Biography of Nora Joyce by Brenda Maddox
"Substantial and thoroughly researched . . . . [*Nora*] emerges as a humanly fascinating and impressive portrait, alive and open."
The New York Review of Books

Rebecca West: A Life by Victoria Glendinning
"As captured in this balanced, stylish biography, Rebecca West seems not only 'the most interesting woman of this century in England' but also the most vital."
The Washington Post

Look Homeward: A Life of Thomas Wolfe by David Herbert Donald
Winner of the Pulitzer Prize for Biography